STUDIES IN
SOCIAL IDENTITY

STUDIES IN SOCIAL IDENTITY

Edited by
Theodore R. Sarbin
and
Karl E. Scheibe

PRAEGER

PRAEGER SPECIAL STUDIES • PRAEGER SCIENTIFIC

Library of Congress Cataloging in Publication Data
Main entry under title:

Studies in social identity.

    Bibliography: p.
    Includes index.
    1. Social psychology—Addresses, essays, lectures.
2. Identity (Psychology)—Addresses, essays, lectures.
I. Sarbin, Theodore R. II. Scheibe, Karl E., 1937–
HM251.S8367 1983   302.5   82-16580
ISBN 0-03-059542-8

Published in 1983 by Praeger Publishers
CBS Educational and Professional Publishing
a Division of CBS Inc.
521 Fifth Avenue, New York, New York 10175 U.S.A.

Printed in the United States of America

CONTRIBUTORS

Vernon L. Allen, Department of Psychology, University of Wisconsin

Michael L. Atkinson, Department of Psychology, University of Wisconsin

Jonathan Cheek, Department of Psychology, Wellesley College

Ki-Taek Chun, Senior Scientist, Office of Research, Washington, D.C.

George DeVos, Department of Anthropology, University of California, Berkeley

Kenneth J. Gergen, Swarthmore College

Mary Gergen, Swarthmore College

Robert Hogan, Department of Psychology, Tulsa University

Joseph B. Juhasz, College of Environmental Design, University of Colorado

Rolf O. Kroger, Department of Psychology, University of Toronto

James C. Mancuso, Department of Psychology, State University of New York at Albany

Daniel R. Miller, Department of Psychology, Wesleyan University

M. Jeanne Peterson, Department of History, University of Indiana

Marvin Rosenberg, Department of Dramatic Art, University of California, Berkeley

Mordechai Rotenberg, School of Social Work, The Hebrew University of Jerusalem

Theodore R. Sarbin, Professor Emeritus of Psychology and Criminology, University of California, Santa Cruz

Karl E. Scheibe, Department of Psychology, Wesleyan University

Kenneth M. Stampp, Department of History, University of California, Berkeley

David A. Wilder, Department of Psychology, University of Wisconsin

Linda Wood, Department of Psychology, University of Guelph

PREFACE

We hold to the premise that the problem of identity is one of the great and central problems of human psychology, although it has not commonly been recognized as such. When science asks how a thing should be called, a taxonomic response is ordinarily called for. That is, one wants to know the order of the matter in question and to know how that order of matter is to be organized in some general hierarchical scheme, such as a periodic table or a phylogenetic outline. This is why geography is such a marginal science, while geology is certainly quite central. For geography cannot be described outside of the context of history, with all its *proper* names—names that are not organized into some hierarchy of dominance or genetic precedence. In this sense, psychology is like geography, for one can go only so far with universalistic types and classes in psychology. In getting down to cases, one must talk of *proper* names—of historically embedded *social* identity. A person's actions are intelligible only by knowing *who* that person is.

The coeditors of this volume have been musing together and writing about this problem for the past 20 years. Now what is very clear and palpable to us, as palpable as this book, was once quite vague, ghostly, without definition. Perhaps we may write a prescription for how such a transmogrification is possible. Start with a shared dream, nurture it through conversation, stimulate it and give it form by discussion with close colleagues, have the courage to give courses on a subject only half understood, schedule a few formal symposia, and finally, invite a set of able colleagues to submit their essays on the subject. Now our topic has something of a history and the beginning of a bibliography. Of course, we cannot pretend to be the first to have discovered the broad and powerful significance of the problem of social identity. But we do think that the essays in this volume make a unique contribution to making that breadth and power demonstrable.

Our first debt as editors is to the authors of our chapters. With two exceptions, the essays here published were prepared especially for this collection at our invitation. Our authors have been subject to the usual editorial goading and prodding, the usual unreasonable requests for cutting and for meeting deadlines. They have been patient and good-spirited. But certainly no more patient and good-spirited than George Zimmar, our editor at Praeger. George has proven to be long–suffering, not just patient. Without his abiding faith in this project, it would have been abandoned long ago.

We acknowledge here with thanks the permission kindly granted by the *Journal of Southern History* to reprint the article by Kenneth Stampp on "Rebels and Sambos," and by *Victorian Studies* to reprint Jeanne Peterson's essay on "The Victorian Governess."

Copious thanks are due to Ona Langer for her typing and retyping many of these chapters. Her promptness and accuracy are legendary. Her constant cooperativeness is a special gift.

Theodore R. Sarbin
Carmel, California

Karl E. Scheibe
Middletown, Connecticut   June, 1982

CONTENTS

PART I
THE IDENTITY PROBLEM

The first essay in this collection has grown out of a project, begun in 1965, to come to grips with the problem of identity in social psychology. The original formulation of the model that appears here was the product of a collaboration of the two editors of this volume with Professor Rolf O. Kroger of the University of Toronto. We were able to spend a considerable time reworking and developing this material during several extended visits by Sarbin to Wesleyan University. Kroger's strong involvement in the initial phases of this work was of critical importance, but because he was not able to participate in the writing of this manuscript, he does not appear as an author. He has contributed a paper, with his coauthor Linda Wood, to the present volume, applying the social identity model to an analysis of suicide.

In the years since the initial formulation of the social identity model, we have had occasion to make applications of it to a number of problems. The ordering of roles along the dimension of ascription and achievement and a consideration of concomitant variation in involvement and evaluation has had an enormous advantage in illuminating such problems as the nature and consequences of social deviance, the reasons for success and failure of institutionalized systems of conduct reorganization, the legitimization of aggression, the nature and significance of group loyalty, the impact of total institutions such as prisons and mental hospitals, and the nature and consequences of social danger. In all of these areas, it is crucial to focus on the question of social identity in order to reach an understanding of the phenomenon in question.

We make no claim, however, that the model we present in the following pages is anything more than a heuristic device. There are other approaches to the problem of identity that will prove fruitful for certain applications. The papers we have solicited for this volume were not intended to adhere to the particular terms of our model but rather were intended to illustrate an even broader range of topics that might fruitfully be subsumed under what we think of as the identity problem. Some of the chapters in the sections that follow will make explicit and direct application of our model. Some will make only passing reference to it. Others will not refer to it at all but will draw their own theoretical conceptions for application to specific issues. In the introductory notes to each set of essays, we make an attempt to comment on the way in which each of the approaches taken may be related and compared to our own guiding model.

In many ways, the direct and elaborate concern with the problem of identity is an outgrowth of a longstanding commitment of one of us (TRS) to role theory. Role theory has seemed to many readers to be of only marginal relevance to individual psychology, perhaps because roles seem somehow located in the collective domain of sociology. Despite repeated claims that role theory is interactive and hence necessarily implicated with characteristics of the person, role theory continues to be alien territory for most psychologists. A focus on identity is meant as a corrective to this condition, for social identity is the obverse of externally structured social roles. A moment's reflection will convince even the most radical behaviorist that answers to the question, "Who are you?" and its reciprocal, "Who am I?" are the very stuff of social life.

Heretofore in psychology the most prominent attempt to describe the problem of identity has been the work of Erik Erikson and some others in the psychoanalytic tradition. The reader will find little reference to that tradition in this book, for our approach differs from that of Erikson in several important respects. Erikson's description of a progression of stages in human development and his characterization of certain identity crises along the way bear the marks of the psychoanalytic tradition, with its emphasis on the nuclear family and on development in early life. Our own approach is to develop a theory of identity without limiting it to any age group or culturally imposed developmental sequence. Our approach is contextualist (see Allen & Scheibe, 1982; Sarbin, 1976) in that we do not prescribe any model course of identity development outside of the context provided by specific social and cultural conditions. By contrast, the psychoanalytic tradition tends to be universalistic and ahistorical in its theoretical pronouncements. Certainly Erikson's contribution to our understanding of identity has been of lasting and positive value. Our own perspective differs from his and has the advantage, we think, of much greater range and flexibility. However, in many ways these two perspectives are complementary. Certainly there is no essential contradiction in principle.

The problem of identity is, we think, one of the most difficult challenges to which social science is called to respond. No single heuristic device is likely to conquer the problem. Even so, we expect that this essay and the fifteen essays that follow it represent a significant advance.

Chapter 1

A MODEL OF
SOCIAL IDENTITY

Theodore R. Sarbin and Karl E. Scheibe

INTRODUCTION

A social psychological theory of identity is a belated development, considering that nineteenth-century writers were already studying such problems as the effects of industrialization and urbanization on personal adjustment. Marx and Durkheim, among others, grappled with problems of social identity in their attempts to illuminate anomie and alienation. It is curious that behavioral scientists have shown so little interest in the personal and social effects of transvaluation. It is not that conceptual tools are not available. William James (1890) and George Herbert Mead (1934), for example, wrote detailed accounts of the development of the self, including discussions of the development of a social self. They saw how personality was formed in interaction with others. Mead, especially, accented the interaction of self and society. But they were obliged to limit themselves to discussions of mental acts, cognitive processes, and the complexities of dyadic communication. For all their liberality and breadth, they remained close to the individual. This was, of course, consistent with their ideological commitment to the genteel tradition. Such a commitment was alien to a search for the not-so-genteel antecedents of selfhood in economic determinism, political forces, and class structure. The search for self, like the search for an elusive mind, was centered on the individual. It was not that James and Mead turned their backs on the broad proposition that the social self was a product of antecedent happenings and doings. Rather, they adopted a narrow focus: the individual and his or her immediate surroundings.

To communicate meaningfully about the social self, a bridge between

We begin from the postulate that people's survival depends on their ability to locate themselves accurately in their various ecologies. Efficient behavior choices depend on the correct placements of self in the world of occurrences. Among the various ecologies into which the world may be differentiated is the social ecology or role system. People are constantly faced with the necessity of locating themselves in relation to others. Misplacement of self in the role system may have embarrassing, perilous, or even fatal consequences.

The self is located in the role system through an inferential process. On the basis of available clues, individuals infer the role of others and concurrently of themselves. A homeward-bound pedestrian, late at night, may locate himself as a potential victim of assault at the same time as he locates another pedestrian as a potential assailant. This process of location in the role system may be described as the formulation of answers to the recurrent question, "Who am I?" The answers to this question mean nothing without explicit or implicit answers to the reciprocal questions, "Who are you?" or "Who is he?"

Mulford and Salisbury (1964) provide an empirical illustration of the way self-conceptions emerge in response to this question. Subjects were asked to reply to the question, "Who are you?" Their answers were commonly constructed in role terms: "I am a physician," "I am a husband," "I am a citizen," "I am a prisoner," and so forth. It must be emphasized that such answers are footless if they are not ratified through actual or symbolic interaction with occupants of complementary positions. The declaration, "I am a physician" requires as a sequel that healing acts be directed to patients. The assertion, "I am a father" is valid only if the person has at least minimal interactions with his children. Thus one's social identity is defined as the multiple product of attempts to locate oneself in the role system—symbolically represented by asking and answering the question, "Who am I?"

It follows that planned or unplanned changes in role relationships will modify inferences about social identity because they provide people with different information concerning who they are. That is, one's location in social space is different when one is interacting with an adult or with a child; with a police officer or with a physician; with a friend or with a stranger; with a victim or with a victimizer. Such induced transitory modifications in social identity should not be confused with the substitution of one identity for another. How far social identity may be modified by changes in social reference individuals and groups is a question that should properly remain open.

Consider these examples. A recent graduate from high school, at large and perhaps alienated in his local version of the Standard Average American culture, applies to enter the Jesuit order and is accepted. He enters the novitiate, renounces all his worldly goods, and goes into retreat. A month later, he emerges a "new man," a Jesuit novice.

A degraded denizen of skid row joins Alcoholics Anonymous. After achieving the "twelve steps," he emerges as a respectable, teetotaling citizen.

A United States army officer is captured in combat. Despite the incontrovertible facts that characterized him as patriotic, loyal, and trustworthy, after six months of "brainwashing," he tapes a series of broadcasts denouncing his country.

Given such well-formed shifts in identity, the proposed model makes it possible to determine their evaluative significance.

The necessary features of the model may be expressed in terms of three dimensions. These jointly describe a solid of roughly specifiable shape. Again, remember that the shaped model is a device for illustrating the relationships we are positing among variables. While the metric significance of the dimensions is weak, the generally important relationships can be clearly represented in this manner. The three dimensions are (1) the status dimension, (2) the involvement dimension, and (3) the value dimension. First, we shall show how the value of a person's social identity is related to characteristics of his component roles. Then we shall take up the problem of transvaluations of social identity.

Status

The term *status* is used to mean position in a social structure. The relationship between role and status is conventionally described as follows. A *status* is an abstraction defined by the expectations held by members of the relevant society. *Role* is a set of behaviors enacted by an individual in an effort to make good his or her occupancy of a particular status. Another way of considering the distinction between these related concepts is to regard status as a cognitive notion—a set of expectations. Role, on the other hand, may be regarded as a unit of conduct characterized by overt actions.

Linton (1936) was the first to make the conventional distinction between ascribed and achieved statuses. Some statuses are given: they are ascribed to a person by virtue of sex, age, race, and kinship. Other statuses are achieved by following decisions made by the person or by other people. This distinction, which many authors have found convenient and acceptable, is not sufficiently clear, since the differentiating criteria for achieved and ascribed statuses have never been explicitly specified. However, even using the major implied criterion in Linton's distinction—the presence or absence of choice—it would seem that the classification of statuses should be more than two-valued.

The term *ascribed* implies granted or given. In the discussion that follows, the term *granted* will frequently be used as a synonym for the more opaque term *ascribed*. The term *achieved* has a surplus meaning in current usage that does not always contribute to the sense of this discussion. The terms *attained* or *selected* will generally be used in its place.

There are two difficulties with Linton's dichotomous conception. First, he specifies no criteria for deciding whether a given status is granted or attained. Second, in many instances, both factors contribute. Is the sex role of the successful transvestite granted or attained? How about the role of the father who deserts his family and establishes himself as a bachelor? Does the natural successor to a king win his position by ascription or by achievement? These and other difficult cases may be dealt with consistently if social statuses are regarded as falling along a continuum based upon the degree of choice prior to entering a given social position. Thus occupying a given status may under some circumstances be a great attainment and under other circumstances be almost completely taken for granted.

The degree of choice for any status may be determined by considering two factors: the number of alternatives available to the actor and the degree to which these alternatives are optional. More choice is exercised entering the position of lawyer than before entering the position of factory worker. The potential lawyer may choose, at least theoretically, many positions below that of lawyer in the occupational status hierarchy. The potential factory worker has fewer occupations below from which to choose. Similarly, less choice is involved in becoming a parent than in becoming a godparent. The social forces toward parenthood are more compelling than those toward godparenthood.

It should be clear that we are using the term *choice* in a sense that is consistent with selectivity. We are not using it to mean freedom or lack of determining constraints. Decisions may be made for or about a person who is placed on the path to great attainments. One may have little sense of choosing one's own destiny. Nonetheless, it is meaningful to consider choice as having operated to a very high degree in the development of virtuoso attainment. For during the course of this person's life many selective decisions must have been made that helped him or her to attain high status.

Social statuses and their corresponding roles, then, may be ordered with respect to optionality. For any society, the position of cultural participants is placed at the granted end of the status continuum—so are sex roles, age roles, and kinship roles. Occupational and recreational roles, such as a member of the Book-of-the-Month-Club, member of the Republican Party, and physician, are placed at the other end.

Granted roles may be further characterized as less differentiated and as applying to many members of society. Thus every person is initially granted the role of cultural participant. As such, the person is expected to act according to certain basic rules of propriety that preempt the requirements of any particular attained position. This grant carries with it legitimate claims to certain inalienable rights.

Each person is born with a birthright. This includes a set of political rights that are bestowed without regard for prior accomplishment or ability. In the United States, the Bill of Rights, together with other written and unwritten principles, comprise a large part of each person's birthright. This initial endowment determines the minimal expectations that are consistent with status as a human being. It also determines the rights and privileges of being human within a particular granting structure—the dominant society. Of course, birthrights are not necessarily bestowed equally. The birthright of slaves in the United States did not include any "human" rights. Slaves were defined as chattels (cattle), and their status was that of a nonperson. The Emancipation Proclamation was an instrument that granted certain minimal human rights for former slaves, that is, it granted them the right to be treated as people. It is sadly instructive to note that legal provisions influence, but do not control, the granting of human rights.

The concept of fundamental human equality, the origin of which Cassirer attributes to the Stoics of ancient Greece (Cassirer, 1946), is a prescriptive injunction against the withholding of a human birthright from any person on a priori grounds. The kind of social progress represented or instigated by the Magna Carta, the Declaration of Independence, the Nineteenth Amendment to the Constitution, and the Civil Rights Act of 1964 is an approach to this ideal.

Let us skip now to the other extreme of the status dimension. Highly attained roles are differentiated and apply to relatively few members of society. Examples are Supreme Court justice, violin virtuoso, or Secretary General of the United Nations. Legitimate power and social esteem accrue to occupants of attained positions.

The placement of a role along the status dimension is a matter of the observers' collective judgment regarding the degree of choice that the person had before entering a social position. Because shared values and experiences are readily apparent, individual portraits of the social structure may be blended into a common conceptualization.

Roles can be placed along the status dimension in another way. A certain probability of attainment exists for every distinct social position. Probability, in this context, has the conventional relative frequency interpretation. The probability associated with a position is determined by the proportion of individuals who opt for a position and attain it. The odds of any American being drafted into the military forces during wartime are perhaps 50 in 100. The odds of becoming an officer are perhaps one in 100. The odds of becoming a general are perhaps two in 250,000. The higher the a priori odds against placement in a given social position, the more attained the role. Thus the degree of attainment is often reflected in the relative number of individuals in various positions. There are always more Indians than chiefs, privates than generals, tellers than bank presidents.

Before an achieved position is occupied, choice may be exercised by several means. A person attains a position by election, nomination, special training, responding to a revelation or "calling," volunteering, or demonstrating some special skill. In each case, the process of promotion to the achieved position is reciprocal. The person must choose (or at least accede), and at the same time the relevant social reference groups must recognize and certify the promotion. The initial choosing is done by the person or by the social reference groups, or by both. Characteristically, then, achievements are a joint product of *choosing* and of *being chosen*. The selectivity involved in both of these choosing processes compounds to form the degree of choice prior to achievement. This degree of choice is the means of indexing the location of a given position on the status dimension.

To recapitulate, a person's social identity is composed of a number of roles located at different points on the status dimension. To approximate a full description of a given social identity, we may begin by listing the person's validated social position. Such listings can be used to infer how much legitimate power the person has, or to predict his or her conduct. However, the significance of status for a theory of conduct must be understood in relation to involvement and valuation. It is to the dimension of involvement that we now turn.

Involvement

The second major dimension to be considered is *opportunity for variation in involvement*, or simply *involvement*. Role enactments vary in the degree to which the actor is involved in the role. But statuses also vary in the extent to which they allow variations in role involvement. Before we discuss this point systematically, it is necessary to define the term *involvement* as it is currently used.

Involvement may be considered a dimension of the intensity with which a role is enacted (Sarbin & Allen, 1968). When involvement is low, role and self are clearly differentiated, few organismic systems are activated, and the actor expends little effort in enacting the role. When involvement is high, self and role are undifferentiated, the entire organism is activated, and the actor expends a great deal of effort. Sarbin and Allen identify eight levels of involvement. An example of zero involvement would be a lapsed club membership in which a person spent no time, by which one would never think to identify oneself, and which required absolutely no effort. An example of midrange involvement would be stage acting, "playing the part." Examples of level eight involvement would be ecstasy, possession, and mystical unions. Cases of voodoo death, bewitchment, and magic-induced illnesses are examples of extremely high involvement in the role of the victim. In these cases, involvement is so total that normal social and physiological regulatory mechanisms are blocked.

Time is an index of role involvement. A role is defined as highly self-involving if the person is "in the role" most of the time. Being "in the role" means engaging in activities that are role specific. Thus, the role of adult female, for example, is highly self-involving because it means being "on" almost continuously. While the organismic involvement required of the Sunday sailor is temporarily very high, this is not a very self-involving role because so little time is spent actually sailing. On the other hand, sailor is an extremely self-involving role for a professional yachtsman, for he devotes a great deal of time to the role enactment.

Some roles (such as person, male, mother, and daughter) demand more or less constant involvement. Others, especially some occupational roles, call for cyclical involvement. Involvement is very high when a worker is on the job. Involvement lapses temporarily with coffee breaks and work stoppages, and may disappear altogether at the end of the day to reappear only when the whistle sounds the following morning. Cycles may be daily (worker), weekly (churchgoer), monthly (lodge or club member), annual (taxpayer), or even longer. Furthermore, cycles may be regular, as in the examples cited, or irregular, as wedding guests, hostesses, or airline passengers.

In short, role involvement varies situationally and temporally. It varies a great deal for some positions and little for others. The problem is to account systematically for these differences. Our observations suggest that variability in role involvement is a function of placement on the status dimension. The closer a status is to the granted end of the continuum, the less potential it has for *differential* involvement. Conversely, the closer a status is to the attainment end of the continuum, the more role involvement will vary.

For the ultimate ascribed role—that of person or human being—it is difficult to imagine less than continuous high involvement. Occasionally people lose involvement in the role of person through meditation, disease, or the use of drugs. But our language has almost no words to describe this condition. People are expected always to behave in a way that is consistent with their culture's definition of human nature. Role enactments that deviate from the cultural definition of human nature cause the actor to be classified as the negative counterpart of civilized humans. This, however, does not relieve the actor of continuous high involvement. He or she is defined as a substandard or beastly being and involvement remains virtually complete.

Attained roles, on the other hand, may be put on and off like cloaks.

Most attained roles are cyclical, and while intense organismic involvement may be demanded for certain periods, it rarely lasts very long. A professional baseball player may be highly involved in his role when he is on the diamond, in spring training, or reviewing batting averages. He may be relatively uninvolved in it when he is attending a funeral, writing letters, or visiting friends.

Involvement can be as high at the attained end of the status continuum as at the granted end. While a man is President of the United States, he is just as involved in that role as he is in the more granted roles of human being, man, and citizen. But any attained role includes the opportunity for complete disinvolvement—for escape. The resignation of Richard Nixon from the presidency is a case in point. Opportunities for disinvolvement are fewer for granted roles.

This posited relationship between potential for variability in involvement and the status dimension is roughly represented by a triangle. The triangle comes to a point at the granted end of the dimension. (See Figure 1.1.) In the relatively totalistic setting of prisons, mental hospitals, and forced labor camps, opportunities for variation in involvement are restricted. In these settings the statuses are heavily weighted with ascriptive features, and involvement is typically high—not by choice, but by the demands of the total situation. The social identity of a member of these classes does not include attained roles, the enactment of which may be cyclical. When one's identity is composed exclusively of granted roles, one cannot obtain role distance (Goffman, 1959). That is, when people are enacting a granted role, they are "on" all the time. They have little or no opportunity to gain distance to view their conduct from the perspective of another role.

Valuation

Positive and negative valuations bear an orderly relation to status and involvement. The valuation dimension is constructed at right angles to the

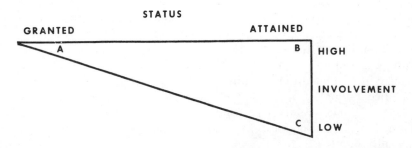

Figure 1.1. Opportunity for Variation in Involvement Related to Status

status and involvement dimensions. Like them, it is a continuum. It is marked with a neutral point and positive and negative limiting extremes. The question, then, is what potential gain and loss in the value of a social identity is associated with various statuses and various levels of involvement?

Before we explore this question systematically, we wish to emphasize the distinctiveness of this conception of valuation. First, the valuation of social identity and corresponding psychological well-being is not unitary. It is a composite whose components have different significance and prominence at different times. On the level of observation, this composite corresponds to mood changes.

Second, the mere identification of a person with a position has no necessary implications for the value the person gains from that position. Thus we may say, for example, "Jones is a philosopher." But the role of philosopher may be more or less attained and more or less involving. Moreover, the constellation of validated roles within which philosopher appears as one component of identity may impart to that component more or less weight. If a person is gaining no social value at all from his or her other statuses, the role of philosopher carries great weight.

Third, physical well-being and psychological well-being are not the same. Consider candidates for martyrdom who feel a lot better than they should according to their objective circumstances, and upper-middle-class neurotics, who feel a lot worse. Both represent paradoxes that will be resolved by the working out of this conception. Now let us examine some specific examples.

Consider first the range of potential valuation applicable to the occupancy of attained statuses, which is the right portion of the straight line in Figure 1.2. Valuations declared on nonperformance or poor performance are near the neutral point. That is, strongly negative valuations are not applied for failures to validate highly attained statuses. The fact that one has been fired from a glee club, dropped from a team, or dismissed from college does not enrage or perturb the community. Such failures are considered to be due to lack of practice, underachievement, poor judgment, limited talent, or misfortune, and are met with verbal expressions of sadness, disappointment, sympathy, regret, and so on. On the other hand, the *proper* performance of attained roles earns tokens of high positive value. These include prizes, public recognition, monetary rewards, and other indicators of public esteem. For attained statuses, then, values range from neutral to positive—there is much to gain and little to lose.

Now consider the range of potential valuation applicable to granted statuses. (See Figure 1.2.) Here there is less to gain and more to lose. One is not praised for participating in a culture as a female, an adult, a mother, or a person. One is expected to enact these roles without positive public

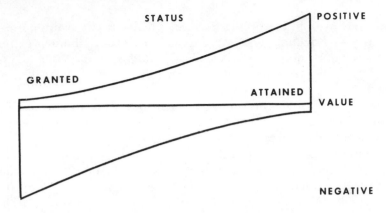

Figure 1.2. Positive and Negative Valuation in Relation to Status

valuations. The *nonperformance* of these roles, however, earns strong negative valuations. Consider the valuations declared on a male who fails to perform according to the expectations for masculine sexuality. He is labeled "sissy," "fairy." Consider the valuations declared on a mother who is indifferent to her children's welfare. She is labeled "selfish," "unloving." Consider the valuations declared on people who fail to act according to age standards. They are called "immature," "childish," or "regressive." Consider the valuations declared on people who act in opposition to fundamental principles of law. They are called "punks," or "outlaws."

It follows that the most universal common expectations for behavior are associated with the extreme granted status of *person*. While there are cultural variations in conceptions of the nature of humans, all persons within a given culture are expected to conform to a basic definition. Especially strong negative sanctions are reserved for acts that held to be nonhuman or "unnatural." Expectations associated with the basic grant of personhood are usually concerned with communication, propriety, and ingroup aggression. People who violate these norms are marked more or less permanently with a strongly pejorative label. Many forms of this label are used. All have the common function of denoting the social identity of a *nonperson*. Once the pejorative label is applied, the society begins to treat the individual as something less than human.

The concept most widely used to represent nonperson status is that of "brute." This concept is sometimes rendered as beast, animal, or low-grade human being (Platt & Diamond, 1965; Sarbin, 1967a). In the vernacular, these valuations emerge in such epithets as "pig," "dog," "worm," "jackass," and "son of a bitch."

The status of a nonperson may be denoted by labels ordinarily used to describe nonliving matters. Examples are "dirt," "clod," and "stone." The vernacular also includes many terms derived from human and animal excrement (Kochman, 1969). Even abstractions of quantity are used to convey the notion of nonperson. Thus, "I am a zero," or "You're nothing but a nothing." It is noteworthy that such terms or their polite equivalents are not a part of the scientific and professional lexicon. In our efforts to be professional and humanistic, we have coined special euphemisms that for a short time conceal the strong negative valuation. Examples of these euphemisms are "disadvantaged," "underdeveloped," "underprivileged," "culturally deprived," "mentally ill," "welfare recipients," "problem families," "patients," "inmates," and so on. These labels carry much of the meaning of nonperson. The person so labeled is likely to be regarded as if he or she were at the lowest grade on the status dimension and at the negative end of the value dimension.

A further qualification must be added to the valuation dimension. This dimension is represented by a single line. However, the quality of the valuation below the neutral point differs from the quality of valuation above the neutral point. Positive valuations of attained roles appear to coincide with esteem, as this term is commonly understood. The public performance of the attained role is the basis for the according of esteem. By contract, positive valuations of granted roles are best denoted by the term *respect*. When people fail to perform ascribed roles, they lose the respect that inheres to the associated status. Motherhood is respected until a mother publicly fails to meet the group's minimal expectations concerning child care. The performance of granted roles, however, earns no special tokens of esteem. One is expected to perform granted roles without special incentives. Disrespect and associated negative sanctions follow nonperformance.

ROLE LINKAGE

So far, we have been discussing components of social identity as if they were independent of each other. At this point, we must dispense with this simplifying fiction. In any social structure certain validated statuses are prerequisite for promotion to achieved positions. What are the social characteristics necessary to become a candidate for a particular achieved validated status? We propose the concept of role linkage to describe these and other functional connections between roles.

First, there are at least two criteria for deciding whether two roles are linked. Is one validated status prerequisite to another? For example, medical students must usually present a college degree among their qualifications for admission to medical schools. Other qualifications of status pertaining to race, religion, or social class may also be effective— unwritten—prerequisites to medical school.

Second, does promotion or demotion on one status affect the valuations accorded the other? Ex-felons are forbidden to hold certain positions in government, for example. In fact, if a person in an attained position is convicted of a felony, he or she is very likely to lose that position. In the 1960s the boxing champion was stripped of his title because he had failed to discharge the military service obligations that were expected of young, male citizens. A former president and a vice president were disbarred for violating laws and customs pertaining to honesty.

Normally, elaborate linkages are set up for entry into those attained statuses in which the actor wields some power or bears some responsibility for the welfare of others. Police officers, judges, physicians, senators, druggists, teachers, and diplomats arrive at their positions only by satisfying the licensing and certifying agencies that they have qualified on a number of prerequisites. For these positions of public trust, there is the uniform requirement that the individuals chosen be of "good basic character," loyal, upright, fair, and so forth.

The example of physicians is illuminating. If a patient dies because of "technical difficulties" in an operation, the surgeon is not charged with murder. However, a physician found to be practicing with a fraudulent license is treated severely and is subject to criminal proceedings, even though that doctor's patients are prospering. It is very difficult for society to view political leaders, magistrates, and surgeons as murderers, even though they sometimes kill people as wantonly as those who lack their attainments. But if a person in such an achieved position can be convicted of a fault on an ascribed and prerequisite status, then he or she is removed from that attained position and prosecuted.

All this implies that the components of identity for promotions are always required in a regular order. Promotion always requires prior validation of roles that are relatively more ascribed. The most selective positions are prerequisite to nothing. No job description would list President of the United States or Nobel Laureate as necessary qualifications. However, a great achievement does serve to exempt the person from the normal qualification rules for somewhat less attained positions. For example, former slave Frederick Douglass was honored by Abraham Lincoln for being a famous abolitionist and distinguished orator.

Attained roles differ greatly in the linkages they maintain with more ascribed components of identity. There are only weak linkages between the highly achieved status of great artist and the more granted status of family man. For some highly attained positions, there are no or only weak linkages to granted statuses. Michelangelo could lack granted status as a family man and still be granted status as an artist. But could Caesar?

Role linkages are governed by rules that can be changed. Through collective social processes, the qualification "male" has been removed from the right to vote, thus destroying a linkage. The linkage between "male" and professional jockey has been severed. Similar social processes create linkages. For example, a university may declare that only Ph.D.s will be employed as professors. In this case the linkage is established between two statuses that are relatively attained. Some universities have created a linkage between granted racial status and the achievement of student status in their black studies programs.

Idiosyncratic Features of Role Linkage

In the preceding sections, we have tried to make clear that the criteria for ascription or grantedness of roles are to a certain extent arbitrary. The criteria of age, sex, and kinship roles are frequently under attack. The validity of such criteria is often questioned, and this questioning is often supported by reference to historical and cultural relativism.

Subcultures arise and the arbitrary criteria for ascribed roles are enlarged to include expectations associated with achievements. Thus a proper child will not only show the filial conduct that is traditionally expected, but will also enter an approved vocation. In this way, the child is maintaining respect at the same time as earning esteem from others. The esteem declarations of others (the public) may be the hidden dimension for the respect declarations by significant others (the parents).

The masculine ideal as a model for validly occupying the status male has been repeatedly challenged, most recently by social groups identified as "gay" or homosexual. The linking of gender to jobs is a cultural arrangement that has the stamp of historical tradition. A midwestern housewife on her first visit to an English pub was outraged that the "man behind the bar" was a woman. A controversy developed over feminist claims that girls should be allowed to participate in Little League baseball. The following conundrum illustrates the traditional linkage between job and gender:

> A man and his teenage son were returning from a holiday. Road conditions were treacherous. Missing a turn in the road, their car ran into a concrete abutment. The father was killed instantly. The son sustained multiple injuries and was taken by ambulance to the emergency hospital. He was wheeled, unconscious, into the operating room. The surgeon, in the act of preparing to operate, glanced at the youth's face and in a state of excitement exclaimed, "I cannot operate on this boy. He is my son."
> Query: Who is the surgeon?

To answer the query, of course, requires a readiness to entertain the possibility that a woman may enact the role of surgeon.

Linkages between ascribed and achieved statuses may be arbitrarily constructed by individuals. In this case, the connection reflects the person's own commitment to certain values. A boy was locked out of his house by his father for having fumbled the ball at a crucial point in a high school football game. Here the father arbitrarily linked the ascribed role, son, with the attained role, football player.

The Protestant ethic has frequently been incorporated into the role linkages. This is particularly apparent in the time-honored expectation that the son will enter the family business. Consider the generations of artists and writers who were regarded as eccentric, indolent, even insane, for refusing such achieved roles as regional manager of sales, production engineer, or executive trainee in the family business. Negative evaluations up to and including disinheritance have been declared on sons for failure to enact such achieved roles. In such idiosyncratic cases, achieved roles take on the characteristics of ascribed statuses.

TRANSFORMATION OF SOCIAL IDENTITY

At any time, a person's social identity is composed of a set of validated statuses. These might be indexed in terms of the extent to which they are granted or attained and in terms of the degree of involvement they entail. These validated statuses determine the social valuations that are applied to a person.

This concept of social validations is intended to illustrate how psychological change depends upon changing social interactions. For convenience, we shall consider the two aspects of social validation separately: the process of degradation and the process of upgrading.

Degradation

The model implies that there are two ways by which the values of a person's social identity may be lowered: *derogation and demotion.*

The root meaning of derogation is to rescind, annul, or reverse a previous privilege. Derogation is the process of transforming a role with potential for esteem to its negative counterpart. To derogate is to identify a person as a "bad actor," an ineffective incumbent of a status. The model accommodates the differential significance of derogation for roles at different points along the status dimension. A person's identity is damaged greatly by allegations of being a "bad person," a "bad daughter," or an "impotent male." Each allegation involves a considerable loss of respect. For a less significant role—like weekend gardener—the loss of status (implied by the allegation "he is a poor gardener") would not necessarily induce any loss of respect.

Demotion is the stripping away from a person of certain attained statuses. This process might also be called "disparagement"—a word whose root sense suggests a comparison between inferior and superior elements. To treat an adult as a child is degrading in this sense, as are actual demotions such as removing an officer from rank or assigning a varsity player to the second team. Demotions from achieved positions deprive the person of opportunities for enjoying esteem.

It follows that the most degrading processes are those which combine derogation and demotion. If a person is relieved of all achieved statuses—professional and avocational—and is derogated with respect to all ascribed roles, including sex, age, kinship, and citizenship roles—he or she is reduced to the lowest possible value. It is the extreme of degradation to treat a person as "nothing but a beast." ("Nothing but" implies demotion, and "beast" implies derogation.)

The following quotation from an 1885 edition of *The Catholic Dictionary* illustrates how the two degradation processes were applied to priests:

> Degradation is of two kinds, verbal and real. By the first a criminous cleric is declared to be perpetually deposed from clerical orders, or from the execution thereof, so as to be deprived of all order and function . . . and of any benefice which he might have previously enjoyed . . . .Real or actual degradation is that which, besides deposing a cleric from the exercise of his ministry, actually strips him of his orders, according to a prescribed ceremonial, and delivers him to the secular arm to be punished.

The first kind of degradation is what we call derogation. The second "real or actual degradation" is what we call demotion. The first is primarily verbal or symbolic; the second is primarily instrumental.

Upgrading

The model applies equally well to the upgrading of social identity. The development of heroes, champions, and successful and self-fulfilling people is typified by the logical opposites to the processes of derogation and demotion. These processes might be called, respectively, *commendation* and *promotion*.

Commendation is positive public recognition. It is given for proper performance in a given status. Commendation is provided in the form of verbal and symbolic acts that serve as social reinforcers. The varieties of commendation are many: the roar of the crowd in athletic contests, curtain calls in the theater, prizes and awards for achievement, honorific titles, and so on. Medals, grades in school, merit citations, and ordinary forms of praise and positive regard are other common kinds of commendation. Often when a speaker is introduced, the audience is informed of his or her

validated statuses—"a mother, a citizen of the commonwealth, a senator"—
and also of the commendations received—"oak leaf clusters, Man-of-the-
Year Award, Guest Prize for Poetry."

A promotion is movement from one role to another, higher status role.
A newly attained status opens up fresh possibilities for gaining esteem. In
general, the greater the jump in rank, the greater the gain in esteem.

The most highly valued human beings, then, are those who have
succeeded in doing two things. They have achieved rare social positions and
have been commended highly for their performances in them. At the same
time, they have also maintained their respectability.

These, then, are the basic mechanisms of social transvaluation. Now let
us explore the implications of the model for various configurations of roles.
We shall begin by discussing the statuses illustrated by the vertices of the
status-involvement triangle. (Refer back to Figure 1.1.)

Extreme Granted Roles (Vertex A)

We have argued that involvement for the most granted role is consistently high. The social category employed at this point is that of human
being, member of a society, participant in a culture, or person. It remains to
consider the values that might be attached to effective validation of the most
granted status—human being—as well as the valuation for insufficient or
improper performance in this position.

The negative consequences of being classified as a nonperson or a
"beast" are very great indeed. Platt and Diamond (1965) have traced the
history of the "wild beast" theory of criminal insanity. Their findings
support the view that no other categorical appellation has had such
consistent negative potency. Partridge (1950) provides evidence that derogatory slang is often a literal allegation that a person is not human.
Nineteenth-century California ranchers disported themselves by exter-
minating "varmints," the remnants of a tribe of Digger Indians. Until the
modern era, death by drawing and quartering was reserved for those judged
to be no better than animals. Hitler decreed that those responsible for the
1944 assassination plot be slaughtered like pigs and their carcasses hung on
meat hooks, and so they were. While Mussolini was given an animal
execution, the world was cheated of revenge on Hitler by his peremptory
human suicide.

Compared to the great negative value of being classified as a nonperson, positive validation of human status carries a weak payoff. In
absolute terms, the difference in value for social identity between person
status and nonperson status is enormous. However, in itself, status as a

person carries no positive value for social identity. Validation of this status is universally expected and is a minimum prerequisite for any form of promotion.

Highly Involving Achieved Roles (Vertex B)

The position of President of the United States is one of maximum achievement and involvement. So are the positions of violin virtuoso, Nobel Laureate, athletic champion, and Pope. Clearly, the maximum possible positive value for social identity is associated with proper performance in these positions. They provide access to power, prestige, and wealth.

What of the negative counterparts of these achieved roles? As examples we might cite an ineffective president, a losing coach, and an incomprehensible philosopher. If society agrees that the failure in each of these cases is *only* with respect to the requirements of the attained role, then the value it declares on the occupant of that position would not be negative. That is, it would not be expressed in terms of *disrespect*. A president's inability to halt inflation, for example, could result in declarations of disesteem, but not disrespect. The president might still be regarded as a kindly and basically honest man and good to his family. The losing coach might still be regarded as an accomplished raconteur, and the incomprehensible philosopher might be regarded as a patriot.

With respect to value, extremely achieved roles that are highly involving present just the opposite case from that of granted roles. (See Figure 1.3) The absolute difference between maximum success and maximum failure for achieved roles is, again, enormous. But most of the potential is for positive value rather than for negative value. *There is much to gain and little to lose in trying for attained positions.* One does not invoke sanctions against a virtuoso for missing a note or playing badly. One does invoke sanctions for a temporary lapse from the requirements of being human.

The loss of attainments can have profoundly degrading consequences. One French pastry chef committed suicide upon learning that his restaurant had lost its four-star rating. Such cases are newsworthy, however, because they are rare. In fact, if we knew the whole story, we would probably discover real or imagined defects in some of the granted components of this man's social identity.

So the negative value attached to the derogatory counterpart of attained roles is not great. We recognize the difficulties contained in this proposition. To strip away a virtuoso designation, championship status, or honorific title is very damaging to the individual so degraded. It is most degrading of all if the person is highly involved in his or her role. (See Figure 1.3.) However, the amount of damage would depend on the density

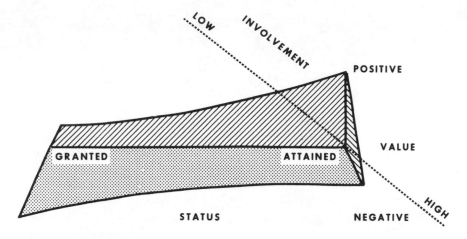

Figure 1.3. The Three-Dimensional Model of Social Identity: Status, Value, and Involvement

of validated statuses in the intervening space between highly attained and less attained, more granted roles. Marilyn Monroe, who believed she had failed as a mother, wife, actress, intellectual, and daughter, and who had given up her original name and family identity, must have suffered a profound identity crisis. Her status as sex queen could not be maintained as she grew older. Her suicide was probably a reaction to a loss of respect rather than to a loss of esteem. An appropriate term for this condition would be "hollow identity" (see Kroger & Wood, this volume).

Minimally Involving Attained Roles (Vertex C)

Sometimes a person is no longer involved in an attained role. Examples would be retired generals and executives, members of honorary societies, and professors emeriti. When this happens, the status that pertains to that role is latent. Zero involvement in a role implies zero value for social identity. Zero involvement in an attained role means that a person is not active in that role, though he or she could again become active.

Obviously, degree of involvement depends on social context. The Grand Plenipotentiary of the Secret Dragons might enjoy great esteem at his conventions and none at all at his place of work. Scholastic honors and publication records mean nothing when one is trying to board a subway. In such cases, the individual can derive satisfaction from implicit role involvement by thinking about personal achievements. However, it seems patent that self-esteem as well as public prestige depend upon valuations assigned by reference groups and individuals. Reference groups and individuals make their evaluations on the basis of the convincingness of the actor's performance. And this, in turn, is a function of involvement.

Linked Roles

Role linkages are very important in the degrading and upgrading processes. For upgrading to occur, the person must have satisfied the formal and informal regulations regarding prerequisite validated positions. Once upgrading has occurred, one must not violate norms pertaining to prerequisite statuses. If a medical superintendent were to admit forgetting medical facts, he or she would probably be demoted. This demotion would occur, not because the forgotten knowledge had any direct function in the discharge of daily duties, but because powerful medical societies have created and supported the linkage between qualified physician and medical superintendent. Similarly, the White House official in the Johnson administration who was revealed to be a homosexual was no longer allowed to function in his attained position. He was demoted from his job and derogated as a man even though he was effective in his job.

Many highly achieved positions are not closely linked with other, more ascribed statuses. Thus a man can attain esteem as a great actor without having graduated from college, without working his way up through the corporation, without being a respectable family man, and without adhering to conventional religious beliefs. However, if he wants to be a politician, he must take care to touch the requisite bases. That is, he must not violate granted role prescriptions before he attempts to gain promotion. Similarly, pecadillos are tolerated with amusement in movie stars that would outrage the public were they exhibited by a magistrate. A well-known musical conductor and a Hollywood actress lived together and had a child without benefit of clergy. There was no public outcry. However, resignation from office was the only option for a high government official who maintained an intimate relation with a "secretary."

Sometimes failure in an attained status is brought about not by incapacity to discharge the demands of that role, but by defect in a granted category. When this happens, the degradation and disgrace are great. Oscar Wilde was not a failure as a playwright, pundit, or writer (attained statuses) but as a man—and at a time in Victorian England when strong implicit linkages existed between masculinity and these attainments. From our point of view, Hitler was not so much a failure as a military leader as he was a failure as a human being. Because of the role linkage between granted and attained positions, failing to meet the requirements of a granted position may bring about derogation and demotion from achieved positions.

The Faust legend provides an excellent example of transvaluation in which the long-term effects of degradation differ markedly from the short-term effects. When Faust bargains his soul away to the Devil in return for earthly favors, he effectively degrades himself with respect to the most ascribed component of his identity—his claim to conventional humanity, to being a normal person. In return, he receives a set of "achievements"— conquests in love and other affairs. In the terms employed here, he has traded respect for esteem. In the modern idiom, he has sold out: he has accepted promotion without legitimizing his claims to the more ascribed component of his identity—his humanity.

The Faust legend illustrates the condition that we have called "hollow identity." The combination of achieved statuses and weak or undefined granted statuses produces a perilous psychological condition. Since there is no solid basis for self-respect deriving from granted statuses, the person is continually dependent on public recognition of personal attainments. As kinship ceases to be meaningful, as sexual adequacy is called into question, as the nation loses respectability as an object of patriotism, and as the established church ceases to provide believable answers to the question, "Who are you?" the only basic grant of respect that remains is challenged by participation in a society that seems to regard human beings as objects to be processed, or as specially adept animals, or as creatures without individual responsibility. Marx made clear that a significant effect of industrialization is the mechanizing of persons along with the personifi-cation of things. A modern man or woman receives much information that says, in effect, that there is nothing particularly special about being human. If this proposition is accepted, and if family, church and nation do not completely contradict it, then one must depend completely upon transitory attainments. When involvement in attained roles lapses, one has no means of earning respect. The hollow man alone is no man at all.

UTILITY OF THE MODEL

The model has not been idle. It has been used to clarify a number of persisting problems. Several essays have paved the way for a new approach to deviance. So-called abnormal behavior (a euphemism for unwanted conduct) takes on a different coloring when viewed through the categories of the social identity model. Persons who acquire labels descriptive of abnormality are seen as responding to shifts in social identity rather than as flawed minds or incomplete psyches. Necessary for a complete under-standing of unwanted conduct is a perspective where not only the conduct of the targeted person is under scrutiny, but also the valuational conduct of persons who have the power to transvalue the targeted individual. Although usually couched in the opaque language of medical diagnosis, the decla-ration of a person as mentally ill, schizophrenic, psychotic, lunatic, etc., is a downward transvaluation of identity. An examination of the actions of professional diagnosticians of unwanted conduct reveals the formulation and delivery of a moral verdict rather than a diagnosis in the usual medical sense (Sarbin, 1968a, 1968b, 1970a; Sarbin & Mancuso, 1980; Shaver & Scheibe, 1967).

The language of social identity has been helpful in understanding the contemporary political facts of terrorism. Available data on terrorists show a set of antecedent political events that have influenced the person to perceive the self as deprived of a claim to national identity. The tactics of terrorism are efforts to restore a lost or never-acquired ascribed status, usually granted as a birthright (Schcibe, 1967).

The model has also served as a heuristic for organizing the ex-communalities in systems of conduct reorganization. Sarbin and Adler (1971) examined widely dispersed methods of changing behavior—religious conversion, psychoanalysis, military indoctrination, and others. All systems are characterized by actions that symbolize the metaphoric death and rebirth of identity. If the efforts at reorganizing conduct are successful, the participant enacts a new set of ascribed roles, and concurrently is accorded a grant of respect.

Among other problems that have been illuminated by the employment of social identity concepts are: social danger (Sarbin, 1967b), the culture of poverty (Sarbin, 1970b), the development of the hippie folk type (Sarbin, 1968a), the effectiveness of children teaching other children (Sarbin, 1975), and the variable social identities of incarcerated felons (Rotenberg & Sarbin, 1971). Central in the clarification of these problems is the transvaluation of social identity. Such transvaluing occurs in historical contexts. The propositions in our model are sensitive to the complexities of historical context—a feature usually absent from the explanations offered by psychologists and philosophers of mind.

CONCLUSION

To summarize, we begin by acknowledging that neither behavioristic nor phenomenological models can convincingly account for personal transvaluations. Current psychological theories—useful as they are for certain purposes—fail to employ as a central construct that form of the self we have called social identity. Without such a construct, we cannot explain why people assign valuations to others and self, except by resorting to post hoc stimulus–response propositions or to idiosyncratic phenomenalism.

The valuation of persons—whether it takes the form of upgrading or of degradation—is a social process. That is, its form and direction depend upon the nature of the social organization in which it occurs. The model of social identity presented in this chapter provides a social psychological language for analyzing valuation. The model itself is a heuristic device. Its utility is to be measured by its success in establishing the processes of enhancement and degradation as knowable events—events to be illuminated by social psychological research and analysis.

We have begun this research process using role theory as a conceptual starting point. We have proposed that a person's social identity may be regarded as a composite of social positions or statuses—the occupancy of which he or she has made good by performing appropriate acts.

The extent to which each of the components of social identity contributes value to the composite depends on two things. The first is the extent to which the position was granted (ascribed) as opposed to attained (achieved). The second is the degree to which the person is involved in role enactment. A person's social identity is not an absolute. Obviously, differently composed reference groups will not assign the same valuations to any particular presentation of self. Valuation is a reciprocal social process. Values do not inhere in either the subject or the object of valuation but emerge from the interaction between them.

From this perspective, *respect* is seen as the maintenance of status grants—birthrights, political and religious orthodoxies, and other minimal expectations for personal conduct. Respect provides a person with a grant of social credit. The loss of this grant of social credit amounts to a loss of respectability. *Esteem,* on the other hand, is earned. It is acquired as the socially proffered wages for attainments. The more selective the attainment, the greater is the esteem.

Social identity is considered to be composed of a complex of references at various points along the status dimension. In contrast to the religious conception of humanity, which emphasizes one's ascribed attributes, and to the economic conception, which values only one's attainments, we argue that the nature of social organization demands that the effectively functioning person have grants of respect and opportunities to gain esteem. Observations of alienation, anomie, depersonalization, and so on, can be conceptualized according to this model, particularly in terms of the improper validation of granted statuses.

PART II
THE TRANSFORMATION OF
SOCIAL IDENTITY

The four contributions in the present section exemplify and extend the ideas presented in the previous chapter.

Although written in the idiom of social history, Peterson's discussion of the Victorian governess provides data that are readily assimilated into the descriptive categories of the social identity model. She makes use of the social-psychological concept "status incongruence," a concept that helps explain the marginal and precarious condition of the Victorian governess. The employment of a governess, Peterson points out, supported the transition of the roles of wife and mother in middle-class households from a domestic emphasis to an ornamental emphasis.

The role of the governess invariably carried little esteem and variable degrees of respect. The enactment of the role of governess, given the lack of options for unmarriageable middle-class women, typically led to identification of self as a nonperson. Victorians, not unlike contemporaries, attempted to solve the problem of a surplus population through placement in institutions, benevolent and otherwise.

The sad and often-tragic lives of Victorian governesses are the determinate outcomes of the downward transvaluation of social identity. So-called personality variables appear to contribute little to understanding the choice of vocation nor the unhappy outcomes. Rather, such macrosociological conditions as the rise of the middle class, the change in family functions, and the residue of a rigid class structure provide the contextual background for understanding the creation of the role of governess, the flawed social identity, and the sorrowful outcomes.

In her contribution, Wood applies the social identity model to a long neglected concept: loneliness. In her effort to describe the phenomena of loneliness, she enriches the conceptual matrix of social identity. She constructs a four-fold typology, making use of the two valuational categories, respect and esteem, and the "quantity" in each category (high or low). The combination of high respect and high esteem is the condition for an optimal identity; the combination of low respect and low esteem is the condition for an "empty" identity; the combination of low respect and high esteem is the condition for a "hollow" identity; and the combination high respect and low esteem is the condition for a "helpless" identity. The typology is helpful in understanding loneliness. It has the potential of becoming a central construction in explaining many forms of conduct often inadequately explained as "personality" variations.

The social identity model is further enriched with the introduction of the concepts of solidarity and status, concepts that lead to the study of emotion as a situated social psychological phenomenon rather than a physiological event or mental state.

Kroger and Wood offer a new synthesis on the baffling problem of suicide. Not content with the Durkheimian social statistics approach, they attempt to solve the puzzle of suicide from the "particulars" of individuals who enact their roles within a specific set of cultural arrangements. Toward this end they make use of ethogeny, a systematic conceptual framework within which social actions can be explained. Among the dominant ideas of ethogeny are the assertions that human beings are agents, that their actions are directed toward solving problems of both the practical and the expressive social orders, and that their actions must meet certain standards of justification and accounting.

The expressive social order—the order of reputation, honor, esteem, and respect—is ordinarily the dominant one. Suicide is the solution for those persons who realize that they have failed to solve the problems posed in the expressive social order and have further concluded that they are without skills or resources to meet such problems in the future.

The social identity model offers categories for communicating about the expressive social order. The transvaluations of social identity that culminate in self-destruction are generally from the "hollow" identity (some esteem, little or no respect) to the "empty" identity (little or no esteem, little or no respect). The case studies and the statistical data lend support to this formulation.

Allen, Wilder, and Atkinson explore the connection between multiple group membership and social identity. They address problems associated with the fact that it is usually the case that an individual is required to answer the "Who are you?" question from multiple perspectives. When the "Who are you?" question is explicitly or implicitly posed, the answer may be: a woman, a teacher, a Catholic, a Greek, a Republican, a Texan, a sister, a tennis player, and so on. While these answers are expressed in the singular, group membership is implied. One is a Greek in virtue of membership in a national identity, one is a Catholic in virtue of membership in a religious organization, etc.

The authors review some of the research carried out by social psychologists to illuminate the solutions to problems posed by multiple group membership. Especially important in their analysis is the effect of the outgroup on the quality of one's identification with the ingrouped. Further, social identity is more than the *effect* of membership in certain groups; social identity is also seen as a *cause* of conduct, an ongoing process in constant flux, changing as social contexts change.

Chapter 2

THE VICTORIAN GOVERNESS: STATUS INCONGRUENCE IN FAMILY AND SOCIETY

M. Jeanne Peterson

The governess is a familiar figure to the reader of Victorian novels. Immortalized in *Jane Eyre* and *Vanity Fair*, she has made frequent appearances as the heroine of many lesser-known novels. And innumerable governesses appear as little more than a standard furnishing in many a fictional Victorian home. While twentieth-century acquaintance with the governess may come purely from the novel, the Victorians themselves found her situation and prospects widely discussed, frivolously in *Punch*, and more seriously in many of the leading journals of the time, so often in fact that one author on the subject of female labor in Great Britain suggested that readers were "wearied . . . with the incessant repetition of the dreary story of spirit-broken governesses" (Martineau, 1859, p. 294; see also Adburgham, 1961, pp. 86–87, 99; Neff, 1929, pp. 269–271). The governess's life is described in what seem today to be over-dramatized accounts of pauperized gentlewomen, "drifted waifs and strays from 'the upper and middle classes,' " who find their way to the workhouse and insane asylum (Martineau, 1859, pp. 307, 316–317; Neff, 1929, p. 159; The Profession of the Teacher, 1858, pp. 5–6; Sewell, 1870, pp. 245–246). And there are condemnations of these accounts as "comic pathos" and "a perfectly, preposterous quantity of nonsense" (Oliphant, 1858, pp. 141, 145). Books on the subject of women as workers, published in growing numbers throughout the Victorian period, devote a large amount of space to the governess.

This article originally appeared in *Victorian Studies*, 1970, *14* (1), 7–26 and was reprinted in *Suffer and be still: Women in the Victorian age*, ed. M. Vicinus (Bloomington: Indiana University Press, 1970), pp. 2–19. Thanks are due to the Indiana University Press for permission to reprint this essay here.[1]

The Victorians' interest in the governess went beyond that of enter-tainment or economic analysis. She was the subject of charitable endeavors, and at least one appeal reveals the sense that the dilemma of the governess was a problem that was expected to touch donors personally: "There is probably no one who has not some relative or cherished friend either actually engaged in teaching, or having formerly been so engaged" (The Profession of the Teacher, 1858, p. 1; see also Belloc, 1865, p. 76; Governesses' Benevolent Institution, 1852, p. 146—hereafter GBI). Lady Eastlake spoke of "the cause of governesses" and urged in 1848 their "earnest and judicious befriending" (Eastlake, 1848, p. 176). In London the Governesses' Benevolent Institution and Queen's College were founded to provide several sorts of assistance.

In terms of numbers alone, this attention to the governess seems somewhat excessive. There were about 25,000 governesses in England in 1851, but there were over 750,000 female domestic servants, not to mention women employed in industry (Banks, 1965, p. 83; Banks & Banks, 1964, p. 31). And when one moves from simple statistics to the conditions of employment of women in this period, the suffering of the governess seems pale and singularly undramatic when compared with that of women in factories and mines. Victorian interest in the governess could not have stemmed from her political importance, for she had none. As militant as women may have been by the turn of the century, there is no trace of militance in the ranks of mid-nineteenth–century governesses. Moreover, the governess had no social position worthy of attention. She was at best unenvied and at worst the object of mild scorn, and all she sought was survival in genteel obscurity.

Modern treatment of the Victorian governess, when it is not set in the framework of literary analysis, takes two forms: either it is a study of the occupation itself without reference to the larger social scene, or the role of the governess is considered within the context of the movement for women's education and women's rights (Barnard, 1961, pp. 22, 156ff; Belloc, 1865, pp. 17, 55–56; Curtis, 1965, pp. 171ff.; Grylls, 1948, p. vii, Chap. 2; Kamm, 1965, pp. 170–173; Neff, 1929, Chap. 5; Thompson, 1956, Chap. 2; West, 1949, Chap. 2–4). In our interest in later historical develop-ments, we tend to ignore the immediate social context of the governess's occupation and the ways in which the dilemmas and contradictions of her employment may have helped to drive women's education and women's employment out of the home. By examining the governess's situation within the middle-class Victorian family, we may approach a better under-standing of how the family functioned and of the values, problems, and fears of the Victorian middle class.

In mid-nineteenth century usage, the term "governess" could refer to a woman who taught in a school, a woman who lived at home and travelled to her employer's house to teach (called a "daily governess"), or a woman who lived in her employer's home and who taught the children and served as a companion to them.[2] The subject of this study is the governess who lived with the family, sometimes referred to as the "private governess." In considering her intimate position within the family, we may see most clearly the problems of the governess's place in Victorian society.

The employment of a gentlewoman as a governess in a middle-class family served to reinforce and perpetuate certain Victorian values. But inherent in the employment of a lady was a contradiction of the very values she was hired to fulfill. The result was a situation of conflict and incongruity for both the governess and the family, a conflict that called forth a variety of responses from governess, family, and society.

From at least Tudor times the governess had been part of the households of the upper classes. In the nineteenth century, increasing numbers of governesses were employed by the English middle classes. The governess was a testimony to the economic power of the Victorian middle-class father, as were servants, carriages, and the other "paraphernalia of gentility." Although the governess was often behind the scenes and not as conspicuous as other items of genteel equipage, there were ways in which the family could indicate her presence in the home and display her as a symbol of economic power, breeding, and station. Drawing room conversations about the governess served to bring her into public "view." If she was foreign, her exotic history might be discussed. Even complaining about a governess was a way of "showing her off."[3]

The governess was also an indicator of the extent to which a man's wife was truly a lady of leisure. The function of the mother had traditionally been, in addition to her housewifely duties, that of educator of the children. Both boys and girls in the middle-class family began their education with their mother. Boys were later sent to school or a tutor was hired for them, but girls continued to learn their roles as women from their mothers. Unlike cooking, cleaning, and scrubbing, the education of children was hardly classifiable as manual labor. For this reason the employment of a governess was even more a symbol of the movement of wives and mothers from domestic to ornamental functions.

Victorian parents sought a woman who could teach their daughters the genteel accomplishments that were the aims of female education. More important, they sought a gentlewoman. But the new ethos of the ideal woman was that of a woman of leisure and, no matter how occupied a lady might have been at home, an outside career was another matter—in Frances Power Cobbe's words "a deplorable dereliction" (Cobbe, 1894, vol. 1, p. 64). If work *in* the home was thought to "pervert women's sympathies, detract from their charms" (The Disputed Question, 1858, p. 366), work for pay brought down the judgment of society and testified to the inferior position of both the wage earner and her family. Sophia Jex-Blake's father told her that if she accepted a salary she "would be considered mean and illiberal, . . . accepting wages that belonged to a class beneath you in social rank" (Kamm, 1965, p. 176). Others put it more strongly: "Society has thought fit to assert that the woman who works for herself loses her social position." The women of the middle classes were very consistent in their attitude toward being paid: "they would shrink from it as an insult" (Sewell, 1870, pp. 238, 279). The image of the lady as a creature of leisure, enclosed within a private circle of family and friends and completely supported by father or husband, was reinforced by the ban on paid employment—a ban so strong that many who wrote for publication, even though writing at home, did so under pseudonyms, or signed their work simply "By a Lady."

The availability of ladies to teach the children of the middle classes depended on the one exception to the rule that a well-bred woman did not earn her own living—if a woman of birth and education found herself in financial distress and had no relatives who could support her or give her a home, she was justified in seeking the only employment that would not cause her to lose her status. She could find work as a governess (GBI, 1852, p. 139; The Profession of the Teacher, 1858, p. 11).[4] The position of governess seems to have been appropriate because, while it was paid employment, it was within the home. The governess was doing something she might have done as a wife under better circumstances. She avoided the immodest and unladylike position of public occupation (Belloc, 1865, pp. 157–158; Female Education in the Middle Classes, 1858, p. 224).

The literature of the 1840s suggests that there was a sudden increase in the number of gentlewomen without financial support in the years following the Napoleonic wars. Middle-class writers attributed the flood of distressed gentlewomen to "the accidents of commercial and professional life" to which the middle classes were subject (Belloc, 1865, p. 76; Eastlake, 1848, p. 176). From the research of twentieth-century historians it is clear that the number of single middle-class women in need of employment was a product not only of the unstable conditions of business in those years but also arose out of the emigration of single men from England to the colonies, from the differential mortality rate which favored women, and from the tendency for men in the middle classes to marry later (Banks & Banks, 1964, pp. 27–30). But the Victorians' belief that economic distress had led to the declining position of these women suggests that problems of social and economic uncertainty were of more immediate concern to them. The Victorian stereotype of the governess, which explained why a lady sought employment, was of a woman who was born and bred in comfort and gentility and who, through the death of her father or his subjection to financial ruin, was robbed of the support of her family and was driven to earn her own living (Cobbe, 1894, vol. 1, p. 51; Going a Governessing, 1858, p. 396; Gosse, 1941, p. 20; GBI, 1852, pp. 19–27).

A word should perhaps be included here about the possibility of upward social mobility through occupation as a governess. There are a few suggestions in the literature of the period that such attempts at social climbing were in fact taking place. Harriet Martineau, in an *Edinburgh Review* article in 1859, noted the practice of "tradesmen and farmers who educate their daughters for governesses" in the hope of raising their station in society (Martineau, 1859, pp. 294 ff.). There is no way of assessing the extent to which this took place, but it is clear that the Victorian middle class regarded such mobility as undesirable (Eastlake, 1848, pp. 179–180; Ellis, 1843, pp. 209–210; *Governess Life*, 1849, p. 127; Sewell, 1870, pp. 259, 275). In the fiction of the period the governesses who were figures of evil or immorality were women of humble origins. Thackeray's Becky Sharp, for example, was the daughter of a poor artist and a French "opera-girl" who, in order to find employment, claimed origins in the French nobility. The wicked Miss Gwilt, in Wilkie Collins' *Armadale*, was an abandoned child whose origins were unknown and who was reared by a "quack" doctor and his wife. As will become clear later in this essay, the possibility of real upward mobility was a chimera. Indeed, employment as a governess was only of very limited use even in maintaining gentle status. It is sufficient here to note that however educated a girl from the lower ranks might be, she was still "ill-bred" in the eyes of those who made themselves judges of governesses. Conversely, however destitute a lady might be, she continued to be a lady (Eastlake, 1848, p. 180; *Governess Life*, 1849, p. 71; GBI, 1852, p. 141; The Profession of the Teacher, 1858, p. 11).[5]

We have been looking at the governess from the point of view of the family that employed her. Her own viewpoint was very different, of course. Once it was clear that she had to seek a post as governess, the task of finding a situation was taken up through a variety of channels. The first source of aid was the help of relatives and friends who might know of a family seeking a governess. If such help was not available or effective, a woman was forced to turn to public agencies—newspaper advertisements or a placement service. Newspaper advertising was disliked, partly because of its public nature and partly because reputable employers were unlikely to utilize such a source. Experience with the falsification of letters of reference among servants obtained through newspapers had brought public advertising under suspicion (Hecht, 1856, pp. 29 ff.). The Governesses' Benevolent Institution, established in 1843, provided a registry for governesses seeking employment, and many seem to have used the service (Going a Governessing, 1858, pp. 386–397; GBI, 1852, p. 15).

Pay was notoriously low. Governesses were, of course, housed and fed, but they were expected to pay for such expenses as laundry, travel, and medical care. They had to dress appropriately, and it was wise for them to make their own provisions for unemployment and old age. A governess often tried to support a parent or a dependent sister or brother as well. According to some estimates, pay ranged from £15 to £100 a year. The larger sum would only be applicable to the "highly educated lady" who could find a position in a very well-to-do family. The average salary probably fell between £20 and £45 a year. To give some meaning to these figures it will be useful to compare them with typical salaries of other groups. The fairest comparison is probably with that of other domestic employees since they were also paid shortly by maintenance:

	Banks, 1848–52	Martineau, 1859
Housekeeper	no data	£40–£50
Cook	£15–£16	£12–£18
Housemaid	£11–£11/13	£10–£14
Nursemaid	£11–£12	£5–£30

Mrs. Sewell, writing in 1865, equated the salary of nursery governess with that of lady's maid, that of an informed but not accomplished governess with that of footman, and that of a highly educated governess with that of a coachman or butler (Banks, 1965, pp. 80–81; Eastlake, 1848, p. 180; GBI, 1852, pp. 139–140; Martineau, 1859, pp. 308–309; Neff, 1929, p. 158; The Profession of the Teacher, 1858, p. 3; Sewell, 1870, Vol. 2, p. 245). If board was worth £30 per year, then governesses were earning £40 to £95 a year (not including the cost of housing). A minimum income for a genteel style of life may be estimated at £150–£200 for a single person (Banks, 1965, pp. 42–45, 72, 120, 173; Belloc, 1865, pp. 83, 105; Cobbe, 1894, vol. 1, pp. 214, 275). It would seem that, under the best of circumstances, a governess's income left her on the very edge of gentility, with no margin for illness or unemployment. Many governesses, between jobs, ill, or too old to work, turned to the "temporary assistance . . . afforded privately and delicately" through the Governesses' Benevolent Institution (GBI, 1852, p. 139; Sewell, 1870, p. 245).

The duties of a governess in a household were as varied as the salary she was paid. In some families, like those of Frances Power Cobbe and Edmund Gosse, the governess had set hours for lessons and her remaining time was free (Cobbe, 1894, vol. 1, pp. 38–39; Gosse, 1941, pp. 103–105, 107–109). The Thackerays' governess acted as a chaperone, accompanying her pupil to French class (Ritchie, 1894, pp. 4–5). Often governesses of adolescent girls would accompany them shopping, read aloud to them while they did fancy sewing, or simply sit in the background to watch over their social activities. Constant supervision of pupils seems to have been a common duty of governesses and would have kept them busy all day, leaving little time for lives of their own. The constant supervision of children and young women resulted from the belief of many parents that indolence and lack of supervision might lead to "immorality" (Hoare, 1872, p. 131; Sewell, 1870, p. 217).[6]

The difficulties that governesses had with their young charges were a well-known occupational hazard. A frequent theme of novels is the mistreatment and disrespect directed toward the governess by children, her lack of authority over them, and the failure of the mother to cooperate in discipline. Evidence about the problems of nonfictional governesses, though sparse, suggests that the novelistic theme was not unrealistic. In the Stanley family's correspondence, for example, there is a casual reference to the scratches and bruises that one of the children inflicted on the governess and the nurse (Mitford, 1939, p. 82; Sewell, 1870, pp. 233, 251).

Occupational problems did not end with finding a position and coming to terms with the duties and the children. A governess always faced the danger of unemployment, either because her work with the children was finished or because her employers were dissatisfied with her. Inadequate preparation for teaching and faulty placement practices were often to blame for the frequent hiring and firing of governesses (Cobbe, 1894, vol. 1, pp. 38–39, 50; Grylls, 1948, p. 13; Zimmern, 1898, pp. 16–17).

The aristocratic practice of continuing to support domestic servants who had outlived their usefulness after long service was not often extended to aged governesses in middle-class families. Long service was much less the rule, and paternalism was expensive. In the event of illness or old age and inability to work, the governess faced the prospect of charity, such as that provided by the Governesses' Benevolent Institution in the form of small annuities for retired governesses. The number was limited, however, and reports of governesses in workhouses or asylums were not uncommon (Martineau, 1859, p. 307; The Profession of the Teacher, 1858, pp. 5–6; Sewell, 1870, pp. 245–246).

In many ways the situation of a domestic servant in the nineteenth century differed very little from that of a governess. But there were no crusades for nursemaids or domestic servants. And in spite of similar work situations, the stereotype of the down-trodden, pathetic governess stands in sharp distinction to that of the warm, jolly nanny who won the affection of her charges and often the sincere regard of her employers.

Occupational conditions seem not to have been the fundamental source of anxiety for the governess and her middle-class employers. The difficulty seems to have been rooted in her special social position rather than in the material facts. An examination of the social circumstances of a governess's life and the way that life fitted into the middle-class social structure and system of values reveals a tension that cannot be explained in terms of hours or wages.

One sensitive observer of the Victorian social scene made the following assessment of a governess's situation: "the real discomfort of a governess's position in a private family arises from the fact that it is undefined. She is not a relation, not a guest, not a mistress, not a servant—but something made up of all. No one knows exactly how to treat her" (Sewell, 1870, pp. 240).

The observation is an acute one because it defines the problem as one of status and role. But one can go further and suggest that the real discomfort arose not from lack of definition but from the existence of contradictory definitions of the governess's place in society. In every aspect of the governess's occupational situation these contradictions in her social status are apparent.

As we have seen, the *sine qua non* of a governess's employment in the Victorian family was her social status as a lady. To quote Elizabeth Eastlake:

> the real definition of a governess, in the English sense, is a being who is our equal in birth, manners, and education, but our inferior in worldly wealth. Take a lady, in every meaning of the word, born and bred, and let her father pass through the gazette [bankruptcy], and she wants nothing more to suit our highest *beau ideal* of a guide and instructress to our children. (Eastlake, 1848, p. 175)

The governess is described here as an exception to the rule that ladies did not work for a living and, in spite of her loss of financial resources (and leisure), she retains a lady's status. But paid employment did bring a lady down in the world.

The Victorian leisured classes were, in part, defined in opposition to the working classes, not because of the work or leisure of the men—for almost all of them worked—but by the leisure of the women. As one fictional uncle said (in Wilkie Collins' *No Name*) about his two well-bred, genteel, but technically illegitimate nieces, as he robbed them of their inheritance: "Let them, as becomes their birth, gain their bread in situations." And, as Mrs. Ellis put it: "It is scarcely necessary in the present state of society to point out . . . the loss of character and influence occasioned by living below our station" (Ellis, 1843, p. 219). Victorians continued to insist that the work of governess was an exception to the "theory of civilised life in this and all other countries . . . that the women of the upper and middle classes are supported by their male relatives: daughters by their fathers, wives by their husbands. If a lady has to work for her livelihood, it is universally considered to be a misfortune, an exception to the ordinary rule" (Belloc, 1865, pp. 74–75). But their own definitions were too potent—and too important to them.

In the paragraph quoted earlier Elizabeth Eastlake says that the truly important components of a woman's social status are those related to birth and education and that the question of wealth is only minor. But in the same article she seems to reverse her position when she says: "There is no other class which so cruelly requires its members to be, in birth, mind, and manners, above their station, in order to fit them for their station." And, later, Lady Eastlake reverts to her earlier position and states emphatically that the governess is "a needy *lady*" (Eastlake, 1848, pp. 176–177, 179). This contradiction, stated or implied, is very evident in mid-century writing about the governess's social position. Mrs. Sewell, for example, quotes a governess who says, "My friends think I am lowered in social position and they are correct." But Mrs. Sewell continues to call the governesses "ladies" and to discuss their gentility and social position in terms that suggest no loss of status (Sewell, 1870, pp. 208, 244–245, 257–258). Sociologists call this conflict in the assessment of a person's social characteristics "status incongruence." The status incongruence of the Victorian governess was more than a matter of conflicting notions about the propriety of paid employment for a lady. It reached into the operations of everyday life.

Earlier it was suggested that the home was the ideal place for a gentlewoman to be employed because she remained in her proper environment. But such employment was, in fact, an aggravation of her incongruent status. While employment in a middle-class home was intended to provide a second home for the governess, her presence there was evidence of the failure of her own middle-class family to provide the protection and support she needed. The structure of the household, too, pointed to the governess's anomalous position. She was a lady and therefore not a servant, but she was an employee and therefore not of equal status with the wife and daughters of the house. The purposes of her employment contributed further to the incongruence of her position. She was hired to provide the children, and particularly the young women of the family, with an education to prepare them for leisured gentility. But she had been educated in the same way and for the same purpose, and her employment became a prostitution of her education, of the values underlying it, and of her family's intentions in providing it. Her function as a status symbol of middle-class gentility also perverted her own upbringing. She was educated to be a "nosegay" to adorn her "papa's drawing room" (Craik, 1861, p. 7), and as a governess she had sold herself as an ornament to display her employer's prestige.[7]

An individual's social position is intimately related to patterns of action—to the way others behave toward him and the behavior expected of him—what social scientists call "roles." Incongruent social status results in confused and often contradictory behavior, both from the individual and his or her associates. As Mrs. Sewell said of the governess, "No one knows exactly how to treat her." If we look at the behavior of the members of the family toward the governess from the perspective of her incongruent position, it becomes comprehensible as a statement-in-action of the contradictions they sensed.

The parents' treatment of the governess was characterized by great variability from family to family, and from day to day within a single family. In one breath the mistress of the house might invite her to participate in some event and in the next would order her to work. Some families, like the senior Ruskins, included the governess in their circle when they entertained. Others required that she eat with the children unless it served their convenience to have her present at the dinner table (Neff, 1929, pp. 165–166; Ruskin, 1949, p. 111). John Ruskin scolded his readers for their behavior toward their governesses:

> What reverence do you show to the teachers you have chosen? Is a girl likely to think her own conduct, or her own intellect, of much importance, when you trust the entire formation of her character, moral and intellectual, to a person whom you let your servants treat with less respect than they do your housekeeper (as if the soul of your child were a less charge than jams and groceries), and whom you yourself think you confer an honour upon by letting her sometimes sit in the drawing-room in the evening? (Ruskin, 1916, p. 60)

It is hardly surprising that "According to general report, the position of an upper servant in England . . . is infinitely preferable to that of a governess" (Sewell, 1870, p. 237). The servant had the advantage of an unambiguous position, and there was apparently no small comfort in knowing one's place.

The behavior of the children tended to reveal and reflect the attitude of their parents. There was sometimes respect and affection, but more often there was disobedience, snobbery, and sometimes physical cruelty. A frequent theme of governess novels was the triangle of governess, parents, and children, in which the unruly children pitted mother against governess and escaped the discipline due them. It is hazardous to assess from novelists' descriptions alone the extent to which these "trials of the governess" were a real problem, but the frequency with which articles and books dealt with the matter of how a governess should be treated and urged parents to support her authority suggests that the domestic dramas of the Victorian era had a firm foundation in English social life (*Governess Life*, 1849; *Hints to Governesses*, 1856; Sewell, 1870, p. 252).

As Ruskin says, servants, no less than parents and children, responded to the incongruity of a lady-employee in the house. Lady Eastlake observed that "The servants invariably detest her, for she is a dependent like themselves, and yet, for all that, as much their superior in other respects as the family they both serve" (Eastlake, 1848, p. 177; see also *Hints to Governesses*, 1856, pp. 26–27; Neff, 1929, pp. 166–168; Sewell, 1870, p. 239). The governess usually had little power over the servants and yet she was to be served by them. They resented her for acting like a lady but would have criticized her for any other manner.

Her relationships with the world outside the family were a further extension of the conflicts within the family. She could expect to lose touch with the friends of her leisured days, because she no longer had either the money or the time for them. Her relations with men and women alike were strained by her position.

> She is a bore to almost any gentleman, as a tabooed woman, to whom he is interdicted from granting the usual privileges of the sex, and yet who is perpetually crossing his path. She is a bore to most ladies by the same rule, and a reproach too—for her dull, fagging, bread-and-water life is perpetually putting their pampered listlessness to shame. (Eastlake, 1848, p. 177; see also Open Council, 1858, pp. 210–211)

Particularly revealing here is the conflict between the gentleman's conduct toward ladies and toward governesses. There was no easy courtesy, attraction, or flirtation between a gentleman and a governess, because she was not his social equal. The pattern of relations between gentlemen and their female domestics was not fitting either, because the governess was not entirely an inferior.[8]

Reared and educated with the same values as her employers and their guests, the governess was the first to be aware of the incongruities of her social position. She tended to judge herself by prevailing social standards and was often uncertain about how she should behave. Two modes of response stand out. One was self-pity, what Frances Power Cobbe calls the "I-have-seen-better-days airs," and an appeal for the pity of those around her. The other was for the governess to present herself to the world with an oversupply of pride, to compensate for the fear of slight or rebuff that she felt. If a governess sought pity, she was a bore; if she was proud, she was criticized for a "morbid worldliness" that make her oversensitive to neglect and disrespect (Cobbe, 1894, vol. 1, p. 51; Eastlake, 1848, pp. 173 ff.; *Governess Life*, 1849, p. 15; Sewell, 1870, pp. 244, 210, 238). Given the inconsistent behavior of others toward her and her own confused self–estimate, it would not be surprising if contemporary observers were correct when they said that the governesses formed one of the largest single occupational groups to be found in insane asylums (Martineau, 1859, p. 307; Sewell, 1870, pp. 245–246).

What look like normal occupational hazards embellished with a Victorian taste for melodrama, turn out to be products of conflict within a complex social structure. The governess was caught in the cross-fire of conflicting social definitions and roles. She and her employers alike sought, in a variety of ways, to solve the dilemma that faced them.

One way of escaping the contradiction of the employed gentlewoman was to deny, or at least minimize, the fact of employment. The governess often viewed her position this way. The central features of advertisements in the London *Times*, for example, were not the occupational dimensions of the work—qualifications, pay, and the like—but the personal position involved. In the words of one advertisement, it was "a comfortable home, the first consideration" (1 January, 1847). The loss of a governess's home, where she should have had not only maintenance, but protection, led her to seek a surrogate home in her employer's house. For both governess and employer this constituted what can be called a retreat to a traditional mode of relationship. The governess entered the economic marketplace, but the employer tried, in his home, to preserve her gentlewoman's position, traditionally defined in terms of personal and familial relationships and not in the contractual terms of modern employment. In the situation of incongruence, rejecting the realities of the modern role was a means, artificial perhaps, of reducing the dissonance of family and employee. Mrs. Sewell captured this attitude when she wrote: "A situation is offered them: a home, in which they are to be quite happy. 'They will be so well treated, and made entirely one of the family.' " In endorsing the attitude of friendliness and respect for governesses by employers, she warned that the alternative was that the governess would become a disinterested paid employee (Gerth & Mills, 1958, pp. 180–195; Sewell, 1870, pp. 211, 250, 258).

The denial of a governess's womanliness—and more particularly her sexuality—was another mode of reducing conflict. The sexual dimension of the relationship of governesses and men in the household is so rarely mentioned in Victorian literature that it is worthwhile quoting a lengthy and rather circuitous description of it from *Governess Life*. In the passage from which this excerpt is taken the author has been discussing a variety of serious breaches of conduct on the part of the governess:

> Frightful instances have been discovered in which she, to whom the care of the young has been entrusted, instead of guarding their minds in innocence and purity, has become their corruptor—she has been the first to lead and to initiate into sin, to suggest and carry on intrigues, and finally to be the instrument of destroying the peace of families . . .

These are the grosser forms of sin which have been generally concealed from public notice . . . but none of the cases are imaginary ones, and they are but too well known in the circles amongst which they occurred. In some instances again, the love of admiration has led the governesses to try and make herself necessary to the comfort of the father of the family in which she resided, and by delicate and unnoticed flattery gradually to gain her point, to the disparagement of the mother, and the destruction of mutual happiness. When the latter was homely, or occupied with domestic cares, opportunity was found to bring forward attractive accomplishments, or by sedulous attentions to supply her lack of them; or the sons were in some instances objects of notice and flirtation, or when occasion offered, visitors at the house.

This kind of conduct has led to the inquiry which is frequently made before engaging an instructress, "is she handsome or attractive?" If so, it is conclusive against her [i.e., she is not employed]. (Governess Life, 1849, pp. 14–15)

Thus one of the stereotypes of the ideal governess came to be a homely, severe, unfeminine type of woman, and this is the image often conveyed in *Punch*. The trustworthy Miss Garth, in Wilkie Collins' *No Name*, had a hard-featured face, a lean, angular physique, and was known for her "masculine readiness and decision of movement."[9] By contrast, Becky Sharp was an example of what havoc could be wrought by an attractive and unscrupulous governess in a family.

These efforts at adjustment through denial of a governess's employment or her femininity were, in large measure, unsatisfactory. A better solution was to avoid the issue of status assessment by employing a foreign governess. Part of the popularity of foreign governesses was, of course, due to the superior training they had had on the continent and the advantage all of them had in teaching a foreign language. But their foreign origins also avoided the incongruence that existed when an English gentlewoman was a paid employee in an English home. As Elizabeth Sewell said:

As a general rule, foreign governesses are much more agreeable inmates of a house than English ones. Something of this may be owing to the interest excited by difference of manner, dress, and tone; something, also, to the imposing influence of a foreign tongue . . . A good Parisian accent will always command a certain amount of respect. But most important, foreigners are less tenacious of their dignity . . . largely because of their ignorance of English customs. (Sewell, 1870, pp. 239–240)

The difficulties of treating a governess both as a lady and as an employee were reduced by importing a woman who was less familiar with English manners and therefore less likely to recognize, and be offended at, a family's failure to treat her properly.

Another mode of coping with the dilemmas of incongruent status was, simply, escape. This might take the form of a governess's day-to-day isolation from the family circle, either by her choice or theirs, in order to avoid for the moment the stresses of conflicting roles. The more permanent way of escape for the governess was to leave the occupation entirely. But for a woman without means, the only way out was marriage. It is difficult to assess how frequently governesses married and succeeded in resolving permanently their status conflicts. Occasionally, Victorian memoirs refer to governesses marrying out of the occupation (Hare, 1869, vol. 1, pp. 176, 248, 250; Ruskin, 1941, pp. 111, 115). But these sources are, by virtue of being memoirs, likely to reflect the mores of a more stable group of upper-middle and upper-class Englishmen, who, although they might have considered it imprudent, would not have seen their status endangered by such a marriage. A more typical attitude is that described by Florence Nightingale and repeated frequently in writings of the time. "The governess is to have every one of God's gifts; she is to do that which the mother herself is incapable of doing, but our son must not degrade himself by marrying the governess . . . " (Strachey, 1928, p. 405). Since one of the functions of marriage was to extend the connections of the family and to add, through the marriage settlement, additional income to the young family, the attractions of an orphaned, poverty-stricken girl would be very limited.

Just as foreign governesses in England served to reduce the problem of status incongruence for the Victorian employer, emigration of the English governess served to reduce conflict for her. She might choose to go to another part of England or, like the foreign governess who came to England, she might, if more adventurous or more desperate, go abroad. Lady Eastlake recognized the advantages of escaping the society and definitions that made a governess's life uncomfortable: "foreign life is far more favourable to a governess's happiness. In its less stringent domestic habits, the company of a teacher, for she is nothing more abroad, is no interruption—often an acquisition" (Eastlake, 1848, p. 178). Such a move, however, would require that an Englishwoman admit the realities of her status as a paid employee and resign herself to the loss of her place in English society.

Between 1849 and 1862 several organizations were established that, among other activities, promoted the emigration of governesses to the colonies, where there were few women and better chances for employment. The organizations involved were the National Benevolent Emigration Society, the Society for the Employment of Women, and the Female Middle-Class Emigration Society. These agencies have been treated as part of the movement for improving the employment situation for all single women of the middle classes (Banks & Banks, 1964, pp. 31, 33). But it seems likely that two other motives were involved. Women escaped to a place where status would be less ambiguous and less painful and where there was more chance of marriage and permanent resolution to incongruence. The other purpose of the female emigration societies was to lure out of England the "half-educated daughters of poor professional men, and . . . the children of subordinate government officers, petty shopkeepers"—those daughters from the lower ranks of the middle class whose fathers had been educating them as governesses in order to raise their station in life. Failing emigration, they were urged to become shop assistants, telegraphists, and nurses (Banks & Banks, 1964, p. 33).

These attempts to resolve status conflict all involved an effort to maintain the traditional place of the woman in family and society. The middle of the nineteenth century saw the beginning, ambiguous to be sure, of the shift toward professional, market-oriented women's employment. The first institutional symbol of this was the Governesses' Benevolent Institution, which, as already mentioned, was founded in 1843. Its purpose was to provide placement service, temporary housing for unemployed governesses, insurance, and annuities to aging governesses—services clearly oriented toward the market aspect of governesses' employment (GBI, 1852, pp. 139 ff.). But the flavor, and often the substance, of the traditional view of the governess is apparent in the activities of the Institution, which still spoke of "homes" for governesses when referring to jobs. The G.B.I. did not agitate for the wider employment of gentlewomen and, in fact, attempted to narrow the profession by including only those women "with character." The institution further reinforced the differences between governesses and working women of lower status by giving governesses a separate source of charity in time of distress. In providing a home for ill and aged governesses, these charitable Englishmen believed they could keep at least a portion of them out of the workhouse, which, bad as it was for the "lower orders," was supposed to cause even greater suffering to a woman of refinement and cultivation (Eastlake, 1848, p. 181). Such genteel charity went some way toward maintaining the fiction that members of the gentle classes were not sinking into the class beneath.

Queen's College, in London, was established in 1848 to provide education for governesses. The founders' purpose was to give governesses a training that would elevate their self-esteem, make them better teachers, and increase respect for them (*Governess Life*, 1849, p. 122; Maurice & Kingsley, 1849, p. 31; Sewell, 1870, p. 209). The school was also open to ladies who were not governesses, but there was no intention to overload an already crowded occupation. It was thought that "every lady is and must be a teacher—of some person or other, of children, sisters, the poor." And Queen's College was to prepare future wives and mothers for a better performance of their traditional role. The other reason for admitting them was related to that social and economic instability that was so often a topic of early and mid-Victorian discussion: "Those who had no dream of entering upon such work [i.e., governessing] this year, might be forced by some reverse of fortune to think of it next year" (Maurice & Kingsley, 1849, pp. 4–5). The author of *Governess Life* saw another benefit arising from the improved education of lady-governesses at Queen's College: "The public will reap this great benefit from the improved mode of instruction, that the ignorant and unqualified will no longer be able to compete with the wise and good, and will therefore have to seek for other means of subsistence" (*Governess Life*, 1849, p. 127; Sewell, 1870, p. 259). Along with the market orientation of professional training for teachers, the establishment of Queen's College was to widen the gap between those "true gentlewomen" who were driven downward into paid employment and the ill-bred, upwardly mobile daughters of tradesmen and clerks who were trying to rise through the governess's occupation (Eastlake, 1848, p. 184).[10]

The mid-nineteenth century saw the beginnings of a movement to broaden opportunities for employment of women. Prominent women such as Harriet Martineau argued for increasing such opportunities, and the *English Woman's Journal* began what amounted to a crusade for this kind of reform. But neither Miss Martineau's call for new jobs nor the journal's campaign were intended simply to give new alternatives to unemployed, needy ladies. The need for more jobs for women, it was argued, arose from the fact that, in the closed market, many "incompetent" women were drawn into governess's work, resulting in "injury to the qualified governesses" (Martineau, 1859, p. 330). The *English Woman's Journal* was quite explicit in the matter: if other occupations were opened to women, "surely then the daughters of our flourishing tradesmen, our small merchants and manufacturers, who remain single for a few . . . years, may find some occupation more healthy, more exciting, and more profitable than the under ranks of governessing." Such girls might help their fathers and brothers in the shop or business, an alternative preferable to "rigidly confining themselves to what they deem the gentilities of private life, and selling themselves to a family but little above their own station for £25 a year" (The Profession of the Teacher, 1858, p. 10). Mrs. Sewell saw that if girls from cultivated, comfortable homes took up occupations without the pressure of poverty, it would help to break down "our English prejudices" against jobs other than governessing as suitable work for ladies (The Disputed Question, 1858, pp. 361–367; Sewell, 1870, pp. 232–233). But such change would not take place until the pressures of female militance, war, and the tensions inherent in the idea of woman as ornament drove the middle classes to resign the leisured lady as a banner and bulwark of their gentility.

NOTES

1. Since the publication of this essay, research on the history of Victorian women has continued at a rapid pace. Among the works that have appeared are some that extend our knowledge of some of the historical issues raised here: Joyce Senders Pedersen, School-mistresses and headmistresses: Elites and education in nineteenth-century England, *Journal of British Studies*, 1975, *14* (1), 135–162; A. James Hammerton, *Emigrant gentlewomen: Genteel poverty and female emigration, 1830–1914* (London: Croom Helm, 1979); and Joan Burstyn, *Victorian education and the ideal of womanhood* (London: Croom Helm, 1980). Middle-class family life is still much in need of historical attention. Patricia Branca, *Silent sisterhood: Middle class women in the Victorian home* (Pittsburgh: Carnegie-Mellon University Press, 1975), takes up the problems of the lower-middle class woman in her domestic environment.

2. Within this category there were such specializations as the nursery governess and the finishing governess, the former responsible for early education of children and the latter mainly for finishing the training of adolescent girls in the niceties of social life, manners, and culture. For examples of how a family mixed the services of a variety of governesses see Cobbe, 1894, vol. 1, pp. 38–39, 50–51; Woolf, 1960, p. 53. The governess should not be confused with the nurse, also called nursemaid or "nanny." The nursemaid, also responsible for child care, was clearly of the servant class. As much overlapping as there might have been in child care, duties, the distinction between the two occupations was always clear.

3. Luomala (1960, p. 195ff.) suggests these means for displaying status symbols. Eastlake (1848, pp. 179–180) calls the governess a symbol of "fine ladyism."

4. In an earlier era such a woman might go to live with relatives and serve some of the same functions as a governess but without pay and be, in a truer sense, part of the family. The job of paid governess may be seen as an institutionalization and movement out of the family of two functions originally performed by the older "extended" family—the education of children, and the support of orphaned or impoverished relatives.

5. The thinking is contradictory—the belief that gentle birth would always tell (and that education or "accomplishments" were only a finish and no substitute for good birth) clashes with belief in the possibility of daughters being corrupted by association with those of inferior birth. Belief in the essential identity of good birth and gentle status may have been an effort on the part of those who had arrived to deny their own movement into gentility—to suggest, at least, that their gentility was not simply a product of well-spent money.

6. This role may be one source of the image of the stern, autocratic governess, which seems to have developed in the late Victorian period—see K. West (1949) for a full discussion. The image of the severe governess is carried to extremes in that piece of pseudo-Victorian pornography, *Harriet Marwood, Governess* (reprinted, New York, 1967).

7. Metaphors of prostitution are not uncommon (e.g., The Profession of the Teacher, pp. 10, 13) and there are hints that some middle-class women were driven into that older profession (A House of Mercy, 1858, p. 25; Sewell, 1870, pp. 245–246).

8. Sexual relations with servants, such as those described in *My Secret Life*, would have been taboo with the governess (Marcus, 1966, pp. 117–118, 130–131). Physical relations with a woman of the working class seem to have carried no social obligations, while sexual relations

with a woman so nearly of one's own class could not be isolated from a whole complex of responsibilities. The sexual tensions may have been one element of what made a governess a better subject for novelists than the lady's paid companion, though the companion was in many respects a similar occupation.

9. *The Governess* (1836) begins with the statement that there are three classes of people in the world, "men, women, and governesses" (p. 1). Some governesses seem to be a fulfillment of the warning, common in the nineteenth century, that work "unsexed" a woman. See for example Belloc, 1865, p. 156.

10. Elizabeth Eastlake opposed the examination of governesses for certificates because she felt the true qualification for teaching was personal moral character, which could not be taught or tested. The qualities she names are those of a good Victorian mother.

Chapter 3

LONELINESS AND SOCIAL IDENTITY

Linda A. Wood

Here was a grown man, educated in the city, who acted like a simple peasant and could not accept the idea that he was alone in the world and could expect no assistance from anyone. Every one of us stood alone . . . It mattered little if one was mute; people did not understand one another anyway. They collided with or charmed one another, hugged or trampled one another, but everyone knew only himself . . . Like the mountain peaks around us, we looked at one another, separated by valleys, too high to stay unnoticed, too low to touch the heavens. (Kosinski, 1978, pp. 249–250)

Loneliness has long been a neglected topic in the mainstream of the social psychological literature, so the increased attention it has received over the past few years is a welcome development. Much of this attention has reflected a cognitive, or more specifically, an attributional perspective (e.g., Peplau, Russell & Heim, 1979) and has focused upon "ordinary" loneliness or loneliness associated with deficiencies in relationships. Work in this vein has certainly contributed to our understanding of loneliness. However, the tendency to focus on such a subjective, individualistic analysis (cf. Sampson, 1981) leads to the neglect of the social arrangements and historical circumstances within which loneliness is experienced; loneliness becomes reified. Further, such analyses give insufficient attention to the social character of loneliness—to the interactional processes involved in

I wish to thank R.O. Kroger, T.R. Sarbin, and K.E. Scheibe for their coments, suggestions, encouragement, and patience throughout the preparation of this chapter and acknowledge gratefully the support of the Social Sciences and Humanities Research Council of Canada, the Rural Development Outreach Project, University of Guelph, and the participants in the rural elderly research project.

both its development and identification, to loneliness as an interpersonal as well as an intrapersonal experience, and to the shared recognition of the inevitable nature and conditions of human life that are the root of existential loneliness. It is perhaps not surprising that the social nature of loneliness is deemphasized; however defined, loneliness in its essence seems to involve the experience of the "not social," the "not shared," of one's separate, isolated individuality, of the "I," not the "we." But to focus only on this aspect of loneliness is to deny its paradoxical, dialectical nature.

The current literature (e.g., Hartog, Audy & Cohen, 1980) identifies other approaches to loneliness. Some point to the importance of social conditions and social structure (e.g., Sadler & Johnson, 1980). Other forms of loneliness besides the "ordinary," such as existential, cosmic, and cultural loneliness, are considered. These approaches are limited in that they lack concepts to connect social structure to the individual experience of different forms of loneliness, to relate the different forms of loneliness to each other, and to account for individual differences in responses to more general social conditions (Wood, 1978b).

The concept of social identity provides a basis for connecting loneliness to social structure. Social identity is useful in another way. Despite the emphasis on loneliness as subjective experience, relatively little attention has been directed to the precise nature of that experience for the individual. How does an individual experience loneliness—as a feeling, a mood, an emotion, an attitude? Is the personal experience different for different varieties of loneliness? Is loneliness a "state" characterized by other subjective experiences, for example, by emotions such as depression? A focus on social identity may suggest some answers to these questions.

The concept of social identity has a long history; it has been interpreted and used in many ways. For the purposes of this essay, I shall mainly employ the model of social identity developed originally by Sarbin, Scheibe, and Kroger (Sarbin & Allen, 1968). Its details are presented elsewhere (Sarbin & Scheibe, *this volume*; Wood, 1978b), so I shall consider here only some general aspects of the model and their implications before focusing directly on loneliness.

TYPES OF SOCIAL IDENTITY

Very briefly, social identity is viewed as a function of all of a person's social positions. It consists of two basic components, respect and esteem, which are derived respectively from ascribed and achieved social positions. Respect and esteem reflect, among other things, the prestige of the positions, the quality of their enactment, and their salience to the person. For some purposes it is appropriate to view respect and esteem as varying in strength in a quantitative fashion, but for the present we may articulate four basic types of identity that are qualitatively as well as quantitatively different (see Figure 3.1).

Optimal identities are those in which both respect and esteem are strong. The person who has a relatively large number and variety of validated, salient, achieved, and ascribed positions is less vulnerable to the exigencies of everyday life. Esteem is important because it reflects social worth; the relatively clear-cut criteria and feedback for validation of achieved positions (in contrast to ascribed positions) mean that high esteem is likely to be matched by high self-esteem. Esteem also means that the person not only has access to the various practical resources associated with social worth (financial and material, knowledge and information, personal contacts) but also is psychologically able to deploy these resources. Achieved positions provide perspective. One can cease to occupy them, they require only intermittent performances and they are not continuously involving. The ability to view one's own life from a variety of perspectives is clearly helpful for problem solving, and for behavioral flexibility. Moreover, for achieved positions, one's role performances *vis-à-vis* the occupants of reciprocal roles are not tied to particular others; as a teacher, for example, one interacts with students, but the particular individuals enacting the student role change from year to year. This is important for individuation, for the maintenance of one's sense of a separate self. The intermittent nature of achieved roles coupled with the possibility of changing achieved positions (either through promotion or substitution) also suggests that identities strong in esteem have potential for growth and change. But the benefits of an identity strong in esteem are only possibilities—the implications of achieved positions for their occupants may be negative as well as positive. The advantages of multiple identity—of multiple senses of self— are moot if at the same time one experiences the self as fragmented, as disunited. The experience of self as separate can mean isolation as well as

Figure 3.1. Types of Social Identity

Esteem

		High	Low
Respect	High	Optimal	Helpless
	Low	Hollow	Empty

Note. "High" and "Low" should be taken to reflect relative amounts of respect and esteem.

individuation. Without the experience of self as continuous, the possibilities of change in identity will not be realized. Such changes can neither be initiated, nor, if imposed externally, can they be coped with.

Continuity, integration, and connectedness are functions of respect, which is why the occupation of ascribed positions is so important for optimal functioning, even though the immediate valuative consequences of occupying such positions are neutral, or are positive only in contrast to the negative consequences of failure to validate. The continuous, nonoptional nature of ascribed positions, and their linkages to particular others (which are often biological, e.g., parent and child) can be seen as providing an essential basis for identity, not least because of their constraints. This is clearly the case developmentally in that all of early experience occurs within the context of ascribed relationships.

The implications of the interrelationships between the components of social identity, respect and esteem, can be illustrated if we briefly consider the other basic types of social identity. Hollow identities are those in which esteem is strong and respect is weak. The term "hollow" indicates the absence of the core of identity, of the continuity and foundation embodied in respect. The hollow identity is thus vulnerable to collapse should there be a threat to esteem (e.g., loss of occupational position). The absence of respect may also create difficulties for the maintenance of esteem to the extent that the effort of achievement is not seen as worthwhile. Helpless identities are those in which esteem is weak, but respect is strong; if a hollow identity is a strong container without contents, a helpless identity is one that consists of contents without a container. It is an unprotected core. The absence of esteem means that the person will lack many of the resources necessary to function in everyday life. Proportionately more effort is expended on the maintenance of relationships without tangible rewards. Yet at the same time, the lack of a sense of social worth combined with perceptions of helplessness and lack of control may mean that such efforts require relatively more energy. Little energy therefore is available for the development of sources of esteem. Helpless identities will thus be internally stable, and any problems associated with this type of identity will tend to be chronic rather than acute.

The fourth type of identity is empty; both respect and esteem are weak. For a person with this type of identity, the validation of those few ascribed positions that are occupied will also require great effort; further however, the consequences of such efforts in terms of creating and maintaining a sense of personal worth may be so minimal that the efforts are not worthwhile (Sarbin & Scheibe, *this volume*). In the absence of esteem, such efforts cannot be viewed as necessary for providing the validation of ascribed roles, which is required for the occupation of linked achieved roles, nor are there achieved positions that might provide quasi validation for ascribed roles. Under these circumstances, the person may cease to perform the minimal activities required for the most basic ascribed positions, for example, by failing to observe the norms of modesty and communication associated with the position of "human being." Or efforts may be redirected toward activities that constitute active violation of norms, for example, injury to other people. The consequences of such failures and violations will frequently take the form of institutionalization—in mental hospitals, old age homes, or prisons. At this point, social identity no longer simply lacks respect; it consists rather of disrespect.

Extreme outcomes of empty social identity may be relatively infrequent in view of the potential associated with large numbers of such identity types. Yet such outcomes do seem to occur. The little public information available concerning assassins of public figures and mass murderers seems quite consistent with an empty identity. John Hinckley, who attempted the assassination of President Reagan, is a clear example of the empty identity. The retrospective judgments of the "instability" of such persons capture an important feature of this identity type. With sufficiently detailed and reliable data on such cases, it should be possible to employ the identity model to specify why these violations have taken their particular form, for example, why they might involve public versus private targets, strangers versus network members, etc.

I have given some attention to delineating the types of social identity without referring to loneliness because the model is intended to be general. But a definition of loneliness as the experience of a discrepancy between achieved and desired (or expected) relationships (Wood, 1978a) suggests that loneliness would be related to deficiencies in respect and esteem, given that these components reflect both the quantity and quality of relationships, as well as the person's desires and expectations (the salience of the relationships).

Further, loneliness should be more strongly associated with low respect than with low esteem, because respect refers to more basic intimate relationships than does esteem. Loneliness should then be associated with types of identity in the following order: optimal (low loneliness), helpless, hollow, and empty (high loneliness). In a previous study (Wood, 1978b), I reported such relationships between loneliness, respect, and esteem, and types of identity. I found only a few people with truly "empty" identities, yet a focus upon this type may be most useful for the understanding of loneliness. It has become commonplace to suggest that loneliness is almost an identifying characteristic of institutionalized populations and further that it is a consequence of institutionalization; it is also among such populations that we would expect to find a high proportion of empty identities. Unfortunately, there has been little systematic study of loneliness in various institutionalized populations, although there are numerous anecdotal reports.

The case of the institutionalized aged in particular deserves attention. The notion that loneliness is essentially a problem of old age (despite the evidence that suggests that loneliness is more frequent among younger populations) may reflect both the perception that the institutionalized aged are lonely and a presumed association between aging and institutionalization. One may argue that most old people are in institutions because of medical problems or "psychiatric" disorders such as senility, and not as a consequence of difficulties in managing an empty identity. Loneliness can thus be seen as a consequence of institutionalization—of being cut off from significant relationships, or of having an empty identity imposed on one because he or she is institutionalized (an imposition that is reflected in the treatment of the institutionalized as nonpersons). Undoubtedly this process does occur. But, as suggested earlier, it may be that an empty identity makes it more difficult to cope with everyday life and medical problems. What is diagnosed as senility reflects a withdrawal of effort in the face of an empty identity as much as the physiological processes of aging. Thus, empty social identity with its corresponding loneliness may precede—indeed precipitate—entry into an institution.

Social identity can also function as a mediating concept to help us articulate the possible associations among isolation, loneliness, and extreme behaviors. Depending on the particular combinations of positions, prestige, quality of enactment and salience that are involved in low respect and esteem, the empty identity type may describe a person who is socially isolated. Such isolation may have negative consequences. It may be reflected as loneliness; it also means that the person is unable to engage in the social comparisons and interactions that help prevent us from developing unusual fantasies (particularly violent or destructive ones) or from turning them into actions. But not all isolated people are lonely; nor do all act destructively. The social identity model suggests that it is those persons whose (few) positions are extremely salient who are likely to experience discrepancies (and thus loneliness) in their networks, and who are most dependent upon social comparisons. Further, people whose positions are highly salient are likely to have to expend more energy to maintain their positions and are thus more likely to fail, and to suffer more negative consequences for failure in terms of disrespect. The identity model helps identify those lonely isolates whose only possibilities for coping with an inadequate sense of worth are limited to violations of the basic requirements of being human.

We expect loneliness to be greater among the young and the old than among those between approximately 25 and 65 years of age. First, younger people have not had much opportunity to earn esteem, and older people have lost esteem through retirement, inability to perform roles adequately with increasing age, etc. Second, young peoply have fewer valued ascribed positions, partly because of lack of opportunity (e.g., have not yet married) and also because of current societal conditions in North America: the deemphasis of institutions such as religion, kinship, and nationality, and the absence of stable communities due to high physical mobility. Older people have fewer valued ascribed positions because of the loss of spouses, friends, and family.

For several reasons, we also expect younger people to be relatively lower on respect and esteem and thus experience greater loneliness than older people. Family relationships appear to become increasingly salient with age. For older people, declining activity levels and retirement are associated with greater emphasis on family relationships and interactions. In contrast, younger people, particularly adolescents, may deemphasize the salience of family positions as part of the process of establishing a separate, independent identity. There is increasing differentiation of people as they age. Thus, the factors conducive to loneliness are likely to apply to most or many young people and much less likely to apply to similar proportions of older people. There will, however, be a subset of older people for whom all the processes that can be associated with aging (declining health, retirement, death of spouse and friends) are relevant. Empty identity and high loneliness would thus be quite likely among this group.

To illustrate the potential for loneliness in a limited combination of positions, we can consider the situation of the elderly male widower. Evidence indicates that people in this category are highly vulnerable to loneliness and to suicide (cf. Haas-Hawkings, 1978). The loss of a spouse seems to be a particularly devastating event for men, because it also often involves the loss of other relationships—friends and children—previously maintained by the wife. Thus, widowhood is likely to result in a hollow identity. For the older man who is retired and has few sources of esteem it will mean an empty identity. Further, this transvaluation of identity is likely to be a massive one, given the hypothesis that high respect and high esteem characterize the identity of employed married men. The transvaluation may be even greater for the man who has retired from a high-status position because it will involve a relatively greater loss of esteem.

Some of these ideas have been assessed in previous work (Wood, 1978b) and in general were supported. For example, I found that loneliness was related to marital status, to sex, to education, and to the interactions between the variables. Loneliness was unrelated to occupation, and was positively related to age, findings that probably reflect the particular nature of the sample. And while the relationships described were statistically significant, they were not strong. Indeed, it would be surprising if they were, given that such tests are limited to a few social positions and do not consider any factors included in the model other than the sheer occupation of position.

In the model, a distinction is made between esteem and respect, and self-esteem and self-respect. I have suggested above that the strengths of esteem and of self-esteem are likely to be roughly comparable because of the public nature of achieved positions. Discrepancies between respect and self–respect are more likely. Since loneliness appears to be related to discrepancies between a person's self-view and the views held by others (or perceived by the person to be held by others)(e.g., Rogers, 1970), we might anticipate that loneliness would be related to the discrepancy between respect and self–respect (since respect reflects the views of significant others). The literature on loneliness also reports consistent findings of an inverse relationship between global self-esteem (as the term is traditionally used) and loneliness (e.g., Wood 1978b). Even stronger relationships between loneliness and self–views might be uncovered if we differentiated between different types of self-views (self-esteem versus self-respect), as well as between different types of loneliness (e.g., of social isolation vs. emotional isolation).

EPISTEMOLOGICAL AND EXISTENTIAL LONELINESS

> To the extent that we are all different, all individual, we are all lonely, every man a stranger, every heart closed to every other heart, and we live and die in this loneliness. (Mannin, 1966, p. 1)

It is in the nature of human existence to be separate from other people, to be unable to share experience completely with others, to be ultimately alone when facing the major events of life. This is the heart of "existential loneliness." Existential loneliness is distinguished from "ordinary" or personal loneliness in that it refers to a condition of all human life, not to a condition of an individual life.

Epistemological loneliness is an aspect of existential loneliness that refers specifically to "the realization that persons all view the world from individualized and idiosyncratic perspectives and that there is no simple criterion of objectivity by which to arbitrate this diversity of points of view" (Chandler, 1975, p. 171). There are several problems with the concepts of existential and epistemological loneliness. It is not clear, for example, how frequent or widespread existential loneliness is. Is it something to be fully endured only by people with an intellectualizing, philosophical bent and only dimly apprehended, if at all, by the rest of the population? College students describing loneliness experiences refer infrequently to existential loneliness compared with personal loneliness (Sermat, 1978). Does this mean that for them existential loneliness is overshadowed by interpersonal concerns, or that existential loneliness is a function of age or of the experiences that come with age? Many of these experiences—making major decisions, birth, and death—would seem to foster existential loneliness, even though it may not be well or frequently articulated. But the recognition of multiple perspectives is required for the attainment of cognitive maturity; epistemological loneliness, in some form, must therefore be quite widespread.

To begin, it seems necessary to make a basic distinction between beliefs and the positive or negative quality of those beliefs. We should, for example, distinguish between existential loneliness as an affectively charged term, and the simple recognition of multiple perspectives or of the impossibility of sharing experience. But how does one specify exactly how or when the former "results from" the latter? The concept of "attitude" might be a useful device for considering this basic distinction and for including the essence of previous work. Loneliness can be viewed as one of a set of attitudes concerning social relationships. A number of advantages accrue to this kind of conceptualization. First, it provides a well-established way for thinking about the distinction between cognitive (belief) and affective (evaluative) components. It also suggests a solution to the problem of specifying the "opposite" of loneliness, through the possibility that the value placed on the object of the attitude could be positive, as well as negative. An additional problem concerns the time dimension of loneliness experiences; by viewing loneliness as an attitude, as part of the cognitive resources of persons, we can temporarily avoid this problem. Finally, the employment of the concept of attitude makes it clear that we are dealing with subject perceptions and not objective conditions such as physical or social isolation.

A preliminary sketch of an attitudinal framework for defining loneliness and related concepts is presented in Table 3.1. The focus of existential attitudes is the nature of the human condition, of human existence; personal attitudes concern the condition of one's own life. I have further classified attitudes as intransitive or transitive. Intransitive attitudes are those without an "object"—they concern the general possibilities inherent in human interaction but are unrelated to any particular relationship or to any particular type of relationship. In contrast, transitive attitudes concern relationships with particular others and thus can be classified as either social (concerning relationships with members of the larger community) or emotional (concerning more intimate relationships). The object in transitive attitudes need not be an existing person, and the relationships

Table 3.1. Beliefs and Attitudes about Social Interaction and Social Relationships

		Intransitive		*Transitive*
Focus	{	Existential (conditions of human life; no object)	Personal (conditions of own life; no object)	Personal (conditions of own life; object)
Belief	{	Existential aloneness	Psychological aloneness	Interpersonal separateness (social; emotional)
		Existential togetherness	Psychological togetherness	Interpersonal connectedness (social; emotional)
Attitude	(+)	Existential solitude	Psychological solitude	Privacy (social; emotional)
		Existential closeness	Psychological closeness	Relatedness (social; emotional)
		Existential isolation	Psychological isolation	Loneliness (social; emotional)
	(−)	Existential deindividuation	Psychological deindividuation	Intrusion (social; emotional)

involved may be possibilities rather than actualities. For example, one may entertain beliefs about the kind of relationship one would have with the "man/woman of one's dreams."

The basic distinction between transitive and intransitive attitudes is reflected in the terms employed for the beliefs identified in the second row of Table 3.1. "Aloneness" and "togetherness" refer to beliefs about the sharing of feeling and thinking experiences—whether this is possible. "Separateness" and "connectedness" refer to beliefs about the ties one does not have or has to other persons and about the nature of those particular ties in terms of communication, understanding, and empathy. In labeling the various beliefs and corresponding evaluations, I have tried to take into account both the current usages and meanings of the terms and their etymology. For example, "together" (to-gather) can be taken to mean simply "with," whereas "connected" (co-nected) means "ties with." Thus, the terms aloneness and togetherness are intended to denote simply the "one" versus the "many." In contrast, the terms separateness and connectedness denote, respectively, the breaking of ties (e.g., a "separated" couple is one that was once "tied" or married) or a denial of or failure to establish ties or bonds, and the establishment or maintenance of ties. The distinctions between the various terms parallel the traditional social-psychological distinction between collectivities and groups.

The difference between transitive and intransitive attitudes is important not so much because of the beliefs themselves but because of the potential for change in the corresponding evaluations. Because attitudes of isolation do not involve beliefs and evaluations about particular relationships with particular persons, they are unlikely to change as a result of changes in the nature and quality of one's relationships. Attitudes of isolation are by their nature attitudes of despair. In contrast, an attitude of loneliness is susceptible to change, to solution, because it concerns beliefs about relationships, beliefs that can change if the relationships change.

Within the proposed framework, beliefs are viewed as distinct from evaluations; that is, it is possible for the cognitive component to exist independently, to be unaccompanied by either a positive or negative affective component. From this perspective, beliefs are viewed as potential, as "awareness without meaning." The concept of social identity helps identify the circumstances under which beliefs are likely to have affective meaning, and whether the evaluation will be positive or negative. Both respect and esteem, the components of identity, refer to sets of relationships, or to attachments. The nature of the attachments, however, differs for the two components. The relationships described by respect are not only close, they are also "tight" in that one cannot move in and out of the relevant (ascribed) positions. In contrast, the relationships described by esteem are more distant; further, they are also "loose" in the sense that one can move in and out of the relevant (achieved) positions and thus attain distance or perspective. These possibilities have several implications for the attitudes described in the framework. Consider first the personal-transitive beliefs. The belief that one is separate from other people in the sense described above will be problematic, that is, negatively valued as loneliness, only in the absence of attachments—that is, in the absence of respect or esteem. Further, the possibility of distancing implied in esteem suggests that a belief of separateness can have a positive evaluation (i.e., privacy). Similarly, a belief of connectedness will be problematic, that is, negatively valued as intrusion only in the context of respect where attachments are close and do not permit distancing. In contrast, the belief may be positively valued (in the form of relatedness) in the context of esteem, that is, of attachments that do permit distance.

Social identity also has implications for the intransitive beliefs delineated in the framework, although slightly different aspects of respect and esteem will be involved. Achieved roles, the source of esteem, serve to emphasize the fact of multiple perspectives from which to view the world; further, these perspectives represent different viewpoints. In contrast, the multiple relationships denoted by respect provide multiple perspectives that emphasize shared viewpoints. The recognition of existential aloneness that may accompany the emergence of formal operational thought will be negative (i.e., will be experienced as "existential aloneness") only for those whose identity consists essentially of esteem. However, if identity consists also of respect, this belief is likely to be experienced as positive, that is, as "existential solitude." A belief in "existential togetherness," that is, in the essential oneness of human experience, will be experienced as a form of deindividuation for those whose identity consists essentially of respect. Again, however, where respect is accompanied by esteem, the belief is more likely to be experienced as positive, that is, as "existential closeness."

A belief of existential aloneness logically also entails a belief of psychological aloneness (although the reverse is not necessarily true), and we can apply the same reasoning concerning respect and esteem to beliefs of psychological aloneness and togetherness. There is, however, a basic difference between existential and psychological isolation, so that the latter is likely to be more severe than the former. First, there can be two degrees or types of existential isolation. I have suggested above that isolation will reflect identities with esteem, but without respect. However, isolation may also be experienced in the absence of both esteem and respect. Existential isolation with esteem is likely to be less severe; although esteem may emphasize that all persons hold different viewpoints, it also means, as suggested earlier, that one may hold different viewpoints about oneself. This possibility of taking different viewpoints means that one may better take the viewpoints of others and in turn perceive that others can take one's own viewpoint. The effects of not being able to share perspectives are likely to be dampened to the extent that one can at least take other viewpoints. However, for psychological isolation, esteem is less likely to have such a tempering effect because taking other's viewpoints is less likely for a person who believes that he or she *personally* is basically different from others. Thus, psychological isolation is likely to be severe whether or not esteem is present. Psychological isolation is likely to be more severe than existential isolation for another reason: in existential isolation one may be alone, but at least he or she shares that condition with others. No such consolation is available to the person who experiences psychological isolation.

LONELINESS AS AN EMOTION

The conceptualization of loneliness as an attitude is unusual; loneliness appears to be viewed most frequently, although often implicitly, as a mood or emotion.

My analysis of emotion from the perspective of social identity draws primarily upon the work of Kemper (1978) and Averill (1980a) and, to a lesser extent, upon that of Lazarus and his colleagues (cf. Lazarus, Kanner & Folkman, 1980).[1] This analysis views emotions in the context of social interaction, and suggests that emotions might arise in connection with the enactment of social roles in two basic ways. First, they would appear as part of the "reading of the script," of the enactment of expectations for a particular social role. Second, they will emerge as a concomitant or consequence of disruptions in role performance. Such disruptions can be of several types; they may reflect role conflicts, inconsistent role locations, inadequate quality of enactment, or self-role incongruence.

Role enactment and disruptions in role performances are not inevitably associated with emotion. The experience, interpretation, and display of emotion is related further to two basic dimensions of interaction, status and solidarity, when status and solidarity refer respectively to concepts of differential value and differential closeness (cf. Brown, 1965). It is important to note that status and solidarity are not the same kinds of dimensions in that they do not apply to relationships in the same way and also are not equally relevant to all relationships. Specifically, status emphasizes inequality and is in essence asymmetrical, whereas solidarity emphasizes equality and is symmetrical. Furthermore, in some relationships (e.g., friendship), solidarity is much more important than status, and in others the reverse is true (e.g., employer-employee; and note that the very terms used to describe this relationship are asymmetrical). In terms of the identity model, the relationships involved in achieved roles are primarily status relationships, whereas those associated with ascribed roles are primarily solidarity relationships. However, this distinction is relative rather than absolute. Considerations of solidarity and status are not irrelevant to (respectively) achieved and ascribed relationships and have implications for the emotions experienced in the context of such relationships.

The basic proposal is that emotions arise in connection with relational outcomes. Whether or not an emotion arises, its intensity and expression, and the particular emotion involved will depend upon absolute (high or low) and relative (one person to another) levels of and changes in status and solidarity, as these are interpreted within the context of the situation, the particular relationship involved (e.g., friend or husband), its salience, and its type. Such interpretations reflect both cultural and idiosyncratic standards. This approach suggests that the emotions generated in interactions involving achieved relationships will be different from those generated in interactions involving ascribed relationships. Emotions such as contempt, pride, and envy are associated with "status" relationships, whereas emotions such as jealousy and love are associated with "solidarity" relationships.

With respect to the nature of emotional experience itself, the identity approach incorporates the traditional notion of emotion as a syndrome involving physiological, cognitive, and behavioral components, although the way in which these components are viewed differs somewhat from that of other approaches. Physiologically, emotion is seen as a combination of specific and nonspecific factors connected with some particular considerations involving status and solidarity as fundamental dimensions of interaction. The cognitive component includes not only the label of the emotion, but also the appraisal of the emotion as "passion" (Averill, 1980a) and a number of specific cognitions relevant to the content of the emotion. Situational appraisals are absent. While situational appraisals give rise to and shape the experience of emotion, they (unlike self-appraisals) are not part of the emotion per se. Finally, there is no necessary relationship between emotional behavior and arousal; the relationship will depend upon the context, the particular relationships involved, and so forth.

I shall attempt to illustrate below how this view of emotion in the context of social interactin (which may be imagined, anticipated, retrospective, or actual) can be helpful for differentiating emotions, and for providing specific links between individual emotional experience and social structure. But I would stress that most of the distinctions to which I have referred are analytical and not material. In the course of everyday life, we do not differentiate between status and solidarity, labels and content, expression and experience, nor do we function at the same level of abstractness.

Consider the idea of loneliness as an emotion. I am now inclined to believe that when people refer to loneliness, they rarely employ the vocabulary of emotion per se. The experience does not seem to involve any particular physiological involvement and the duration tends to be too long. This is not to say that loneliness is never an emotional experience. In some circumstances such a classification is appropriate—when there is an acute reaction containing some physiological components (at the moment unidentified) and a set of cognitions about one's own state *vis-à-vis* another person (e.g., "I miss you," "I cannot talk to/reach you") that imply separation and that may or may not include the cognition "I am/feel lonely"; further, the reaction implies movement towards the other and occurs in response to a perceived absence of solidarity in the context of interaction, an absence that is the result of a previous loss or decline in solidarity. Such reactions can occur in imaginary interaction (retrospective or anticipatory), for example, when one thinks of a deceased spouse, or absent lover, or contemplates the imminent death of someone close. (And such imaginary interaction may occur during the course of actual interaction with "irrelevant" others.) The reaction may also occur during actual interaction, for example, where the absence of solidarity is signaled by a "breakdown in communications" (or where the latter is interpreted as a sign of the former). This view of loneliness as an emotion should be sufficient to distinguish it from other emotions.

The distinction between loneliness and grief might be taken as an example, for they are often discussed together. Grief occurs in response to the *loss* of a loved one and gradually subsides over time, whereas loneliness occurs in response to the absence of a loved one and thus continues until the relationship is replaced (Weiss, 1973). Thus grief can be seen as a response to the loss as opposed to the absence of solidarity. It might be further distinguished from loneliness in terms of the cognitive component; that is, grief will include cognitions about the future, such as "I will never see him again," "I will never meet anyone like her again." Because the loss of solidarity and the absence of solidarity can occur together (or be perceived that way), we might expect loneliness and grief to co-occur. On the actual occasion of a major loss, grief overwhelms loneliness in intensity and as a focus of attention. As the event of the loss recedes in time and the intensity of its memory declines, loneliness becomes the dominant emotion.

The social identity model itself contains some implications for considering loneliness as an emotion. First, loneliness would appear to be a stigmatized emotion (cf. Gordon, S. 1976) so that its display is usually viewed negatively, except for very limited circumstances (e.g., when displayed by the recently widowed). However, an additional complication is that the experience and display of negative emotions may nonetheless be expected for people in certain positions defined by "failure." Without overemphasizing the importance placed in North American culture on being part of a pair or of a couple, it seems that the single, "unattached" person faces a particular dilemma. If the person does not display the "appropriate" emotions with respect to being single (e.g., loneliness, depression) he or she may be viewed as odd or insufficiently sensitive to social expectations or even as missing some element required in normal men or women. On the other hand, the display of negative emotions such as loneliness may simply reinforce the impression of having failed.

Second, the prestige of a social position may constrain the expression (and experience) of emotion by the occupants of the position; as prestige increases, the emotions considered appropriate for display will become more positive, fewer in number, and less likely to concern solidarity, and the intensity and frequency of emotional display will decrease. This would account, for example, for the expectation held by some people that females will be more emotional than males and that the expression of loneliness is more acceptable in females and the aged.

Third, both the general concept of "role skills" and the specific social identity dimension "quality of enactment" suggest that one factor involved in the maintenance of solidarity through successful enactment of relevant roles, and thus in the prevention of loneliness, is the ability to express the emotions associated with different roles. For example, some capacity to display love is clearly necessary for the continued enactment of the spouse role.

CONCEPTUALIZING LONELINESS

the real definition of loneliness: to live without social responsibility. (Gordimer, 1979, p. 77)

What conclusions might we draw about the nature of loneliness? I think first that we must view loneliness as a term describing a multitude of experiences that are different not only in their sources and intensity but also in their fundamental nature. As Audy (1980) has suggested, "Loneliness is a vague idea which comprises episodes or states that should be considered separately" (p. 115).

Although I have suggested above that loneliness is infrequently experienced as an emotion, this does not mean that it is rarely an affective experience, that is, that it does not involve a sense of pleasantness or unpleasantness about one's own state or the world in general. In fact loneliness often corresponds to a feeling or a mood—experiences that are distinct from emotion in that they do not involve any special physiological arousal. Nor do these feelings or moods necessarily arise in the context of interaction; they are likely to be transsituational and of longer duration (particularly moods). But they are not related to a specific other and thus do not imply movement toward, against, or away from the other. (That is, feelings are "intransitive"; if they involve an "other," it is only in a most general sense, as in "I feel good about you.") Following Ewart (1970), I would further distinguish between feelings and moods in that, in the former, there is differentiation between the self and the world with the focus on the self, while in the latter there is not such differentiation. Feelings may be further divided into those in which the focus is on one's "state of body" and those in which the focus is on one's "state of mind" (Arnold, 1960). Feelings of loneliness are likely to be of the latter type, to involve the "emotional colouring (pleasant/unpleasant) of conscious contents" (Ewart,

1970, p. 233), when such contents involve a particular set of cognitions about one's relationships to others or to the world and when the cognitions concern separation or distance (e.g., "I have no one to talk to," "I am alone in the world," "People don't like me"). To refer to loneliness as a feeling rather than as an emotion is not to suggest that it is somehow less serious, because extreme feelings of unpleasantness can be experienced as "pain" (Arnold, 1960).

I am less certain about whether it is appropriate to consider loneliness as a mood, that is, "as a temporary disposition toward a broad set of behavioural *and* private or subjective events" (Nowlis, 1970, p. 264), because it seems to me that moods are too global, too undifferentiated with respect to content to apply to something as specific as loneliness, that they involve only general orientations of good/bad, pleasant/unpleasant, happy/sad. They may nonetheless set the stage for experiences of loneliness as feeling or emotion.

In an earlier section, I discussed the possibility of conceptualizing loneliness as an attitude. This fits quite well with the present scheme. In comparison to feeling or emotion, loneliness as an attitude involves a relatively permanent cognitive structure in which the evaluative component is attached to the object of the cognition rather than to the self. As Arnold (1960) has suggested, such attitudes (which she calls "emotional attitudes") may derive from or be the residue of affective experience; they may in turn influence such experience by providing part of the context of the interpretation of later events.

Finally, loneliness may be used to refer to a condition, that is, it may be used as a description of a person's life over a certain period (defined in terms of events, life stages, particular locations), in which feelings of loneliness are frequent, in which attitudes related to loneliness are dominant, and in which circumstances are conducive to loneliness (e.g., separation from spouse or illness). Aside from the actual frequency of feelings or emotions of loneliness, such a condition is characterized by a potential for such experiences. As one participant in my current research stated,"Loneliness is always with you if your spouse has died" (Wood, 1981).

Whether loneliness is experienced as an emotion, feeling, attitude, or condition, it would always seem to involve considerations of solidarity—its absence or loss. This may not always be apparent, because such considerations can arise in "status contexts." For example, people may report feeling lonely after taking an exam or in connection with a loss of face. But the loneliness itself concerns solidarity, that is, the absence of closeness to others with whom one may share one's experiences of failure or who may restore one's feelings of worth. More generally, status is indirectly important for loneliness, because it influences one's evaluations concerning solidarity and because it may constitute a basis for solidarity (Brown, 1965).

Status also affects the possibilities of enactment of relationships involving solidarity (for example, where losing one's job deprives one of the opportunities to interact with friends in the workplace).

Because of its implications for solidarity, the utility of the social identity model for understanding loneliness is not restricted to the analysis of loneliness as emotion or attitude. For example, certain types or patterns of identity (e.g., hollow) are likely to be associated with frequent feelings of loneliness and, further, may also provide a picture of a condition of loneliness. And the concept of transvaluation of identity has implications for the intensity and frequency of loneliness as feeling or emotion and for changes in loneliness as a condition, as well as for changes in attitudes concerning loneliness.

Using this approach, loneliness might be differentiated from other emotions, feelings, attitudes, and conditions. Apart from any specific physiological differences, emotions can probably be differentiated on the basis of combinations of factors rather than on any single factor. Thus, we need to consider levels and changes in both solidarity and status, as well as combinations of these, the specific relationship involved, and the specific cognitions involved. For example, depression might be distinguished from loneliness in the following ways: it involves the loss of both solidarity and status and includes the cognition that recovery of status or solidarity *vis-à-vis* relevant others is not possible in the future either through their efforts or one's own (i.e., hopelessness). This preliminary distinction might provide one way of integrating psychoanalytic and attributional approaches to depression. The inclusion of the status dimension would distinguish depression from grief, include losses in both the ascribed and achieved realms (the latter of which has implications for control), and provide a link with guilt in the form of a secondary emotion. And it is quite compatible with the results of a recent study by Weeks, Michela, Peplau, and Bragg (1980), which suggest that loneliness and depression are not causally related but share common origins.

Distinctions between loneliness and other emotions might draw upon some of the attributional literature concerning the relationship between attributions about the causes of loneliness and other emotions associated with loneliness. For example, it has been suggested that hostility and anger will be associated with ascriptions of "loneliness to external factors, such as being excluded by other people" (Peplau et al., 1979, p. 63). An advantage of the present approach is that by considering systematically the specific relationships involved (which is not done in the attribution approach), we might be able to distinguish between those instances where "being excluded by others" constitutes an unacceptable level or loss of solidarity and where it does not.

Finally, feelings of loneliness can be distinguished from such feelings as boredom, homesickness, and restlessness on several dimensions. We can consider, for example, the specific cognitions involved and whether these concern solidarity, as well as the extent to which the focus on the self is directed towards a "state of mind" or a "state of body" (e.g., as in restlessness).

Attempts to deal with the personal pain subsumed under loneliness will obviously benefit from a greater understanding of the sources of such experiences, but we may well be able to achieve some more immediate success simply by identifying more precisely what is meant by loneliness. For example, the loneliness of some older people might be alleviated more effectively by transportation and health programs than by social programs, to the extent that such loneliness is in fact boredom created by immobility.

Some general suggestions for intervention can also be derived from the social identity model. Perhaps training in social skills requires a greater emphasis on the specific obligations and expectations associated with different relationships (and less emphasis on the direct elimination of loneliness or on the direct pursuit of happiness). We may need to give greater attention to solidarity and to rethink the notion of success in interpersonal interaction with its implied transformation of ascribed relationships to achieved relationships. Finally, the current emphasis on misperceptions and the success of attribution therapies should not blind us to objective or structural contributions to loneliness, such as unemployment and poor health, that bring about direct losses in status and solidarity.

CONCLUSION

The major theme of this discussion has been that loneliness is an extremely complex phenomenon, susceptible to analysis from a number of perspectives. I have suggested several ways in which concepts of identity might be helpful in looking at loneliness for locating what seems to be a most private experience in a broad social context. As we attempt to extend our understanding, we must consider the implications of our analyses. To what extent does a focus of self, identity, and loneliness contribute to broader social trends, for example, "narcissism" (if such indeed exists; cf. Lasch, 1979) and, in turn, the perpetuation of loneliness? Much of the current social science literature—for example, that on social networks and social support (which contains many hitherto unexploited parallels to social identity theory)—seems to involve one-way relationships, to neglect the necessity (and benefits) of attention to the needs of others. In contrast, one advantage of a role-theoretical perspective is its stress on mutual rights and obligations. If there has been a decline of interest in social role theory, perhaps it is a reflection of an emphasis on individualism versus interaction, on independence versus interdependence, another "trend" that has been implicated in loneliness (Slater, 1970). We need to apply a systematic developmental, historical, and cross-cultural perspective not only to loneliness but also to our approaches to loneliness. Most of the literature on loneliness, including parts of the present discussion, views loneliness as a problem susceptible by definition to solution. In many ways it is. But we must also consider loneliness as a more or less inevitable fact of life. We must ask, how do we maintain the delicate and fragile balance between acceptance and longing?

> I held the receiver to my ear; . . . somewhere at the other end of the wire there was someone who wanted to talk with me . . . I felt an overpowering desire to speak.
> I opened by mouth and strained. Sounds crawled up my throat . . . I spoke loudly and incessantly . . . convincing myself again and again and again that speech was now mine and that it did not intend to escape through the door which opened onto the balcony. (Kosinski, 1978, pp. 250–251)

NOTES

1. I wish to acknowledge my indebtedness to these authors for the general stimulation that their work has provided. I am unable in the space of this chapter to document the specific ideas that I have employed, nor to specify the similarities and differences between their approaches and the social identity analysis, but I would be pleased to provide such details upon request.

Chapter 4

ETHOGENY, SOCIAL IDENTITY, AND SUICIDE

Rolf O. Kroger and Linda A. Wood

to be no part of any body, is to be nothing. (John Donne)

Our purpose in the present chapter is to locate the study of suicide in a systematic conceptual framework and, in so doing, to stake out a territory of research, to develop ideas about where empirical studies can be done and what they might be. To accomplish our purpose, we shall employ the concepts of social identity, especially the notion of the transvaluation of social identity, and shall draw as well on the emerging strategy of ethogeny. We hope to show how these concepts may serve as the social–psychological link between societal conditions, such as anomie, and individual actions, such as suicide, and thus address an essential ambiguity in sociological theories of suicide, an ambiguity that has come to be known as the ecological fallacy (Douglas, 1967) or, simply, as the Durkheimian fallacy (Harré, 1980). Before proceeding, we pause to consider in more detail some of the difficulties in the traditional approaches to the study of suicide.

SOME PROBLEMS OF TRADITIONAL APPROACHES

Regularity and Explanation

We already know a good deal about suicide. We know that suicide rates constitute a nonrandom pattern, that suicide is not "accidental." We know that men commit suicide more often than women, Hungarians more often than Canadians, whites more often than blacks, otolaryngologists more often than radiologists, and so forth.[1] We owe this knowledge to Durkheim and to his followers who, in the pursuit of his thesis, have identified various social categories whose members are at special risk. But the identification of regularity is only the first step in scientific inquiry; it constitutes the occasion for asking the question, "Why?" but it cannot provide the answer because the identification of regularity in itself cannot reveal the processes that produce the regularity (Harré & Secord, 1972).

It is true that the Durkheimians have established "constant connections," or correlations, between suicide and such societal conditions as unemployment, anomie, racial group membership, etc. Their mistake has been to assume that these "Humean regularities" have explanatory force. The problem is that this view compels us to ask the wrong questions: "What is it about Hungary that makes for a higher suicide rate than in Canada?" Or, "What is it about life in the inner city that makes for a higher suicide rate than does life in the small town?" "What is it about British Columbia (or Los Angeles) that makes for a higher suicide rate than in Newfoundland?" And so forth. We suggest that these are the wrong questions because they urge us to treat relations between collective properties as cause and effect, if they show Humean regularity. For example, Durkheim might have said, "Urban anomie makes people kill themselves" to account for the high suicide rate in Los Angeles. But how are we to account for an individual suicide by invoking this "constant connection" between abstracted collective properties and individual actions? MacIntyre (see Harré, 1980) has noted that Los Angeles had the largest number of rental accommodations of single people of any city in the United States. Perhaps those unfortunate souls bent upon suicide migrated to Los Angeles to do it. Perhaps there is nothing about Los Angeles that "induces" people to commit suicide there. But we will never know whether this is so if we cling to the Durkheimian paradigm and its associated methodology. We could, of course, collect more data and attempt to control for the "confounding variable" of immigrant status. But this approach involves infinite regress. Here, as elsewhere, we are not faced with a problem that is primarily empirical in nature—there is an abundance of data on suicide—but with a problem of "conceptual naivete" (Harré & Secord, 1972). Conceptual analysis must do more than "organize the facts," after the fact, as the logical positivists would have us do.

People who have encountered suicide intimately in the circle of their families or of their friends profess to be profoundly baffled in the face of suicide ("he was not the kind of person who . . . ," "she would never . . . ") and they react with incomprehension to the suggestion that their husband, their daughter or their friend committed suicide because he or she belonged to a certain social category or was exposed to certain abstract social conditions. And this is not simply because they are laypeople. They are rightly baffled because it is unclear, if not mysterious, how the abstract societal conditions postulated by the Durkheimians can be seen as the determinants of individual actions, including suicide.

This difficulty has appeared in another way. The Durkheimian scheme has not been able to tell us the reason why most individuals in high-risk categories do *not* kill themselves. Or, as Choron (1972) has put it, " . . . the overwhelming majority of people in similar circumstances do not commit suicide. The question then is why these particular people do kill themselves" (p. 61). The truth is that we do not know. But what we, as social psychologists, want to know is why individuals kill themselves. Otolaryngologists as a group have a very high suicide rate (95.2;[1] Craig & Pitts, 1968), yet most otolaryngologists die in an ordinary way. The Archduke Rudolf of Austria committed suicide "because" he could not marry the woman he loved while about half a century later King Edward VIII chose abdication in similar circumstances. Hemingway killed himself, but Sinclair Lewis, an equally famous author, died of natural causes. These examples could be multiplied endlessly. The point is that they all raise the same question. It seems that we must follow the realist philosophers (e.g., Harré & Madden, 1975) in abandoning the externalist, Humean conception of causality embodied in the Durkheimian approach as a sufficient basis for the explanation of individual social action. We must return to the level of the individual to identify the "powerful particulars"[2] that generate actions such as suicide.

The Data Problem

Individuals, of course, cannot have high suicide rates. The rates are summations of the social categorization of individual actions. Does a focus on the individual as suggested above imply that we should ignore the data on suicide rates? Not at all. Such rates constitute part of the critical description of the phenomenon of suicide; furthermore, while they cannot count as explanations of suicide, they must be accounted for by our explanation. There is, however, the "data problem" (Harré, 1980 p. 113). To obtain reliable data, we must have "transparent" instruments—that is, instruments that allow us to "see" the property we are studying "through" the instrument. Unfortunately, our present instruments are almost totally opaque, and we cannot be certain to what extent the "data" are artifacts of the methods used for recording the data. In the study of suicide, this problem presents itself in the assumption that self-inflicted death is so unambiguous a phenomenon that official suicide rates may be taken to be transparent instruments for the recording of the phenomenon. But, as Douglas (1967) has argued, suicide is not an objective fact but rather the assignment of an occurrence to an interpretive category for certain practical purposes. It is the upshot of a complex process of negotiation between the parties attending the occurrence. Where a priest might argue for a verdict of accidental death, a medical examiner might argue for a verdict of suicide, and so forth.

We are persuaded by Douglas's argument that verdicts of suicide are not generated in a social vacuum, but we are reluctant to accept his conclusion that official statistics are almost wholly useless for scientific purposes. Our hesitation is two-fold. First, the force of Douglas's argument is greatest when directed at statistics of absolute incidence, especially for the historical periods considered by Durkheim himself. Nearly everyone agrees that the absolute incidence of completed and especially of attempted suicide is underestimated by the official rates (Stengel, 1964). But for some theoretical purposes the underestimation is not a problem. It is a problem only if it can be shown that the bias operates selectively with respect to certain social categories. For example, if it were shown that the three-to-one gender ratio (Choron, 1972; Stengel, 1964) is the result of official reluctance to admit that women commit suicide, except when that conclusion becomes inescapable, then the use of the ratio for analytical purposes would be problematic. Douglas's argument is even more difficult to accept in the face of the results of certain other studies. For example, it would not seem reasonable to argue that the vastly higher rate for otolaryngologists as compared to that for radiologists (95.2 versus 7.5; Craig & Pitts, 1968) is due wholly to differences in the negotiation process, to the attitudes of coroners vis à vis otolaryngologists as compared to radiologists, or to the greater resources of the survivors of otolaryngologists to influence the final verdict. We may be able to rescue these sorts of data if we are able to show the theoretical necessity that lies behind the differential rates, as we hope to do in this chapter.

Second, our acceptance of Douglas's conclusion must be further constrained by Sainsbury's (1972) finding that immigrant groups to the United States retain the patterns of suicide characteristic of their country of origin. This finding is clear evidence that official statistics are not wholly a function of local cultural practices. None of this is to say that we should not maintain a healthy skepticism vis à vis the official rates.

The Definition of Suicide

We do not intend to become involved in the thorny problem of the nominal definition of the term "suicide" at this point in our inquiry. These have been discussed at length by Lester and Lester (1971), by Neuringer (1962), and by Choron (1972).

However, we wish to point out that in other languages there are extant multiple terms for suicide, reflecting a variety of conceptions of the act of suicide. The term "suicide" (or self-murder, a conception more explicit still in the French *"homicide de soi-même"*) was introduced into English in about 1650 as a neologism. The emphasis on violence implied by the reference to the concept of murder is absent in the German *"Selbsttötung"* (self-killing) and *"Selbstvernichtung"* (self-destruction). Totally absent from English terminology is the idea of suicide as *"Freitod"* (freely chosen death), an idea also embodied in the French *"mort voluntaire,"* as is the idea of the suicide as a *"Lebensmüder"* (one tired of life). The concept of *"Lebensmüder"* contradicts the emphasis on aggression in the term "suicide," focusing our attention instead on a disposition toward resignation, helplessness and hopelessness.

The absence from English of such terms as *"Freitod,"* of course, does not imply that the idea of suicide as freely-chosen death, seen by some as the highest expression of man's freedom and autonomy and, like true language, as a uniquely human potential and capacity, is unknown to speakers of English. What it does imply, psycholinguistically, is that speakers of English have felt less compelled, for whatever resons, than their French and German counterparts to identify in a linguistically differentiated manner the possible varieties of the act of suicide.

These terms deserve attention because they figure in the accounts people give of suicides and so embody folk theories about the nature of suicide. While we must be careful to distinguish people's accounts from scientific explanation, it is a basic methodological tenet of ethogeny that accounts given by people of their own actions and of the actions of others must be part of any systematic study of social life. The definition of suicide cannot be undertaken apart from a coherent theoretical framework. Certainly, the definition cannot be an "operational definition."

SUICIDE IN PERSPECTIVE

We must keep suicide in perspective. We must not lose sight of the personal tragedy that lies behind every statistic entered into the official record. To say this is not to succumb to maudlin sentimentality. Rather it is to say that we must begin our inquiry into the puzzle of suicide from the particulars of individual lives lived through the particulars of the local culture. And these particulars must then be viewed and reviewed from the vantage point of some system of concepts that can be assembled into a model or image of the processes that must underlie the superficial variations in the act of suicide. There is a further and simple reason for the initial emphasis upon particulars and that is that suicide is an action whose "cause" must be sought ultimately *in rerum persona* and not in stimuli, external reinforcement contingencies, societal conditions, or even in the automatic powers of repressed contents as delineated by Freud. For what we take to be sound reasons (see Harré, 1980; Harré & Madden, 1975), we find the automata theories of both Skinner and Freud unfruitful for the study of suicide, and we find implausible, as we have said, the social determinism of Durkheim.

These are several possible sources of particulars about suicide. There are suicide notes, left by about 25 percent of suicides. They are not very informative. In general, they appear to be intended to make certain that the survivors interpret the act as the suicide himself sees it, as part of the suicide's attempt to determine the "form of the future" (Harré, 1980). Better are biographies of famous suicides (e.g., Baker, 1969), particularly the footnoted, academic sort. They sometimes permit a retrospective psychological autopsy, though they do not always contain all the data one might wish to have for the evaluation of a particular theoretical perspective. Finally, one can look at the autobiographical ruminations of articulate failed suicides (e.g., Alvarez, 1971). In their nature, such statements are rare.

We present first a suicide note from a man who died by slashing his throat and wrists (identifying proper names have been changed):

> Dearest Grace,   6:55 AM Thursday March 9/66
> The comptroller has accused me of embezzling and has discharged me. I can see no other way out than that which I have done. Call Mr. Ross, turn over to him all insurance policies. His name is in a letter in the new house agreement file. Other data in the blue box in the bar. I have got a new will therein in the event my mother has mislaid the original one.
> There will be bills coming in—Mum and Dad can carry you over. Have Mr. Ross contact Mr. Jenkins of Prudential Life, Ron Miller branch who can no doubt arrange for interim monies. *Do not* sign any documents pertaining to the house or my estate except on Ross's advice or that of his lawyer. The car loan account, the outstanding loan at the GMC I believe will be paid off by their own insurance. There is an outstanding with the Bank of Canada, check credit department—I believe this may also be covered by their own insurance.
> With Mum's help, $150. must be placed in the current chequing account at the Bank of Quebec, Warren and Taylor Streets. I would recommend that you start another account in your name and ask that the mortgage cheques already written on First Trust Bank be debited to your account. This way there will be no tie-ups.
> I recommend Mum and Dad—whom I love dearly—to sell their house for $30,000. minimum. Rely on Mr. Brown and his legal advisors.
> You and Frank have been the loveliest things that could happen to any man. I am so proud of Frank—he is growing into a lad the likes of which I wish I had been. I hope he can continue his education and eventually become an architect or similar. I have always loved you and with my last breath, You are my all. May God forgive me and rest my soul and may you

forgive me for the heartache I am giving you in the months to come. Goodbye my dearest,

Love, John

I wish to be cremated and family only [illegible]

And a second one from a person who died by pulling the trigger of a shotgun held in his mouth:

My brother, Mom, Jane, Alice, my   May 1, 1969
dearest wife and daughter,
Warren Smith my last will and testament
Nova Scotia Life Insurance Policy at my bank—Montreal Imperial Bank, Tremont and Hedge Road. Insurance agent Anderson. Policies in office.
God forgive me, Warren

These notes are not what we expect, yet they are not atypical. We do not find ruminations regarding the nature of life, death, fate, or God. What predominates are mundane concerns. Yet, given the tragic occasion, they shock by their very mundaneness. They cannot fail to convey the message that this was a genuine suicide, projecting the suicide's "definition of the situation" into the future.

Let us now look at the account given by the poet and critic, Alvarez (1971). Alvarez entitled the epilogue to his study of suicide, "Letting Go." It contains his personal account of how he detached himself from life, bit by bit. It contains his account of how he committed what would have been a "successful" suicide had it not been for the high technology medical care available to the inhabitants of major Western cities. Alvarez prepared the act for a long time (technically by having multiple prescriptions filled on both sides of the Atlantic, by bamboozling unsuspecting fellow-travellers into sharing their supplies and by hoarding it all). He had a plan and he acted on a strategic principle. One day he realized that he meant it when he found himself repeating ritualistically, "IwishIwasdead, IwishIwasdead." It became a constant focus of his life and marked his " . . . steady descent through layer after layer of depression" (p. 291).

The bare facts are ordinary enough. The poet, compelled to supplement his precarious income by academic teaching, moved his wife and child to the United States on a visiting professorship. There, ignored by the university, they inhabited a cavernous house ten miles from the campus. His wife, unable to drive, was confined to the house. After watching a rented television for two months, she packed her bags and, with her son, returned home. In his words, "The action was nil." No longer just a social drinker, Alvarez "went at the bottle with a pure need" (p. 294). Alcohol, so long seen by the mental hygienists as a "cause" of suicide, became the crutch, the last line of defense against the enveloping depression, against a course of life already so diminished as to have rendered ineffectual the prophylactic force of marriage and of fatherhood. Christmas loomed and, in a final attempt at reconciliation, he trekked back across the Atlantic. There he faced, in addition, the special burden of holidays: the removal of the fragile structure of routine, the hollowness of an encapsulated existence. Christmas began with a raw shot of whiskey meant to steel him against the day. He felt brief exuberance at the delight of the three-year-old son among the gift wrappings. There was then the traditional noon meal with the in-laws, an elegant dinner party later on and, later still, a wilder party. And there was always the booze; "without the booze, we would have splintered into sharp fragments" (p. 295). There was a final quarrel and his wife left to bed down elsewhere. He swallowed the 45 pills so assiduously hoarded on two continents.

He was 31 years old. The medical diagnosis was "deeply unconscious, slightly cyanosed, vomit in mouth, pulse rapid, poor volume" (p. 298). And it became worse, "deeply cyanosed," Tory blue. There was a three-day gap and a week of shadowy recovery; " . . . in some way I had died" (p. 301).

Afterwards the transformation occurred, "The overintensity, the tiresome excess of sensitivity and self-consciousness, of arrogance and idealism, which came in adolescence and stayed on and on beyond their due time, like some visiting bore, had not survived the coma", and the new beginning, "I began gradually to stir into another style of life, less theoretical, less optimistic, less vulnerable. I was ready for an insentient middle age" (p. 302–303).

There are allusions in Alvarez's account to a kind of Freudian deficit from childhood, which colored his later perspective, including his relationship with his wife. It is impossible to tell from these allusions what really transpired, nor is it perhaps really necessary to know all that went before. The suicidal path is not straight; it meanders from an amalgam of hurts vaguely remembered from the past and of present difficulties only vaguely understood. What is clear is that we, as dispassionate but also concerned observers, must bring to bear all our intelligence to try to understand why this obviously talented man (and so many others equally talented in their own ways) tried to end his life. Our inquiry, no matter how abstract it will ultimately seem to be, must never stray from the center of particular, individual lives, as they are lived and sometimes ended.

THE ETHOGENY OF SUICIDE

At the outset, we proposed to locate the study of suicide within a systematic conceptual framework. The framework we chose is the new theory for social psychology, ethogeny (Harré, 1980; Harré & Secord,

1972). Ethogeny is not a deductive system; it is rather a system of concepts within which a variety of social forms can potentially be explained, much as the Darwinian system of concepts explains a variety of organic forms. Ethogeny attempts to articulate the relationship between the personal and the social. It revives the Veblenian distinction between the practical and the expressive social orders, emphasizing that the latter is far more pervasive in human social life than we have been led to believe by the various reductionist accounts of human nature. Ethogenists see social action as a form of problem solving whose meaning depends upon the place it has in systems of public conventions, rather than in any private causal history. It views social action on the model of language, assuming that there are syntactic and semantic rules that govern the production and comprehension of socially meaningful behaviors. It puts to use the competence/performance distinction that has served so well in structural linguistics. Before we can say anything about how intentions are translated into performances, we must develop a theory of social competence and an inventory of the social repertoires ordinary folk are able to bring to bear upon the problems offered by the vicissitudes of social life.

Such a view cannot be sustained without a conception of persons that . acknowledges the unique capacities of the species. The ethogenic injunction is: " . . . treat people, for scientific purposes, *as if they were human beings* . . . " (Harré & Secord, 1972, p. 87, italics in original), that is, not animals, not machines, not subroutines in some computer program. People are agents. They are agents in the special sense that they have the capacity to shift among and to bring their actions under an indefinite number of lateral and higher-order principles. Thus, one may deliberately abandon a principle of civility, ordinarily followed, to assert one's autonomy. Principled revolutionaries, for example, make just these sorts of moves, as do children who sometimes engage in "perverse" actions to counter the power held by parents.

What we require and what is not readily available from traditional sources are concepts for the analysis of synchronic or short-term activities of people in society. These are needed for the analysis of the immediate circumstances of suicide. But we require even more urgently concepts for diachronic analysis, that is, for the study of changes in people. We hope to show that it is not the static conditions surrounding the individual that precipitate suicide, but rather certain dynamic changes in the life history of the individual.

The Expressive/Practical Distinction

The distinction between the practical social order and the expressive social order (Harré, 1980) is not a material but an analytic distinction, for in social lives as they are really lived, the two are usually inextricably intertwined. Yet, for many analytic purposes the distinction is indispensable.

In the practical social order people direct their practical reason toward the maintenance of life, toward the solution of problems arising from our evolutionary history, and from the conditions we find on earth. In the practical order, we try to solve the problems of subsistence, of shelter, of the protection of the young, of the procreation of the species. As basic and as demanding as these practical aspects of social activity are, anthropologists have estimated that for most of historical time and for most preindustrial societies only between eight to ten percent of living time is devoted to the maintenance of life (Harré, 1980).

The expressive social order is concerned with the creation and maintenance of honor, reputation, and dignity, with the development of personae that may show the individual to be a person worthy of the respect of his or her peers. The expressive aspects of social life are often revealed in the way practical activities are carried out or in the adverbial qualification of action, as in "he scored the goal effortlessly," "she typed the letter resentfully," "she looked at her results despondently," and the like.

In this view, suicide may be seen as the realization of the failure to meet the problems posed in the expressive social order and as the realization of the incapacity to do so in the future. Much of what we know about suicide accords with this hypothesis. The expressive social order is dominant in almost all phases of human cultural activity. The practical order comes to dominate only under special conditions, in general those that actually threaten the maintenance of life: war, famine, and other natural or manmade disasters. The reduction of life to its bare bones leaves little room for expressive concerns. When people have to put their shoulders to the wheel, honor and reputation, and, at times, even dignity take a temporary back seat. It is in this way that we must see suicide as a civilized and peculiarly human act. It is not to be found among those temporarily or permanently reduced to a less than civilized existence.

We do not find the highest rates of suicide among the economically destitute, among those daily threatened with extinction (e.g., inmates of Nazi concentration camps), or among those in the midst of war. It is instead in those reaches of social life where expressive concerns predominate that we find the suicides. Hemingway was not threatened by problems of subsistence, nor was Marilyn Monroe destitute. In Canada, the highest suicide rates are not found in the poorest provinces (e.g., Newfoundland) but in the most affluent ones (e.g., British Columbia). In the United States, it is not West Virginia but California that leads in the number of suicides.

Blacks are poorer but have a lower suicide rate than whites, and black women, the most disadvantaged of all (in a gender × race table) also have the lowest suicide rate of all. North American Indians, poorer still than blacks, have very high suicide rates. Their actions thus *seem* to contradict our hypothesis. For the Indians, the Metis, and the Innuit, poverty is only the byproduct of the systematic curtailment of the possibility for expressive activities that we have imposed upon the aboriginal people. For black people in North America there is still the possibility of the creation of personae that will command respect, albeit in a circumscribed world. For some blacks there is the hope, by dint of sheer effort and extraordinary talent, of "making it" even in the white world of entertainment, sports, academia, or jurisprudence though even now rarely in the world of business. None of these expressive possibilities exist for the members of the Native American societies. The destruction of the indigenous culture has meant that there are no indigenous "moral careers" available, no layers of local expressive activities that can be traversed to accumulate honor and reputation. The possibilities of alternative careers in the white world are virtually nonexistent for native people. We may predict a drastic reduction in the native suicide rates for those groups who manage to "return to the land," to cut themselves off from the welfare system, and to reconstitute their religious and other cultural practices. And this prediction can be made though such groups would be even "poorer" by white standards than they are now.

Is the practical/expressive distinction equally illuminating with respect to other long-established differences in suicide rates, for example, to the three-to-one gender ratio? This ratio has been remarkably stable over time, though there have been some changes in the female rate, possibly representing the "dark side" of the women's liberation movement. And it has been remarkably stable cross-culturally, though there are some country-by-country differences that may be susceptible to understanding in terms of the practical/expressive distinction itself. This regularity may be understood in terms of the relative involvement of men and women in social activities tilted toward practical and toward expressive ends.

For purposes of the present discussion, we assume that the possibilities for earning honor and reputation through the successful meeting of hazards is greater for those individuals engaged actively in the "marketplace," as these matters are still judged in our culture. That is certainly so for individuals who may be said to be "having a career" as opposed to those who may be said to be merely "holding a job," be they men or women. Honor, in the form of high incomes, medals, prizes, recognition, even adulation accrues to those in the public arena. The corollary of this idea is that where there are hazards there is also the possibility of failure, of incurring the contempt of one's fellow moralists. To the extent that men continue to be more heavily involved in the shadowy world that bisects the practical and the expressive social orders, they may be expected to suffer in greater numbers the sort of expressive losses we see as figuring in the cognitive preparations for suicide.

Is this the reason for the lopsided gender ratio in suicide rates? Or are matters more complicated still? Because, as Wood (*this volume*) and others have noted, women also carry expressive burdens not carried by men. In the intimate, familial realm it is more often the women who create and maintain the expressive network of social relations with family members and friends, which, on other grounds, we see as prophylactic and as immunizing against suicidal action. On this count, widows seem to fare better than widowers who not only lose their spouses but an entire intimate network whose fragile existence has depended upon remembering anniversaries, sending Christmas cards, baking the special cake; upon doing the myriad things that have no practical import yet are essential for the sustaining of that corner of the expressive order.

What we must consider is the relative value of work for the sustenance of human life in the public and private arenas. Perhaps it has to do with life stages. Once past adolescence, people see their existence as being primarily in the practical order (though in fact it never is), as a struggle for establishing economic security. It is only in the later stages of life that expressive concerns once again come into ascendance. So we have real-estate tycoons acquiring football teams (that keep losing money), captains of industry endowing hospital wings (not just as a tax dodge), and aging stimulus-response theorists turning to the investigation of religious feelings, to the study of the immutable chemistry of the brain, or the verities of long-standing issues in the philosophy of science; that is, to anything that might have some transcendental value. From the contemplation of these aspects of social life, we must address the question of the life-sustaining values of activities in the public and private domains and how the value of these activities changes with changes in the cycle of life.

SUICIDE AND THE SOCIAL IDENTITY MODEL

We turn now to the implications of the Social Identity Model (see Sarbin & Scheibe, this volume) for the understanding of suicide. Although the Social Identity Model was originally drawn from social role theory (Sarbin & Allen, 1968–1969) and, more generally, from the symbolic interactionist tradition, it may gain in force by being placed in the context of ethogeny (Harré, 1980). We have already explored the utility of the expressive/practical distinction, and we shall attempt to exploit additional ethogenic concepts to supplement the insights to be gained from the Social Identity Model.

The Social Identity Model is multidimensional. Unlike traditional sociological conceptions based on SES indices and unlike status-congruence models (Sampson, 1969), it recognizes the importance of the person's activities in the ascribed realm, in that part of the social order constituted by one's intimate relationships and one's most basic attributes. In addition, the Social Identity Model takes into account changes in the life of the individual, as well as the person's subjective evaluations of his or her present condition and of his or her future prospects. Unlike those earlier models, it also takes into account the relationships between the ascribed and achieved realms. We shall argue that it is the balance or imbalance achieved between the two realms of living that has profound implications for the understanding of the genesis of suicide. To consider the one at the expense of the other is to court misunderstanding. We must elucidate the conditions of a person's life, both public and private, and the interdependence of that life with the lives of significant others, be they located in the ascribed or in the achieved realms.

Even though this is a social-psychological essay, we cannot disregard sociological conceptions in trying to understand social actions. In the ethogenic theory we locate the causes of actions in the individual. That is *not* to say that individuals can display their "powers" without constraints. The expression of a person's powers is facilitated by the presence of "enabling conditions" (Harré & Secord, 1972) and constrained by disabling conditions. We see these conditions as being part of the sociological macrostructure. Thus, during the radical 1960s, many entrepreneurs felt constrained to camouflage their greed as rendering some public service; under the impact of Reaganomics the unabashed accumulation of wealth has become once more a laudable enterprise. In a similar vein, changes influence the sorts of social identities people can fashion for themselves, enabling or preventing them from furthering their projects.

In the Social Identity Model, ascribed positions are marked by respect (or disrespect), achieved positions by esteem (or disesteem). The total value of one's social identity is the sum total of respect, disrespect, esteem, and disesteem incurred by the person from his multifarious affiliations in the ascribed and achieved realms. This array of affiliations may be reduced for analytic purposes to a simple typology of social identities (see Table 3.1, Wood, *this volume*).

We said earlier that we require not only synchronic but also diachronic concepts if we are to understand suicide. It is not the static, synchronic conditions of a person's life that seem primarily implicated in suicide but rather certain dramatic changes in that life. In this context, we find useful the concept of the transvaluation of social identity, especially transvaluations in the negative direction, as found in various processes of degradation (see Sarbin & Scheibe, *this volume*). We are not concerned with relatively minor changes in the amounts of respect and esteem an individual may be able to earn but with larger changes (e.g. loss of an important job, loss of spouse) that affect significantly both one's public standing and one's private definition of self. In order to understand fully the nature of such trans-valuations it is necessary to recognize that the many social positions held by an individual are not necessarily independent of each other, that is, there is role linkage (see Sarbin & Scheibe, *this volume*). If a person occupies an achieved position that is linked to an ascribed position, and "fails" in the ascribed position, it is only a matter of time before such a failure is discovered and before he or she loses the linked achieved position. For example, to be a teacher in the public schools one must not only have professional credentials, one must also be a moral person. If one is derogated from one's ascribed position of moral person to its counterpart, "bad person," by conviction on a marijuana possession charge one will also be demoted from one's achieved position of teacher, at least in Canada. In such cases, the change in the person's social identity would be quite large; he or she would lose both respect *and* esteem.

We said earlier that the causes of social actions, including suicide, must be found *in rerum persona*, in individuals. It must therefore be our task to discriminate between individuals in high-risk categories, between those likely to commit suicide and those in the same category who are not likely to commit suicide. If we can do this, we could provide an answer to Choron's (1972) basic question: why it is that most people who are in similar situations—to those of suicides—do not commit suicide.

As discussed earlier, we must not be misled by the form of Choron's question, which seems to imply that it is something in "the situation" as such that "causes" suicide and that might lead us to look in the wrong places for answers. But we still want to show that the people in high-risk categories who kill themselves are *not* in "similar situations" to those members of the category who do not kill themselves. It is in this task that the components of the Social Identity Model and especially the diachronic concept of transvaluation can be put to work usefully.

It is our most general hypothesis that suicide is a function of the transvaluation of social identity from the hollow to the empty category. We believe those persons to be at high risk who have achieved high-status positions and who, in doing so, have neglected their ascribed positions or sources of respect. We do not wish to imply that our hypothesis does not hold for suicides by young persons who have not yet achieved positions of status. We believe that in those cases aspiration to high status positions, rather than their actual achievement, is implicated in the genesis of suicide. For example, despair over ever becoming a leading cinematographer may figure in a young person's preparation for suicide.

Neither do we wish to imply that suicide may not be a function of transvaluation from the helpless to the empty category. We would argue, however, that such transvaluations occur more rarely than those from the hollow to the empty category. We would do so by pointing to the differential nature of the ascribed and achieved realms. It would appear to be easier to lose one's sources of esteem than one's sources of respect, especially in the radical way that constitutes a major transvaluation. It is usually the case that one's sources of respect are more diffusely and pervasively distributed than one's sources of esteem. Even if one loses one's spouse there are still parents, children, friends, colleagues, neighbors who may shore up a person's social identity in times of personal crisis. Esteem tends to be derived from very limited sources, such as one's occupation. It is thus more vulnerable to catastrophic change. This is not to say that transvaluations from the helpless to the empty category, when they do occur, will not have consequences that are as serious as those from the hollow to the empty category.

Note also that it is the shift in social identity that appears to be crucial in the genesis of suicide rather than the possession of an empty social identity as such. The shift may be relatively sudden, though more often it seems occasioned by the gradual realization of one's incapacity to solve the fundamental problems of one's life, even in the future.

It is a basic tenet of ethogenic theory that human beings, as social persons, must always show themselves to be rational beings if they wish to be counted as such (Harré, 1980, ch. 1). The strategic and tactical social devices available for this purpose are the range of excuses and justifications that are contained in any cultural repertoire for action (Austin, 1962; Backman, 1976) and that are called upon whenever one's rationality is questioned. Those who fail or who are unable to proffer acceptable excuses and justifications are classified, after a process of social negotiation, as either criminal or insane. In the language of the Social Identity Model they are derogated from the ultimate ascribed social position, that of human being, to its counterpart, an identity bereft of the essential attributes of what it is to be human.

To lose this part of one's identity is to become highly vulnerable, as attested by the suicide rates of people classified as mentally ill. They may kill themselves, not because they are mentally ill but because they have given up the battle of excuses and justifications and have accepted the definition of others that they are unworthy, that they are "beings devoid of value," as the Nazi Rassenhygienists put it (Chorover, 1980). Fortunately, most people manage to cling to the ultimate ascribed role and to the other ascribed roles that demand continuous involvement with others (as in parenting) and so reduce the feelings of isolation, of existential loneliness (see Wood, *this volume*) that forever threaten existence.

In this sense, achieved roles are precarious. Even for workaholics, their demands are intermittent, leaving spaces of vulnerability. Moreover, their value can come to be questioned in a way that the value of parenting, for example, cannot. A psychiatrist may come to the realization in middle age that his professional skills do not really cure anyone, a dentist that there must be more to life than filling yet another cavity. Ascribed roles, in contrast, contain their own justifications, which are immutable except in rare cases. In this way they do their prophylactic work.

We can safely say that any condition that militates against the cohesion of the circle of ascribed roles is conducive to furthering the kind of transvaluation we see as being implicated in suicide. On this basis, it is possible to identify groups whose members may be at high risk but who have not been so identified on more traditional theoretical grounds. Professional athletes who are frequently traded, leading to the erosion of their ascribed networks, and who suffer the termination of their professional identities at a relatively early age may constitute one such group.

SOME IMPLICATIONS FOR PATTERNS OF SUICIDE

Is it possible in light of these views to make the pattern of suicide rates more intelligible? Is it possible to discern behind the suicide rates some of the individual factors that must have produced them? We look at some selected patterns below to explore these possibilities.

We stated earlier our reservations with respect to the trustworthiness of the official statistics but also the reasons why we believe them to have retained some residual usefulness for the purpose of elucidating the nature of suicide. We are mindful of Cicourel's (1968) discovery that the largely unexamined hypotheses held by public officials will influence their judgments regarding the causes of the social activities of members of various social groupings (e.g. the "causes" of delinquent behavior of young people coming from broken versus intact families) and that these judgments are reflected in the official statistics. This kind of hypothesizing or bias, if it operates uniformly across a given domain of data does not necessarily invalidate the data for internal comparisons, that is, within countries rather than across countries, within occupations rather than across occupations, and the like. For example, we may assume that coroners across Canada share roughly similar theories about the genesis of suicide and that their theories will influence their classifications of the causes of deaths. If this assumption is at all reasonable, we might still be able to make sense, for example, of the variations in suicide rates across the provinces of Canada.

In this light, how do we explain a rate for British Columbia of 13.4 compared with a rate for Newfoundland of 2.6? In line with our general hypothesis, we suggest that British Columbia contains, as it were, more hollow identities than Newfoundland, which contains more helpless identities than British Columbia. British Columbia is the Canadian counterpart to California. Many people move there in search of a "better" life and indeed the job opportunities in British Columbia are golden in comparison to those in Newfoundland, a notoriously economically depressed area of Canada. Moving across the continent almost necessarily means abandoning one's network of ascribed relationships—family, friends, neighbors. Those who move are left then with the sorts of relationships that tend to make for hollow social identities. In Newfoundland, people still do not lock their doors and there are virtually no strangers. The "incorporation of the stranger" (Harré, 1976) in Newfoundland involves a ceremony swiftly conducted, after which bed and board are offered as a matter of course; it is the "understood" thing to do. As economically deprived people, Newfoundlanders are helpless but not hollow. In the centers of Newfoundland these conditions are likely to change as the off-shore oil comes on stream, with corresponding implications for the number of suicides. This prediction can be verified by careful monitoring over time.

In the Yukon, the rate was 27.4 when it was 9.3 for the rest of Canada. For males in the Yukon it was an astounding 48.9 (13.6 for males in the rest of Canada). For females in the Yukon the rate was only 5.3, far below the usual three-to-one gender ratio. Why? What produces these differences? The Yukon in Canada even today is a bit like the Old West. Men, mostly single, go there from Southern Canada "to make their fortune" (actually, all most of them can get is extra hardship pay and overtime in construction and mining). Their hope is to return in glory. More often their hopes are shattered. Gambling and drinking to ward off the tedium of living temporarily in the North take their toll, as does the sheer inflated price of food and shelter. The dream becomes empty and, in the absence of sources of respect, life becomes perilous.

Women who go to the Yukon are likely to be married, perhaps helpless but not hollow. They are not fortune hunters, more likely they are wives of civil servants or company executives on fixed rotations, though all of this may be changing.

Given the state of the art, our suggestions are necessarily speculative. But they are not beyond empirical verification. To gain purchase on the true state of affairs would require determining the demographic mix of Native Americans and white, of married and single people and of occupations and the like. This is a task not beyond a determined investigator.

Let us look at one more pattern, this one drawn from the occupational world. Craig and Pitts (1968) examined carefully the suicide rates of male members of various medical specialties in the United States. The highest rate was found for otolaryngologists (95.2), the lowest rate for radiologists (7.5). Psychiatrists also ranked high (66.9) and internists and general surgeons low (29.4 and 15.4). How were these marked differences produced? Surely, as we pointed out earlier, whatever sources of bias operate among the recorders of the official statistics will tend to operate uniformly with respect to the different medical specialties. We are not concerned here with whether these figures reflect accurately the absolute incidence of suicides in these groups. We are concerned with the generative processes that must underlie the differences in rates.

Our hypothesis is that many medical specialists create for themselves hollow identities. There is the long period of arduous training, years beyond medical school. There are then the pressures of setting up a practice and of meeting the expectations for high income that seem to surround those at the top of the medical profession. There is very little time to shore up sources of respect, to fulfill adequately one's ascribed obligations. Wives are bought off with large homes, fur coats, club memberships; children with flashy automobiles and other accouterments of affluent living. The picture we draw is a caricature only in that it does not fit all medical specialists. More seriously, insofar as it is true, it would apply equally to all medical specialties when the rates show clearly that it does not. What we require are additional generative elements. We propose that these are to be found in the differential probabilities for transvaluation, which we may attach to the different specialties.

One of these additional elements is the degree to which the skill and the performance of the specialist is likely to increase with age or decline with age, given that there is always competition from the "youngsters" coming up from behind. What internists, general surgeons, and radiologists have in common is an increase in expertise with age. Diagnostic success and therefore effective treatment are enhanced by experience. After having seen thousands of x-rays, the Gestalt of a particular disorder is more likely to leap out at the seasoned practitioner than at the relative novice.

The situation of the psychiatrist and otolarynogologist is quite different. The psychiatrist, as we have noted, may experience a crisis of confidence in middle age, given the precarious foundations of that specialty. The otolaryngologist, as well as the ophthalmologist (rate 63.3), requires great manual dexterity, a skill that declines with age. They are thus faced with competition from younger colleagues, which may reach crisis proportions.

Our argument thus far still fails to explain why most medical specialists, even those in the very high-risk categories, do not choose suicide as a solution to the problems they face. Our further hypothesis is that those who do not succumb are individuals who have maintained an optimal social identity, which allows them in times of crisis to fall back upon the solace provided by a rich ascribed network. Having maintained that network over time opens up several options not available to those less happily situated.

Those with optimal identities may accept reduced incomes without construing that reduction as a reduction in personal worth. Or they may choose to divert their energies to administrative posts, to government service and the like, with a similar positive construal of their place in life. It is those who insist on keeping all their eggs in one basket who are at peril.

There is much empirical checking to be done. But we need not despair. Certainly, it cannot be beyond the ken of some ingenious investigator to reconstruct the biographies, for example, of otolaryngologists who have committed suicide and of otolaryngologists who have managed to harvest the fruits of their training well into a ripe old age. We would anticipate from the findings of such investigations confirmation of much that we have suggested.

Our account would be incomplete without touching upon some particular case histories that may be drawn from the biographies of famous suicides. The suicides of famous, accomplished people arouse great interest because they go against the grain, as it were. The average person (and no less the professional) is baffled. The famous have everything the culture defines as the ultimate good—money, fame, adulation, extraordinary privileges. Why, then, suicide?

Let us take the case of Marilyn Monroe. According to Guiles (1970), her biographer, Marilyn Monroe saw herself as having failed as a mother, wife (several times), daughter, intellectual, and actress. Born Norma Jean Baker, she gave up her original name, perhaps the most important link to an anchored ascribed identity anyone can have. To be a sex queen of one's age is to be in a perilous condition, totally dependent upon the fickleness of public opinion. What is a person in that condition to say to herself in the dark of the night? How is one to bridge the gulf between public and private definitions of self? We believe that more detailed examination would reveal that Marilyn Monroe represents the paradigm case of a hollow identity who suffered the drastic transvaluation to the empty identity we see as productive of suicide.

Ernest Hemingway is another particular exemplar. For Hemingway, his identity as a writer was paramount. Whenever ascribed obligations interfered he would shed them to continue his writing. Wives who stood in the way were divorced; children who became bothersome were shipped off to private schools. It is true that fidelity and fatherhood were not valued highly in the circle in which Hemingway moved, though we can see that he disregarded them to his peril. Hemingway became vulnerable when he came to doubt what he defined as the core of his existence: his creativity as a writer. The ink ceased to flow. There are those agonizing accounts of Hemingway taking one more shot at the current unfinished manuscript, standing at his stand-up desk at Key West, Ketchum, Idaho, and those other places where he desperately sought to reestablish the sort of inner peace that must ultimately rest upon something other than public recognition. At the time of his suicide, Hemingway was paid more than ever. His fame with the public was unimpaired. But in his heart, Hemingway appeared to know that he could no longer do what he had once done, a desperate conclusion for a man hollow at the center.

IMPLICATIONS

It must be emphasized that our thoughts regarding the nature of suicide are not aimed at prediction and control. Prediction of improbable events, such as suicide, may be impossible in any case (see Boulding, 1980). And the notion of control involves technological and ethical questions that are essentially extrascientific.

Rather we believe, along with other writers, that the central aims of science are concerned with the search for understanding, with making social life intelligible. This view of science involves looking for the processes that generate the observed patterns of events, including patterns of suicide. It involves the use of the imagination under the control of plausibility, that is, the imaginative guessing at the processes that must be there but are as yet unobservable as well as the subsequent empirical checking of those guesses (cf. Boulding, 1980; Harré, 1980; Toulmin, 1961). Even though we may never be able to predict the occurrence of any particular suicide, our investigations may yet yield an understanding of the conditions that led to any particular suicide and beyond that, with patience, to increasingly more general insights into the nature of suicide as such.

Our most promising general research strategy is that of reconstructing the biographies of individuals who have committed suicide and of individuals who have not but who are otherwise comparable in relevant characteristics. So, otolaryngologists who have committed suicide should be compared to otolaryngologists who have not; Hemingway should be compared with Sinclair Lewis or Theodore Dreiser, and so forth (cf. de Waele & Harré, 1976; Glazer & Strauss, 1967).

As we have seen, it is a basic tenet of the ethogenic theory that individuals must show themselves to be rational beings at all times, if they wish to be recognized as persons, as full members of the human community. People do this by engaging in principled actions and by offering Austinian excuses and justifications if the intelligibility and warrantability of their actions are challenged. On this view, suicide involves principled action. The principles involved may differ from case to case, but they must be part of the "powerful particulars" that people bring to bear in their attempts at solving the problems of living and, where those attempts fail, in solving the ultimate problem. Our scrutiny of biographical materials must be focused upon finding those principles that will eventually lead to deeper understanding, an understanding that goes beyond the flux of particular events to the essence of the phenomenon at issue.

NOTES

1. All rates cited are per 100,000 persons of the relevant population. Unless otherwise specified, the suicide rates cited have been taken from Canadian Government publications.

2. The causal powers of individuals may be described as "powerful particulars." The concept combines the idea of formal cause with that of agency (Harré & Madden, 1975). It draws attention to the idea that causal powers exist as potentials, awaiting the appropriate occasion for their expression, and that they are particular rather than general. Furthermore, the realization of a powerful particular is seen to be under the control of the person, as an agent (Harré, 1980). For example, if a person has the power to speak French, as well as English, that power exists in potential form; it *may* be expressed in the presence of other French speakers and it is particular to that specific kind of action, namely, talking with French speakers. The concept of the powerful particular thus stands in direct contrast to the concept of trait, which, based on the model of the Pavlovian reflex, implies automaticity of response upon an appropriate stimulus and transsituational generality.

3. Perhaps surprisingly, those general surgeons whom we have interviewed insist that manual dexterity is relatively unimportant in their profession. As one of them put it, it is more a matter of "*schneiden und sehen*" (cut a large hole and have a good look), of diagnostic skill, etc.

Chapter 5

MULTIPLE GROUP MEMBERSHIP AND SOCIAL IDENTITY

Vernon L. Allen, David A. Wilder, and Michael L. Atkinson

We are not amused. (Queen Victoria)

Properly speaking, a man . . . has as many different social selves as there are distinct *groups* of persons about whose opinion he cares. (William James, 1890)

All good people agree
  and all good people say
All nice people like us are we
  and everyone else is they:
But if you cross over the sea,
  instead of over the way
You may end by (think of it!) looking on we
  as only a sort of they. (Rudyard Kipling)

These three quotations illustrate variations of the basic theme that will be addressed in this chapter: the centrality of group membership in the problem of social identity. Queen Victoria's remark reveals the existence of the perception of a total redundancy between self and social group in her cognitive system. Perceiving the lack of a boundary between self and group means that the two entities are equivalent and, therefore, are adequately encompassed by a single term— the royal "we."[1] Social identity is so intimately enmeshed with one's membership in social groups that it is with great difficulty indeed that the "I" can be distinguished from the "we." The second quotation, from William James (1890), also points to the importance of the social group in an individual's identity and introduces some additional complexities into the subject as well. Two points are made salient by James concerning the nature of social identity in the quotation taken from his famous chapter, "The Consciousness of Self." First, he immediately recognizes that the social environment should be concep- tualized as consisting of groups rather than of individuals. Most authors who refer to James's passage usually quote the first portion of the section, which mentions only individuals: "Properly speaking, a man has as many social selves as there are individuals who recognize him and carry an image of him in their mind." He goes on to note the potential impact of these images by saying: "To wound any one of these his images is to wound him." Then, as James's next sentence makes clear, he prefers to use the social group as the basic conceptual unit: "But as the individuals who carry the images fall naturally into classes, we may practically say that he has as many different social selves as there are distinct *groups* of persons about whose opinion he cares" (italics in original) (p. 294). Furthermore, James identifies some of the behavioral complexities and problems of consistency versus situational specificity of social behavior arising from multiple group membership, which are still the subject of active research in psychology at the present time. As he says in a continuation of the same passage, multiple group memberships may produce different patterns of behavior dependent upon the social setting. Moreover, concerning one's "several selves," James remarks that the person

> generally shows a different side of himself to each of these different groups. . . . We do not show ourselves to our children as to our club- companions. . . . From this there results what practically is a division of the man into several selves; and this may be a discordant splitting, as where one is afraid to let one set of his acquaintances know him as he is elsewhere; or it may be a perfectly harmonious division of labor. . . .

We have quoted rather extensively from James because in the space of only a few sentences he has succeeded in delineating some of the central issues concerning group membership and social identity; these problems still intrigue investigators who are interested in this area. He also raises explicitly some of the problems associated with the structure existing between two groups (or among several different groups).

The third quotation—the poem by Kipling—focuses on a particular type of relationship existing between the two groups: a dichotomous categorization that effectively bifurcates the social world into two parts, creating a cleavage between one's own membership group and some other specifiable group. Although it is theoretically possible to divide a thing into three parts (like Caesar's Gaul) or more, it seems that the human mind is predisposed toward the most fundamental and the simplest operation with both social and nonsocial stimuli—dichotomizing (Foss, 1974). (Consider the ubiquity of "taking sides," for example.[2]) The dichotomous categorization of social groups brings with it additional psychological baggage not found in nonsocial categorization, namely it entails (or implies if the situation is ambiguous and relevant information is lacking) a special and usually complementary relationship between the two groups. Often, the relationship is perceived as being one of competition or rivalry; and even in the absence of explicit rivalry differential attribution is brought to bear regarding one's own membership group relative to the other group in such a manner that the resulting evaluation will almost always be distinctly more favorable to one's own group. This process is well known, and long ago Sumner (1906) apparently first coined appropriate terminology (which is still in use) in connection with his discussion of groups in primitive society—"ingroup" and "outgroup." (Sumner also used the terms "we-group" and "others-group," which did not attain wide currency.) Complementarity between the two groups in question was explicitly assumed by Sumner: "The relationship of comradeship and peace in the we-group and that of hostility and war towards others-groups are correlative to each other . . . The exigencies of war with outsiders are what make peace inside . . . " (p. 27). The relativity and perceptual selectivity inherent in any ingroup/outgroup relationship is the basis of the irony so effectively conveyed by Kipling's poem.

The present chapter will discuss three major aspects of the basic theme alluded to in the quotations cited above: (1) the role of multiple group membership in social identity, (2) the structure of multiple group membership in social identity, and (3) the function of the outgroup in social identity.

Before turning to a direct discussion of the theme of the present chapter, a few preliminary comments are in order. The editors have already clarified the concept of social identity and other related concepts such as "self," and that terminology will be adopted here. Social identity depends upon one's being placed in a set of broad social categories; that is, the positions one occupies in the social structure—role, status, and group memberships. Although social identity is not synonymous with "personal" identity or self-concept—which contains nonsocial components such as physical attributes—it is probably the most prominent or salient aspect for most people. Thus, research using the "Who am I?" technique typically has found that the first responses given are social categories. For most people, then, social identity is practically equivalent to personal identity.

To say that social identity is, in final analysis, derived from or is a reflection of a pattern of social interaction might appear to be a tautology that annuls the need for any further discussion. But not all social interaction involves group memberships, which is our basic concern. Nor does a general statement to the effect that social identity is based on group memberships constitute a satisfactory explanatory statement, since such a global assertion does not specify the psychological processes responsible for social identity outcomes nor the nature of the outcomes. When we move beyond the consideration of a single group membership to multiple group memberships, a host of complicated questions arise that are relevant to an understanding of social identity. Is social identity merely the combined effects—the residue—of all of one's group memberships? What determines the impact on identity of one group membership relative to another at a particular point in time? How does the nature of the structure existing among membership groups affect social identity? (The structure among membership groups may take several forms that can be characterized in terms of, e.g., degree of inclusiveness of one group with others, degree of harmony or conflict, membership marginality, and a complementary ingroup/outgroup relationship.) We cannot begin to answer adequately all of these and other questions in this chapter; but we hope, at the least, that the reader will become more aware of the potential of multiple group memberships for making a contribution toward our understanding of social identity.

Multiple group memberships provide a substantive answer to the question, "Who am I?" in terms of social status or social structure; they also give an answer to the question, "How well am I doing?" (i.e., the evaluative dimension). Group membership gives a substantive identity for an individual and conveys affective or evaluative significance as well. The groups I belong to not only are such-and-such groups, which provide a basis for identity—for *who* I am; in addition, I also obtain information about how good, excellent, kind, etc. the such-and-such groups may be. Social identity is enhanced by belonging to groups that are positively evaluated by self or others. In this way, the "we" contributes to the enhancement of the "I"— the individual's self-esteem (Cialdini, Borden, Thorne, Walker, Freeman & Sloan, 1976). That is to say, the affective component of group membership cannot be separated from the cognitive. In the individual's effort to maintain a positively evaluated identity, membership in a group that receives positive valuations (due to achievement or other reasons) is one way of ensuring that these benefits will accrue to the individual as well. The positive valuation accorded to the general "we" is conferred to each of the individual "I's", who would not experience such positive valuations in the absence of membership in the group.[3] Take the following recent example drawn from the frenetic world of college sports. The University of Wisconsin ice hockey team had just defeated both North Dakota and Harvard to gain a position in the semifinals of the national tournament and with it a chance to repeat as national collegiate champions. A male fan of the team was talking to a television reporter and obviously was deliriously happy. His commentary was characterized by numerous exuberant expressions such as "We're the best; we are great, we played a terrific game," etc. He had not played; he was only a spectator. But the joy and pride felt by this individual through the medium of his "we-ness" with the team would probably not have been surpassed had he actively participated in the game.

THE STRUCTURE OF MULTIPLE GROUP MEMBERSHIPS

The Quantitative Dimension

Beginning with the simplest possible operating assumption that social identity is merely a straightforward reflection of group membership, we shall first explore very restricted conditions and then examine the complexities introduced when structural or organizational factors are considered.

If a very simple society existed in which only a single group membership were possible, social identity would be highly predictable on the basis of the group's attributes and would be highly stable across situations and over temporal periods. In such a case, as Nobles (1973) has observed about certain African societies, "oneself and one's people . . . are one and the same." An industralized society produces social fragmentation, division of labor, and a heterogeneity of interests; as a consequence social identity is determined by membership in many different types of groups. Not only are there kinship, ethnic, and religious groups in complex societies, but a variety of political, economic, and recreational groups exist as well. The antecedents of social identity under such conditions are much more complicated than those found in a simple society. Some of these problems will be discussed later, but for now attention should be directed to the importance of the mere number of membership groups without regard to organizational considerations.

Assuming that membership groups are true psychological groups for the individual, the quantitative dimension has several implications for social identity without regard to the type of organization among them. To take the simplest case, contrast the situation of one's membership in a single group as opposed to membership in many groups. The latter case holds the potential for a far greater degree of variation in social identity over time and across place than does the simpler case of membership in one group only. Further, the greater the number of group memberships possessed by an individual the greater the likelihood of the occurrence of conflict, ambiguity, or other strains among them. One can also speculate that the substantive content of social identity is likely to be more complex and subject to perturbations in response to a shift in the importance given to particular groups from time to time.

Having a large number of group memberships is not without its advantages, however. Membership in a large number of groups offers an individual the possibility of alternative sources of positive social identity when membership in one important group is lost or if it is downgraded; these alternative resources would be less likely to be utilized in a simpler group membership system. Furthermore, evidence suggests that membership in a more differentiated social environment may be positively related to social adjustment and the ability to deal effectively with problems in everyday life (Cameron, 1947; Stephan & Stephan, 1971). Cognitive flexibility and the ability to adapt to situational contingencies are acquired in the course of the frequent modulations of social identity that occur when multiple group membership exists.

Discordant and Concordant Identities

The sheer number of group memberships plays an important part in social identity particularly in helping define limits of the impact of other structural factors. Of more direct interest, however, is the effect of the nature of the organization or structure among multiple groups. The degree of discrepancy in social identities created by a system of group memberships is one important problem. Minor discrepancies of social identity associated with membership in multiple groups are not likely to cause much difficulty since a single identity of sufficient breadth can incorporate slightly shifting but basically harmonious social identities. Concordant social identities associated with multiple group memberships is probably more common than conditions of severe discrepancy. The better-integrated a social network the greater the likelihood of association among members of different groups; the overlapping of membership of others across different groups should help prevent the development of strongly discrepant identities associated with membership in different groups.

William James was quite aware of the problem of severe discrepancies between groups when he mentioned (further along in the quotation cited earlier) that a youth who is "demure enough" in the presence of his parents apparently holds a very different and discrepant social identity among his "tough" young friends, as indicated by his piratical behavior ("swears and swaggers like a pirate"). We may infer that these two membership groups are associated with different social identities; if these or other multiple identities are discordant in terms of their content, then problems of coordination may arise.

Social identities associated with two different group memberships are discordant if they are inconsistent or contradictory in a logical or psychological sense. If one's identity in group A consists of the elements of kind, self-effacing, generous, and "demure" (referring again to James's example) and in group B of cruel, arrogant, miserly, and "tough," then the two do not seem to be in a harmonious relation one with the other; it is not easy to reconcile them into a single identity in terms of their content. To construct a merged or composite identity that would result from these two sets of characteristics would not seem easy to accomplish. Yet, it is well known that people do behave in ways that appear to be highly discrepant and contradictory, and apparently they possess the corresponding discordant self-identities without suffering undue cognitive and social strain.

Lack of harmony among the different identities created by membership in different groups poses a problem for the creation of a composite identity, but other solutions can be found. Perhaps the easiest way to avert the problem is to ensure that discrepant group memberships are activated only when they are sharply separated by time and place. William James recognized this possibility when he implied that the two discrepant identities of "tough" and "demure" existed because the youngster was unlikely to be part of such different groups as "young friends" and "family" at the same time. In interviews with children, Hartley, Rosenbaum, and Schwartz (1948) found that multiple group memberships did not seem to cause problems. The reply of a five-year-old child illustrates one novel, but workable solution: "I'm Jewish when I am awake; when I sleep I'm American." In short, the potential for confusion and conflict due to discrepant social identities connected with different groups may rarely materialize if a satisfactory degree of temporal and spatial segmentation among the groups is maintained. In the absence of cues that divulge (to self and others) that one has membership in a group other than the one activated during the interaction, even discrepant group memberships need not pose a problem for a person's social identity in the course of everyday life.

Averting potential cognitive strain and behavioral conflict due to discordant social identities by ensuring that an adequate amount of distance (psychological, physical, and temporal) is maintained between them will not always be feasible. A clear hierarchy of personal values can be applied to the discrepant identities and used as a behavioral guide in conflict situations that may arise. Thus, the relative centrality and importance of two social identities that are associated with the potential conflict evoked by multiple membership groups was clearly indicated by the remark of E. M. Forster that " . . . if I had to choose between betraying my country and betraying my friends, I hope I should have the guts to betray my country. . . . "

It is not always possible to conceal one's group membership even if it does not constitute the focal group that forms the basis of an interaction. Thus, group memberships based on criteria such as race, sex, caste, or criteria such as those of the Japanese "mafiosi" (a criminal organization that requires a member to be tattooed over his entire body) among many others present cues indicative of a particular group membership at all times—making it more difficult to avoid problems that may arise when potentially discordant social identities are made explicit.

Gender and race provide illuminating examples of problems in social identity produced by the visibility of multiple group membership. On the basis of extensive data provided by direct observation and other techniques, Schofield (1981) presents a fascinating analysis of the social identity associated with gender and racial group membership in a desegregated middle school. For preadolescents in the United States there is a pronounced separation between males and females and also between blacks and whites in school. Thus, friendship groups are formed primarily on the basis of commonality of individuals in terms of sex and race.

Gender was readily acknowledged by both teachers and students in Schofield's study as being important to social identity in the school, and there was a sharp cleavage also between groups of boys and girls. Both staff and students agreed upon the elements that comprised male and female social identities. The racial group membership of these students was, of course, equally as obvious to staff and students as gender membership. Unlike gender group membership, however, the staff maintained that race should not be used as an important element of social identity; accordingly, teachers attempted to ignore racial group membership of the students and treated it as an inappropriate and even illegitimate aspect of the students' social identity.

Thus, gender was seen by the staff and students as being an important component of identity that was legitimate to consider; by contrast, racial group membership was considered to be irrelevant to identity by both black and white staff members. A quotation from a (black) vice-principal at the school expresses this position: "I don't address myself to group differences when I am dealing with youngsters . . . I try to treat youngsters . . . as youngsters and not as black, white, green or yellow . . . children are children . . . " (p. 73). Race was only mentioned in the school on rare occasions in connection with the staff's urging the students to ignore race. Yet, a child's membership in a racial group (black/white) could not be concealed because of the easily identifiable differences in physical characteristics.

Although teachers tried to ignore race, it was clearly not ignored by the children and was an extremely important element in their social identity. They thought of themselves as black or white, and friendship groups were segregated by race. For example, when an interviewer asked about the degree of friendliness of the children at this school, the interviewee (a white female) responded with the inquiry, "The black kids or the white kids?" (p. 74). Racial group membership was strongly associated with certain identity elements by the students. Thus, the whites were seen as being more intelligent and academically motivated than the blacks; blacks were seen as being physically strong, tough (aggressive), and more dominating than white. Males and females of both races seemed to share these images associated with racial group membership.

It should be obvious that another group membership that cuts across race, namely, social class, probably accounted to a large extent for any racial differences in intellectual ability and academic motivation among the students. But social class membership is a less visible characteristic than race; the omnipresence of cues indicative of race makes it very difficult for the children to ignore this group membership in spite of the effort made by teachers to be "color blind" and to convince the children that racial group membership was not a legitimate basis for social identity. (In contrast to the attitude toward race, gender was readily acknowledged by staff and teachers to be an important basis of social identity.)

Nesting: Containing and Contained Groups

One possible type of organization among multiple groups is of particular interest—the group-within-a-group arrangement. Analysis of groups in terms of their inclusiveness-containedness structure is the subject of discussion in a small (and apparently neglected) treatise by the Norwegian sociologist, Odd Ramsöy (1962). In this thin volume Ramsöy shows that a large number of group phenomena in the context of both small groups and the broader society are amenable to analysis according to this particular type of structure—the location of one group inside another.

Examples abound of such structure, in which one group is part of a larger containing system, which in turn is part of a still more general system. Many organizations are explicitly designed in this way. Political divisions provide a clear-cut example that illustrates the principle: the city, the county, state, nation—each lower level entity is contained within the higher one. Religion also offers many examples: there are subsystems of sects within the more inclusive group of Protestants, but the Protestant and Catholic groupings are part or subsystems of a more inclusive category. The significance of this type of structure lies in the fact that a person is at the same time a member of each of the groups that exist at different levels of the complex system. Does the relation between an inclusive social system and a subsystem have implications for social identity? We are citizens of the nation and of the state and the city. What is the influence of such nested subsystems on social identity? Conflict will sometimes force a person to focus more sharply upon the relation between the contained and containing groups, and may require an excruciating decision about loyalty. General Robert E. Lee placed his subgroup identity of Virginian ahead of his identity of American during the civil war; he chose to fight for the South (the subgroup membership) instead of the United States (the inclusive group), although he was serving as an officer in the U.S. military forces at the time. More common, perhaps, is the subordination of a subsystem identity in deference to the inclusive group identity, especially in the face of threat or imminent danger. Thus, when facing a common danger antagonistic groups experience little difficulty in ceasing their hostility and forming an alliance. Subgroup identity is submerged and made subserviant to the more inclusive group membership, which the erstwhile enemies now share.

Interesting differences between the perceptions of persons inside and outside complex systems may occur that have implications for social identity and social interaction. Outsiders often do not see an inclusive system as being divided into subgroups, whereas the subgroup boundaries may be very important to insiders; or if noticed, outsiders often fail to attach any significance to subgroup divisions that are viewed by insiders as being extremely significant for social identity. Thus, outsiders usually see Islam as an inclusive group, without being aware of the existence or the crucial distinctions among Omar's "two and seventy jarring sects"—distinctions important enough for believers in the subgroups to sacrifice their lives for the sake of their sect. The failure of U.S. foreign policy in Iran may be related to the non–recognition of important distinctions in Islamic religions.

ROLE OF THE OUTGROUP IN SOCIAL IDENTITY

Despite the complexity of our social identities, we seldom consciously consider the various possible groups and categories to which we belong. Moreover, we usually consider social identity from a rather egocentric viewpoint. We tend to focus on the attributes of the ingroup (both in terms of self- and other-perception), while the role of the outgroup is largely ignored. Just as Tajfel and Turner (1979) have described group identity as an epiphenomenon of intergroup conflict in traditional theories of inter-group relations, the outgroup frequently is seen as a secondary construct— as the complement of the ingroup. Recent work by Tajfel and his colleagues (e.g., Tajfel & Billig, 1974; Turner, Brown & Tajfel, 1979) suggests, however, that the outgroup is not so passive an element in group identification. The mere existence of an outgroup under the most superficial of conditions may result in a positive attachment to the ingroup. Furthermore, subjects categorized into these "minimal" groups often display favoritism toward the ingroup—a bias similar to that associated with ethnocentrism. Of concern to us here is the role of the outgroup in determining our sense of social identity. For purposes of social identity it may be even more important to emphasize those groups in which we do *not* hold membership as it is to specify those to which we belong. Thus, according to this line of thought, outgroups can play an important part in contributing to social identity. As a case in point, consider the following statement by Spiegel (1968): " . . . in behavior such black people are occupied in defining what they are *not*: how they are not like whites and don't like whites; how they are not like middle-class people and reject their values; how they are not of western European origin, with several choices of alternative origins, cultures, and languages" (p. 152). In the following section, we shall examine the role of the outgroup in social identity.

The "Minimal" Group Situation

Most groups that we belong to are "substantial"—they have existed for some period of time and perceived norms for group behavior are well established. Identification with the ingroup is seen as the result of intergroup competition (for scarce resources), a functional behavior that increases positive attachment to the ingroup while justifying derogation of the outgroup. In the minimal group situation, however, there is no competition for resources. In fact, there is no intergroup interaction. Yet, we still find evidence of ingroup bias, suggesting that subjects have, indeed, identified with the ingroup. Consequently, factors other than intergroup competition must contribute to the perceived group identity.

The experimental paradigm involves the division or categorization of subjects into two groups, ostensibly on the basis of some superficial task (e.g., preference for paintings). Group assignment is actually random. Following this categorization manipulation, subjects are given the opportunity to distribute resources (usually money) between pairs of other subjects, identified only by a code number and group membership. The task is arranged so that the subject can allocate the money in a variety of ways that reflect several distribution strategies. For example, subjects may choose to give an equal amount of money to both the ingroup and outgroup member, or the choice can favor either group (ingroup or outgroup bias). Other strategies include maximizing joint profit (the choice that results in the dispersal of the greatest amount of money) and maximizing the difference between the two groups (relative ingroup bias). (The reader is referred to Brewer (1979) or Tajfel, Billig, Bundy & Flament (1971) for a more complete discussion of this allocation task.) The consistent finding from a large number of studies (Allen & Wilder, 1975; Billig & Tajfel, 1973; Tajfel, 1970; Tajfel & Billig, 1974; Tajfel et al., 1971) is that subjects choose to distribute the money in a manner that favors the ingroup. Moreover, the dominant strategy is to maximize the difference between ingroup and outgroup, even if this choice sacrifices both personal and group monetary gain (Brewer & Silver, 1978; Turner, Brown & Tajfel, 1979). Thus, the unequal distribution of money serves to differentiate ingroup and outgroup, rather than simply to provide the ingroup with a greater share of the profits. Several authors have reported that a positive ingroup bias also is observed in evaluative trait ratings (e.g., Brewer & Silver, 1978; Doise, Csepely, Dann, Gouge, Larsen & Ostell, 1972; Rabbie, Benoist, Oosterbaan & Visser, 1974; Rabbie & Wilkins, 1971), and the allocation of meaningless points (Turner, 1975).

Subjects in these minimal group situations behave in much the same fashion as members of more substantial groups. However, in the absence of any intergroup interaction, we must conclude that ingroup bias results not from competition but from categorization into groups per se. Several studies bear directly on this point. For example, Rabbie and Wilkins (1971) categorized subjects into two groups and led them to believe that they would subsequently interact competitively or that they would interact but not competitively (there was also a no-interaction control). Subjects then rated ingroup and outgroup members both before and after the intergroup interaction. Results indicated that all subjects showed ingroup bias in their ratings before the interactive task, although ratings were higher for those subjects expecting to interact as compared to the control group. Ingroup bias was enhanced following the experimental task but equally in the competitive and noncompetitive conditions. Billig and Tajfel (1973) also have demonstrated that social categorization (the division into groups) is sufficient to produce ingroup bias regardless of the perceived similarity with ingroup members. In their study, half the subjects were categorized and told that the rationale for this division was on the basis of painting preference (similarity conditions), or that group designation was entirely random (no similarity condition). The remaining subjects were not categorized (no mention of two groups being formed) but were told that code numbers were assigned either by painting preference or by chance. All subjects then distributed money in the manner described earlier. Ingroup bias was found in both categorization conditions regardless of similarity, but no favoritism was observed when subjects were not categorized. Allen and Wilder (1975) reported parallel findings, even when subjects explicitly were informed about dissimilarity (rather than lack of similarity) between their own and other ingroup members' opinions.

How does the mere categorization into groups result in favoritism toward the ingroup? Tajfel (1970) has suggested the operation of a social norm for discrimination—individuals realize that two groups have been formed and that one should favor the ingroup. Although this explanation has intuitive appeal, it is somewhat tautological. Furthermore, subjective reports from the Allen and Wilder (1975) study indicate that ingroup favoritism is not the ideal distribution strategy (although subjects did expect both ingroup and outgroup members to be biased). Perhaps other factors are involved.

A more general theory is offered by Turner (1975) and, recently, Tajfel and Turner (1979). Briefly, ingroup bias results from a social comparison process based on an individual's need to maintain a positive social identity. Social categories provide an individual with a system of reference: identification with a particular group allows a person to locate himself or herself in the social milieu. A category has some associated positive or negative value (along a specified dimension), and thus alignment with a particular group results in a corresponding positive or negative social identity. Furthermore, one evaluates the ingroup through social comparisons with relevant outgroups. Positively discrepant comparisons (i.e., favoring the ingroup) result in a positive group-and-self concept, while negatively discrepant comparisons yield a negative group-and-self concept. Thus, an individual is motivated to achieve positively discrepant comparisons between one's own group and relevant other groups in order to maintain a positive social identity.

When considering existing (or what we have referred to as "substantial") groups, maintenance of a positive identity is a relatively easy task. Positive (and negative) attributes of group membership are, for the most part, known, and thus the consequences of group alignment are apparent. Indeed, when several possible group structurings are available, an individual may compare various in- and outgroups on relevant dimensions and identify self with the group that results in the largest positively discrepant comparison.[4] But such freedom is not available in the minimal group situation. Subjects have been categorized into an ingroup and an outgroup along some superficial dimension or, in the extreme case, randomly. Since the maintenance of a positive ingroup identity requires the achievement of a positively discrepant comparison, this comparison will be made along whatever dimension is available, for example, the distribution of money. This attempt to differentiate ingroup and outgroup Turner (1975) has called social competition—intergroup behavior results not from a real conflict of group interests but from a mutual competition by comparison for positive ingroup identity.

A social comparison perspective highlights the importance of the outgroup in the establishment and maintenance of social identity. Consider what is happening in the Tajfel/Turner situation. Subjects are divided into two groups—groups that did not exist previously in the social environment. In most cases the subject has little or no information about value-laden attributes of the groups and, consequently, cannot engage in social competition on any existing dimension.[5] When presented with an opportunity to discriminate against an outgroup, however, positive social identity may be achieved by favoring the ingroup. Thus, the outgroup represents more than the antithesis of the ingroup: the fact that the outgroup exists forces individuals to identify with the ingroup if they are to maintain a positive social and self–identity. In effect, the presence of the outgroup generates ingroup camaraderie—Lewin's strong "we-feeling."

Variations in the Outgroup: Effects on Social Identity

The presence of an outgroup member may affect one's social identity by any of several means. Most directly the outgroup may behave in a manner that demands a consideration of the ingroup's contribution to one's identity. The outgroup may treat one as a member of the ingroup, thereby establishing a role relationship commensurate with ingroup identification. For example, consideration of the ingroup's contribution to self-identity should occur when an outgroup member addresses a person by the ingroup name or treats him or her in a manner consistent with the behavioral norms of the ingroup. Thus, we may experience a stronger identification with our department when members of other departments call us psychologists or ask for our opinions about human behavior. On a more fundamental (and more subtle) level, however, the salience of an outgroup may cause one to think rather automatically of the complementary ingroup. This process may occur in much the same way as the presence of a member of an associated pair of opposites conjures up the other (e.g., up-down, night-day, negative-positive). Furthermore, one may argue for the complementary process as well; that is, removal of a salient outgroup should reduce the probability of identification with the relevant ingroup. These hypotheses concerning the propensity of outgroups to arouse ingroup identification will be examined in light of some recent literature dealing with the effects of categorization on intergroup perceptions and behavior.

Increasing Salience of Outgroups

To test the implication of mere salience of the outgroup for social identity, a situation must be created in which an outgroup is psychologically salient yet does not interact with the person in any manner. We have conducted some research that meets this criterion.

In one experiment (Wilder, 1981), subjects were categorized into one of two mutually exclusive groups allegedly on the basis of their preferences among the paintings of two artists (ingroup/outgroup condition). Actual assignment to the groups was random, as in the Tajfel et al. (1971) procedure. Other subjects were all assigned to the same group, so there was no outgroup salient for them (ingroup-only condition). Finally, in a third condition subjects were not categorized into groups at all (control condition). All subjects were unaware of which of the other persons were members of either the ingroup or the outgroup. Following the categorization manipulation subjects predicted the beliefs on a variety of issues of either the anonymous outgroup members (ingroup/outgroup condition), other anonymous ingroup members (ingroup/outgroup and ingroup-only conditions), or the anonymous others in the session (control condition). Some of the issues directly pertained to the criterion for categorization (artistic preferences) and others were less relevant (e.g., political beliefs).

As expected, subjects in the ingroup/outgroup condition assumed greater belief similarity between their own beliefs and those of other ingroup members than of outgroup members. This pattern of differential assumptions of belief similarity emerged most strongly on items that were relevant to the criterion for categorization. Subjects in the ingroup-only condition also assumed greater similarity between their beliefs and those of the anonymous ingroup members than did subjects in the control condition in which categorization had not occurred. Of greater interest to us was the finding that persons in the ingroup/outgroup condition assumed more similarity between themselves and the ingroup than did those in the ingroup-only condition. Thus, the salience of a specific outgroup (ingroup/outgroup condition) caused persons to assume greater similarity between themselves and fellow ingroup members in comparison to the situation when no outgroup was salient (ingroup-only condition). The outgroup's salience augmented the subjects' perceived similarity to fellow members of the ingroup.

On another set of measures in this experiment, subjects estimated the range of opinions that others probably held on a variety of issues (e.g., artistic preferences, political beliefs, opinions about a legal case). Overall, subjects assumed relatively greater homogeneity among members of an outgroup than among members of the ingroup. Consistent with the findings reported above, the salience of an outgroup affected subjects' estimates of ingroup homogeneity. Subjects assumed greater homogeneity in the ingroup when an outgroup was present (ingroup/outgroup condition) than when no specific outgroup was salient (ingroup-only condition). Moreover, these effects were stronger on items most relevant to the categorization criterion (painting preferences), although the same pattern emerged on some of the less related items (e.g., political beliefs).

In another, related experiment (Wilder & Allen, 1978) subjects were either categorized into one of two groups, a single group, or not categorized at all in the manner described above. Then they ranked their preferences among several types of information that would be available for viewing about the beliefs and opinions of others in their experimental sessions. When an ingroup/outgroup categorization existed, subjects preferred to view information that indicated ingroup similarity and outgroup dissimilarity relative to themselves (ingroup/outgroup condition). Subjects also preferred to view information indicating ingroup similarity when all persons were members of the same group (ingroup-only condition). Interestingly, preference for information indicating ingroup similarity was stronger when an outgroup was salient (ingroup/outgroup condition) than when no outgroup existed (ingroup-only condition). Thus, the salience of a specific outgroup enhanced preferences for information that drew subjects closer to their ingroup.

In summary, the psychological presence of an outgroup enhances feelings of oneness with the ingroup as indicated by: (1) greater perceived belief similarity within the ingroup, (2) smaller assumed variance of ingroup members' beliefs, and (3) preference for information indicating similarity with fellow ingroup members. These findings suggest that one's relationship to an ingroup can be affected by the salience of an outgroup.

Decreasing Salience of Outgroups

Thus far, we have focused on consequences for ingroup identification of the increased salience of an outgroup. An alternative approach would be to consider the opposite situation. Suppose the outgroup were made less salient in a situation. Would this lessen the likelihood of an individual identifying with the corresponding ingroup? Evidence relevant to this question can be found in research on intergroup contact.

Favorable contact between groups may reduce ingroup/outgroup bias by replacing negative stereotypes with positive experiences (c.g., Amir, 1969, 1976; Riordin, 1978). But contact with the outgroup may or may not have an impact on one's identification with the ingroup. To the extent that ingroup identification is based on negative relations with the outgroup (e.g., coalition to combat a common foe), the improvement of relations between the groups may weaken ingroup identity. On the other hand, in other situations one may feel stronger identification with the ingroup following positive contact with the outgroup. This may be due to pride associated with the ingroup's part in improving intergroup relations. Most research on intergroup relations has focused, however, on attempts to produce harmony from discord. Rarely has attention been given to consequences of contact for ingroup identity. We hypothesize that the form taken by contact between groups will affect ingroup identity. If outgroup salience serves to enhance ingroup identity, then cues that reduce the salience of the outgroup should lessen ingroup identification in the contact setting.

To recapitulate, we hypothesize that cues that lessen the salience of an outgroup as an entity should, in turn, lessen ingroup identification and thereby reduce the individual's proclivity to favor ingroup over an out-group. A portion of this chain of inferences was examined in three experiments by one of the authors (Wilder, 1978). In these experiments one or more members of an outgroup behaved in a manner that made the outgroup appear to be a heterogeneous collection of individuals rather than a homogeneous unit. In one experiment, some outgroup members be-haved in a manner contrary to that expected of the outgroup. In the other two studies, outgroup members revealed information about themselves that accentuated their uniqueness. In all studies the individuating behavior of the outgroup members fostered a significant reduction in ingroup favoritism when subjects later divided rewards between the groups. The lack of homogeneity in the behavior of the outgroup may have reduced the extent of identification with the corresponding ingroup. With ingroup identity relatively diminished, subjects had no need to maintain a positive identity for the ingroup by favoring it at the expense of the outgroup. These experiments are discussed more fully below.

Dissent in the Outgroup

Dissenting from the expected behavior of the outgroup should enhance the salience of individual outgroup members. Dissent has the effect of partitioning persons from their ingroup by abrogating the unit relationship between them and the group (Heider, 1958). In the first of three ex-periments (Wilder, 1978), subjects were arbitrarily categorized into two groups by the experimenter. Each group was led to a different room and was informed that the members of the other group were adjudicating two legal cases. Supposedly, subjects would be evaluating the outgroup's performance at a later time in the experiment. Subjects then worked on a few filler tasks until the outgroup had finished deliberating the cases. Feedback from the outgroup indicated that either all members agreed on both cases (unanimous condition), one member dissented on both cases (dissent condition), or feedback was obtained from only one person (alone condition). Subsequently, subjects completed dependent measures, in-cluding several reward matrices that divided earnings between members of the two groups (Tajfel et al., 1971).

Subjects in the unanimous and alone conditions displayed significantly greater ingroup favoritism than subjects in the dissent condition. Overall, subjects in the dissent condition divided rewards almost equally between the ingroup and the outgroup. Moreover, subjects were more likely to describe the outgroup as a collection of independent individuals than as a single entity in the dissent condition than in the other conditions. Dissent apparently altered the perception of the group from a simple entity to a collection of heterogeneous individuals.

Disclosure of Personal Information

Another method of individuation consists of disclosing personal information about oneself. Information that is relatively unique to a person should encourage a more complex and differentiated view of the individual. Such information should prevent or compensate for overly simplified categorizations. In two experiments Wilder (1978) varied the distinctiveness of information that subjects had about members of an outgroup and assessed the impact of this information on measures of ingroup/outgroup bias. Subjects in these experiments were divided into two groups and were instructed to perform several problem-solving tasks. On one of these tasks, subjects in all conditions received highly critical feedback from the outgroup. Later, after discovering that they did not have sufficient information to complete another task, they sent a message to the other group requesting assistance to complete the task. The reply each group received from the outgroup constituted the experimental manipulation.

Groups of subjects were assigned to one of four conditions, with some receiving all the help they had requested (cooperative condition), others receiving no help whatsoever (uncooperative condition), others receiving partial assistance from half of the outgroup acting as a unit (partially cooperative group condition), and, finally, others receiving some aid from half of the outgroup acting as individuals (partially cooperative individual condition). Specifically, feedback in the partially cooperative group condition came from the entire outgroup as a unit. But in the partially cooperative individual condition, the assistance came in the form of individual notes signed with the initials of those helping. The primary dependent measure of interest was a reward matrix that subjects used to divide earnings between the ingroup and the outgroup.

As expected, subjects showed the most ingroup favoritism on the reward distribution task when the outgroup was uncooperative and the least bias when the outgroup was fully cooperative. These conditions were included to set the range of bias expected to be observed in the experiment. The partially cooperative conditions fell between the others. Significantly less ingroup favoritism occurred when the outgroup was heterogeneous (partially cooperative individual condition) than when they responded as a group (partially cooperative group condition), even though the outgroup's behavior did not differ between the two conditions. When assistance came from the individuated outgroup members, bias against the outgroup did not differ substantially from the amount observed when the outgroup cooperated completely.

In summary, intergroup discrimination was eliminated in the preceding series of studies by providing cues to enhance the perceived diversity or heterogeneity of the outgroup. There are several ways to account for these findings. One explanation relevant to the thrust of this chapter would be that the reduced salience of the outgroup as a single entity also reduced the salience of the ingroup as a component of the subject's social identity. Maintenance of a positive social identity did not, therefore, necessitate favoritism of the ingroup. Thus, subjects discriminated less in favor of the ingroup than if the situation had been clearly drawn along simple ingroup/outgroup boundaries. Moreover, the diversity present in the outgroup may have encouraged subjects to reflect upon the heterogeneity inherent in their ingroup as well, thereby reducing their identification with and desire to benefit the ingroup over the outgroup.

Some anecdotal evidence from beyond the laboratory is consistent with these results. For instance, hostage situations often involve two mutually exclusive groups—the hostages and their captors. Indeed, hostages are frequently chosen because they represent an outgroup despised by their captors. In examining the hostage literature, we have read several accounts of hostages receiving more favorable treatment when they have acted in a manner that individuates themselves from the narrow category of outgroup member. Consider, for instance, the case of Gerard Vaders.

In December 1975, Mr. Vaders was held hostage on a train commandeered by South Moluccans near Groningen, Netherlands (Ochberg, 1977). Frustrated because their demands were not being met, the terrorists decided to execute Vaders as an example to the authorities. Before shooting him, he was allowed to dictate a final letter to his family. In that letter Vaders talked about his life and his family, his accomplishments and shortcomings, his dreams and concerns. It is important to note, however, that he was not maudlin and did not plead for sympathy in the letter. When he had finished dictating the message, his captors decided not to execute him after all. Instead, they ushered out another hapless hostage and shot him without benefit of a farewell letter. The change in behavior directed toward Vaders can be explained in several ways. Certainly his captors may have felt some empathy for him as he revealed information about himself—information about successes and failures that probably had parallels in the lives of his captors. In addition, empathy for Vaders may very well have reduced feelings of strong ingroup identity among the captors, at least with regard to him.

It is tempting to take these speculations one step further and wonder if successful contact between groups can only occur if ingroup identification is lessened in the contact setting. To go directly to the heart of this proposal, consider Sherif's (1967) classic research on intergroup contact. One wonders if the effectiveness of superordinate goals in reducing bias was not partially a consequence of reducing ingroup identification among the subjects. Sherif reported that mere contact between the groups, whether in spirited competition (e.g., baseball tournament) or in a positively valued environment (e.g., dining room), was unsuccessful in reducing bias. Indeed, such contact tended to inflame passions. Perhaps, this should not have been surprising if we consider that the contact occurred in situations where group boundaries were highly salient (e.g., groups segregated to different sides of the baseball diamond or to separate dining tables). In such contact environments, the salience of both the ingroup and the outgroup should serve to enhance ingroup identification and conformity to perceived ingroup norms—which included denigration of the outgroup and positive enhancement of the ingroup. By contrast, consider the superordinate goals introduced by Sherif and his associates (e.g., attempt to fix broken water supply). These tasks were such that individuals from the groups most likely mingled with one another across group boundaries; the task environment did not allow a simple division of effort along group lines. If individuals pitched in and interacted more across group boundaries in pursuit of the common goal, it seems probable that the salience of the ingroup and outgroup as a determinant of social identity and as a guide for behavior was relatively reduced.

To be most successful, then, contact between groups should eliminate cues that structure the encounter as an intergroup interaction situation in favor of cues suggesting interindividual interaction. To generalize a bit further, failure to reduce antagonism in some desegregated school systems may be partly due to the manner in which the contact between racial groups occurs. When schools integrate, students often enter as members of existing segregated groups of friends. They chat in segregated groups, eat at different tables, study separately, and so forth (Schofield, 1981). Thus, interracial contact often occurs between these small groups with little opportunity to alter the perception of the interaction as one between groups as opposed to between individuals. Persons in these interactions define themselves in terms of their highly salient racial ingroups and act according to prevailing group norms.

Identifying Social Categories: Which Outgroup?

Social identity depends, in part, on the perception of social categories: to identify with a particular ingroup, one must realize that groups exist (or, at least, that the potential for group division exists). This perception is almost automatic in a highly structured intergroup interaction, such as a sporting event. Two uniformed teams appear on the playing field, each defending a particular area. Spectators will often express group alignment by wearing the team's colors or by sitting on the ingroup's side of the field. The group division is so obvious that we are often surprised when someone fails to notice it. (Consider the novice sports fan who asks, "Who's playing here?" or "Which team is in white?") Furthermore, the categories have been established prior to the interaction and, as several authors have noted (e.g., Brewer, 1979; Hamilton, 1979; Turner, 1975), individuals tend to structure the social environment in terms of existing categories.

In less structured settings, identification of the social groups may not be so unambiguous. Most social interactions offer the possibility for multiple–group structurings and in the extreme minimal group situation, categories exist only because they have been created by the experimenter. How do we decide what groups exist in a particular social interaction?

We can represent an individual by a set of features (height, sex, political philosophy, etc.). The salience of each feature is determined by its intensity and diagnostic value, and the perceived similarity between individuals is some linear combination of their common and distinctive features. But an important difference between social and object similarity judgments is that one of the elements in social comparisons may be self. This is the relevant comparison (self versus others) for group identification.[6]

Tversky (1977) has commented on the "two faces" of similarity—causal and derivative. Similarity may be used as the basis for categorization, but at the same time categorization influences perceived similarity through the diagnosticity principle. This aspect is important when considering group identification. In some social situations, an individual must first decide what categories exist (using perceived similarity); in others, the categories have already been formed (e.g., sporting events, the minimal group situation). In one case, categorization (and identification with the ingroup) results from a comparison of salient features; in the other case, the salience of features result from the categorization.

When multiple group structurings are possible, the choice of a particular dimension for categorization is often attributed to the salience or singular importance of that dimension. While this may be true in some situations (e.g., a highly prejudiced person categorizing on the basis of race), it is far too general a rule. We propose that an individual assesses the similarity between self and others, and then structures the social environment in a manner that maximizes similarity within the ingroup and, simultaneously, maximizes dissimilarity with respect to the outgroup. Note the critical role that the outgroup plays in defining social identity. The ingroup is constructed not just on the basis of perceived similarity among potential ingroup members, but also on the ability of those individuals to provide a distinct identity from the outgroup. Indeed, the overall similarity of ingroup members may be sacrificed in order to maximize the difference vis à vis the outgroup. In an extreme case, ingroup members may have little in common other than the fact that they do not share the features of the outgroup.

The influence of the outgroup is even more important in the minimal group situation. The subject has been identified as a member of one of two superficial groups. He or she has no information about either group (with the exception of some assumed quality, e.g., picture preference). There is only one feature available for comparison: a feature low in intensity, but high in diagnostic value—the group designation per se. Thus, we would expect an increase in perceived similarity among individuals when categorized into an ingroup and outgroup (compared to a noncategorized baseline) because they now share a common, salient feature, and data consistent with this notion have been reported by Wilder (1981). Interestingly, our feature-matching analysis suggests that the perceived increase in similarity is not so much an ingroup bias as an accurate assessment of the intergroup situation. The ingroup members really are more similar in the presence of the outgroup.

People provide a rich source of information, and, most likely, individuals will have many common and distinctive features. According to the cognitive model outlined here, we can see ourselves both as similar to and different from other individuals, depending on whether we attend more to common or distinctive features. The question arises as to which is more important—sharing common features with the ingroup or maintaining distinctive features with respect to the outgroup. While one cannot deny the importance of ingroup similarity, several studies indicate that subjects will attempt to differentiate the ingroup from the outgroup even though they know that ingroup members hold dissimilar opinions (Allen & Wilder, 1975) and even at the cost of ingroup and personal profit (Turner, Brown & Tajfel, 1979). Thus, differentiation appears to be of primary importance, indicating that social identity rests squarely on the shoulders of the outgroup.

A recent study by McGuire, McGuire, and Winton (1979) demonstrated the role of distinctiveness in social identity. Subjects (school children) were asked to describe themselves to the experimenter by responding to two, open-ended questions: "Tell us about yourself," and then the complementary question, "Tell us what you are not." The verbal descriptions were tape-recorded, and the protocols were coded for reference to the subject's gender. McGuire et al. (1979) predicted that the children would be more likely to mention gender in their verbal descriptions to the extent that opposite sex predominated in their own family. For example, boys from households with females in the majority should be more likely to mention gender as part of their self-concept than boys from households where the sex distribution is more equivalent. Such skewed distributions (predominately female or predominately male) provide information about the distinctiveness of one's gender and, consequently, increase the probability that gender would be a salient aspect of social identity. Results supported this prediction. Both boys and girls from predominately opposite-sex families mentioned gender in response to the question, "Tell us about yourself," more than children from families with equal numbers of males and females. It is important to note that the crucial factor influencing the salience of gender was not the skewness of the gender distribution per se but, rather, the possession of a nonshared feature. Neither boys from a predominately male household nor girls from a predominately female household mentioned sex in their verbal descriptions more than the control group (equal numbers of males and females). Thus, a particular feature is more salient to individuals in the minority as compared to the majority.

This conclusion seems somewhat paradoxical, as McGuire et al. (1979) have suggested. One forms a sense of social identity by noticing what one is not. Indeed, responses to the question, "Tell us what you are not," produced stronger effects for distinctiveness than the affirmative, "Tell us what you are." Implications of these findings for the intergroup situation are clear. From an individual's perspective, outgroup members share at least one feature that ingroup members do not possess (namely, group membership). As we have already seen, this alone may provide a basis for group identification. However, we would expect the strength of group identification to increase as the distribution of features becomes disproportionally larger in the outgroup relative to the ingroup. Thus, ingroup identity may be related directly to characteristics of the the outgroup. We may even speculate that the critical dimension for group categorization would be defined in terms of proportionality—the feature most disproportionally represented in the outgroup will form the basis for ingroup social identity.

Envoi

Our discussion of the structure of multiple group memberships has proceeded as if the individual behaves within a static and preexisting system that he or she did little to create and can do little to change. We hasten to say that we are well aware that social reality is not so simple nor so docile as may have been suggested by our previous discussion. It would be more correct to say that the system of membership groups in which the individual participates is in a state of flux, being subject to changes brought about by the intentional efforts of the individual as well as by external processes outside his control. Social identity is not conceived of as being only a pale shadow, as it were, of a set of group memberships—as an effect only. On the contrary, we conceive of social identity not only as a product but as an important cause of social behavior, as an ongoing process that is constantly changing and being transformed. Moreover, the attempt to modify or support social identity frequently underlies the individual's active attempts to seek out particular kinds of group memberships. Sir Isaiah Berlin (1982) shows clearly the critical role of group membership in his felicitous essay on the life of Disraeli:

> The life of Benjamin Disraeli . . . is one of the most vivid illustrations of a desperate search . . . for a group loyalty, a regiment with which he could identify himself, in whose name he could speak and act, because he could not face the awful prospect of speaking in his own—indeed, he could not be certain that, if he tried to find what was his own, he would find an answer (p. 275).

Nor can we all.

NOTES

1. To avoid propagating a popular but erroneous myth, we must hasten to the service of truth by sadly reporting that there is no evidence that Queen Victoria actually ever used this expression in spite of its being popularly attributed to her. It is possible that she might have done so, however, since the earliest record of the use of the royal "we" to refer to one's self can be attributed to Richard I, whose reign preceded Victoria's by a considerable margin.

2. Goffman (1959) notes the prevalence of dichotomizing in social interaction: "I do not know of any general reason why interaction in natural settings usually takes the form of two-team interplay, or is resolvable into this form, instead of involving a larger number, but empirically this seems to be the case. Thus, in large social establishments, where several different status grades prevail, we find that for the duration of any particular interaction, participants of many different statuses are typically expected to align themselves temporarily into two groupings" (pp. 57–58).

3. We should not fail to note the obvious fact that group membership can also provide unwanted negative valuation to the "I" due to the person's being part of the "we" of a group that is despised or derogated by others or self. See for example, Lewin's (1948) discussion of the causes of self-hatred among Jews.

4. The situation may arise in which no positively discrepant comparisons are available. In this case, the individual may cognitively restructure the evaluative dimension so that the discrepancy now favors the ingroup. The slogan, "black is beautiful" is a classic example. See Tajfel and Turner (1979) for a more detailed discussion.

5. We might expect that subjects in this situation would feel a little anxious. They have been identified as belonging to a group that they have relatively little information about—they cannot reliably predict the behavior of others. Such uncertainty should motivate subjects to seek information that will reestablish predictability (Heider, 1958).

6. A similarity judgment involving self and others may not be the same as one involving two other individuals. To the extent that we focus on self, that is, take self as the referent in the judgment, the greater the similarity. A variant is more similar to the prototype than the prototype is to the variant.

PART III
HISTORY, POLITICS, AND SOCIAL IDENTITY

It follows from the conception of social identity set forth in Parts I and II that human personality takes form within a particular historical and political context. History provides us with major social categories—the forms of ascription as well as the structure of opportunities for attainments. If by politics we mean the series of power relationships among social groups and the question of access to power, then social identity must be considered in relation to political reality. Nationality, racial, ethnic, and religious questions then become psychological issues, as mediated by their political meaning.

The chapters in this section are unified by their concern for specific historical and political questions that have to do with a prime contemporary definition of human birthright grants—the major determinant of what we currently think of as the inalienable rights and duties of human beings. Stampp's essay is a critical appraisal of earlier attempts by historians to characterize the dominant personality pattern of American slaves. Stampp uses role theory to argue that previous writers have failed to appreciate the complexity of the social identity of the American slave—that neither "rebels" nor "Sambos" were dominant character types, but that both of these roles were present in the pre-Civil War South, as well as a complex of other roles presented by the historical and political circumstances of the time.

Stampp presents data that invalidate any claim to a racial or biological basis for the Sambo stereotype. Antebellum blacks were adept at employing a form of self-presentation that included apparent stupidity. "Playing dumb" is a form of impression-management widely used by whites as well as blacks, by men as well as women. "Playing dumb" may protect the self, frustrate the goals of others, and—from the perspective of a disinterested observer—may be categorized as purposive behavior. (See Gove, Hughes & Geerken, 1980.)

A similar argument against simplistic and universal conceptions of human personality is provided in Rotenberg's chapter. The Protestant Ethic is an example of how historical processes provide a definition of how it is possible to live a meaningful life—to achieve assurance of salvation through work. Rotenberg argues that the eighteenth-century Hasidic revolution among European Jews provided a double and seemingly opposed set of possibilities for human fulfillment—the merchant and the scholar. So both vertical means of ascending in life and horizontal means of moving to a differing system of self-actualization are products of historical invention. Like Stampp, Rotenberg argues for a conception of social identity as a composite, rather than for a fixed and stable personality typology.

Both Chun and De Vos take up the discussion of ethnicity as a controlling feature of identity. Chun notes the contradiction between the American ideal of assimilation and the fact of ethnic diversity and pluralism. It is obvious that this conflict is at once historical and political, for the unification of ethnic groups in the United States is often a means of gaining political power or escaping the domination of an oppressive majority. Chun argues that this struggle is also expressed psychologically. Similarly, De Vos's cross-cultural examination of ethnic identity yields an appreciation of the complex and multiform ways in which historical and political realities translate into the psychology of ordinary people. De Vos gives particular emphasis to the individual's sense of placement in historical time—the relationship between one's sense of historical origins, one's current state of malaise or well–being, and one's aspirations and expectations for the future.

Chapter 6

THE PSYCHOLOGY OF NATIONAL IDENTITY

Karl E. Scheibe

Ernst Cassirer concludes *The Myth of the State* with a Babylonian legend, according to which the god, Marduk, uses the limbs of a monster serpent he has slain as the material for the creation of mankind and the world. Cassirer suggests this myth as a simile to the development of human culture:

> It could not arise until the darkness of myth was fought and overcome. But the mythical monsters were not entirely destroyed. They were used for the creation of a new universe, and they still survive in this universe. The powers of myth were checked and subdued by superior forces. As long as these forces, intellectual, ethical, and artistic, are in full strength, myth is tamed and subdued. But once they begin to lose their strength chaos is come again. (Cassirer, 1946, p. 298)

The name of the Babylonian monster serpent was Tiamat. But there is no proper name for a force that may arise in many guises or modes of expression. And in many of its forms, this mythic force will not appear so recognizably evil as a monster serpent. The main difficulty in discussing the psychology of nationalism derives from a similar distinction between a general but unnamed human disposition and an historically particular form. Nationalism is a named form, but surely it is not an essential name for that which it manifests in human nature. Nazism has been seen by some as an exaggerated or extreme form of nationalism. Let us surmise that Nazism is the monster serpent that Cassirer had in mind, for his work was written just at the conclusion of World War II. But nationalism also appears in more favorable colors, for it has been the principle force at work in the massive postwar trend toward the decolonization of territories formerly dominated by European powers.

The basic premise of this chapter is that nationalism is linked to the psychology of the person because it comprises a functional response to the general problem of social identity. But it cannot be supposed that this connection is a necessary or timeless one. In fact, the importance of the nation in providing a partial solution to the problem of identity is completely dependent upon historical context. So a discussion of nationalism or national identity is secular psychology. I take it as given that the psychological dispositions that make nationalism in its many forms possible must be more general than any historically dated phenomena.

This is not to say that the behavior of a person as a member of a nation can be reduced to universal psychological traits or needs but rather that the psychological functioning of modern humanity must be understood, in part, in national terms. In the present dispensation, men and women are members of nations, and their lives are strongly influenced by the particular form taken by this relationship. Understandably, the leaders of the "superior forces" decided at the conclusion of World War II to pronounce an official condemnation of proud and expansive nationalism. The founding of the United Nations was an attempt to demonstrate the earnestness of this judgment. However, the postwar years have shown that the states comprising the United Nations really did not believe in universalism or in the death of nationalism. Indeed, there is increasing evidence that nations will remain *the* fundamental political reality for a long time to come.[1] It is my belief that the nation will long remain a fundamental psychological reality and that it is time for psychologists to recognize it as such.

WHAT IS THE PSYCHOLOGICAL INTEREST IN THE QUESTION OF NATIONALITY?

A dependent relationship between national identity and psychology takes two basic forms. Either political behavior is considered to result from psychological dispositions or else psychological functioning is considered to depend on the political or national ambiance.

Certainly, attempts have been made to extend general psychological theory to cover or render an account of political behavior. The general stock for this borrowing consists mainly of psychoanalytic theory and some of its variants. The term psychohistory has been coined as a collective name for a set of efforts to render psychological accounts of major political figures or conspicuous political types (De Mause, 1982; Erikson, 1969; Freud & Bullitt, 1966; George & George, 1956; Keniston, 1965; Pomper, 1973). These efforts are ambitious, often stylistically elegant, and in some cases genuinely original, especially when the reductive pressure is temporarily dismissed and the writer presents a discussion of a particular form of political behavior or character in its own terms.

It is my view that the borrowing into psychological theory by political scientists and historians has been hampered by misconceptions about the current state of psychological theory and consequent unrealistic expectations about the power of traditional personality theories as means of accounting for the lives and careers of major historical figures. In the traditional style of nineteenth-century positivism, scholars have sought to ground their own disciplines in something more fundamental. Psychologists are looked to for the real (inner) reasons for a political assassination, for the intransigence of Wilson at Paris, or for Hitler's destructive mania. If one accepts the Freudian premise that all important character traits are laid down prior to puberty and if one adopts the common belief that actions are expressions of inner dispositions, then it seems logical to expect psychology to provide some answers to major historical problems. But each of these beliefs—in preformation and in behavior as trait expression—is highly questionable, if not out of date, in contemporary psychological theory (Hunt, 1965; Mischel, W., 1977; Scheibe, 1979).

Also, the several premises leading to the expectation that one discipline may be grounded in another is questionable. In particular, the notion that historical and political occurrences can be accounted for in the idiom of personality theory is perhaps the strongest reason for the failure of psychology and history, both as separate and conjoint disciplines (cf. Gergen, 1973; Gergen & Morawski, 1980).

Within psychology a small subdiscipline has developed that is concerned with the obverse problem of studying the dependency between psychological functioning and the political ambience. It is possible for psychology to borrow from history and political science but without repeating the mistake of thinking of this borrowing as a grounding. Psychology might employ the idiom of political science or history in order to fulfill its own purpose—that of rendering a satisfactory account of contemporary human behavior.

Psychologists have for a long time considered the nuclear family to be the fundamental institutional reality in human life. Psychological theory has been built up largely on this premise. However, the premise is quite obviously time and culture bound, and a partial truth even within a given culture and epoch. For the last 200 years in Western society, the nation has been an institution of varying salience for human beings, and yet psychologists have treated this institution as if it did not exist, or as if it were one of a general class of "group identifications," or as if attachments of the person to the nation could only be viewed as a kind of mistake or aberration from the "normal" dependency of the person on the nuclear family. The most difficult whale for psychologists to swallow is that what is psychologically essential is often accidental. That is, while the nuclear family played an essential role for millennia, it is a role that could be played by another institution that is clearly not a nuclear family. As historical and cultural developments occur, the substantive content of psychology actually changes, if not the nature of basic processes.

The idea of a nation in a psychologically salient sense—that is, as an idealized entity with which the person truly identifies—is not a historical constant but a recent human invention.

> What now seems natural once was unfamiliar, needing argument, persuasion, evidences of many kinds; what seems simple and transparent is really obscure and contrived, the outcome of circumstances now forgotten and preoccupations now academic, the residue of metaphysical systems sometimes incompatible and even contradictory. (Kedourie, 1961, p. 9)

This is not to say that the identification of the person with the nation was something that emerged suddenly and full blown at a given date in Europe. But whatever the date or mode of transition, the nation today is a psychologically fundamental reality for most human beings. Our actions as well as our self–conceptions are highly conditional upon our particular conception of the nature of our nation—its history and present reality.

Psychological theory can either be extended to account for political occurrences or else it can be expanded by the inclusion of historical and political factors as determinants of psychologist functioning. The former enterprise is by now familiar and has earned a label if not broad recognition of success. This latter enterprise is more novel and has been given the provisional label of "historical psychology" (see Morawski, 1982). It is the aim of the next section to suggest what kind of success might in the future be realized.

PSYCHOLOGICAL QUESTIONS REQUIRING AN EXPANSION OF PSYCHOLOGICAL VOCABULARY TO INCLUDE THE CONCEPT OF NATION

Men go to war and face the prospect of death for reasons that are obscure and impersonal. Some Buddhist monks destroyed themselves by fire as a political gesture and the gesture was imitated by a few throughout the world. An American Jew conducts a shootout in a mosque in Jerusalem for reasons he considers to be above reproach. Our President urges greater expenditures for defense and for nuclear arms against all instrumental reason, but rather so that our nation will never be in a "relatively weak" position *vis à vis* our adversaries. A civil war rages in El Salvador; Argentina claims sovereignty over the Falkland/Malvinas Islands, and Great Britain goes to war to defend her national honor.

All of these events, all of these observations have a psychological aspect. The decision to leave one's country is profoundly significant (Taft, 1966). The decision to revolt against one's country entails a complete psychological transformation, similar to a religious conversion. The nation functions as protection for the person—a source of power. Or it can be an object of fear or hatred. The state is a guardian, but as such it may either be protector or tyrant. What determines the manner in which personal destiny and national destiny are intertwined? How does the state extend or limit the life aspirations of a person?

At certain times and in certain places there is evidence of a strong and positive patriotism. Current examples can be found in Poland, in El Salvador, in Afghanistan, in Israel, and in Argentina. What is the function of such displays for the individual? Why is it sometimes important to celebrate the nation? Why and under what circumstances does a manifest hatred of one's nation become psychologically functional?

What is the psychological significance of compatibility or incompatibility between church and nation? Between race and nation? What are the effects of foreign travel, acquaintance with foreigners at home, and information about other countries on self-conceptions? What are the psychological consequences of insults to the nation? What are the psychological consequences of national successes in wars, Olympics, the World Cup, Nobel prize competition, treaties, or the United Nations?

Does a person derive part of his self-conception from clauses contained in the national charter regarding "natural human rights"? To what extent does the nation ultimately define the rules of guilt or shame for the person? What are the psychological consequences of the transformation of an individual into a citizen of a newly developing nation?

What are the psychological consequences of universalism—of the possibility of the disappearance of all national boundaries?

Obviously, it is not possible to consider more than a few of these questions in this brief essay. But the foregoing set should serve to illustrate the range of problems to which a psychology of national identity should be responsive. It is obvious that the nation plays a role in the psychological task of self-definition, and similarly it plays a role in critical, personal decisions, such as whether or not to go to war, leave home, engage in an act of sabotage, or drop out of college.

PAST PSYCHOLOGICAL PERSPECTIVES ON THE PROBLEM OF NATIONAL IDENTITY

Modern psychology has displayed a characteristic antipathy to strong national identification. Perhaps Freud (1930) set the tradition within psychology of regarding with distrust all strong attachments between the person and external social institutions.

Floyd Allport (1927) presents the classic behavioristic view of the development and function of nationalism and patriotism. According to Allport, the young child is frequently exposed to symbols of the nation— the flag, photographs of leaders, anthems, and so forth—in connection with positive emotional stimuli that were established within the family setting; i.e., smiles, expressions of pleasure and approval. Thus, the young child is conditioned to react favorably to national symbols as he would to symbols having to do with his own family. Thereby the child is woven into a connection with the nation by repetition and variation of the conditioning mechanism. At a later time, the national symbols can be used to elicit loyalty and obedience. Allport applied the label "nationalist fallacy" to the view that nationalism consists of anything more than the result of conditioned obedience to authority. One may see a more modern version of this same understanding of national identity in Skinner's (1948) *Walden II*, in which citizens are securely conditioned into the proper regard for their form of governance. In this scheme of things, people are not loyal out of choice but because they have to be loyal to that which they have been conditioned—there is no other possibility.

A variation on this view was presented by Ross Stagner (1946). Stagner similarly considered national loyalties to be a result of direct conditioning but suggested that a person can gain some insight into the mode of conditioning and thereby achieve some rational control over automatic impulses.

> Self-insight is integrally related to the preservation of World peace because it is only with insight that reason achieves control of human behavior. A man who lacks understanding of his own emotions easily falls prey to propaganda . . . he may be induced to project aggression onto foreign peoples and . . . act in an irrational manner. (Stagner, 1946, p. 895)

It is not far from this view to a psychoanalytic conception of national identity, in which the identification with the nation is viewed as a form of narcissism extended outwards from the self to the family, to the clan, to the tribe, and finally to the nation. The similarity is in the conception that national narcissism is inevitable, automatic, and, from the standpoint of the individual or the collectivity, disadvantageous in the long run. Appel (1945) views nationalism as a form of neurosis. Nationalism is considered to be an irrational dependency between the person and the nation. Psychological health is truly compatible only with a world community to which humankind must move in any case if peace is to be preserved.

The same kind of argument was presented by Alexander (1941) who suggested that world peace can be achieved only by a dilution and extension of narcissism to cover all of humanity. He favored the establishment of a world government empowered to enforce law and order over the entire globe. He saw the need for such a police force diminishing as nations become educated away from narrow self-interest and dedicate themselves voluntarily to world democracy.

More modern social psychological views of national identity may be found in Guetzkow (1955) and Klineberg (1964), but the major features of the position remain unchanged. National identification is seen to result from a process of direct tuition, with a strong connection to the emotional needs of the person. Nationalism is considered to be consistent neither with maximal psychological health nor with the progress and well-being of world civilization. Again, education and accompanying self-insight are seen as mechanisms for replacing nationalism with a more extended loyalty to humanity.

The psychologist has tended to view national identity and nationalism in the same way that racism is regarded. As a scientist he considers beliefs in the inherent superiority of racial or national groups to be without scientific support. As a political being he is aware that these myths of superiority are destructive—accounting in large measure for the antagonism that threatens the existence of humankind. So his work has been a moral enterprise—the condemnation of the primitive and aberrant belief in racial or national superiority. But in the process he has largely forgotten the interesting question of the functional significance of beliefs in native superiority.

Psychologists have had the view that if only men could be saved from certain primitive errors in thinking, then one world of universal brotherhood and mutual respect would more or less automatically follow. As professionals, they have shown a generous piety—a willingness to formulate universal declarations for the United Nations about the lack of scientific support for any unflattering belief that people have about each other. But aside from reference to "primitivism," "irrationality," and "neurotic narcissism," they have ignored the question of why individuals acquire a very salient set of beliefs about the unique virtue of national or ethnic identification.

The anger behind this piety is expressed most clearly by Erich Fromm:

> This incestuous fixation not only poisons the relationship of the individual
> to the stranger, but to the members of his own clan and to himself. The

person who has not freed himself from the ties to blood and soil is not yet fully born as a human being; his capacity for love and reason are crippled. . . . The average man today obtains his sense of identity from his belonging to a nation, rather than from his being a "son of man." His . . . reason is warped by this fixation. . . . Nationalism is our form of incest, is our idolatry, is our insanity. . . . Man—freed from the traditional bonds of the medieval community, afraid of the new freedom which transformed him into an isolated atom—escaped into a new idolatry of blood and soil, of which nationalism and racism are the two most evident expressions. (Fromm, 1955, pp. 58ff)

This is very close to a standard position on the question of nationalism. "Nationalism is in our day the chief obstacle to the extension of social cohesion beyond national boundaries. It is therefore the chief force making for the extermination of the human race" (Russell, 1951).

The psychological literature lacks a convincing and sympathic explanation of why individuals in the modern world identify so strongly with their nations. Very little discussion of the problem of national identity places the problem in the context of a more general consideration of social identity and the requirements of psychological functioning. Nationalism has been associated with racism and with religiosity (both positively and negatively, see Fessler, 1941) but rarely with family and occupational roles.

A PSYCHOLOGY OF NATIONAL IDENTITY

What does it mean to state that an individual is identified with a nation or that nationality is a component of his identity? What psychological functions are performed by this form of identification? Answers to these questions can only be formulated in the context of a more general psychological theory. The theoretical framework of choice for this task is social role theory (Sarbin & Allen, 1968–1969).

It is not necessary here to describe again the model of social identity that Sarbin and I have presented in Chapter One of this volume and elsewhere (Sarbin & Scheibe, 1980). Suffice it to say that, in the terms of that model, national identity falls near the granted end of the "granted-achieved" continuum. Hence, involvement with national identity is relatively constant and the contribution of national identity toward the evaluation of social identity has more to do with the maintenance of respect than the possibility of gaining esteem. It is worth noting finally that nationality, like other ascribed components of identity, is relatively resistent to change.

Social identity is a composite of that which a person is by right of birth and that which he has become through social promotions. That which he is, prior to the enactment of any achieved roles, is a result of the birthright.

The nature of this contract is quite variable over time and cultures. Whatever its form, the birthright forms the critical basis for the social understanding of human nature. A child may be born slave or free, born as one of the "chosen" or one of the "heathen," born as an animal or as a human being with "inalienable" rights. In general, the terms of a birthright—rights, duties, or liabilities—are inalienable, for the granted component of social identity is a point of continuous involvement.

Not only does the nature of the birthright grant determine the respect in which a person is initially held (and, in turn, the self-respect that generates) but it also determines the possibilities for the individual to gain access to attained positions within the society, because of linkages that are explicitly or implicitly codified within a society to regulate the promotion process. Thus, the rule "no Irish need apply" constitutes a barrier to promotion resulting from the particular character of a granted component of identity.

The minimal characteristics of granted birthrights are not specified by role theory. Each society has some working definition of human nature that it uses as a basis for granting the charter of humanity to newborn infants produced within its domain. Whether there are universals of human birthrights is an open question. Certainly enormous variation is found over cultures. The Xavante tribe of Brazil practices infanticide and doubtless with full moral justification, since the birthright grant is withheld from deformed children, excess females, or any child who cannot be supported by its mother (Neel, 1970). The controversy over abortion laws in this country devolves to a controversy over the arbitrary point in time at which a fetus may be regarded as a human being with inalienable rights to "life, liberty, and the pursuit of happiness." African slaves imported to the Americas were regarded by their European masters as chattel (cattle) and as such entitled to humane but certainly not human treatment.

The rewards of respect that accompany a birthright are enormously important, but they are silent. The child growing up becomes fully adapted to the birthright. Since the child is born with the birthright but without knowledge of it, learning of it is the most powerful lesson about identity. A child must come to recognize membership in gender, caste, family, race, and nation. The description of this recognition process is an important subject of psychological research. (See Clark, 1963, on race; Jahoda, 1963, on nationality.)

Commonly, more than one social institution grants its charter to an individual at the same time. The terms of their charters under ideal circumstances are mutually consistent; the basic duties, rights, and obligations laid down may be compatible. But commonly the terms of institutional charters come into conflict with each other, particularly in societies that are undergoing rapid changes. The resulting conflicts generate intrapsychic problems with a clear social origin. For example, a child in nineteenth-century rural United States was expected by his family to have primary responsibilities in working on the home farm, while the state, as represented in the schools, expected educational priorities to be more basic. Such conflicts may assume epic proportions, as in the case of a Thomas More or a Thomas á Beckett.

Questions of conflicting institutional loyalties comprise a set of classical legal issues. Courts may, by what amounts to establishing a social convention (albeit a mightily significant one), determine the arrangement of priorities of conflicting granting institutions. For example, in a 1940 decision(Minersville School District vs. Gobitis), Justice Frankfurter declared:

> The mere possession of religious convictions which contradict the relevant concerns of a political society does not relieve the citizen from the discharge of political responsibilities. The necessity for this adjustment has again and again been recognized. . . . We are dealing with an interest inferior to none in the hierarchy of legal values. National unity is the basis of national security. . . . The ultimate foundation of a free society is the binding tie of cohesive sentiment. (Walhke, 1952, p. 25)

The issue was the school expulsion of a Jehovah's Witness student for failure to salute the flag and recite the pledge of allegiance. Just three years later a contrary opinion on the ordering of loyalties was expressed by Justice Jackson (West Virginia State Board of Education vs. Barnette):

> [The] ultimate futility of such attempts to compel coherence is the lesson of every such effort from the Roman drive to stamp out Christianity as a disturber of its pagan unity, the Inquisition, as a means to religious and dynastic unity, the Siberian exiles as a means to Russian unity, down to the fast failing efforts of our present totalitarian enemies. Those who begin coercive elimination of dissent soon find themselves exterminating dissenters. Compulsory unification of opinion achieves only the unanimity of the graveyard. (Walhke, 1952, p. 34)

No "natural" test can resolve the question of the relative priority between church and state, and, where the two institutions are not aligned, conflicts of the sort illustrated by this example are bound to arise. Membership in any other identity granting group, such as a revolutionary political party or a hippie communal family, can and does produce similar conflicts among institutionalized rights and duties (see Scheibe, 1974).

In a society characterized by a high degree of institutional change and demographic mobility a large number of individuals suffer considerable confusion about their birthright. In the United States, where one of three marriages ends in divorce, where one of five families move every year, where religious institutions are often of vestigial importance, where material affluence creates the impression that the person is supported not by a social agreement but by money, and where the political structure for many provides only the vaguest sense of identity and basic human rights, it is not surprising that many authors should note a desperate search for "collective identity" (Klapp, 1969; Lofland, 1969). Bennis writes in *The Temporary Society* (Bennis & Slater, 1968): "Somehow with all the mobility, chronic churning, and unconnectedness we envisage, it will become more and more important to develop some permanent or abiding commitment....This means that as general commitments become diffuse or modified, a greater *fidelity* to something or someone will be necessary to make us more fully human" (p. 128). Keniston (1965) makes a similar suggestion in *The Uncommitted*. He notes a strong unconscious desire of youth to " . . . merge, to fuse with, to lose themselves in some embracing person, experience, or group. This fantasy of mystical fusion involves the unconscious desire to lose all selfhood in some undifferentiated state with another or with nature, to be totally embraced and to embrace totally" (p. 190). As Kedourie (1961) has argued, this is precisely what nineteenth-century romantic nationalists promised: "that the state should be the creator of man's freedom not in an external and material sense, but in an internal and spiritual sense" (p. 47).

In classical nationalist doctrine, a primordial essence is supposed to manifest itself in language, culture, race, and religion; it is the true, the God-given nation. The psychological appeal of such an institution is the exact complement of the kind of identity-anxiety expressed by Bennis, Keniston, Klapp, and others. The early nineteenth-century philosopher and apologist for German nationalism, Schleiermacher, states the case as follows:

> How little worthy of respect is the man who roams about hither and thither without the anchor of national ideal and lover of fatherland; how dull is the friendship that rests merely upon personal similarities in disposition and tendencies, and not upon the feeling of a greater common unity for whose sake one can offer up one's life; how the greatest source of pride is lost by the woman that cannot feel that she also bore children for her fatherland and brought them up for it, that her house and all the petty things that fill up most of her time belong to a greater whole and take their place in the union of her people." (quoted in Kedourie, 1961, p. 73)

This declaration sounds archaic, and, given its national source, it resonates forward to Nazism. But if one attributes these words to a contemporary "Third World" statesman, they might appear to set a very proper sort of ideal.

Lest the point be lost in the examples, it bears repeating that the psychological mechanisms of national identification are presumed to be universal. In some manner the developing individual must seek to establish an identity by becoming aware of the nature of the birthright. Psychological problems result from conflict among institutions concerning the specific content of that birthright and also from ambiguity or vagueness about *any* birthright. When the individual conceives the question, "Who am I?" an answer is both expected and deserved. In some societies and under some circumstances, one hears nothing in reply or in reply one hears "nothing," so one has to seek out or build a social collectivity in which to find "the self."

The desire of the individual to find a common birthright or to seek a collective identity need not be construed as an attempt to obliterate uniqueness or individuality. Instead, when a person finds a "natural" identity, he is redeemed from insignificance, and a basis is provided for the development of an authentic individuality. It is the sense of significance in the collectivity that gives importance to the individual—the person has a sense of the contextual meaning of individuality. The nature of this apparent paradox as it applies to the question of self-sacrifice is illustrated in an essay by George Orwell:

> Brotherhood implies a common father. Therefore it is often argued that men can never develop the sense of a community unless they believe in God. The answer is that in a half conscious way most of them have developed it [a sense of community] already. Man is not an individual, he is only a cell in an everlasting body, and he is dimly aware of it. There is no other way of explaining why it is that men will die in battle. It is nonsense to say they only do it because they are driven. If whole armies had to be coerced, no war could ever be fought. (1968a, p. 17.)

Of course, there are many occasions when appeals to duty and *patria* fall on deaf ears and arouse no response. Men are not willing to die for institutions to which they feel psychologically alien. It is that dim awareness of being an organic part of an institution that makes legitimate, if not fully reasonable, its demands for loyalty. That awareness, in turn, must derive from having accepted a grant of identity from the institution (see Scheibe, 1974).

One consequence of this complex conception of social identity is that it is possible to envisage intrapsychic conflict as a conflict between components of the same social identity—as in some previous illustrations—traceable to conflicts between social institutions. In addition, the individual develops a self-conception connected not to a particular social institution but to a composite experience with the physical and social environment. William James (1890), besides describing the social self in its many manifestations, posited a material self; a psychological conception to be sure, but intimately tied up with the actual flesh of the body as well as its material possessions. Orwell expresses in vivid terms a conflict between this self and the part of a person that could respond favorably to a call to arms:

> If you look into your own mind, which are you; Don Quixote or Sancho Panza? Almost certainly you are both. There is one part of you that wishes to be a hero or a saint, but another part of you is a little fat man who sees very clearly the advantages of staying alive with a whole skin. He is your unofficial self—the voice of the belly protesting against the soul. (1941, p. 163)

If most political rhetoric is of the Don Quixote kind, a good deal of the normative ethics emerging from psychological writing is partial to the interests of Sancho Panza.

The importance of national identity in one's psychological makeup depends on the composition of the remainder of self and social identity. Certainly there are other institutions—family, clan, race, church, university, or company—that might be the functional equivalent of a nation. The central psychological function of these institutions is seen here as being the provision of a valid birthright to the person on which one can build the achieved components of one's identity. If competing birthrights are given or if the character of what can be "taken for granted" is never clear to the developing person, then the person may never have a sense of belonging to a human entity that extends beyond the limits of the physical self. In this condition, individuals will tend to seek or form collectivities with which to identify, so that a working birthright may be forged (see Kanter, 1972).

NATIONALISM

While there are certainly differences in the views of historians on the question of the social and ideological origins of nationalism, the consensus is that modern nationalism is a phenomenon of the nineteenth and twentieth centuries (Snyder, 1968). The emergence of nationalism in the nineteenth century is often described as a transformation in consciousness or, on a different level, a transformation of collective identity. What were the preconditions for this transformation, and how may the change be characterized in functional terms? What follows here is an abstraction of what some historians have said, in psychological terms, about the emergence of nationalism (see Hayes, 1926; Kedourie, 1961; Kohn, 1962; Minogue, 1967; Snyder, 1968).

In primitive and stabilized cultures, social structures are supported by universal consensus within the community. In addition, a characteristic mythic and legendary tradition is passed on from generation to generation, providing the basis for the authority of the priesthood as well as functionally satisfactory answers to cosmic psychological questions concerning the origins of life, the meaning of death, the nature of purpose in the universe. Technically speaking, societies that are describable in these terms are also likely to be unprogressive and unsophisticated in their ability to use their own resources for development. Social strata are likely to be strictly demarcated, and positions in society are likely to be based upon heredity; hence there is discrimination exercised at the level of bestowing the birthright on newborn infants within the community.

Exogenous technological development, ideological change, and changes in mobility and communication tend to be destructive of this kind of stable psychological environment. Rationally, of course, little case can be made for the maintenance of such cultures, since it is often quite easy to see how they might be improved in a material sense, i.e., in terms of percentage of surviving infants, caloric intake per person, life expectancy, or incidence of communicable disease.

But the "satisfactoriness" of a given birthright depends upon the stability of the institution that bestows it. One does not have much confidence in a contract made with a company created yesterday, which is likely to be replaced next week. The destruction of feudal society left men free, but it also left them with deficient identities. While the medieval period is said to have terminated with the European Renaissance in the fifteenth and sixteenth centuries, it may be that the full psychological consequences of the disruption of medieval society were not generally felt in Europe until the beginning of the nineteenth century. The political revolutions in the very late eighteenth century were truly fundamental challenges to the old order. Men became aware that they were living in subjugation to myths of dominium, which could in fact be challenged. Of course, they might have discovered that same truth hundreds of years before; but it is one thing to know that the social institutions to which you are subject are not divine and quite another to believe that you have the power to overthrow those institutions.

What then is nationalism? I think there is good psychology in this characterization by a political scientist:

> The formula that I find most convincing is to say that nationalism provides an escape from triviality. Implicitly or explicitly, men suffering from a social upheaval put to themselves the question: what is happening to us? The nationalist answer is clear: our nation is struggling to be born; it is fighting for independence against its enemies. This answer is never the whole truth, and sometimes it has absolutely nothing to do with the truth

at all. But that does not matter. The nationalist struggle is a noble one which dignifies a man's sufferings, and gives him a hopeful direction in which to work. (Minogue, 1967, p. 32)

Nationalist struggles are attempts to be born or carried into a new identity. The dissatisfactions that fire nationalist movements often have purely material or economic aspects, but those who become revolutionary leaders are typically drawn from the classes most favored by the old established system. Nationalist ideology is romantic, transforming each prosaic setting into a stage of destiny. The German concept of *Volk*, championed by such writers as Herder, Schleiermacher, Fichte, and the Grimm brothers, comprised not only a collective folk name, but a mysterious *fons et origo*—an essential force that manifests itself in a particular set of great men, a distinct language, a folklore, artistic creations, and so forth. It hardly matters that such an idea is nonsense from a scientific point of view. The point is that such a conception provides a viable psychological reference for the most fundamental problem of identity—what is my birthright?

At times, the ideology of nationalism has been combined with that of racism, though such a connection is hardly a necessary one. Joseph de Gobineau (1816–1852) presented a thoroughgoing theory of racial inequality, which challenged political ideals of democratic nationalism as well as religious and moral values. His was an attempt to show that nobility inhered in the Aryan, who is ordained by nature to superiority. "A man is great, noble, virtuous, not by his actions but by his blood. The only test that our personal work has to stand is the test of our ancestors. It is his birth certificate that gives to a man the certainty of his moral value. Virtue is not a thing to be acquired" (quoted in Cassirer, 1946, p. 236). But de Gobineau recognized that Aryans do not comprise a separate nation. Rather, he considered Aryans to be a kind of natural aristocracy—the only legitimate aristocracy—in whatever land they happened to live. While the ideological seeds for Nazism were clearly present in these ideas, it remained for later German ideologues to work out the theory that the Aryan race ought to be coextensive with the German nation, and that this nation should rule the world by natural right as manifested in their material power.

Early nineteenth–century German nationalists of a romantic persuasion were in favor of making political states coextensive with natural nations—indeed such was the major logic in European political partitionings throughout the nineteenth century and finally in 1919 in the Treaty of Versailles. But these same early nationalist writers were also universalists in that they respected the moral legitimacy of other nations and did not initially set themselves apart as superiors. This benign attitude led to a kind of appreciative descriptive anthropology, resulting in the collection of songbooks, folk tales, and typical artifacts by means of which other nations might be known. However, it was the clear duty of a person to cultivate those modes of speech and custom that are natural, and these derive from the nation.

It is but a short step from this cosmopolitan nationalism to a more "advanced" variety. Orwell describes a more vulgar nationalism as it was expressed in England:

> All peoples who have reached the point of becoming nations tend to despise foreigners, but there is not much doubt that the English–speaking races are the worst offenders. One can see this from the fact that as soon as they become fully aware of any foreign race, they invent an insulting nickname for it. Wop, Dago, Groggy, Squarehead, Kike, Sheeny, Nigger, Wog, Chink, Greaser, Yellowbelly—these are merely a selection. (1939, pp. 431–432)

Surely such attitudes must give tremendous satisfaction to those who hold them. All kinds of hardships might be endured with forbearance and patience if one has this kind of confidence in natural superiority—and that superiority is granted with the birthright, not attained by some test of performance or adequacy.

Individuals who do not possess any such natural surety of their own blessedness should be susceptible to appeals to seize the advantages of natural superiority. With rapid institutional change, the young find it difficult to engender such self-respect in themselves by imbibing the myths that nurtured their elders. It is the young, then, who will experience a need for a new nation. Kedourie notes that nationalist movements are dominated by the young:

> Their very names are manifestoes against old age: Young Italy, Young Egypt, the Young Turks, the Young Arab Party. When they are stripped of their metaphysics and their slogans—and these cannot adequately account for the frenzy they conjure up in their followers—such movements are seen to satisfy a need, to fulfill a want. Put at its simplest, the need is to belong together in a coherent and stable community. Such a need is normally satisfied by the family, the neighborhood, the religious community. In the last century and a half such institutions all over the world have had to bear the brunt of violent social and intellectual change, and it is no accident that nationalism was at its most intense where and when such institutions had little resilience and were ill-prepared to withstand the powerful attacks to which they became exposed. (1961, p. 101)

If such a characterization applied to Mazzini and his Young Italy followers, it applied with equal validity to the Woodstock Nation and its prophets—Jerry Rubin, Abbie Hoffman, or their academic apologists, Theodore Roszak and Charles Reich. All the elements are present for the emergence of a new nationalism in the United States—rapid institutional change, affluence that allows a large segment of the middle class to discover their more fundamental poverty, and the strange metaphysical promise that you can be transformed and reborn into a natural human being if you will but "do it." A unique feature of this new nationalism is that the oppressor is not identified as a foreigner or alien influence, but as an endogenous entity—the Establishment, or Technocracy.

Another problem beset the new American nationalists. Revolutionary leaders knew better than to refer to some common origin of language or race as a way of creating a new mystique of nationality. Instead, reference was made to difficult abstractions such as "consciousness III" or the "psychedelic generation" or the "counterculture." Except for black revolutionaries, no radical political movement in the United States can hope to establish that romantic and mysterious sense of automatic brotherhood that characterized European nationalist movements in the nineteenth century. Such a mood may be established for brief intervals at music festivals or in a political campaign; but until a way is found to make such episodes a permanent feature of society there will be no way of nurturing that mood from artificiality to reality.

The interpretation of nationalist movements that makes most psychological sense is that they are searches for missing birthrights, or as replacements for birthrights that have been invalidated by the withdrawal of the granting institution or of the individual from the institution. As such, these human ventures affect primarily the granted components of social identity. The great facility with which one can "achieve" an identity in contemporary American society merely means that institutional deficiencies can be papered over. But one's condition is much more significant for one's self-respect than is one's situation. Consequently, it is inevitable that there will be attempts, psychologically homologous to nationalist movements, to redeem that condition.

For a long time now, but especially since the advent of nineteenth-century deterministic science into biology and the human sciences, the human birthright has been eroded away. Scientists have long ceased to regard birthrights as having any real meaning at all—anthropologists are forever giving assurances that fundamentally everybody is just like everybody else. Early nineteenth-century romantic nationalism did not destroy birthrights, yet it was universalistic. Scientific universalism, on the other hand, gives to humans no sense of their own significance, except insofar as one can be a scientist, which, unfortunately, is an attained identity.

The novelist, Kurt Vonnegut, replied as follows when questioned about the impact of science:

> When I went to school everybody was jeering astrology, congratulating each other on escaping these lies. Maybe we should get back to the lies and see if there is anything there after all. You have a problem in a lonely society. People think they are nobody, and somebody says when is your birthday. My God, this guy's a Leo, and pretty soon you find out who's compatible with him and life becomes very vivid because science has been abandoned and everybody's agreed to go nuts. (*New York Times Magazine* interview, January 24, 1971)

For someone who has been reading about the history of nationalism, there is a familiar ring to these words. The excitement of self-discovery, the discarding of rational caution, the willingness to be guided by forces only vaguely understood—these characteristics appear to be common to cult initiation and participation in nationalist movements.

THE NATIONALISM OF INTELLECTUALS AND SCIENTISTS

The motto of my undergraduate college is *Pro ecclesia et patria*, a sentiment that must have seemed quite legitimate in the first quarter of the nineteenth century when it was adopted. But today, as the last quarter of the twentieth century approaches, such a motto is likely to appear at best quaintly absurd and at worst fiercely insulting to those who study and teach under the banner on which it is inscribed. Educated men and women in developed countries have for some time been in a profound dilemma with respect to the granted components of their identities. They have acquired the belief that the institutions into which they were born have been, historically, guilty of monstrous crimes while deluding themselves into self-righteousness. Much of the literature, poetry, and art of the modern era has been a steady work of breaking down illusions, of revealing hypocrisy, of demythification and deracination. It has become part of maturity to reject the naive myths of childhood.

Once disillusionment begins, the educated person develops an insatiable appetite for arguments, evidence, and illustrations on how political indoctrination "imprisons innocent children to lies." The educated person quite often succeeds in gaining liberation from the primitive emotional bonds into which he was accidentally born. But what is the psychological sequel to this liberation?

An example might be found in Orwell's characterization of the left-wing English intelligensia:

Their obedience depended on the mystique of the Revolution, which had gradually changed itself into a nationalist loyalty to the Russian state. The English left-wing intelligensia worship Stalin because they have lost their patriotism and the religious belief without losing the need for a god and a fatherland. (1943, p. 286)

The Communist party provided intellectuals with something to believe in—something on which they could hang their identity. But this is only one of the many options that exist for intellectuals. One of the more attractive options is to become a heteronationalist, that is, an ardent nationalist for some country other than one's own. Emerging nationalism in Africa, in the Middle East, in Eastern Europe, along the Sino-Soviet axis, and in Latin America not only fulfills economic and social needs for the regions directly affected by these changes, it also provides the observing intellectuals of developed countries a rich variety of causes in which to believe.

Another option for the redemption of a lost birthright is presented by science, which in the ideal is supposed to be no respecter of national boundaries or ethnic identity and hence is a universalist institution. Unfortunately, the plain facts of the history of scientific development spoil this illusion (Lasswell, 1970). While it may be true that a small number of scientists in the history of the world have been true universalists working entirely without regard to national interests, it is surely safe to assert that most science has been and is being done as a means of promoting national interests, into which scientists have been willingly co-opted. In practice, most scientists willingly conform to the going political ideology in their countries since quite obviously they owe their very livelihood and "freedom of inquiry" to those political institutions. As Kedourie (1961) has said in a slightly different context, "It is not philosophers who become kings, but kings who tame philosophy to their use" (p. 50). *Mutatis mutandis* certainly seems true for science.

Hitler was able to command the support of a large segment of the scientific community in Germany in the service of his war machine. He was even able to command congenial racial theories from his anthropologists, which along with Lysenko's brand of genetics, we are quick to label pseudoscience. It is an open question as to how much of our currently accepted scientific dogma is similarly a matter of political conformity and expediency and might with equal rapidity be called pseudoscience from another national-ideological perspective.

If science has been guilty of facilitating the development of auto-nomous nationalism, while all the while posturing as something universa-listic, history is guilty one-hundred fold, if perhaps less pretentiously universalistic. The same is true for political science and the social sciences in general. The peculiarity of the practitioners of these arts is that they may maintain the illusion of gaining their birthright from their discipline and not from something so restrictive as a nation or a religion. Of course, the disciplines, themselves, are chartered by the nations in which they prosper, and their continued existence is at the sufferance of those nations; their efforts are largely in the national service.

NATIONALISM, RATIONALITY, AND THE PIETY OF THE SOCIAL SCIENCES

At the base of this formulation about the functional significance of nationalism is a psychological premise that may seem gratuitous from the rationalistic point of view characteristic of the social as well as the natural sciences. If people are viewed, correctly enough, as animals, it is not obvious from a comparative point of view why there should emerge with the human species a psychological need for a birthright—a fictional grant of identity that is supposed to remain with an individual throughout life. When psychologists speak of the most fundamental human needs, they are likely to present a list that can be coordinated with specifiable biological states, such as tissue deficits or optimal patterns of neural stimulation. Even such humanistic psychologists as Fromm and Maslow put such needs as hunger, thirst, and sex at the base of the hierarchy of human needs. Only in the last two decades has attention been directed to the elaborate social organization of primates in their natural habitat (Goodall, 1965; Washburn, 1961), so that one may begin to see some respectable evolutionary anchorage for such a phrase as the "need for stable identification with a social collectivity." For human beings it may be that motives deriving from the problem of identity are at least as fundamental as those drives that are customarily considered biological, such as sex. When a man's stomach is empty his only problem is an empty stomach. When his stomach is full, he has leisure to pursue a possible unrewarding series of contemplations about such problems as the meaning of his life and the importance of his efforts. At the human level, mere organic survival potential is not the ultimate evolutionary value, however useful this concept may be when applied to the entire animal kingdom.

Nationalism is but one of the mythic enterprises by which men and women have been enthralled in what amounts, functionally, to attempts at detrivializing their existence. But because this special kind of human need frequently leads to behaviors that are noneconomic, from a narrower biological point of view (wars, crusades, religious movements, committee meetings, games, and sporting events) there has been a tendency for scientists to consider birthright needs as distinctly secondary or pathological, or both. Also, the monster serpent of superstition was supposed to have been laid to rest by the Enlightenment, by the industrial revolution, and by such intellectual companion movements as positivism. But the very success of these movements in serving humanity's tissue deficit needs has given the monster surcease from persecution, so that he may be in the ascendancy.

More recently, Freudian psychology has made the mistake of placing sex at the base of all human motives. Eighty years later a youthful revolutionary would proclaim, "General liberation is general copulation." Yet surely it is not a naive observation that human beings who copulate *ad libitum* discover that they have other problems. By a revision and extension of the "when a man's stomach is empty . . . " cliché, it may be that the success of the sexual revolution will expose a much more fundamental and universal human problem—and I think that this will be the problem of the birthright grant.

This leads me to be highly critical of an easy liberal piety among social scientists. In the general introduction to the "World Perspectives" series of historical essays, Ruth Nanda Anshen asserts: "It is the thesis of "World Perspectives" that man is in the process of developing a new consciousness which, in spite of his apparent spiritual and moral captivity, can eventually lift the human race above and beyond the fear, ignorance, and isolation which beset it today." Further she states, "Beyond the divisiveness among men there exists a primordial unitive power since we are all bound together by a common humanity more fundamental than any unity of dogma. . . . Science, when not inhibited by the limitations of its own methodology, when chastened and humbled, commits man to an indeterminate range of yet undreamed consequences . . . " (Kohn, 1962, p. ix). These are phrases worth pondering, for they express the belief that if only people will be sensible, they can be led from fear, ignorance, and isolation into a condition of human fulfillment, with science the humble handmaiden to the enlightened progress of humanity.

These sentiments translate the hope that people will be sensible and see what is best for them into the expectation that they surely will. Such vapid optimism is revealed even more clearly in Hans Kohn's conclusion to the very same volume:

> The 1960's are not a period of intellectual and spiritual sterility. Great works of art may not be created at present, but the treasures of many centuries in poetry, music and painting are today far more accessible to greater multitudes than they were in the past. . . . The rapid progress of science will not only change our knowledge and mastery of the outside world, it will refine and broaden our concern with our fellow man; it will alter and improve the scope and methods of human welfare and psychological understanding. In the 1960's, men are pushing forward, beyond any previous experience, toward higher forms of international

integration—in the Inter-American Alliance for Progress, in Asian and African unity conferences, in the European Common Market, and the North Atlantic Community, in the United Nations. No one foresaw these developments in 1940. They are experiments in building new frameworks for coexistence and cooperation, for mastering problems on the solution of which the survival of a great part of mankind may depend. (Kohn, 1962, pp. 166–167)

In fairness to Kohn, these words must have had a different sound two decades ago, at the beginning of the Kennedy years. That most of the regional organizations to which he pointed would have come to grief along precisely nationalist lines could not have been obvious in 1960. But surely now our hopes for such a millennium should be chastened.

To return once again to Cassirer, I think one may obtain a clearer vision of the future. It is indisputable that political myths, many of them in the form of nationalist doctrines, have been at the source of many of the great troubles of the twentieth century. Ample basis for fearing trouble again from this ideological quarter. But Cassirer notes his reservations about the facile combination of wish and reason:

It is beyond the power of philosophy to destroy the political myths. A myth is in a sense invulnerable. It is impervious to rational arguments; it cannot be refuted by syllogisms. But philosophy can do us another important service. It can make us understand the adversary. . . . To know him means not only to know his defects and weaknesses; it means to know his strength. All of us have been liable to underrate this strength. When we first heard of the political myths we found them so absurd and incongruous, so fantastic and ludicrous that we could hardly be prevailed upon to take them seriously. By now it has become clear to all of us that this was a great mistake. We should not commit the same error a second time. We should carefully study the origin, the structure, the methods, and the technique of the political myths. We should see the adversary face to face in order to know how to combat him. (1946, p. 296)

Among other things, this is a call for a certain kind of intellectual courage. Political and social developments that seem to be regressions to primitivism and myth are not to be reviled or dismissed as irrelevant because they do not appear to spring from respectable sources. It must be recognized that when people are in a certain condition, the invitation to danger and destiny is psychologically far more powerful than the invitation to a life of ease. Don Quixote may awaken when Sancho Panza sleeps.

Orwell, to whom reference has been made several times in this chapter displayed the kind of courage of which I am thinking. He was capable of seeing the evil in that which he loved—socialism—and the genuine appeal of that which he hated—totalitarianism.

Hitler, because in his own joyless mind he feels it with exceptional strength, knows that human beings *don't* only want comfort, safety, short working-hours, hygiene, birth-control, and in general common sense; they also, at least intermittently, want struggle and self-sacrifice, not to mention drums, flags, and loyalty parades. However they may be as economic theories, Fascism and Nazism are psychologically far sounder than any hedonistic conception of life. The same is probably true of Stalin's militarized version of Socialism. . . . After a few years of slaughter and starvation 'Greatest happiness to the greatest number' is a good slogan, but at this moment, 'Better an end with horror than a horror without end' is a winner. Now that we are fighting against the man who coined it, we ought not to underrate its emotional appeal. (1968a, p. 14)

Those who dare to look an enemy in the face are in danger of being suspected by more timid observers to be on the point of embracing their adversary. Certainly Orwell has been criticized in precisely this way. But his is a psychology less flawed by sentimental blindness and doctrinaire ideology than that produced by the bulk of psychologists and other social scientists. Not only do most psychologists refuse to take national identity seriously as a legitimate problem for research, those who do write on the problem seem bent on explaining it away in the course of preparing their moral case for universalistic utopianism. This is a condition that ought to be corrected, and this is a problem to which philosophers, in the broad sense of that term, can apply themselves to good effect and perhaps gain thereby some sense of legitimacy in their own calling.

NOTES

1. In 1945, there were 51 members of the United Nations. By July, 1981, there were 154 member nations. There is no sign that the number of nations on the face of the earth will be reduced by voluntary consolidation. Rather, divisive pressures of the sort evident in Northern Ireland or Quebec continue to have prominence. Whatever the psychological or social relief provided by the end of colonialism, in a certain rough empirical sense the world is much further away from universalism now than it was a generation ago.

Chapter 7

REBELS AND SAMBOS:
THE SEARCH FOR THE NEGRO'S
PERSONALITY IN SLAVERY

Kenneth M. Stampp

What we know about slaves and their masters we have learned mostly from the business records, diaries, letters, memoirs, and autobiographies of slaveholders; from travelers' observations; from contemporary newspapers and periodicals; and from various government documents, including court records. Direct evidence from the slaves themselves is hopelessly inadequate. Well over 90 percent of them were illiterate, and even the small literate minority seldom found an opportunity to write or speak with candor. Travelers in the South occasionally interviewed slaves; in the 1850s Benjamin Drew, a white New England abolitionist, interviewed a group of fugitives who had settled in Canada (Drew, 1856); and a few ex-slaves left autobiographies of varying quality. But I know of not a single slave diary; and letters written by slaves are rare. For more than sixty years after emancipation, no one made a systematic attempt to record the narratives of former slaves. Three belated efforts in the 1920s and 1930s appear to have come too late to be of much value to historians, though the narratives are of considerable interest to folklorists.[1] Historians have no doubt failed to make as much use of the Negro's oral tradition of songs and folklore as they should; but this material, as a source for slavery, also presents problems. Among other things, the songs and folklore are ever changing; and, since the collections were made for the most part after slavery, we can seldom be sure that what they contain are true expressions of the slaves.[2]

Inevitably, then, our knowledge of the life and behavior of American Negroes in slavery comes mainly from the testimony of white observers. The letters written by slaves were usually written to white men; the slave

Reprinted, with permission, from The Journal of Southern History, 1971, 37(3).

autobiographies were often dictated to and written by white men; and the early collections of slave songs and folklore were put together by white men, who may well have missed the nuances in this often subtle material. In short, the ubiquitous white man, as master, editor, traveler, politician, and amanuensis, stands forever between slave and historian, telling the historian how the slave was treated, how he behaved, what he thought, and what sort of personality he had. However imaginative the historian may be, he will always have trouble breaking through this barrier, and he will always be handicapped by the paucity of firsthand testimony from the slaves themselves.

This being the case, it is hardly surprising that historians who have studied the behavior and personality of the Negro in slavery have failed to agree on the meaning of the evidence and have left many problems unsolved. Indeed, two of the books that address themselves directly and explicitly to this problem—Herbert Aptheker's *American Negro Slave Revolts* (1943) and Stanley M. Elkins's *Slavery* (1968)—arrive at opposite conclusions. Aptheker, whose purpose is to depict "in realistic terms the response of the American Negro to his bondage," found "that discontent and rebelliousness were not only exceedingly common, but, indeed, characteristic of American Negro slaves" (p. 374). Elkins, focusing more narrowly on plantation field hands, suggests that characteristically they were not rebels but Sambos, with personalities very much as they were described in southern lore:

> Sambo, the typical plantation slave, was docile but irresponsible, loyal but lazy, humble but chronically given to lying and stealing; his behavior was full of infantile silliness and his talk inflated with childish exaggeration. His relationship with his master was one of utter dependence and childlike attachment: it was indeed this childlike quality that was the very key to his being. (p. 82)

These two portraits of the southern slave, one as the discontented rebel, the other as the passive Sambo, are worth examining, because together they define the two extremes—the outer limits—of possible slave behavior.

Of the two portraits, Aptheker's is the easier to evaluate. From his empirical research, mostly in newspapers and government documents, he claims to have uncovered approximately 250 revolts and conspiracies, each involving a minimum of ten slaves and having the winning of freedom as its apparent goal (p. 162). He makes no attempt to explain slave behavior with any personality theory; but implicit throughout the book is an assumption that when a mass of people are as brutally exploited as the southern slaves, discontent and rebelliousness against the ruling class are bound to be endemic.

We are indebted to Aptheker for providing a useful corrective to the view, still prevalent when his book was published in 1943, that the slaves were almost uniformly contented. He presents detailed accounts of a few rebellions and of a number of authentic conspiracies; but above all he shows how persistent the *fear* of rebellion was among white southerners and how frequently insurrection panics drove them to near hysteria. However, the book has three major shortcomings. First, it fails to use sources critically; second, it argues beyond the evidence; and, third, it does not distinguish between slave discontent, which was probably widespread, and slave rebelliousness, which was only sporadic and always local. A more accurate title for this book would be *American Negro Slave Revolts, Conspiracies, and Rumors of Conspiracies*, for it is the last of these things that most of the book is really about.

Elkins, in a decidedly more influential counterhypothesis, offers the placid and contented Sambo as the typical plantation slave. He is concerned almost entirely with describing and explaining Sambo's personality and behavior rather than with offering empirical evidence of his existence. He disposes of the problem of evidence in two sentences: "The picture [of Sambo] has far too many circumstantial details, its hues have been stroked in by too many different brushes, for it be denounced as counterfeit. Too much folk-knowledge, too much plantation literature, too much of the Negro's own lore, have gone into its making to entitle one in good conscience to condemn it as 'conspiracy.' " Beyond this, at several points, Elkins simply tells his readers that the widespread existence of Sambo "will be assumed," or will be "taken for granted," and then proceeds to his explanation (1968, pp. 86–86, 88–89).

Since the Elkins thesis is familiar, I will only summarize the three chief points of his strategy, which are (1) his use of comparative history, (2) his use of personality theory, and (3) his use of analogy. Elkins argues, first of all, that the Negro with a Sambo-type personality was not a universal product of slavery in the Americas but, because of certain unique conditions, a peculiar product of slavery in the United States. The principal differences between North American and Latin American slavery, he believes, were the latter's relatively greater flexibility and openness, the far greater opportunities it gave the Negro to escape into free society, and the presence of not one but several centers of authority: church and state as well as slave master. In the antebellum South slavery grew unchecked by church or state; its form was dictated by the needs of the planter capitalists; and state laws treated the slave essentially as property, thus depriving him of his identity as a human being. Southern slavery operated as a "closed system" in which the slaves had only limited contacts with free society and little hope of becoming part of it. It was this closed system that produced Sambo (pp. 81–82, 84, 134–137).

Second, to explain how southern slavery had this devastating effect on the Negro, Elkins utilizes some of the literature on personality theory. Using Freud, he points to the impossibility of a "meaningful relationship between fathers and sons" and to the difficulty of becoming a man without "acceptable male models to pattern yourself after" (pp. 130, 242). But he relies chiefly on a blend of certain aspects of the interpersonal theory of Harry Stack Sullivan and of role psychology. Sullivan maintains that personality can be studied only as it manifests itself in interpersonal relations,[3] and he stresses the manner in which personality is formed in relationships with so-called "significant others"—that is, with those in positions of authority or otherwise capable of enhancing or endangering one's security. Out of anxiety concerning the attitudes of these significant others a person learns to behave in ways that meet their expectations. Eventually, some of this behavior is internalized and becomes part of the personality. Role psychology emphasizes the roles, or models of behavior, that are extended to individuals throughout their lives by organizations, or by groups, or by society at large.[4] There are rewards for playing the expected role well and penalties for playing it badly or not at all. How well an individual plays a role depends in part on his skill, on his motivation, on his "role knowledge," and on "role clarity," the last requiring a condition of general agreement about proper behavior. The more clearly a role is defined the better it is likely to be performed, and the greater its impact is likely to be on the personality of the performer. Thus, it may be that to some degree one's personality consists of the roles one plays.

Applying these ideas to the southern plantation slave, the Elkins hypothesis runs something like this: In a closed system from which there was virtually no escape, the master, whose authority was absolute, who dispensed rewards and punishments, was the only significant other in the slave's life. The master defined the slave's role, provided him with a clear and simple script, judged his performance, and rewarded him according to its quality. The result was Sambo, the perpetually dependent, irresponsible child. Elkins does not claim that Sambo was the universal slave personality, for he recognized that there were "a great profusion of individual types." A "significant number," including house servants, skilled craftsmen, slaves who hired their own time, slave foremen, and those who lived in single families on small farms managed "to escape the full impact of the system and its coercions upon personality." For these slaves "there was a margin of space denied to the majority . . . ," and few of them took on the character of Sambo. But of the mass of field hands on large and small plantations, though Elkins recognizes that some did not fit the classic Sambo type, it is clearly his intention to suggest that Sambo embraced the majority (1968, pp. 86–87, 137–138).

Finally, to illuminate certain aspects of southern slavery, Elkins resorts to the analogy of the Nazi concentration camp. He warns that an analogy must not be taken literally, for things that are analogous are not identical. His purpose is to examine two situations which, in spite of their "vast dissimilarities," contain "mechanisms that are metaphorically comparable and analytically interchangeable." In this analogy the mechanism was "the infantilizing tendencies of absolute power" (pp. 104, 225). Elkins sees a rough similarity between the Sambo produced by slavery on the southern plantation and the human product of the concentration camp, whose experiences often led to personality disintegration, infantilization, and even a tendency to look on SS guards in a childlike way as father figures.

Both the master of the plantation and the commander of the concentration camp were the sole significant others in the lives of the people under their control. Both could mete out punishment or grant protection, while the slaves and inmates were reduced to complete dependence. "A working adjustment to either system," Elkins concludes, "required a childlike conformity . . . "; the crucial factor

> was the simple "closedness" of the system, in which all lines of authority descended from the master. . . . The individual, consequently, for his very psychic security, had to picture his master in some way as the "good father," even when, as in the concentration camp, it made no sense at all. But why should it not have made sense for many a simple plantation Negro whose master did exhibit, in all the ways that could be expected, the features of the good father who was really "good"? If the concentration camp could produce in two or three years the result that it did, one wonders how much more pervasive must have been those attitudes, expectations, and values which had, certainly, their benevolent side and which were accepted and transmitted over generations. (pp. 128–130)

It is no small tribute to Elkins's achievement that his essay should have provided the focus for virtually all scholarly discussion of slave personality for the past decade and that a volume of commentary, with a response from Elkins, has recently been published (Lane, 1971).[5] I doubt that any future historian of slavery will fail to recognize Sambo as an authentic personality type among the slaves on southern plantations. More generally, Elkins has contributed much to arousing interest in the problem of slave personality and to making historians aware of the possibility of dealing with the problem through an interdisciplinary approach. On the other hand, I believe that the discussion has been rather too much preoccupied with his hypothesis; that, in consequence, we have made little additional progress during the past decade; and that the time has come for renewed investigation. Elkins, after all, intended his essay to be the start of a new approach, suggestive rather than definitive; and, accordingly, he left plenty of work for others to do. Moreover, his essay contains a number of flaws, which give the remaining work a special urgency.

Because of their fascination with the essay's methodology and conceptualization, many scholars seem to have overlooked its lack of empirical evidence—its bland assumption that the prevalence of Sambo on the plantations can be taken for granted. The concentration-camp analogy, of course, proves nothing; at most, Elkins can argue that *if* the typical plantation slave was a Sambo, the literature on the camps might suggest an explanation of *why* he was a Sambo.[6] Elkins, as I have noted, takes Sambo for granted because Sambo appears so prominently in antebellum plantation literature. But most of this literature was written by white men, and much of it is in defense of slavery. To accept it at face value would be only slightly more justifiable than to accept at face value a body of literature on the concentration camps written not by former inmates and competent scholars, such as Bruno Bettelheim, but by the SS guards. Moreover, the public testimony of white witnesses does not by any means invariably support the Elkins hypothesis, for contemporary writers often speak of the resourcefulness and guile of Negroes, and numerous essays on the governing of slaves warn masters never to trust them.[7] Elkins is certainly mistaken when he asserts that the prevalence of Sambo was part of the Negro's own lore. Neither the slave narratives nor the Negro's oral tradition give validity to Sambo as the typical plantation slave; rather, their emphasis is on the slave dissemblers and the ways in which they deceived their masters.

In an essay on sources, Elkins explains why he did not use manuscript plantation records, which constitute the private testimony of the white slaveholders. Manuscripts, he writes, "are useful principally on questions of health and maintenance, and they have already been worked over with great care and thoroughness by eminent scholars" (1968, p. 224). But the plantation manuscripts are in fact quite valuable for the study of slave personality, and even information on maintenance and health (including mental health) is decidedly relevant. If the manuscripts have been worked over by other scholars, that is really of little help to Elkins, because no one has used them for precisely his purpose and with his hypothesis in mind. He offers no explanation for his failure to examine other sources, especially newspapers, with their extremely revealing fugitive-slave advertisements, and contemporary periodicals, with their countless essays on the management of slaves and their descriptions of slave behavior. As a result, Elkins is obliged in the end to offer corroborating testimony from sources such as John Pendleton Kennedy's *Swallow Barn* (1832), where we learn that the slave had "the helplessness of a child—without foresight, without faculty of contrivance, without thrift of any kind"; and from Edward Pollard's *Black*

Diamonds Gathered in the Darkey Homes of the South (1859), which assures us that "The Negro . . . in his true nature, is always a boy, let him be ever so old . . . ." "Few southern writers," Elkins concludes, "failed to describe with obvious fondness . . . the perpetual good humor that seemed to mark the Negro character, the good humor of an everlasting childhood" (pp. 131–132).[8]

David C. McClelland, one of Elkins's authorities on personality, devotes two chapters of his book to the problems of collecting and interpreting data. In one of them, McClelland observes that an individual's personality may change "as he changes or as the scientist's insights improve (1951, p. 70). This is an important point, for the accumulation of an ample supply of data is often the beginning of improved insight. Eugene D. Genovese, after paying tribute to Elkins's achievement, reminds us "that all psychological models may only be used suggestively for flashes of insight or as aids in forming hypotheses and that they cannot substitute for empirical investigation" (1967, p. 314).

The remaining shortcomings of the Elkins essay concern its conceptual and methodological strategies and its apparent misunderstanding of the life of plantation slaves. Several critics have already questioned Elkins's comparative approach, particularly his exaggerated notion of the success of church and state in Latin America in protecting the slave's humanity. They have also demonstrated that Sambo was not a unique product of north American slavery, for he appeared in Brazil, in the French colonies, and in Spanish America as well. "On close inspection," writes Genovese, "the Sambo personality turns out to be neither more nor less than the slavish personality; wherever slavery has existed, Sambo has also" (Genovese, 1967, pp. 255–298; see also Davis, 1966; Degler, 1970; Harris, 1964). Since the antebellum South did not actually produce a distinct slave personality, the explanation for Sambo may be sought not there alone but everywhere in the Western World.

Elkins's concentration-camp analogy, as I will try to demonstrate, may help to illuminate the condition of one small group of plantation slaves, but it is of little value as an aid to understanding Sambo. He would be quite justified in using his analogy for limited purposes, provided, first, that he could establish a controlling mechanism that is in truth "analytically interchangeable," and, second, that the obvious and admitted elements of dissimilarity between slavery and the concentration camps did not themselves have an important bearing on the formation of personality. To Elkins, the "shock and detachment" experience of adult camp inmates—an experience that slaves born into the system did not endure—was less crucial to personality than adjusting to "the requirements of a 'closed system' of absolute authority" (1968, p. 229).

However, Elkins dismisses far too easily certain vital elements of dissimilarity that did have a profound impact on adult personality, and first among them is the systematic policy of terror and brutality in the concentration camps. Slaves were rarely treated as cruelly as camp inmates. The realities of slavery dawned on them gradually over a period of years, while the realities of the concentration camp hit the inmates with one stunning and often disintegrating blow. Moreover, plantation slavery was a rational institution; it had a logic and purpose that was utterly missing in the camps, where life, with its total unpredictability, had about it a nightmarish quality. The extermination policy eventually adopted in the camps destroyed all belief in the value of human life. Everybody in the camps, as Bettelheim observed, "was convinced that his chances for survival were very slim; therefore to preserve himself as an individual seemed pointless" (1960, p. 138).[9] It was this hopelessness, rather than the absolute authority of one significant other, that explains the phenomenon of inmates walking without resistance to the gas chambers. Slavery, though its influence on personality was severe, still afforded its victims something a good deal closer to normal life, and therefore it did not ordinarily have anything like as shattering an impact on personality as did the concentration camps.

The most momentous difference between the two institutions is evident in the fact that only about 700,000 out of nearly eight million inmates survived the camps. Elkins declares that he is necessarily concerned only with the survivors, but among those he thus eliminates from consideration are nearly all who in some manner resisted the system and whose personalities were not crushed by it.[10] To establish a comparable situation in slavery, one would have to imagine that the system had become vastly more brutal in the 1850s and that, in consequence, only 400,000 rather than four million slaves were alive in 1860, the rest having been murdered by their masters for resistance or rules infractions, or in medical experiments, or as victims of a Negro extermination policy. One could hardly argue seriously that such a profound change in the nature of slavery—in terms of the slave's expectations of survival—would have had no significant impact on personality. Nor would one then want to limit a study of slave personality to the cringing 400,000 survivors. It would appear, therefore, that absolute power was not the controlling mechanism as much as the manner in which the power was used.

Turning finally to the theoretical foundation of the Elkins essay, the important question is whether personality theory, when applied to the available data, points unmistakably to Sambo as the typical plantation slave. This does not seem to be the case, for there are important aspects of the theories that Elkins uses, together with much data, that suggest other plausible hypotheses.[11] In addition, personality theory contains more than a few ambiguities. For example, role psychology does not provide a clear answer to the question of whether the Sambo role played by many plantation slaves was internalized and became part of their personalities, or whether it was a form of conscious hypocrisy, a mere accommodation to the system. David McClelland asserts that the roles an individual plays are part of his knowledge "and therefore part of his personality" (1951, p. 296; see also Hartley & Hartley, 1952, pp. 509–511).[12] But Ralph Linton thinks that playing a role proves nothing about an individual's personality, "except that he has normal learning ability." The psychologist must be able "to penetrate behind the façade of social conformity and cultural uniformity to reach the authentic individual" (1945, p. 26). Two recent writers on role theory, Theodore R. Sarbin and Vernon L. Allen, illustrating a new trend, hardly touch on the matter of role and personality. They are far more interested in the interaction between role and social identity, and they state explicitly that they "are not using 'social identity' and 'self' as synonyms. Selfhood . . . embodies more residuals of behavior than those generated through role enactment" (1968–1969, pp. 550–557).

At times Elkins approaches this problem warily, suggesting only that the roles an individual plays are internalized to "an extent," or that "deliberate" role-playing and "natural" role-playing grade into each other "with considerable subtlety." Returning to the problem in an appendix, Elkins again refuses to generalize: "The main thing I would settle for would be the existence of a broad belt of indeterminacy between 'mere acting' and the 'true self' "; to the extent that they "grade into one another" it seems "permissible to speak of Sambo as a personality 'type' " (1968, pp. 86n, 125, 227–228).

These cautious statements are hardly disputable, but they do not represent the tone of the essay as a whole. The clear inference to be drawn from Elkins's comparison of North American and Latin American slavery, from his introduction of the concentration-camp analogy, and from his use of personality theory is that Sambo was not a dissembler but a distinct personality type and the typical plantation slave. Indeed, in one footnote, Elkins explicitly rejects the possibility that the Sambo role was only a form of conscious accommodation. Not until after emancipation, he insists, did the Negro's "moral and psychological orientation" permit the development of "the essentially intermediate technique of accommodation . . . as a protective device beneath which a more independent personality might develop" (1968, pp. 132n–133n).[13]

Yet the theory of role psychology, when applied to the information we have concerning the life and behavior of plantation slaves, provides plenty of room for personalities other than Sambo. This theory, which stresses the importance of "role clarity," holds that adequate role performance will be unlikely if there is uncertainty concerning the nature of an appropriate role. In addition, role conflict occurs when a person finds himself occupying more than one status at a given time, each requiring different behavior, or when there is more than one source of advice about how a role is properly played. Conflicting obligations or conflicting expectations may lead to a personal crisis and to difficulty in playing any role successfully (Hartley & Hartley, 1952, pp. 521–532; McClelland, 1951, pp. 316–318; Sarbin & Allen, 1968–1969, pp. 540–544). These were problems that troubled plantation slaves in their daily lives—problems whose psychic strains they resolved in ways that varied with their individual natures and experiences.

Harry Stack Sullivan's model of interpersonal relationships, when fully utilized, also provides theoretical support for a variety of plantation slave personalities. Sullivan describes a highly complex and subtle interplay between an individual and the significant others in his life. One side of it— the side that Elkins explores—is the anxiety that helps to mold an individual's personality as he behaves in certain ways to meet the expectations of authority figures. But there is another side, which involves the conscious manipulation of significant others to the individual's own advantage. By the time a child is ready for school, Sullivan observes, he has "evolved techniques" for handling his parents "with only a modicum of pain"; he now encounters other adults "who have to be managed" (1947, p. 18).[14] In addition to manipulation, there is still another and less fortunate way that a person deals with tendencies in his personality that are strongly disapproved by his significant others. These tendencies are neither lost nor resolved but simply "dissociated from personal awareness." In the process of dissociation they are "excluded from the self" and become part of the "extra-self." But the tendencies still remain an integral part of the personality, manifesting "themselves in actions, activities, of which the person himself remains quite unaware" (1947, pp. 13, 21–22).

Sullivan's concept of dissociation describes a condition which, at a certain point, may lead to serious psychic problems. Generally speaking, he believes that the "healthy development of personality is inversely proportionate to the amount, to the number, of tendencies which have come to exist in dissociation" (1947, p. 22). In Elkins's conceptualization we encounter the significant other of Sullivan's interpersonal theory but not the phenomena of manipulation and dissociation; yet all three concepts are relevant to the problem of slave personality.

I believe that a historian utilizing the available evidence on slave behavior and master-slave relationships and taking account of all aspects of the personality theories used by Elkins will be forced to abandon his hypothesis that Sambo was the typical plantation slave. Several historians have already briefly suggested other possibilities (Fredrickson & Lasch, 1967, pp. 315–329; Genovese, 1967, pp. 293–314, 1970, pp. 34–43; Levine, 1971, pp. 99–130; Rose, 1970; Stampp, 1970, ch. 3, 8), and at present several have more ambitious projects under way. The following is my own sketch of an alternative to the Elkins hypothesis.

I would begin by accepting Elkins's description of southern slavery as a closed system from which few escaped and in which the slaves had only limited contacts with free society; his emphasis on the dehumanizing tendencies of slavery (though not in North America alone); his belief that the system had built into it powerful pressures toward dependent, infantilized, emasculated personalities;[15] and his conception of the master as a formidable significant other in the life of nearly every slave—partly an object of fear, partly a Freudian father figure. But I would reject his assertions that the master's power was absolute; that he was the only significant other in the lives of his slaves; that he was the sole author of the role, or roles, they played; and that southern slaves were almost totally dehumanized. Finally, I would suggest that plantation slaves encountered significant others in their own families and communities; that dissembling, manipulation, dissociation, role conflict, and lack of role clarity were important ingredients of slave behavior; and that plantation life enabled most slaves to develop independent personalities—indeed, provided room for the development of a considerable range of personality types.

In his concentration-camp analogy Elkins observes that a small minority of the inmates, who held minor administrative jobs, was able to escape the full impact of the system on personality. This minority could engage in petty underground activities, such as stealing blankets, getting medicine from the camp hospital, and negotiating black-market arrangements with the guards. These activities turned out to be crucial for the fortunate prisoner's psychological balance. For him the SS was not the only significant other, and the role of the child was not the only one open to him—he was able to do things that had meaning in adult terms (1968, pp. 134–135).[16]

If these trivial activities could preserve the psychic balance of camp inmates, then the plantations afforded the great mass of field hands infinitely greater opportunities to preserve theirs. Though plantation slaves were exposed to influences that encouraged childlike dependency and produced emasculated personalities, the system nevertheless permitted them a degree of semiautonomous community life and the opportunity to do many things that had meaning in adult terms. They lived in their own separate quarters where they could escape the constant scrutiny of their master. Unlike the slaves on the sugar and coffee plantations of Brazil and Cuba, where men outnumbered women by as much as three to one, those on the plantations of the Old South could experience something like a normal sex life, because the sexes were usually evenly divided. Though slave marriages had no legal support and families were ever in danger of being broken up by sales, southern slaves nevertheless lived in family groups more often than those on the commercialized plantations of Latin America. In fact, it was customary for them to live in family groups.[17]

Slave families, because of their relative lack of economic significance, their instability, and the father's severely restricted role, may well have been less important in the lives of slaves than the broader plantation slave communities. The latter provided opportunities for self-expression in their celebrations of holidays, in their music and folklore, and in other aspects of community life. Historians have perhaps viewed religion among plantation slaves too much in terms of the nonreligious uses to which it was put. We know that masters used religious indoctrination as a means of control and that slaves found in their religious services subtle ways of protesting their condition. But there were other and deeper ways in which religion served them. It provided a system of beliefs that comforted and sustained them in their bondage, and it afforded additional means of self-expression that helped them retain their psychic balance. I do not believe that a truly autonomous Afro-American subculture developed in slavery days, but some of the ingredients for one were certainly there.

Both the family and the community provided plantation slaves with roles other than that defined by the master, and with significant others besides the master. For the very young child the mother, not the master, was the significant other in the sense that Sullivan uses this concept. Though the near impossibility of fathers acting as true authority figures was of great psychic importance, meaningful relationships did sometimes exist between fathers and sons. As the child grew, the master's role as a significant other became increasingly vital, but he was always in competition with significant others in the slave community: with husbands, wives, fathers, and mothers; with religious leaders; with strong male models, some of whom may even on occasion have served as substitute father figures;[18] with slaves believed to possess mystical powers; and with those whose wisdom was respected. Few planters had any illusions about being the only authority figures on their estates; as one of them noted, there were always slaves who held "a kind of magical sway over the minds and opinions of the rest" (*Southern Cultivator*, 1851).

In his community, in the presence of these significant others, the slave could play a role decidedly different from the one prescribed by his master. This situation often led to the psychologically important problem of role conflict. An obvious illustration is the dilemma of a slave being questioned by his master concerning the whereabouts of a fugitive. Here the rules of proper conduct that the master tried to instill in him came in conflict with the values of his community. If we can trust the testimony of the masters themselves, community values usually triumphed, even though punishment might be the consequence.

Was there any sense in which the master's power was really absolute? Only in the sense that if a master killed a slave by overwork, or by cruel punishment, or in a fit of rage, it was nearly impossible to convict him in a court of law. But southern state laws did not themselves give the master absolute power over his slaves, for the laws recognized their humanity and attempted to control the degree of punishment that might be inflicted, the amount of labor that could be required, and the care that was to be provided. Where the laws failed, the master might be restrained by his own moral standards or by those of the white community. If law and custom were not enough, he was still confronted by the fact that, unlike the inmates of a concentration camp, his slaves had monetary value and a clear purpose—to toil in his fields—and therefore had bargaining power. The master got work out of his slaves by coercion, by threats, by promises of rewards, by flattery, and by a dozen other devices he knew of. But if he were prudent, he knew that it was not wise to push slaves too far—to work them too long, punish them too severely or too often, or make too many threats. Slaves had their own standards of fair play and their own ways of enforcing them.[19] The relationship between master and slave was not one in which absolute power rested on one side and total helplessness on the other; rather, the relationship was one of everlasting tensions, punctuated by occasional conflicts between combatants using different weapons.

If the master had the *de facto* power of life and death over his slaves, the slaves knew that he was most unlikely to use it. They knew that rules infractions and certain forms of resistance did not ordinarily lead to death but to milder and often quite bearable forms of punishment, or to sale to another master, or, on occasion, to no penalty at all. In the conflicts between masters and slaves, the masters or their overseers sometimes suffered defeat, and the resulting collapse of discipline led inflexibly to economic disaster. To read the essays "On the Management of Negroes" that frequently appeared in southern periodicals is to appreciate the practical limits of the master's power. Clearly, for the slave, as he responded to the problems of his existence, the choices open to him were a good deal more complex than a simple one between life and death.

Role psychology, as those who have written on the subject observe, tempts one to view the whole problem metaphorically as drama.[20] But in slavery the theatrical situation was seldom one in which the master wrote the script and the slaves played their roles and read their lines precisely as their master had written them. The instructions masters gave to their overseers, which describe the qualities they hoped to develop in their slaves, suggest something quite different. Significantly, the model slave described in these instructions is not Sambo but a personality far more complicated. Masters wanted their slaves, like Sambo, to be docile, humble, and dependent; but they also wanted them to be diligent, responsible, and resourceful—in short, as Earle E. Thorpe has noted, "to give a very efficient and adult-like performance" (1962, pp. 174–175).[21] The slaves in turn had to find ways to resolve the obviously incongruent role expectations of their masters, and many of them responded as persons troubled with this or other forms of role conflict often do. They resorted to lying and deceit.

Eugene Genovese, in an otherwise valuable essay on slave personality, is not very perceptive when he argues that slaves who tricked their masters, rather than coping with problems of role conflict and role definition, were merely playing a game which the masters enjoyed and had themselves written into the script (1967, pp. 310–311). True, a master might occasionally be amused when a house servant outwitted him, but there is scant evidence that he enjoyed this "game" when played by field hands. This was certainly not in the script, and masters frequently expressed their anger or perplexity at the "untrustworthiness" of Negroes. Their appreciation of the slave trickster was confined mostly to their public defenses of slavery and to sentimental plantation literature. In private they were seldom amused.

Plantation field hands, finding no escape from slavery but plenty of elbow room within it, usually managed to preserve their individuality and therefore revealed a considerable variety of personality types. Among the types, there were, to be sure, genuine Sambos who seemed to have internalized much of the role, for some slaves simply lacked the psychic strength to withstand the infantilizing pressures of the system. They looked on the master as a father figure, accepted his values, identified with him, and perhaps even viewed themselves through his eyes.

We may assume that the slave who internalized the Sambo role did accept his master as his only significant other and that he was relatively untroubled by the problem of role conflict. But he must have been sorely disturbed by the psychic process of dissociation—that is, exclusion from the self of disapproved personality tendencies, which then become part of what Sullivan calls the "extra-self." Such dissociated tendencies, we must remember, still remain part of the personality; and, therefore, Sambo was Sambo only up to a point—in Genovese's words, "up to the moment that the psychological balance was jarred from within or without . . . " (1967, p. 312). Plantation records often reveal the astonishment of masters when slaves, who had long given evidence of Sambo personalities, suddenly behaved in disturbingly un-Sambo ways.

Another personality type was evident on certain large plantations, especially on those of absentee owners in new areas of the Southwest, where labor was sometimes exploited ruthlessly and punishments were brutal. This type displayed none of the silliness of Sambo, none of his childlike attachment to master or overseer; rather, he was profoundly apathetic, full of depression and gloom, and seemingly less hostile than indifferent toward the white man who controlled him. One slaveholder observed that slaves subjected to overwork and cruel punishments were likely to fall "into a state of impassivity" and to become "insensible and indifferent to punishment, or even to life . . . (De Bow's Review, 1858). These brutalized slaves had their counterparts on Latin American plantations, where extreme cruelty produced in some a state of psychic shock manifested in apathy and depression. In colonial Brazil this condition was sufficiently common to be given a special name: *banzo* (Davis, 1966, p. 238). It is this condition that seems to be analogous to the concentration camps, where life had lost its meaning, and to prisons and asylums, where "situational withdrawal" is a form of institutional adaptation.[22]

More numerous among plantation personalities were the men and women with sufficient strength of character to escape the emasculating tendencies of the system, a group whose size Elkins seriously underestimates. These slaves were not only not Sambos, but they did not *act* like Sambos—their behavior was in no respect infantile. Though observing all the niceties of interracial etiquette, they maintained considerable dignity even in their relations with their masters. Judging from plantation diaries, masters often treated slaves of this kind with genuine respect and seldom made the mistake of regarding them as children. Slaves such as these were not troublemakers; they were rarely intransigent as long as what was asked of them and provided for them was reasonable by their standards. They worked well and efficiently and showed considerable initiative and self-reliance. They tended to be fatalistic about their lot, expected little of life, and found their satisfaction in the religious and social activities of the slave communities. No doubt their psychic balance and their relative tranquillity was sometimes disturbed by a certain amount of role conflict; and they could hardly have escaped the phenomenon of dissociation described by Sullivan.

Herbert Aptheker's rebels must also be included among those whose personalities were far removed from the traditional Sambo. I would not limit these to the organizers of or participants in rebellions, for their number was very small.[23] Rather, I would include all who were never reconciled to the system and engaged in various acts of resistance: running away, arson, the damaging of crops and tools, and sometimes even assaults on masters, overseers, or other whites. Needless to say, it is often impossible to distinguish conscious resistance from the unconscious carelessness and indifference of slaves, but the evidence of genuine resistance is clear enough in some cases (Bauer & Bauer, 1942, pp. 388–419; Harding, 1969, pp. 179–197; Stampp, 1956, ch. 3). Genovese argues that the slaves did not develop a genuine revolutionary tradition, that their acts of resistance were usually nihilistic, and that at best they came out of slavery with a tradition of recalcitrance—"of undirected, misdirected or naively directed violence." George M. Fredrickson and Christopher Lasch object even to calling the acts of slave rebels "resistance" and insist that it was only "intransigence." They define the former as organized, purposeful political action, the latter as mere "personal strategy of survival" which can easily lead to "futile and even self-destructive acts of defiance" (Genovese, 1966, pp. 7–11; see also Fredrickson & Lasch, 1967, pp. 317, 326). Surely, little that was done by the rebels could form the basis for a revolutionary tradition or satisfy so narrow a definition of resistance; but these were rebels, nonetheless, who never internalized the masters' standards of good conduct and never dissociated from their conscious selves all the disapproved tendencies of their personalities.

All of these slaves types, with myriad individual variations, were recognizable on the plantations. But I believe that the personalities of most slaves are less easily classified, because their behavior when observed by whites was usually that of conscious accommodators. They played the role of Sambo with varying degrees of skill and consistency,[24] but, in contrast to the authentic Sambos, most characteristics of the role did not become part of their true personalities. For them the Sambo routine was a form of "ritual acting"—that is, they went through the motions of the role, but with a rather low degree of personal involvement (Hartley & Hartley, 1952, p. 493; Sarbin & Allen 1968–1969, pp. 492–496).

Several aspects of role theory support this hypothesis. One assumption of this theory is that the average normal person plays not one but several roles, and often two or more simultaneously. To think of the slave as playing but one role—that of Sambo—is to assume that he responded to a single social situation, which was clearly not the case. Moreover, when a role performance is demanded primarily in terms of the pains and penalties for nonperformance, as it was on the typical plantation supervised by an overseer and run as a business enterprise, the role is likely to be enacted with little conviction and minimal personal involvement. The Sambo role doubtless was performed more convincingly and with more feeling in a paternalistic situation. Finally, the extent to which a given role makes an impact on the self depends on its "preemptiveness"—on how much of a person's time is spent playing the role (Hartley & Hartley, 1952, p. 498; Sarbin & Allen, 1968–1969, pp. 491, 496–497, 535). Therefore, one must ask how preemptive the Sambo role actually was. During the week the plantation field hand spent most of his waking hours as an agricultural worker, planting, cultivating, or harvesting, and the demand on him was for a responsible adult performance. He spent evenings and holidays in the slave community playing a variety of roles, only occasionally being observed by master or overseer. The one occasion that called for the Sambo role was that of a direct contact with a member of the white race, when the Negro was forced to acknowledge in some way not only that he was a slave but that he belonged to a degraded caste. However, for the average field hand such contacts were brief and relatively infrequent; therefore the pressures on him most of the time were to play roles other than Sambo.

In short, most plantation slaves avoided the internalization of Sambo, first, because they were able to play different roles in their communities; second, because the Sambo role was not unduly preemptive; third, because masters were not the only significant others in the lives of slaves; fourth, because slaves found abundant opportunities to behave in ways that had meaning in adult terms; and, last, because conditions on the average plantation were not so brutal that they were destroyed as human beings. In consequence, slaves could use the essentially external Sambo role, in Elkins's words, "as a protective device beneath which a more independent personality might develop" (1968, p. 133n). Those who consciously and purposefully acted the part of Sambo, thereby reducing sources of friction and putting limits on what would normally be expected of them, were in no sense being childish or infantile; rather, their behavior was rational, meaningful, and mature.

In an essay based on studies of other total institutions, George Fredrickson and Christopher Lasch suggest that conditions in prisons and asylums are more analogous to slavery than conditions in concentration camps. They note that the inmates of such institutions do not usually internalize a sense of obligation to obey their rules and accept their values. In the case of slavery, they conclude, "a system that rigorously defined the Negro slave not merely as an inferior but as an alien, a separate order of being," could hardly have instilled in him "the sense of belonging on which internalized obedience necessarily has to rest" (Fredrickson & Lasch, 1967, pp. 320–323).

However, I think there is a better approach to understanding the personalities of plantation slaves than that provided by either of these analogies. Much more can be learned from a study of ex-slaves and their descendants in the rural South in the decades after Reconstruction, when, for all practical purposes, the system was still a closed one from which few escaped, and when powerful forces again generated tendencies toward emasculated personalities. Now their humanity was assaulted and their race denigrated by the most extreme forms of prejudice, segregation, and discrimination; and they felt strong pressures, both subtle and crude, to internalize the white man's opinion of them. After emancipation there was still a white landlord to serve as a counterpart to the slaveowner as a significant other. More important, the whole white community now became, collectively, a significant other, imposing a subservient and dependent role on the Negro and enforcing an etiquette of race relations with sanctions equal to those available to masters in slavery days. Yet, most Negroes, as in slavery days, found ways of maintaining a degree of psychic balance. Through their churches, their music, and a great variety of organized social activities, they gradually developed a semiautonomous Afro-American subculture; in their communities and families they responded to their own significant others; and in their mature years they had a variety of adult roles to play, even though whites persisted in calling black men boys and black women girls.

In circumstances whose psychic impact had many parallels to slavery, Negroes once more resorted to conscious accommodation. The investigations of twentieth-century social scientists provide much evidence that most post-Reconstruction Negroes did not internalize the Sambo role they played before the white community. For example, in the 1930s, John Dollard observed that the southern Negro played two roles:

> one that he is forced to play with white people and one the "real Negro" as he appears in his dealings with his own people. What the white southern people see who "know their Negroes" is the role that they have forced the Negro to accept, his caste role. . . . It is perhaps this fact which often makes Negroes seem so deceptive to white people; apparently our white caste wishes the Negro to have only one social personality, his caste role, and to *be* this with utter completeness. (1957, pp. 257–259)

The testimony of post-Reconstruction Negroes themselves, especially in their music and folklore, also suggests a prevalent pattern of conscious accommodation.[25]

Similarly, the slaves, in their scattered records, and the masters, in their private papers and published essays on the management of Negroes, indicate that conscious accommodation was a widespread behavior pattern on the antebellum plantations. Whatever the masters may have said about the loyal, childlike "darky" in their public defenses of slavery, the dissembling pseudo-Sambo was the most common reality that confronted them in their daily lives. As one planter wrote: "The most general defect in the character of the Negro, is hypocrisy; and this hypocrisy frequently makes him pretend to more ignorance than he possesses; and if the master treats him as a fool, he will be sure to act the fool's part. This is a very convenient trait, as it frequently serves as an apology for awkwardness and neglect of duty" (*Farmer's Register*, 1837, p. 32).[26]

However, the fact that some masters saw through the Sambo act, as this one did, suggests that slave accommodators may often have missed their lines. Playing this intricate role could never have been easy, and it may have caused even the most skilled of them serious psychic problems, especially if there was a basic incongruence between the self and this role (Sarbin & Allen, 1968–1969, p. 524). I suspect that many had profound difficulties with role conflict, as the weaker characters who internalized the Sambo role suffered from dissociation. Those who study slave personality would be well advised to watch for signs of character disorders in these seemingly gay dissemblers. I want to point again, as I did in *The Peculiar Institution*, to the astonishing frequency of speech problems among slaves. Time after time, owners advertising for runaways reported that a slave "stutters very much," "stammers very much," "speaks quickly and with an anxious expression of countenance," or is "easily confused when spoken to."[27] Such data are open to several interpretations, but one respectable theory suggests that speech impediments are symptoms of buried hostility. Dr. Murry Snyder of the Speech Rehabilitation Institute of New York City believes that "Underneath the cloak of inhibition and mild manner, the stutterer often seethes with anger" (*Time*, 1970, p. 42; see also Sarbin & Allen, 1968–1969, p. 527). In the case of slaves, speech problems may also have been a manifestation of role conflict or of incompatibility between self and role.

The art of conscious accommodation, along with all its psychic consequences, is one of the skills that Negroes carried with them from slavery to freedom. Accommodation continued to be a part of life for many of them, especially in the rural South, for another century. Being obliged to wear the mask of Sambo, whatever they may have been inside, doubtless they were, as in slavery days, troubled to an extraordinary degree by the problem of role conflict. To escape this problem seems to be one of the aims of the present black revolution, for the search for black identity is in part a search for role clarity. To end the dissembling, to be all of a piece, to force the white community to accept them as they really are, not as it so long wanted to see them, is quite obviously one determined goal of the new generation of blacks.

NOTES

1. Cade, 1935, pp. 294–337; Fisk University Social Science Institute, 1945; Botkin, 1945. See also Yetman, 1967, pp. 534–53. My evaluation of these collections of slave narratives is based on the above published extracts. A careful study of the more than two thousand narratives collected by the Federal Writer's Project in the 1930s may lead to a more favorable assessment of their historical value.

2. A good case for the value of this material is presented in Levine, 1971b, pp. 99–130. See also Stuckey, 1968, pp. 417–37.

3. Sullivan defines personality as "the relatively enduring pattern of recurrent interpersonal situations which characterize a human life" (1953, p. 111).

4. "A role is a cluster of traits (or pattern of behavior) which serves as the culturally normal or modal solution to recurrent, usually social problems peculiar to a particular status of position in society" (McClelland, 1951, p. 293; see also Hartley & Hartley, 1952, pp. 485–6).

5. In his response, except for one important point mentioned, Elkins concedes very little to his critics. Therefore, since he has neither changed his position significantly nor added any supporting empirical evidence, my comments on his use of analogy, his use of personality theory, and his view of the life of plantation slaves are as relevant to the new essay as to the old.

6. It is unlikely that Elkins thought of his analogy as more than an explanation. Yet he creates a small ambiguity by labeling one of the sections of Appendix A (p. 225) "*Analogy as evidence*."

7. Winthrop D. Jordan has called my attention to an important question about when Sambo first began to appear prominently in southern plantation literature. He was not the

typical slave depicted in the seventeenth and eighteenth centuries. In those earlier years the slave was more often thought of as a dangerous element in the population—a threat to the peace and safety of the English colonies. Of course, it is possible that the Negro's personality had changed by the nineteenth century, when Sambo first became important in southern literature; but there may have been a connection between the appearance of Sambo and the growing moral attack on slavery. Sambo was always one of the proslavery writer's major arguments for keeping the Negro in bondage.

8. It hardly needs to be said that Elkins does not endorse the racist implications of these statements. He uses them merely to illustrate the Sambo character that slavery allegedly forced on the Negro in the South. Still, it is worth noting that, except for the racist overtones, his description of the plantation slave is almost identical with that found in the writings of Ulrich B. Phillips.

9. For statements of the crucial differences between slavery and the concentration camps see Genovese, 1967, pp. 308–309; and Thorpe, 1962, p. 173.

10. The literature on the camps indicates that there was resistance, but such behavior is not taken into account in Elkins's essay (Genovese, 1967; Kogon, 1950; Thorpe, 1962).

11. Since psychologists cannot agree on a definition of personality, the literature gives the historian plenty of latitude. One psychologist compiled a list of almost fifty definitions of personality (Hall & Lindzey, 1957, pp. 7–10). Though I am not here considering the personality theories that Elkins does not use, I do question whether he was justified in making so little use of Freud, especially Freud's emphasis on the molding of the child's superego through experiences with the parents. Elkins explains why he thinks that Freud is not very useful in understanding the impact of the concentration camps on personality, but he never explains adequately why he thinks that Freudian concepts would not help us to understand the personality of the slave. While on the subject of what Elkins has neglected, I must note his failure to use the decidedly relevant writings of Erik H. Erikson on the problem of identity.

12. However, it is important to note that those who relate roles to personality are usually writing about children and the role the parents prescribe. In the case of the slave child, it was the mother or the father or a slave nurse, not the master, who taught the child a role in his early years. The master's direct involvement in child training did not usually begin until the child was old enough to perform some chores—say, at the age of seven or eight. By that time a large part of the child's personality had been formed. In the early formative years the master was not so much the one who prescribed a role as he was an object whom the child was taught to cope with in one way or another.

13. In his recent essay Elkins claims that his statement about "a broad belt of indeterminacy between 'mere acting' and the 'true self' " expresses the position he had taken in the original essay (Lane, 1971, p. 359). However, in my opinion, this claim represents a shift in his basic position rather than an accurate statement of his original point of view.

14. Speaking of the child and his relations with his parents, Sullivan notes the child's "realistic appreciation of a necessity and a human development of devices to meet the necessity. . . . that marvelous human thing, great adaptive possibilities applied successfully to a situation" (pp. 19–20).

15. My study of slavery also called attention to these pressures: "Ideally [slavery] was the relationship of parent and child. . . . The system was in its essence a process of infantilization . . . ." (Stampp, 1956, p. 327).

16. I suspect that the ability of these petty administrators to escape the full impact of the terror and brutality of the camps was even more crucial to their psychological balance.

17. In her unpublished paper, "Childhood in Bondage," Willie Lee Rose argues that historians have underestimated the importance of the slave family, especially the role of the father in raising children (see also Genovese, 1970, pp. 37–38).

18. In discussing the problem that boys without fathers have in learning the male role, Eugene and Ruth Hartley note that the situation changes quickly when such boys find other

opportunities to observe the male role: "They learn from their playmates and from any adult males with whom they come into repeated contact" (1952, p. 504).

19. Fredrickson and Lasch, (1967, pp. 322–325), suggest that slaves developed their own standards of fair play through their varying experiences with different masters and overseers.

20. "*Role*, a term borrowed directly from the theater, is a metaphor intended to denote that conduct adheres to certain 'parts' (or positions) rather than to the players who read or recite them" (Sarbin & Allen, 1968–1969, pp. 489, 547–550).

21. This is an excellent example of one kind of role conflict—the kind that results when an authority figure holds "simultaneous contradictory expectations for one role" (Sarbin & Allen, 1968–1969, p. 540).

22. See Fredrickson and Lasch (1967, pp. 325–327), and their sources for behavior in total institutions, especially Goffman, 1961.

23. For persuasive explanations of why there were relatively few insurrections in the antebellum South see Degler, 1970, pp. 1013–1016; 1966, pp. 4–6. I believe that a major factor contributing to the larger number of insurrections in Brazil was the imbalance of the sexes on the plantations, whereas most southern slaves lived in family groups. The presence of a large number of young men without women and the absence of the stabilizing influence of the family on Brazilian plantations were bound to create a condition highly conducive to rebellions.

24. Sarbin and Allen note the great qualitative differences in role performance among individuals: "One person may enact a role convincingly and skillfully, while another may be inept" 1968–1969, p. 514.

25. See, for example, Levine, 1971a, pp. 125–147.

26. For an excellent analysis of "Quashee," the Jamaican counterpart of Sambo, and of the degree to which he was a conscious role-player, see Patterson, 1967, pp. 174–181.

27. One must, of course, ask whether runaways were not exceptional slaves with special psychic problems. I do not think that this was the case, because many kinds of slaves ran away for a variety of reasons. But this is a matter that requires further investigation.

Chapter 8

THE HORIZONTAL AND VERTICAL STRUCTURE OF SOCIAL IDENTITY: APPLICATIONS TO THE HASIDIC REVOLUTION

Mordechai Rotenberg

When we think about the process through which people acquire their social identities we must obviously qualify the resulting identities in relatively positive or negative terms. That is, based on role enactments we would rank a person's social identity on the ladder of respectability according to our preconceived cultural criteria as to what constitutes a negative or positive identity. If, for example, a particular society exclusively values mystic meditation as a legitimate actualization goal, the valuative consensus of a person as a competent scholar or as a constructive industrialist would probably not grant him a positive social identity whether or not this activity provided him with personally satisfying actualization outlets. In a society that essentially prescribes only one ideal actualization role, say, constructive industrialist, an "idle person" would probably be assigned negative identity labels, "no-good," "lazy bum," etc. (regardless of his scholarship or his meditation skills).

From a social structural point of view one could predict the proportional ratio of people who would be able to acquire positive social identities—from the number of equally valued positive social identities available and from the degree of accessibility of these identities. In the first part of this essay the differences between what will be termed multiple-actualization systems (in which many ideal social identities are available for actualization) and mono-actualization systems (in which essentially only one positive ideal social identity is available) will be outlined and discussed. To demonstrate how a multiple-actualization system minimizes the casting

Portions of this chapter have been adapted from the author's previous works (Rotenberg, 1978, 1982).

of people into deviant or low-grade social identities, I shall discuss the eighteenth-century Judeo-Hasidic identity relabeling movement, a social movement that legitimized divergent and attainable ideal social identities and preserved the horizontal balance among members of a social system.

The number of negative versus positive ideal social identities available in a social system—a component of social structure—is identified here as the horizontal dimension of social identity.

While the structural component of multiple ideal social identities may indeed minimize the number of people forced into negative social identities in a given society, psychological barriers may hinder one's enactment of such positive prescribed ideal identities. That is, one's motivation to acquire available positive social identity may be vertically contingent on the degree to which one's basic psychological identity as a human being is being threatened or respected.

The psychological dynamic component that considers the congruency between one's basic primary age and sex identity and one's social identity will thus be termed here the vertical dimension of identity. The vertical dimension deals with the meaningfulness of one's social identity as contingent on one's psychological self-identity as a human being. The second part of this essay will introduce the "contingent being" theory to illuminate the vertical dimension of the present social identity perspective, following Linton's (1945) distinction between ascribed (primary-psychological) and achieved (secondary-sociological) roles.

I shall attempt to show how the acquisition of various sociological-achieved identities is contingent on the degree of compatible fulfillment of their concomitant psychological-ascribed roles such as those related to age and sex statuses. To illuminate the dynamics of the contingent relationship between achieved identity and ascribed identity, the social typing of a person system will be analyzed. It will be demonstrated accordingly how the provision of a new achieved "rehabilitation" identity may become irrelevant as long as one's psychological ascribed age and sex statuses are being threatened, frustrated, or demolished.

THE STRUCTURAL-HORIZONTAL COMPONENT OF SOCIAL-IDENTITY: THE SOCIOLOGICAL DIMENSION

The term "ideal identity," as used here, refers to a positive or derogatory label used by societies to socialize, label, and relabel their members relative to an ideal type. An ideal identity or label refers to a set of culturally desirable or nondesirable behavior systems in the sense of Max Weber's ideal type concept. Ideal identities differ from role models in that ideal identities do not refer to concrete people and, consequently, do not entail the charismatic components implicit in the definition of role models. Similarly, ideal identity labels differ from social types (Strong, 1943). The latter term refers to idiosyncratic, transient types emerging in small groups. Ideal identities are derivations from cultural normative prescriptions for actualization and socialization transcending the existence of small groups. As all people do not have equal opportunities or are not equally endowed or motivated to pattern their behavior according to various ideal identities, the scarcity and rigidity of positive ideal identity labels in relation to negative identity labels might be crucial in determining the proportion of people suffering from degraded identities in different social systems. Hence it is not only the derogatory labeling process, as labeling theorists have hitherto posited, that would maximize the prevalence of deviance and degradation of people's identities, but also the scarcity of positive ideal identity labels. By scarcity and plenitude of ideal identity labels, I do not refer to the ranking of various social roles available to people in the Western materially-oriented success systems. Indeed, I regard the typical Western society as a mono-ideal-identity system, precisely because of the exclusive materialism criteria used to evaluate the constructive industrialist or the well-paid scholar or the rich member of the leisure class alike. By contrast, the term multiple-ideal-identity system will be used to refer to societies where actualization via materialistic, ecstatic, scholastic, or other salvation modes are equally valued as legitimate means for the acquisition of positive ideal identity labels.

More specifically, to elucidate the mono-identity society, I use the example of the Western actualization ideal through constructive material- ism, which is traceable to the Calvinist-Protestant work ethos (Weber, 1930). To construe the dynamics of a multiple-identity society, I use the case of the Judeo-Hasidic "Zebulun and Issachar" pluralistic actualization system. Very briefly, continuous with the Jewish tradition that was based on the legendary contract between the Biblical tribal brothers; Zebulun (the merchant) who supported Issachar (the Talmudic scholar), eighteenth- century Hasidic-identity revolutionary movements developed the plural- istic egalitarian "matter-spirit" actualization system. Accordingly, the Zebulunian "people of matter" acquire their positive social identity by working and supporting the Issacharian "people of form" who acquire their positive social identity through scholastic Talmudic studies or through ecstatic worship. The assymetric actualization exchange between them, is, however, so structured that no one can degrade the other's identity by turning him into an oppressed, degraded debtor because these divergent identity actualization modes, while indirectly benefitting each other, are nonetheless not measurable by the same yardstick (Rotenberg, 1982). One can best assess the functionality of a monolabeling versus multilabeling identity system by examining how such systems maintain or regain their horizontal and functional equilibrium during or after a period of radical change or social crisis. To assess the Western monolabeling actualization system, I have chosen the surplus free-time crisis created in the West by contemporary automation. To assess the functionality of a multilabeling social system, I examine the social-economic crisis that preceded the emergence of the eighteenth-century Hasidic movement in Eastern Europe. Let us begin by examining how the man of leisure was assigned a positive value in the Western automated society.

Automation, Leisure, and the Mono-Material-Identity Ideal

Plato believed that:

> God alone is worthy of supreme seriousness, but man is made God's plaything....Therefore every man and woman should live life accordingly, and play the noblest games....Life must be lived as play, playing certain games, making sacrifices, singing and dancing, and then a man will be able to propriate the gods, and defend himself against his enemies, and win in the contest. (Laws VII, 796, quoted in Huizinga, 1949, p. 119)

In his classic study of the play element in culture, Huizinga (1949) tells us that the word "school" did not always refer to systematic, time-restricting work. "School" originally meant "leisure" (as many rebellious students might be interested to know). Consequently, in ancient Greece, school was not "an educational system designed to train the citizen for useful and profitable occupations. For the Greek, the treasures of the mind were the fruit of his leisure" (p. 147). Thus, self-actualization or salvation in life must be reached through playing noble games. Huizinga points out that Aristotle shared this view. "Nature requires us not only to be able to work well, but also to idle well. This idleness or leisure is the principle of the universe for Aristotle. It is preferable to work; indeed it is the aim of all work" (p. 161).

While for the free man in ancient Greece, the labels "player" or "leisure man" symbolized salvation, liberation, self-actualization, and attainment of the highest ideals of the Greek culture, after the Industrial Revolution, laments Huizinga, "Work and production became the ideal, and then the idol, of the age" (p. 192). Similarly, in ancient Greece, states B. M. Berger (1963),

> [w]ork as instrumental or productive activity was regarded below the dignity of a free man, fit only for slaves and women....When Calvinism sanctified work and industrialism ennobled it, what followed was the separation of work and leisure ... and the relegation of leisure to the status of spare time—time especially vulnerable to the ministrations of the Devil." (p. 25)

What we have, then, in both of these cultures—in ancient Greece and in contemporary Western civilization—is essentially only one predominant ideal identity for salvation or self-actualization. Thus, if the productive worker in ancient Greece was looked down upon as a lower-class slave and the unemployed or "lazy bum" in Western society is degraded as a deviant outcast, then, as we have argued, the proportion of people assigned deviant identities may be expected to be relatively high due to actualization scarcity and rigidity, as suggested above.

A critic might question whether in Western society the "lazy man of leisure" is an "idle ideal man" rather than a degraded man. A more systematic examination of the meaning of leisure in our society reveals, however, that it is only the member of the leisure class who can prove that somehow he is active or industrious in a Calvinist sense and who, therefore, can constantly provide material-success signs (Rotenberg, 1978), usually in the "conspicuous consumption" manner described by Veblen (1934). The state of grace of a rich but idle hobo or hippie is confirmed only after he displays extravagant, consuming ability; it seems, however, that for the real poor, although the road to salvation through leisure is with good intentions paved, it leads him not to be among the saved.

The difference between behavior motivated by culturally institutionalized actualization norms and ad hoc behavioral goals designed to "keep the masses busy and off the street" receives full expression when examining the paradoxical connection between automation and leisure in Western technological society. Sociologists and economists interested in social problems arising from the growing automation of Western technology have repeatedly claimed that it is not lack of income maintenance but lack of sufficient employment and the consequent excess in free time that threatens to create new and serious behavioral and social problems (Soule, 1955).

On the other hand, President Kennedy, who considered automation to be the "major domestic challenge of the 1960s," maintained that in the United States, 25,000 new jobs would be needed each week to meet the demands of automation and population growth. Arthur Goldberg, Kennedy's Secretary of Labor, testified before a House subcommittee "that 1,800,000 workers would feel the impact of automation in 1962 alone" (Francois, 1967, p. 77). According to sources cited by Cloward and Piven (1974), "In the years between 1950 and 1965 alone, new machines and new methods increased farm output in the United States by 56% and reduced farm employment by 45%" (p. 201).

It seems that it is not the lack of sufficient funds to provide everybody with a minimum income,[1] but lack of sufficient employment that increases social gaps. Paradoxically, however, most relief and economic security programs are, in most Western countries, linked mainly to work records as a major indicator, if not sole moral criterion, for income eligibility (Macarov, 1980).

It is not my purpose here to take a stand on the difficult social issue of whether there are sufficient funds in a particular country to assure a minimum income for everybody or whether the funds are sufficient but simply not available to the right people. Rather, my goal is to point out that wherever there are sufficient sources of income but not enough working hours, "forced leisure" becomes "false leisure" because of the predominating single ideal "salvation through work."

As indicated above, increases in income and productivity forced workers to redivide their time between labor (for additional income) and leisure. As Faunce (1968) pointed out:

> In the non-governmental sector of our economy, output per manhour has approximately doubled over the past twenty-five years. The benefits of this increased productivity have been distributed between income and leisure on roughly a 60-40 basis, 60% going into greater income and 40% for more leisure time. (p. 73)

Faunce further suggested that, although various industries are differently susceptible to further automation and mechanization, "Reductions in hours worked per week have occurred at varying rates in different industries in the past and will undoubtedly continue to do so" (p. 74). Thus, whether in a leading Western country like the United States, increased productivity and automation has destroyed more jobs than it has created, as many labor leaders insisted, or whether the contrary is true, as many business leaders believed (Francois, 1967), the question that concerns us here is whether "forced leisure" or paid unemployment in the United States means freedom from involvement in work or freedom to become involved in leisure (the former does not necessarily lead to the latter) or whether it leads to self-actualization or to social deterioration, and whether the identity labels "man of leisure" and "working man" are equally acceptable as social identity ideals. B. M. Berger (1963) admitted that the concern of cultural elites over mass leisure reflected their fear of the power of the disengaged poor. Accordingly, leisure for dependent groups that is designed to keep them busy is subjected to the attacks of liberal and radical intellectuals alike. They "accuse the suppliers of mass culture of catering to the lowest levels of popular taste in order to achieve the highest of net profit" (p. 24) and of serving as a device for distraction and intoxicating escape from the hazards of boredom. Thus, compared to the time of ancient Greece, leisure today is no longer the privilege of a few, but the problem of many. It seems that the masses did not learn to purchase their salvation by playing Platonic noble games, nor did leisure become their new existential ideal for self-actualization. The problem seems to be much deeper and embedded in the unsettled, inherent contradiction between what Berger (1963) termed the value system and the social system. The Protestant value system, which condemned the "lazy man," is incapable of honoring the "leisure man" produced by the situational requirements of the social system. Indeed, if leisure as paid unemployment "fails to give to men . . . the feeling of personal adequacy . . . that only work provides for most adult male Americans" as Weiss and Riesman claimed (1963, p. 169), and if membership in the new Calvinist leisure class can be bought only through conspicuous consumption, then it should not be too surprising that taking another part-time job of a very different sort is rationalized by many as being recreational (Weiss & Reisman, 1963, p. 172). After all, the Protestant purpose of leisure is mainly to recreate, restore, or refresh the organism for its primary purpose, work (Berger, 1963, p. 25). Thus, a vicious circle of "democratic unfreedom" (Marcuse, 1966) is created. In the "free" leisure class, people are forced to work during their free time in order to have, as Marcuse (1966) pointed out, a "free choice between brands and gadgets" (p. 7) to be freely and conspicuously consumed. Faunce's (1968) plea to post-industrial society is to create a new "identity ideal" by deemphasizing vocational training and instead teaching more leisure skills in order to break the binds created by Protestant work values.

My aim here is not to represent the naive, antiindustrial revolution that takes modern technological comforts and life-saving devices for granted (Rand, 1970), but to point out how social inequality, social gaps, and deviance cannot be expected to decrease in a mono-ideal-identity culture. Thus, I have shown that the inflexible predominance of one ideal identity label is incapable of contracting itself (Rotenberg, 1982) in order to allow another ideal label to take its place equally alongside the old one, even when circumstances (e.g., excessive free time) prescribe such a need in the interest of system stability.

The point made in the foregoing discussion stresses that, in Western society, new, existential, self-actualizing roads to identity salvation through leisure activities are disconnected from the deep-rooted ideal identity "successful worker." Hence, the new leisure-salvation movements including psychedelic and sex-involvement movements (as one sociologist stated, "Kinsey studying sex is surely studying leisure") appear to be sufficient for keeping people temporarily busy and off the streets, but otherwise they are considered transient, semideviant, and subordinate to the ideal identity label "productive supermaterialist."

In a multiple actualization culture, the proportion of degraded identities is minimized, and horizontal social equality is maintained even in the face of an identity labeling crisis. The sociohistorical background of the emergence of the Jewish ideal identity label *Hasid* in eighteenth-century Eastern Europe is a foremost example of how this may be accomplished.

The Convergence of the "Issachar and Zebulun" Identities and the Emergence of Hasidism

An Israeli professor of education listed a number of Jewish ideal identity types (labels) that he believed emerged throughout the nation's history (Dushkin, 1939). These included the Talmudic Scholar, the *Hasid*, and the farmer type, Pioneer. Dushkin believed that each of these types was equally important, and each should serve equally as an ideal model in socialization and education. Accordingly, declared Dushkin, "we should not concentrate on one type even if he is most favorable to us" (p. 89).

By and large, the principle of socialization toward multiple-ideal-identity labels was maintained throughout Jewish history. Thus, the Issachars (the Talmudic scholars) and the Pioneers (*Halutzim*) were not only equal in status to the Zebuluns (the merchants) who supported them, but the merchants actually had to struggle to keep their equal place alongside the poor Talmudic scholars and the Pioneers. Likewise, the Talmudist did not feel subordinate to the kibbutz Pioneer. This does not mean, however, that such a multiple-ideal social structure did not face periodic predominance of one positive ideal identity when the concomitant degradation of the others widened social gaps and increased the probable incidence of deviance.

During the sixteenth and seventeenth centuries, Jews in Eastern Europe, especially in Poland, lived a prosperous and autonomous life, "a nation within a nation" (as some historians phrased it), with their own courts and synods fully recognized by the Polish government. Education was compulsory and the teacher-rabbis were paid by the council. All young men, including those from poor homes, could equally study the Talmud. The relationship between the Zebuluns and the Issachars was a living testimony to the functionality of the horizontal egalitarian actualization system (Dubnov, 1975).

In 1648, the Greek Catholic peasants of the Ukraine, led by Chmelnitzki, rose up in revolt against their tyrannical Roman Catholic lords and in the process slaughtered Poles and Jews alike (Dresner, 1960, p. 24). These terrible massacres, known as the Chmelnitzki pogroms, wiped out much of Ukrainian Jewry and brought terrible suffering and harsh decrees to large sections of East European Jewry. The central government of Poland was considerably weakened, and, as a result, the situation of the Jews worsened.

The external problems that shattered the Polish central government were soon reflected in an internal decay of the Jewish communities in Poland. The local councils gradually became the government's perverted and corrupted vehicle for extorting taxes from the masses. Thus, since nothing could be done without bribery, including appointments of council members, communal leaders, and rabbis (Dubnov, 1975), the "bought" oligarchy of rich rabbis and leaders created, in fact, a sociological situation that can be best described as a convergence of Issachar and Zebulun into one ideal identity, "rich-scholar," for now only the rich could afford to study the Talmud. Consequently, the road to salvation merged into one narrow alley, open only to the privileged few who, by divorcing themselves from the ignorant masses, shattered the horizontal basis of the egalitarian multiple-identity system. Indeed, in the eighteenth-century only a minute minority was privileged to attend the *yeshiva* (Talmudic college), and for the masses the Torah became a closed book. Thus, contended the historian Dubnov (1975), "the gap between the Talmudists and the masses was continually widening and whoever belonged to the camp of the scholars would look down on the masses and the masses would concede to their worthlessness vis-a-vis the students" (p. 22).

The social system regained its functional horizontal balance through a structural breakthrough of a new ideal identity for actualizing-salvation. The label *Hasid*, which was used since Talmudic times to designate pietists, was assigned a new meaning by the eighteenth-century Hasidic movement. The term now operationally referred to religious self-actualization through group-oriented, ecstatic, and joyful adherence to God, especially during prayers. The movement's founder, the Baal Shem Tov ("Master of the good Name," 1700–1760) who is known by the acronym Besht, is said to have stated that "divine matters were revealed to him not because he studies many Talmudic Tractates and Responsa, but only due to the prayers, as he was always praying with great intention" (Besht, 1975, p. 44). This was a revolutionary change in traditional Judaism, for by exalting prayer the Besht challenged the major scholastic socialization ideal of Talmudism. Hasidism thus reversed traditional scholasticism and ascetic Kabbalism by designating sadness and self-torture as the worst of sins and by sanctifying, similar to some Eastern mystical practices, the emotional, ecstatic, and joyful adherence to God through the art of meditational praying as a countervailing ideal practice to rational Talmudism.

It is here where the multiple-ideal-identity label system receives its full functional expression in terms of social survival. According to the monistic functional relationship between the weak, deviant social elements and the stronger conforming group members, the labels ignoramus (*Am Haaretz*) or sinner were not idealized (as false messianism dictated), neither did the label *Hasid* substitute for the old ideal label "Talmudist." Nonetheless, after a long and bitter struggle (Wilensky, 1970) between Talmudic rationalism and Hasidic emotionalism, Hasidism succeeded in relabeling the derogatory label *Am Haaretz* by putting the new ideal identity label *Hasid* (which now required adherence to the divine but not to scholarship) on the same level with the old positive ideal labels[2] without degrading or substituting them. This is not to suggest that ignorance and poverty became the new ideals for actualization. Tevyeh, the heroic poor *Am Haaretz* in Shalom Aleichem's *Fiddler on the Roof*, admits that according to Jewish ethics it is no shame to be poor, but "it's no great honor either!"

Thus, sociologically, the new identity label *Hasid* strengthened the old Issachar and Zebulun social contract by forcing contraction on other ideal labels in order to make room for it. Hasidic salvation ethics might then explain the difference between functional, lasting Hasidism and the dysfunctional, transient, "messianic" movements (i.e., the Sabbatean movement in the late seventeenth century and, especially, the Frankist movement in the early eighteenth century). These movements, like Pauline Christianity in the first century A.D., attempted in fact to substitute, rather than complement, the old Jewish ideal labels with a new, single ideal label ("Sabbatean," "Frankist," or "Christian").

It should, however, be pointed out again that the new Hasidic road to salvation set upon by the ignorant Jewish masses in eighteenth-century Eastern Europe was not paved by an economic revolution even though they were similarly not only very poor, but persecuted and tortured by both the hostile general environment and their own community. The Hasidic identity revolutionary movement may thus represent a most significant and far reaching case in the sociological history of successful revolutionary movements.

Eighteenth century Hasidic relabeling movement was thus used to demonstrate how the horizontal structural dimension of multiple ideal identities, with its monistic conception of man must allow the periodic reabsorption of potential "dropouts" into its mainstream by legitimizing new modes for actualization. Our structural analysis has thus shown how sociological processes that widen and increase actualization outlets may contribute to the upgrading of people's social identities.

To demonstrate how people's total (self and social) identities may be reshaped, we turn now to examine how social identity might be vertically contingent on its dynamic relationship with basic psychological personality dimensions. We examine the effectiveness of rehabilitation systems that are structured to offer new sociological positive identities for people whose basic personality identity has been essentially mortified. The conceptual model of "contingent being" requires a shift from the sociohistorical consideration of structural variables determining the nature of social identity to a more psychologically oriented assessment of dynamic personality dimensions impinging on the effectiveness and meaningfulness of any given social identity.

THE VERTICAL (DYNAMIC) COMPONENT OF SOCIAL-IDENTITY: THE PSYCHOLOGICAL DIMENSION

It is not enough to describe identity in terms of a horizontal (structural) perspective. A full account of identity formation must include vertical (psychological) constructs.

I present herewith a model that notes the connection between basic identity problems and "secondary opportunities." It begins with the concept of "contingent being." The term "being" is a verb and a noun. The verb "to be" means to exist and noun "being" refers to the sum total of components comprising a person. In a sense, the verb "being" connotes existence from the actor's perspective, and the noun "being" connotes existence from the other's (or others') perspective. "Being," then, includes the objective and subjective aspects of identity: the way one is *being* identified by others and the way he identifies his own *being*. "Being" encompasses one's total existential experiences, which constitute an individual's personhood. These experiences may be construed as needs, role opportunities, and interactions with others. The construals may be formed out of valuations, labeling, and other acts as the actor and others see them.

The model of "contingent beings" assumes (1) two basic levels of existential or experiential beings—a primary and secondary level, and (2) social identity—the secondary state of "being"—which is contingent on the primary state of being—self identity. (Compare with Juhasz, *this volume*).

The concept of "contingent being" can be operationally subdivided into several primary-secondary dimensions, which are expanded derivations from existing theories. These derivations include two major dimensions—one pertaining to actions and the other to reactions: (1) primary and secondary roles (actions), and (2) primary and secondary labels (reactions). They also contain two subdimensions, again one of actions and the other of reactions: (3) primary and secondary others (reactions), and (4) primary and secondary involvement (actions).

Primary and Secondary Roles

Linton's (1945) much-cited simplistic distinction between ascribed roles (e.g., age, sex, kinship) and achieved roles (e.g., social position acquired by skill and merit) is a starting point. Since ascribed roles, which relate to the undifferentiated role " person," form one's basic personality structure, Linton's simple dichotomy renders difficult the classification of some achieved roles that carry a heavy freight of ascribed features. For example, the achieved role of a teacher is more imbued with undifferentiated, ascribed components than the achieved role of mathematician. Conversely, the role "Casanova" carries achieved components, although it is derived from an ascribed sex-role. Moreover, since role is a relational concept, any role definition must encompass both the role and its reciprocal. Characteristic of the ascribed roles of person, age, and kinship are primary face-to-face relations in which other's valuations are declared undifferentially to the total person, while valuations of achieved roles are presumably more differentiated and related to specific skills. But here again others' valuations of a teacher are applied more on the basis of his/her general personality and empathic primary interpersonal abilities than valuations of the "crazy mathematician," although both are achieved roles. Since ascribed roles are basic, it would seem that all other roles should be seen as being contingent on the basic ascribed role, *person*, whether these are characterized as achieved or ascribed features. In this sense, it is "basic" that one first be a person, a human being, before he becomes a carpenter or a doctor. For this reason I have introduced the terms primary roles and secondary roles to replace Linton's ascribed and achieved role conceptions (Rotenberg & Sarbin, 1971).

Primary and Secondary Labeling

Roles are engendered by actions; social labels arise from reactions. Very closely related to primary and secondary roles is a feature of social life that relates to the compatibility of identity labels and subsequent social labeling. Either adjectives or nouns can be employed as a reaction to role performance. For example, the descriptive label "schlemiel," denoting the perennial loser or "fall guy," may be assigned to anybody in its adjectival form if his established identity label is not that of a successful striver. It would be useful therefore to expand our conceptual scheme and distinguish between primary labels and secondary labels.

A primary (categoric) label refers to one's established social and self–identity and is related to position, rank, and class. It categorically classifies the individual, in his own eyes and in the eyes of others, as a "success" or "failure" as "in" or "out," "good" or "bad" (Rotenberg, 1978). A primary label is not synonymous with a primary role, since it is not related to any specific roles but rather to the dominant personality-evaluative features attributed to a person in the ongoing process of social typing. A secondary label refers simply to a new, or additional label to be assigned to a person. A secondary label may be descriptive or categorical, positive or negative. Secondary labels can "stick" from the actor's perspective only within the category. If one's primary label is that of an "intellectual," the added secondary label "intellectual bum" is still compatible with this primary label, although it is negative. But the secondary label "bum" cannot stick unless the person is first delabeled as an intellectual. Here it might be noted that in some societies the label "unemployed," or even "schizophrenic" is not necessarily incompatible with the role of respected head of household. The rejecting categorical degradation of "laziness" (Davis, 1938) or of schizophrenia (Goffman, 1961) seem to be more characteristic of Western societies. If a secondary identity label is compatible with one's primary identity label, it may be incorporated into the self identity if the labeler is of primary significance to the labelee. Thus, secondary labels are contingent on the nature of primary labels.

Primary and Secondary Others

How significant must a significant other be in order to have an impact on an actor? The terms significant and relevant other have also been used in the literature without any attempt to differentiate empirically between degrees of significance that various others need in order to affect various actors. In contingency terms, the significance of valuations applied by A to B's secondary role performance is contingent on the kind of valuations applied by A to B's primary role enactment and also on the level of B's acceptance of A's valuations. If B accepts A's definition of himself as a "male" or "person" he is also likely to accept his valuations of him as a teacher. It is a matter of common observation that others may possess varying degrees of significance for an actor, ranging from zero to situationally significant others (e.g., a prison guard to prisoners) to highly significant others whose valuations are incorporated into one's self-identity. Those others whose valuative reactions are incorporated into the self-identity are termed primary others. Audiences who have power or prestige for the actor and whose reactions are situationally significant (e.g., prison guard) are not necessarily incorporated into the self-identity and are here referred to as secondary others (Rotenberg & Sarbin, 1971).

Primary and Secondary Involvement

It has been demonstrated empirically that degree of intensity in role enactment, in terms of time spent, or in emotional and visceral participation, reflect as well as influence one's self-identity (Sarbin & Allen, 1968–1969). Thus, even the best process of anticipatory socialization will have little meaning for self-identity if not validated by actual organismic role involvement,[3] especially if one has been "stripped" of his established identity components. That is, the claims concerning "who I am" will become progressively empty if not supported by my enactment of what I claim to be. Involvements in a role may also range from zero, in which role and self are presumed to be completely differentiated, to maximal involvement, where role and self are presumably fused. Involvement in role behavior or assigned labels may be voluntary or involuntary. In contingency terms, involvement in secondary roles or labels becomes meaningful to self-identity to the extent that involvement in secondary roles is compatible with primary role involvement. If I have a chance to be properly involved in my sex and age roles, and I am evaluated by my primary others as a "person" and a "male," the secondary role "teacher" is meaningful. Similarly, involvement in the masculine role (e.g., Casanova) might be relatively high, even if masculinity was inadequately valued by others or one has had limited opportunities to enact this role previously, because the masculine role is a primary role. Conversely, if I enact the primary role of a "nonperson," the secondary role of "nosy trouble-maker" or "psychotic" is compatible with that role. Thus, for parsimony and conceptual consistency, primary involvement is being used to refer to the nature (intensity, degree) of one's actual enactment of his primary roles and labels, and secondary involvement is being employed to refer to involvement in secondary roles or identity labels.

In summing up the briefly sketched four dimensional "contingent being" model, the usefulness of a culturally linked identity hierarchy could be demonstrated. Based on cultural differentiations between primary personality roles (PPRs) and secondary sociological roles (SSRs), a contingency hierarchy may be so constructed that by arranging identity roles according to their PPR-SSR combinations, the individual's location in an identity hierarchy might be determined. In that sense, age and sex roles will be at the basis as pure primary personality roles and an educator or a priest might be considered as a secondary personality role (as skills required and valuations relate to personality qualities), and a Casanova's role would comprise a primary sociological role. At the top we will find a more pure secondary sociological role, such as a mathematician's role in which socially achieved criteria are the major definers of role-valuations (compare with Sarbin & Scheibe, *this volume.*)

Since ideal identity labels and role valuations are essentially normative and cultural units, PPR-SSR combinations can be roughly located on a continuum between the following two cultural poles. In general, we might assume that on the traditional side most identity roles would require a wide charismatic personality basis (including both some masculine figures in urban slums who might expect to be respected as heads of households even without enacting achieved-occupational roles, and the highly skilled witch doctor) and on the modern side most secondary achieved roles would require a minimal basis of charismatic-personaltiy components (e.g., technicians and mathematicians). In modern societies, however, some primary personality roles might nonetheless require highly complex secondary achieved skills (e.g., the Casanova), and some secondary-achieved roles might require a wide primary-personality basis (e.g., the teacher).

Prison Social Types and Contingent Being

To demonstrate how the model of contingent being may explain vertical dynamic relationships between social and self-identity, I use the example of prison social types.

Prison social types are identity labels associated with specific actions and reactions that prisoners assign to each other. The "right guy" refers to the idealized convict (Irwin, 1970) "who pulls his own number," who is loyal, honest, criminally oriented, and tough. The "inmate" is also a criminally oriented type, but one "who cannot be trusted," who is a "nosy trouble-maker," and one who "would sell his own mother." The "square" type refers to one who "doesn't know anything," who is unfamiliar with both the criminal and the prison system, and who is not criminally oriented. The "politician" is a "big shot," a "con-boss," highest in the prison hierarchy (Mitchell, 1966), and is considered to be a smart inmate who can manipulate others and communicate with both administrators and prisoners without endangering himself.

Reviewing the repertory of prison-labeled identity types, two major questions arise that have direct bearing on the age-old queries about the genesis of the prison culture, on the one hand, and on society's efforts to formulate effective and applicable rehabilitation theories, on the other hand. The first question asks why did the "right guy" become an idealized identity label in the prison in the first place? The second question asks why are the efforts to offer prisoners rehabilitative goals admittedly so unsuccessful in reducing criminal orientation not only of committed criminals but also for incoming "squares"? (Clemmer, 1958; McCorkle & Korn, 1962).

The prison reality can be better explained with the vocabulary of vertical contingency. Since one's secondary being (e.g., rehabilitation roles) is contingent on the state of his primary being, the functionality of social typing has to be examined in the way it relates to the primary or the secondary levels of identity. Based on Cloward and Ohlin's (1960) "differential opportunity" theory, one may assume that in the extramural world the right guy's illegitimate primary being (self-identity) was positive. That is, his primary involvement in age and sex roles (e.g., the pimp lover, etc.) was positively evaluated by criminal primary others. Contingent upon his "positive" primary being, his illegitimate secondary being (underworld professional activities) may also be positive. We may assume also that outside prison walls the "square" type experienced a normal legitimate primary and secondary being (e.g., conventional sex and occupational life). The "inmate" type may have experienced a negative primary and secondary being on the outside, and the politician, on the outside, may have had a chance for both legitimate and illegitimate options for positive primary and secondary being. Upon entering the prison, processes of identity stripping, degradation, and negative reactions are set in operation, largely mortifying the primary identity of all prisoners. That is, prisoners are denied the opportunity to enact age, sex, and kinship roles. Secondary rehabilitative opportunities become irrelevant and meaningless as long as the problems of being, of primary identity, are not solved. To solve the problem of primary identity, the "incoming" prisoner must choose between two general identity options: (1) to accept the nonperson role and the degraded valuative reactions assigned by prison guards and other prisoners, or (2) to enact a quasi-primary role for which he can receive some respect valuations from other prisoners and consequently also from some guards. The psychotic role and the "inmate" social type (e.g., homo, snitch) represent those who have chosen the first alternative. The idealized "right-guy" identity type represents those who have chosen the second option. Consequently, the "right guy" idealized behavior refers to a set of situationally functional role responses to deprivations on the primary identity level of being, which, due to their highly valued status in prison, everybody strives to enact (in front of other prisoners as Rotenberg & Sarbin [1971] have demonstrated), and the "inmate" (distrusted type) behavior is an alternative response to the same problem by those who "cannot make it."

Thus, most criminally oriented prisoners will be preoccupied in trying to enact the quasi-primary role (right guy) and secondary roles will be irrelevant for them. "Inmates" tend to enact prison-oriented quasi-secondary roles compatible with their negative primary being (e.g., stool pigeon, peddlar). Politicians will enact quasi-illegitimate roles compatible with their quasi–primary right guy behavior (e.g., clerk, con-boss), and the "squares" will be severely stressed, being unable to use secondary legitimate opportunities due to their degraded primary identity.

It should be noted that while most prisoners seem to resolve their deprived state of primary being to some extent by enacting substitute quasi-primary roles ("squares" the least and "politicians" the most), secondary roles compatible with prison primary identities are functional only inside the prison and dysfunctional for extramural rehabilitative roles. Moreover, criteria for successful post-institutional adjustment are in general defined exclusively in terms of occupational (secondary) role behavior. Virtually ignored is the crisis involved in reentering primary roles: male, husband, father, etc. Thus, the complexities of conduct can be understood by assessing how performances and evaluative reactions affect the vertical contingent relationship between one's primary identity and secondary identity. Prison social types are used here as a case in point, but the model is applicable to other deviant or conforming types as well. Moreover, assuming that "involvement" and "others" affect states of being, directed or managed involvement in selective roles with selective others may have important implications for rehabilitation and identity transformations.

CONCLUDING IMPLICATIONS

A transformative relabeling model, conceptualized in terms of the "contingent being" framework, requires an operational strategy that brings about drastic changes on the primary level of being (i.e., a new sense of being and a new answer to "who am I?"). Such can be attained only through disinvolvement in the old primary label via differentially directed involvement in an alternate primary identity and with a different set of primary others.

In reviewing the diverse literature describing self-reconstitution processes, such as conversion, shamanism, thought reform, Synanon, and military indoctrination, Sarbin and Adler (1971) identified specific operational phases common to most change systems. These include destruction of the old identity, influence of others, and ritual involvement in a new identity.

Indeed, socialization in early Christian groups (Mowrer, 1964), in contemporary Hasidic groups (Buber, 1958), or in Messianic cults (Katcher & Katcher, 1967) are well marked by ritual processes in which the individual is totally and organismically involved to foster specific labeled identities pertaining to the primary level of being. This involvement is accompanied by an enlarged sense of community or comraderie ("others").

In order to change a person in desirable directions, it is not sufficient to subject him to degradation ceremonies (Garfinkel, 1956) to destroy his primary being, and then to "cage or store" him, even if supportive therapy is offered as is the case in most prisons or mental institutions. The reconstruction of identity fails to take place because an authoritarian social structure enhances the inevitable social distance between the formal and the informal systems in the institution, which, in turn, prevents staff members from becoming primary others for inmates. Moreover, it exposes the uninvolved, available, and frustrated prisoner or patient to the managed involvement of other prisoners or patients. In the case of the prison social structure, the management of involvement creates the conditions for the "right guy," a quasi-primary identity.

Such a conception of directed involvement to change contingent beings was inadvertently applied with considerable success by Synanon groups (Yablonsky, 1965). In these groups, resocialization was accomplished by first drastically forcing the newcomer to switch from the right guy primary being to that of enacting the dependent "child" primary role, and only later in a developmental sequence was he helped to establish his compatible secondary roles.

Thus, delabeling of a negative primary type must be followed by a complete process of desirable primary relabeling, as in Pygmalion. This requires constant involvement in that identity (e.g., dancing, singing, meditation, working) and reinforcement by specially labeled others (e.g., gurus, coaches, "brothers") who become increasingly significant due to their functional modeling power and support. Only after the new primary being is relatively established via positive relabeling (e.g., I am a monk, "hippie," or "Hasid") do compatible secondary occupational roles become more relevant and more readily enacted.

Here our vertical perspective might contribute new insights to our Hasidic case, which was discussed in the first section, mainly from the sociological structural angle. While the revolutionary effectiveness of eighteenth–century Hasidic identity relabeling movement may, indeed, be attributed to the structural multiple identity dimension, one must remember that its power as an actualizing system followed to a great extent from the fact that it helped people to change their primary identity and regain their self-respect as human beings.

Since Hasidism did not offer people an economic secondary occupational salvation, it is only the total ecstatic involvement process in the new identity, Hasid, which was highly valued by selective significant others. This construction throws light on why secondary occupations of low status lost most of their degrading effect for these people.

Thus, by drawing together the implications contained in both cases presented above we may now conclude that both the Hasid and the prison "right guy" became ideal and even idealized identity labels because they offered relabeling solutions to primary identity deprivations. While any secondary ideal identity might entail actualizing power if it is not incongruent with one's primary identity, the positive relabeling of the derogatory identity label "ignoramus" was possible because of the structural multilabeling breakthrough and legitimation of the new positive ideal identity label, Hasid, which prescribed actualization through adherence to the ecstatic and not to scholarship. Analysis of the "right guy" identity suggests further that in a mono-ideal-identity system increased frustration and scarcity in primary identity fulfillment will increase the number of negative ideal identity labels.

Additional ramifications pertaining to horizontal and vertical components of social identity are beyond the scope of the present chapter and are treated elsewhere (Rotenberg, 1978, 1982). I have tried to show how a sociological perspective is necessary to explain the proportion of people with negative identities, and the dysfunctional effects may be structurally minimized through the horizontal expansion of the multiple ideal identity system. From a psychological point of view, the personal meaning of such multiple-ideal-identity labels is contingently dependent on the vertical congruency between secondary ideal labels and their concurrent actualization outlets for primary identity roles.

NOTES

1. According to the official figures of the Social Security Administration, actual per capita income continues to grow in the United States, and hence the rate of poverty will continue to decrease. The dispute between Utopians, Dystopians, and Socialists as to how to calculate the poverty line (Gendron, 1977) is not central to the present perspective.

2. With the decline of Talmudic studies in the eighteenth and nineteenth centuries, the label *Haver* was bestowed upon people in Eastern Europe and especially in Germany, not on the original criterion of Talmudic scholarship, but simply to express respect to good, conforming congregationalists.

3. To use an extreme example: it would seem inconceivable that one could become a combat soldier through correspondence.

Chapter 9

ETHNICITY AND ETHNIC IDENTITY: TAMING THE UNTAMED

Ki-Taek Chun

Intended as a prelude toward a psychological study of ethnic identity, this essay considers pertinent background issues and proposes that ethnic identity be conceptualized as a socioepistemic self-emplacement. By exploring some of the ensuing implications, we show that the proposed conceptual framework helps us tame the phenomena of ethnicity and ethnic identity into a manageable inquiry.

ETHNICITY: NEGLECT, DISCOVERY AND ABUSE

Recalling some of the bestsellers published in the late 1960s and early 1970s or popular television shows of the same period, one would have to agree that the 1970s was indeed a decade of ethnicity. Based on an overview of books published, new journals formed, and prominent journal articles, Williams observed in his 1975 *Annual Review of Sociology* chapter that a "rediscovery of ethnicity was evident by 1968 and increasingly conspicuous thereafter" (p. 127). The trend has continued to gain momentum so that observers noted, "a wave of ethnic feeling is . . . sweeping over America" (Glazer, 1974, p. 55) "resulting in a great reordering of identities . . . among

For his enlightening companionship in moments of solitary pursuit and his ready supply of clarifying questions and edifying references, I am indebted to Theodore R. Sarbin. My appreciation extends to David J. Harris and Howard H. Garrison for stimulating discussions, and to Sandra S. Tangri for her support in the early days of my interest in ethnicity. This essay gained immeasurably in coherence and readability from the thorough editing rendered by the editors of this volume and the helpful comments by Margaret G. Hodge. I am also grateful to Cathy Somers for those long hours she spent at the WANG terminal.

all kinds of Americans" (Isaacs, 1972, p. 76). In short, American society was being "reethnicized" (Alter, 1972; Friedman, 1971, pp. 15–53; Meister, 1974).

The celebrative mood of rediscovery is puzzling to some and sobering to others. The subscribers of "melting pot" and "Americanization" ideology would either question the genuineness of a resurgence or consider it a "dying gasp" (Steinberg, 1981, p. 51). On the other hand, the believers in the notion that the United States remains a nation of immigrants and immigrant ethnic groups are amused by the innocent excitement of discovery. For example, while some investigators were "surprised by the persistence and salience of ethnic-based forms of social identification and conflict" (e.g., Glazer & Moynihan, 1974, p. 33), others continued to deplore the long tradition of neglecting ethnicity as a respectable topic. Novak (1977) points out that

> For over a generation most social scientists in America have considered ethnicity a fading dysfunctional variable; the emphasis of their research has fallen upon terms such as race, class, and caste, to the exclusion of ethnicity. Since the early 1970's a burst of work has attempted to bring the discussion of ethnicity to comparable sophistication, but the state of this discussion is nevertheless still primitive. (p. 26)

In a similar vein, Greeley (1969) remarks,

> The historians of the future will be astonished that American sociologists, the product of this gathering in of nations, could stand in the midst of such an astonishing social phenomenon and take it so much for granted that they would not bother to study it. (p. 5)

Speaking on this matter, the eminent historian Oscar Handlin also observes that "only a handful of scholars glanced at ethnic problems between 1940 and 1960" (Handlin, 1979, p. 401).

To the theme of general neglect, Himmelfarb (1974) adds a new dimension:

> Fifteen and twenty years ago, when ethnicity was thought to be dead or dying, and anyway of little importance, I suspected that the news of its death had been exaggerated . . . Now that the pendulum has swumg, I am perversely inclined to suspect that the news of ethnicity's robust health has been exaggerated. (p. 69)

He suggests that the resurgence of interest in ethnicity is not so much indigenous to the intrinsic needs of intradisciplinary inquiries, as it is the product of the time and its particular alignment of economic and political forces. These forces, which indirectly mold and fashion social scientists' inquiry into ethnic phenomena, are the topic of our next section. In the meantime, we need to make explicit two contemporary connotations or surplus meanings associated with ethnicity since they are disruptive to a sustained inquiry.

In its contemporary usage, ethnicity, or interest in ethnic phenomena, is often used synonymously either with anti-civil-rights philosophy and neoconservatism, or with the self-serving pursuit of narrowly defined group interests. It is also viewed as a white backlash in disguise against the civil rights movement, or as the advocacy of one group's self-interest over another's.

The benefits of the civil rights developments were perceived to accrue only to the "visible" minorities (blacks, Hispanics, and Asian Americans), and this perception has triggered a sharp reaction from those of European descent. Schermerhorn (1974) observes that their plaint became louder: "We never get our way by burning down buildings, by using brute force or mob violence. Until we have law and order, nobody will get what he wants." He concludes that "it was in this overheated atmosphere that the new ethnicity was born" (pp. 8–9). Meister (1974) makes a similar point when he notes

> At times black gains came at the expense of the blue-collar workers. The white working class felt oppressed, felt as if it were made solely responsible for the sins of racism. Ethnicity became a means to counter it. (p. xvii)

In addition, partly because "liberals believed that ethnicity had disappeared" when ethnicity began to manifest itself, liberals saw it "only as a cover for racism" (Meister, 1974, p. xviii). Novak (1971) provides some concrete examples of how civil rights movements sometimes conflicted with the interests of working white ethnics. (Recent incidents where minorities ended up in adversarial positions are discussed by Perlmutter, 1980.)

Another connotation derives from the demand of white ethnics that they be recognized as victims of past discrimination and holders of "separate but equal" heritages, entitled to special consideration and protection by governmental agencies. As their demands were recognized, it was natural that a new class of "professional ethnics, self-appointed and unemployed former civil rights fighters" came into being (Isaacs, 1972, p. 76). With the rising rhetoric and political maneuvering, the extent of the underlying grass-roots support was questioned (Edwards, 1977). The recognition of such politics of self-interest led Senator George McGovern to identify the pluralism of the 1970s as the "politics of interest groups" (1977).[1]

Needless to say, neither of these imputations is conducive to developing a sustained, unbiased inquiry. They tend to trivialize ethnic phenomena by deflecting our attention from their crucial psychological and sociological aspects, and diminish interest in scholarly work on ethnicity. Being aware of such connotational trappings might help us safeguard the legitimacy of scholarly interests in ethnicity.

ETHNICITY: OVERSHADOWED BY DEMOCRATIC IDEOLOGY AND ASSIMILATIONISM

Central to our purpose is the observation that the ideas of ethnic diversity and pluralism have long been considered alien to the premises of Western democratic ideology. Enloe (1973, pp. 35–83) reminds us that every ideology seeks to define the basic unit of society: Marxism points to class, a collective entity, and the democratic tradition focuses on individuals apart from any collective body with which they may associate. Since it is as individuals that people are born into this world to inherit rights and obligations, to treat individuals as members of ethnic, religious, and other groups and to accord rights, obligations, and opportunity based on group membership is fundamentally foreign to democratic ideology. Western democracy is potentially hostile to ethnicity and favors deethnicization. This inherent dilemma is what prompted Bell to observe wryly that "the . . . attack on discrimination was based on its denial of a justly earned place to a person on the basis of an unjust group attribute. . . .[But] the demand for [proportionate] representation on the basis of an ascriptive principle is [a] complete reversal" (Bell, 1973, p. 418).

Operating within the broad framework of democratic ideology, scholars in the field of world development and international affairs have been persuaded by the assimilationist perspective. They assumed that, with modernization and industrial development, ethnicity would eventually disappear and be replaced by universalism. If ethnicity persisted, it was a transitory phenomenon, hence, unworthy of serious attention. Consequently ethnicity was relegated to the sidelines of our intellectual arena. Connor (1977), Lijphart (1977), and Cheung (1979) all describe how undue optimism was placed on the future development of supranationalism replacing nationalism and other regionalisms, and how such assimilative outlook led to ignoring the signs of persistent, sometimes increasing, ethnic assertions and then to missing the warning signals of ethnic conflict. Huntington had in mind such assimilationist willful neglect of ethnic factors and its consequent insensitivity when he said, "The concept of political development serves in effect as a signal of scholarly preferences rather than as a tool for analytic purposes" (1971, p. 304).

The dominance of the assimilationist perspective has been undisputed throughout the history of our nation in all fields of intellectual endeavors, as well as in our national policies regarding immigrants. In recent years, many authors have articulated the deep-rooted nature of assimilationist dominance and its prohibitive impact on the alternative perspective of pluralism (Gleason, 1979; Greenbaum, 1974; Higham, 1975; Mathews, 1970; Swierenga, 1977; Wacker, 1979).[2]

Metzger (1971), Singer (1962), and Taylor (1979) among others have shown how assimilationism has both shaped the tenor of sociological thinking and circumscribed the range of research questions on race and ethnic relations in the United States. According to Metzger (1971), this assimilationist bias is partly responsible for the failure of the social sciences to anticipate the turmoils of the late 1960s. The assimilationist's implicit definition as well as image of U.S. society is essentially one of Horatio Alger and the melting pot: ethnic and racial groups are inevitably incorporated into the mainstream of culture; minority problems, therefore, are problems of provision of opportunity for minority members to ascend as individuals into the mainstream; the ascendance to full participation in the "American way of life" is facilitated by, and presupposes, discarding one's ethnicity. In short, assimilation serves as the "embodiment of the democratic ethos" (Metzger, 1971, p. 628).

Once the diminishing importance of ethnicity and the inevitable assimilation of ethnic groups are assumed, one's attention naturally turns to questions of language learning, adjustment, acculturation, social and economic mobility, integration, etc. One asks, for example, how English language acquisition influences upward social mobility rather than asking whether English can be learned effectively in a bicultural, as opposed to Americanization, setting. One becomes disinclined to ask if learning English could be effective without discarding one's non-English, home language: such questions on multilingual learning would strike the assimilationist as quaint and distractive. One may study residential relocation in terms of occupational achievement and attributed personality characteristics rather than in terms of social support, which the potential relocators derive from membership in an ethnic community. One could celebrate the rising rate of interethnic marriages without wondering either about the conditions under which interethnic and intraethnic marriages take place or about the consequences of these marriage patterns. Nonconforming behaviors are likely to be categorized as adjustment problems, and, once so categorized, they are studied in relation to a host of demographic and psychological variables. But they are not studied in terms of whether ethnic communities may have been providing a basis for social self-definition and behavioral norms.

As a result of the assimilationist dominance, the study of ethnicity has either been neglected or tended to be externalistic, reflecting the pre-dilections of "outsiders." In pointing out such built-in insensitivity, we do not intend to invoke the etic–emic dilemma or to allow ourselves to slip into what Merton labels the "doctrine of Insiderism" (1972, pp. 11–30). For the purpose of rebalancing our perspective, we merely wish to note that assimilationism has restricted the range of permissable questions and has encouraged only the most obvious questions. It is on this ground that Nobles (1973) objects to the traditional approach to the psychology of black selfhood.

In addition to intellectual bias, the atmosphere of assimilationist domination has wrought another insidious consequence—the climate of ethnic denigration. Ethnic artifacts and interest in ethnic phenomena were viewed as insignificant, as residual oddities. At best, ethnicity was some-thing to outgrow and discard—something to play down. At worst, ethnicity was a source of shame. The climate of ethnic stigmatization was indeed pervasive: it is reflected in novels from different periods; it is echoed repeatedly by many citizen testimonies; and it is equally evident in autobiographical recollections.[3]

In this connection, Vecoli (1971) provides one of the most telling accounts of the constrictive effects on academic professionals brought about by the climate of ethnic denigration. He notes that although sons of European immigrants began to enter social science professions in the 1920s and 1930s (the first generation of Ph.D.s being largely from middle-class Protestants of old stock), the primary function of higher education in the United States was to "assimilate talented youth from all segments of society to the Anglo-American core culture . . . .As emancipated intellectuals, [the scholars of ethnic background] reject[ed] the narrow parochialisms and tribal loyalties of their youth" (pp. 174–176). In illustration of this point, he cites the response of one of the Italian-American scholars who were invited to participate in a study of Italian-Americans:

> I am too concerned with trying to erase all national boundaries—and nationalisms—to be enthusiastic about activities delineating any national groups . . . .I do not believe there is room for an Italian minority. I suggest that Italians or persons of Italian origin have no recourse but to merge into the majority. (Vecoli, 1971, p. 176)

Recognizing that the academic milieu has generally not encouraged the pursuit of ethnic interests, he ponders "how many graduate students have shied away from research topics for fear they would be suspected of ethnic chauvinism?" (p. 177). Even if the situation may have changed in the 1970s, his observations remain a sobering warning.

ETHNIC IDENTITY: A CONTINUING CONCERN

Despite the atmosphere of general neglect by scholars, and despite ethnic denigration and assimilationist domination discussed earlier, a discernible stream of interest in ethnic phenomena has persisted. This flow of interest constitutes the backdrop of contemporary developments and, if explored historically, could yield considerable dividends. It would not only lead us to a rich source of the raw materials of ethnic phenomena, but also instill an awareness of historical continuity. Our examination of some of these historical materials indicates that an underlying, central theme has been the question of ethnic identity. Until historians provide us with a detailed history of ethnicity that brings the earlier works into contemporary scholarship, an emphasis on historicity is in order to prevent conceptual impoverishment.

We begin with a few examples of early work. First, always prominent in the pages of the *Menorah Journal* (see Alter, 1965, for an epitaph of the *Journal*), the predecessor of *Commentary*, were topics of immigrant and descendent groups in U.S. society and their social status, their settlement patterns and relationships with the host society, and the question of their self-definition.[4] Second, themes of anticipation and frustration, success and disappointment, and pains and agonies of immigrant life filled the literary works of early twentieth-century ethnic writers such as Louis Adamic, Abraham Cahan, and Anzia Yezierska.[5] Third, Horace Kallen's advocacy of cultural pluralism, spanning over a period of three decades starting from the 1910s, was permeated with a prominent motif of securing one's selfhood in full recognition of ethnic heritage. In one of his early essays "Democracy versus Melting Pot," he wrote

> Man may change their clothes, their politics, their wives, their religions, their philosophies, . . . [but] they cannot change their grandfathers. Jews and Poles . . . would have to cease to be . . . . The selfhood which is inalienable to them . . . is ancestrally determined, and the happiness which they pursue has its form implied in ancestral endowment. This is what, actually, democracy in operation assumes. (1924, pp. 122–123)

Remaining close to the pulse of cultural diversity in our society, Louis Adamic wrote on the elusive quest of identity by immigrants in a new setting and on the disquieting effects of new identity. At one point he said

> They have got rid of their badges of alienism and become "Americans," but they are not at ease. In secretly discarding their 'foreign' labels. . . . [they] are severed from what are normally the most vital influences in one's

life . . . . They pretend to be something they are not. Behind their fronts and new handles they are still Hunkies, Litvaks, Kikes or Wops. (p. 60)

To many people the problem of their own identity is inextricably concerned with that of finding their natural place. (Adamic, 1942, p. 75)

In 1960, by way of extending the "triple melting pot" theory introduced earlier by Kennedy (1944), Herberg suggested that traditional ethnic groups were merging into three religious groups (Protestants, Catholics, and Jews). In this influential study of American ethnic groups he noted that "belonging" depends on the concrete situation. Religious affiliation, according to him, is one expression of a person's "belonging." With changing situations the underlying imperative for "belonging" may take on another form of expression. Religious or ethnic affiliations, then, are variants of self-location in the larger social fabric. Whether one defines oneself in reference to religious groups or to ethnicity is determined by the constraints of societal forces operating at a given time in history. When religious, ethnic, and national identities are not coterminous, they are potent sources of conflictful mobilization. Recent troubles and tragedies in Iran and Egypt may be viewed as instances of such competing identity mobilization.[6]

The 1970s expression of this imperative to belong, or define one's self, is ethnic identity. To borrow some catchy phrasing, it is said that "the new ethnicity is an expression of their [i.e., ethnics'] identity crisis along with their repudiation of the Wasp cultural soul" (Tolzmann, 1972, p. 22) and also that "the major premise of the New Ethnicity is the primordiality of ethnic identity, that is, ethnicity is the core of human identity" (Stein & Hill, 1977, p. 41).

Moving forward now, the example of the third generation hypothesis illustrates our points of historical discontinuity and its impoverishing consequences. In its simplest form, it proclaims "what the son wishes to forget, the grandson wishes to remember."[7] As Abramson notes, for some 30 years now this third-generation hypothesis has been "a provocative and persisting question in the social sciences in the United States" (1975, p. 163). The historian Marcus Lee Hansen elaborated on the theme in 1938 (Hansen, 1952).

However, writing in the 1930s about ethnic people in the United States, the Slovenian-American writer, Louis Adamic, mentioned in passing,

Some time before I had read in a magazine that second-generation Americans, children of immigrants of most nationalities, had a tendency to feel ashamed of their parents and repudiate their racial background, to draw away from people of their own blood; while third-generation

Americans, the immigrants' grandchildren, tended very strongly to return—or, rather, to seek out people of their racial strains and discover their backgrounds. (1935, p. 85)

Apparently Adamic did not consider the idea worthy of special documentation or elaboration since it was in popular circulation. Our concern here is not the issue of original authorship, but the consequence wrought upon our contemporary scholarship by a narrow historical perspective. An awareness that the idea was in popular circulation around 1930, long before its formalization by academicians, would have directed students of ethnicity to the popular culture and to the ethnic literature of earlier periods, thereby recognizing the complexity of the third-generation phenomenon.

Had the raw materials of earlier ethnic literature been within the boundary of social sciences, we might not have had to wait until ethnographers reminded us that ethnicity is entangled with class phenomena (e.g., Sennett & Cobb, 1972). Nor should we have had to wait for empirical researchers to speculate on the effects of education and social mobility on the return of the third generation (e.g., Abramson, 1975, p. 172). Our impoverished contextual comprehension of the phenomenon as well as our neglect of its historicity seems to have caused the delay in recognizing the moderating effects of class, occupation, education, and socioeconomic status on the third-generation phenomenon. These demographic variables contribute to the self-perception of a person, as a member of an immigrant/ethnic group, in relation to other groups or their members. The nature of one's resulting ethnic self-definition may determine the acceptance or rejection of ethnicity at any generational point (see Section V for further elaboration of this point). Clearly, future studies of ethnic identity would benefit from an explicit accommodation to its historicity.

ETHNIC IDENTITY AS SELF-EMPLACEMENT IN SOCIOEPISTEMIC ECOLOGY

It is disappointing to read the literature on ethnic identity and ethnicity for clues on alternative conceptual approaches: one is struck by the lack of attention to definitional and conceptual aspects. Ethnic identity has surfaced as a "celebrity" concept, hiding the underlying definitional ambiguity with its glitter and intimidating the raising of questions on terminological imprecision and conceptual boundaries. The meaning attached to ethnic identity varies widely: at one extreme it is a mere demographic ascriptive category, a classificatory label; at the other extreme it refers to the core of personality, the Eriksonian basic stratum of one's selfhood. Sometimes, the meaning shifts from one to the other extreme for individual authors.[8]

In recent years, however, we have begun to recognize the over-extended use of the term *ethnic identity*. Harold Isaacs provides a picturesque description that captures the state of enthusiasm and its accompanying imprecision. In 1975, he observed that

> In recent seasons especially, there have been dozens of academic safaris in the field, especially American safaris, tracking the snowman of "ethnicity," everyone sure by now that it exists and is important, more important than most thoughts, but no one sure what it looks like, much less whether it is abominable or not.... It also has to be partly due to the fact that the reality represented by all these terms is in fact imprecise, full of contradictions and uncertainties.... (p. 27–28)

Glazer and Moynihan (1974) also make a similar observation in their commentary "Why ethnicity." The situation did not seem to improve much, and in 1978 Pettigrew was led to note that "like time, we are agreed upon its [i.e., ethnicity's] importance," but unable to measure it or "rescue it fully from heated ideological usage" (p. 25).

The enormity of this loose usage and conceptual imprecision is easy to see. Based on an analysis of 65 studies,[9] Isajiw (1974) concluded that "very few researchers ... ever define the meaning of ethnicity.... [Of these 65 studies] only 13 included some definition ... and 52 had no explicit definition at all" (p. 111). Definitional inattention is obvious even in those studies whose explicit purpose is quantification of ethnic identity. According to a recent review of ethnic identity measures (Chun & Harris, 1977), more than half of the measures in current usage (i.e., 11 out of 20) had no provisions for what is being quantified, and only nine of the 20 measures had what may be considered a definition (or sometimes a rudiment of a definition) of the subject matter (p. 52).

Terminological imprecision and definitional inattention may have been encouraged in part by the tendency of some researchers who, out of respect for the complexity of the phenomenon itself, refused to be bogged down with definitional matters. This purposive reluctance at definitions reached its articulate height in none other than Erikson himself. Isaacs describes well the sophisticated complexity of such reluctance:

> Erikson's deliberate imprecision ... speaks to the complexity and elusiveness of the matter he seeks to deal with—even the term "identity" itself is never pinned down in pages but allowed, as he says, to speak for itself in its various connotations. (1975, p. 25)

Indeed Erikson himself is clear about the undefinability of the concept:

> [Ethnic identity] alternately circumscribe[s] something so large and so seemingly self-evident that to demand a definition would almost seem

petty, while at other times they designate something made so narrow for purposes of measurement that the overall meaning is lost, and it could just as well be called something else. (1968b, p. 150)

Because of a tendency for overenthusiasm and an accompanying inattention to the underlying logic of inquiry, basic theoretical work on ethnic identity has been scarce (Herman, 1970, p. 13) and its paucity persisted throughout the 1970s (Kelman, 1977, p. 9). Basic work in this area has begun only in recent years (e.g., Dashefsky, 1975, 1976; Devereux, 1975; Epstein, 1978; Herman, 1977; Horowitz, 1975; Isajiw, 1974; Obidinski, 1978).

Insistence on definitional matters, if premature, could easily constrict the breadth of one's perspective, trivialize issues, or oversimplify the phenomenon under scrutiny. Moreover, definitional products tend to be viewed as givens inherent in the phenomenon—after all, names outlast "things" named, taking on a life of their own through reification (Chun & Sarbin, 1970; Sarbin, 1968c). In a spirit of tentativism, we propose in this section a socioepistemic approach to ethnic identity as a component of social identity and examine in the next section some of the implications that stem from this approach.

As an implicit axiom, we assume that as creatures living in a world of relationships and meanings, we continually strive to place and define ourselves in this world. This world of relationships and meanings consists, on the one hand, of social role relations and, on the other, of persistent existential questions. The questions may center on social and political issues, or philosophical and cosmological perplexities. Not all questions are equally operative in all of us; the answers may be normative in that they are socially provided or unique in that they have been arrived at individually.

The way our role relations are construed and the way the epistemic questions are answered lead to the construal of the sense of a person being a distinct individual or a member of a distinct group. To place oneself in this world of social relationships and ontological questions—which for expository convenience I will call a socioepistemic world—is to define oneself in terms of each relationship or question as well as the total configuration; that is, to clarify *who one is* and to articulate one's stance from other stances. Self-emplacement, viewed as such a clarification, is to become aware of a particular socioepistemic configuration among possible alternatives and to recognize one line of differentiation as distinct from others. By social identity we mean this awareness of socioepistemic configuration and the recognition of a particular differentiation as distinct from other placement possibilities. We speak of *ethnic identity*, then, when the markers of effective differentiation and the underlying symbols of configuration are ethnic.

Having proposed ethnic identity as self-emplacement in a socioepistemic world inhabited by ethnic markers, several comments are in order regarding this definition. First, with the inclusion of epistemic components in its domain, social identity—a component of which is ethnic identity—takes on an aspect of self-knowledge. This usage is not as unusual as it may seem. In elaborating on the proximate, social, and cosmological ecologies as the embedding context in which a person answers the questions "Who am I?" and "What am I?," Sarbin and Scheibe (*this volume*) included those self-defining cognitive elements. Langbaum (1977) writes that modern literature's concern with identity is essentially a quest for self-knowledge. Through ample illustrations he shows that this quest involves defining one's place in the universe in terms of relationships to people and issues. This striving for self-knowledge and self-awareness, for self-definition, for self-emplacement in the socioepistemic world, seems basic and enduring.[10]

Second, we should note that to become aware of socioepistemic differentiation is to distinguish one role relationship from another and to impose a boundary between oneself and others, between "we" and "they," between one stance and other contrasting stances. As Barth (1969) has done with ethnic groups, to emphasize demarcation and boundary as effective definiens is to view social or ethnic identity as primarily a matter of boundary setting. The question of how a boundary gets set has priority and the question of what is contained within and enclosed by the boundary is secondary. It is, therefore, important to separate ethnic identity from the characteristics or traits commonly associated with ethnicity: that is, to distinguish the sense of boundary from what is enclosed by the boundary. Ethnic characteristics (such as the elaborate form of handshaking among urban blacks, the "grunting" expression of greeting or slight bowing on social encounters among Asian Americans, the combination of hugging and handshaking among Chicanos) may be mere, inconsequential characteristics observable among members of an ethnic group. Or they may be symbolic markers with which the members themselves draw a line of differentiation. Symbols and markers of ethnic identity are seldom invariant: identifying the operative symbols is a vital task in understanding the dynamics of ethnic identity.[11]

Third, the awareness of a "we" and "they" separation is likely to lead to its corollary: "they" treat "me" not as "I" but as one of the "we" group. This realization of ascriptive dumping, the recognition of ascriptive categorization prevailing over individuals as unique social objects, gives rise to the distinction between ethnic identity at the individual level and ethnic identity at the collective group level (see Parming, 1976, for a recent effort at this distinction). In this connection, we may note that the assertive manifestation of collective ethnic identity and its effective mobilization has been the hallmark of recent ethnic phenomena (for example, see Clark, 1967, regarding the case of the black movement). To the extent that collective ethnic mobilization is mediated by group ethnic identity, the resulting distinction between the individual and the group version of ethnic identity is crucial in comprehending the consequences of enhanced ethnic identity in the contemporary scene.

IMPLICATIONS OF SOCIOEPISTEMIC CONCEPTION OF ETHNIC IDENTITY

Once we advance ethnic identity as a self-emplacement, or a sense of differentiation, whose boundary is set off by ethnic markers and sustained by appropriate symbols,[12] several questions confront us for clarification and elaboration. These questions have to do not only with the process of differentiation, but also with the multiplicity of social identities or socio-epistemic differentiations and the situational specificity of ethnic identity.

To begin with the multiplicity issue, because there are many social roles and role relationships, the socioepistemic differentiation mediated by ethnic markers is merely one of many differentiations. Although the idea of multiple social roles has been recognized from the time of William James, a systematic effort at the problem of differentiating among constituent selves has been scanty. The extent to which ethnic identity can be studied in isolation from other social identities remains unexplored. When social commentators note that ethnic identity is replacing occupational identity, do they mean the salience of ethnic identity over other social identities as a center of one's self-definition? Or do they mean the overriding dominance of ethnic identity over other identities that are at best so underdeveloped that ethnic identity alone serves as the exclusive source of self-definition? The review by Isajiw (1974) did not find any indication as to how ethnicity is to intersect with social class, occupation, political party affiliation, and the like. Thus, it remains unknown how ethnic identity is to be viewed in relation to class, occupational, and political party identities. The review of ethnic identity measures by Chun & Harris (1977) notes that none of the 20 measures adopted a configurational approach in quantifying ethnic identity, an approach that would pay explicit attention to the configuration of ethnic identity with other social identities. Behavioral problems such as the fanaticism and rigidity of, say, ethnic/religious extremists in the Mideast, which are characterized by the failure to respond to varying demand characteristics across situations, may be looked at in terms of a configuration of constituent identities. If one's identity set consists of one strong identity and others that are weak, there will be a greater likelihood of intersituational rigidity (Turner, 1978). Likewise, obsession with racial discrimination irrespective of the nuance of each situation may be a case wherein only ethnic/racial identity has been propelled into an operative dominance at the expense of other identities.

While it remains a future challenge, the multiplicity issue of constituent identities also raises a corollary question of situational specificity. Does one's identity change with changes in situation? As is well demonstrated by research on role demands (Sarbin & Allen, 1968–1969) and the recent debate on the situational determinancy of behavior over personality disposition (see Ekehamman, 1974, and Mischel, 1979, for updating reviews), it is not new to say that one's behavior changes in line with the perceived demand characteristics of changing situations. However, the demonstration of situational potency and the specification of situational cues remain a task for future research. For example, is a Chicano youth's self-definition governed by the same markers when he/she interacts with an exclusively Anglo group, an exclusively Chicano group, or a mixed group? Questions of this nature are legion, but their answers are scanty. Accounts of both multiple constituent identities and their situational markers are necessary to pursue a configurational approach. A useful beginning in charting the multiplicity of constituent identities has been provided by Bell (1975) and Young (1976). Recognizing that multiple sociological units serve as bases of social identity, Bell discusses macrosocial units (e.g., nation, religion, class, color, and language) and suggests a list of micro- as well as intermediate-level social units (neighborhood and family as examples of microunits, and political party and geographic region as intermediate units) (1975, pp. 152–160). Using an example of a hypothetical Native American Indian, Young demonstrates the drawing of a role-identity map that consists of occupational, social status roles at one end and national, religious roles at the other (1976, pp. 38–39). In deliberating the issue of multiple identities, both Bell and Young maintain that identity choice or claim is situationally determined:

> At particular times . . . one specific identification becomes primary and overriding. . . . But there is no general rule to state which identification it might be. (Bell, 1975, p. 159)

> The role selected in response to any given situation depends upon the definition and perception of the particular events, the context in which messages are received, and anticipation of the possible consequences which the events may have. (Young, 1976, p. 38)

Cultural anthropologists report observations which indicate that operative identities indeed change in conformance with situational requirements and identity claims vary according to situation and audience.[13] In our future pursuit, we might do well to remember that the configurational approach would center around the theme of "integrative identity": that is, how constituent identities are organized in relation to each other.

Germane to considering the process of differentiation are three issues: (1) the source of differentiation, (2) the markers that set boundaries and symbols that sustain existing boundaries, and (3) the context in which differentiation takes place. The impetus for ethnic differentiation may originate either from within, choosing to set oneself apart from others (i.e., self-initiated), or from without, being set apart involuntarily by others (i.e., externally imposed upon by others).

Self-initiated ethnic differentiation usually involves a self-serving element. Setting oneself apart or separating one's ingroup from the rest enhances one's social status or group solidarity, or protects the privileged position, which may be social, economic, or political in nature. A most detailed illustration of such self-generated differentiation can be found in the account given by Woods (1972). She shows how the Letoyant Creoles (the descendants of a Frenchman named Letoyant and a woman of African ancestry, now living in Riverville, Louisiana) set themselves apart from other blacks despite the latter's hostility against such separation. A sense of common history can also accelerate the process of ethnic differentiation (Blu, 1977; Yinger, 1964).

If the self-initiated differentiation enhances the position of either oneself or one's ingroup, the externally imposed differentiation has in general the effect of social degradation, that is, the effect of assigning a position of lower status or less power. While the self-generated differentiation may constitute a self-enhancing mark of distinction, the externally imposed one often creates social barriers that help preserve the existing social stratification and the status quo of privilege and position. In fact, the split labor market theory of ethnic relations explicitly rests on the notion that external differentiation is motivated by the differentiator's desire to preserve its economic advantage over the differentiated (Bonacich, 1979). Because of its devaluing consequence, the externally imposed differentiation has debilitating effects on children. A youngster who has been unaware of ethnic or racial differentiation may one day be forced to realize that his/her peers consider him/her, not as one of them, but as one belonging to a social outgroup. This discovery of externally imposed emplacement into a socially devalued, degraded group is a frequent occurrence in those minority youths who have grown up in a protective family atmosphere of assimilationist orientation. The pleas by minority adolescents that "I am an American, too," a popular theme of mass media coverage in the 1970s, are reverberating reactions to this discovery (see Chun, 1980, for a review of Asian-American youth).

Once the forces favoring a particular differentiation are set in motion, certain cues like physical appearance, language, religious and food preferences, and the like are seized upon as markers to guide differentiation and then to reinforce and confirm existing differentiation. Choice of particular markers is almost incidental to the underlying forces pushing for particular differentiation. As such, markers may be substituted; chosen markers serve as symbols rather than as markers that enforce a particular differentiation by virtue of their intrinsic properties. Potential markers encompass a wide variety: they may be a common historical memory, a sense of common fatedness, a particular language or dialect, dietary habits and preferences, or other cultural practices and traits. But little is known of how one cue is selected over other cues as markers and symbols of ethnic identity.

Because markers are often characteristic of the ethnic group being circumscribed, it is tempting to view ethnic identity in terms of the group's characteristics. That is, since the markers of boundary as well as what is enclosed by the boundary are characteristic of the group, it is easy to lump together the boundary markers and the enclosed characteristics. To view what is enclosed by ethnic boundary as definers of ethnic identity, however, is not only to miss the essence of ethnic identity, but to commit a serious logical error. If a paper-and-pencil measure of ethnic identity consisted of items descriptive of the enclosed characteristics such as ethnic food preference, use of ethnic language or dialect, and cultural or religious practices, the gradual diminution over time of these habits, preferences, and practices is likely to lead to the inference of declining ethnic identity. Ethnic habits, preferences, and practices are likely to weaken over the years and across generations, but the sense of ethnic identity or ethnic self-definition may be determined or reawakened by a totally different set of factors.

The studies by Masuda and associates may serve as a case in point. Although many test items in their Ethnic Identity Questionnaire have to do with ethnic habits, food preferences, and cultural practices,[14] the test's total score is alleged to reflect the strength of ethnic identity. Not surprisingly, these investigators confirmed their hypothesis of successive generational erosion of ethnic identity from the Issei (i.e., the immigrant generation) to the third generation (Masuda, Matsumoto & Meredith, 1970; Matsumoto, Meredith & Masuda, 1970). However, an undetermined portion of this "erosion" may be due, not to the weakening of Japanese-American ethnic identity, but to the dilution of ethnic food preferences and cultural practices. Our point here is that the use of content-based measures of ethnic identity is vulnerable or possibly bound to the logical trap of having to infer the demise of ethnic identity from the diminishing level of the enclosed traits and characteristics.

Unless self-definition has to do with purely epistemic issues, ethnic differentiation takes place against the background of power relations and ascriptive social valuations. As we noted while considering the source of differentiation, the externally imposed variety commonly brings about social devaluation and assignment of lesser economic and political power. (One may think of the history of the Irish, Italian, and other Euroethnic immigrants from an earlier period, and of Asian immigrants in more recent years.) These power and valuation aspects of the context of differentiation deserve a special note. Differentiation in a setting of strict economic and power balance would be of a different nature, but as long as the context of differentiation remains one of imbalance, to force a differentiation or create a new social category is to accord a position of social devaluation and less power. In any multiethnic society, the context of ethnic emplacement is likely to remain one of imbalance. It is for this reason that to recognize a differentiation from without in United States society is to discover that one has been involuntarily assigned, either as an individual or as a member of a group, to a position of lower status and less power, tinged with social stigma.

Thus, when a child of immigrant parents from a non-English-speaking country realizes that his peers consider him as not quite belonging to their group, he is making a simultaneous discovery that the group he is bound to by birth occupies a devalued status and a position of political weakness. To view ethnic self-emplacement in terms of social valuation and relative political power suggests that the core of the third-generation phenomenon is not so much a generational issue as an issue of the perception of social status and relative power. If guided by this approach, one would examine signs of returning to and searching for ancestral ethnicity, not in terms of generation, but in terms of the *perceived valuation* accorded to one's ethnic ingroup. The second generation would not necessarily develop rebellious antipathy toward its parents and parents' ethnic background unless the parents' background is accorded devalued and weakened social status: even the third generation would not try to reclaim or return to its grandparents unless it no longer feels the devaluation. It follows that the alleged generational variation could be explained not by generational standing, but by perceived location of one's ancestral ethnicity on social valuation dimensions. Reasoning along this line, one would predict that within each generation, irrespective of the generational position, it is the perceived social valuation that determines the posture of psychological escape from or return to their ethnic self-definition.

The potent role that the sense of collective deprivation can play in understanding social movement and disorder has been well documented (Pettigrew, 1967; Williams, 1976). Using his 1972 mayoral election data, Pettigrew (1978) presented a convincing case for separating "egoistic" (i.e., personal) from "fraternal" (i.e., collective) deprivations (pp. 32–37). We suggest that collective ethnic identity, like any other entrenched system of differentiation, serves as an organizing cognitive schema and as such plays a key role in forming a sense of collective deprivation. To the extent that ethnic self-emplacement is embedded into the context of differential power, collective ethnic identity contributes to the sense of relative group deprivation.

The cumulative, festering sense of relative group deprivation would be a necessary condition leading to the eventual social disorder and divisive upheaval which many critics of ethnicity seem to envision. However, the process of political development and social revolution does not lend itself to a simple explanation in terms of one or two master variables: consider all those intervening conditions such as the cohesiveness of the ethnic group and its economic-political resources, the perceived weakening of governmental authority, the perceived instrumental efficacy of collective action, the group's organizational capability, and the like. Accordingly, to link in a causal chain the rise in collective ethnic identity to eventual, disruptive consequences such as separatism, social fragmentation, Balkanization, and so forth, is to make an unnecessary logical leap. In addition, by creating a specter of disastrous consequences, such a leap transforms itself into an insidious force of intellectual oppression.

In summary, the phenomenon of ethnic identity is an aspect of our times, unavoidable in a multiethnic society, inseparable from the society's undergirding sociopolitical forces. The socioepistemic approach proposed in this essay makes it imperative that the social, political, and economic forces associated with ethnicity must be brought into the purview of an ethnic identity theory. Intended as a prelude toward a psychological theory of ethnic identity, I have sketched the broad background against which the phenomenon of ethnicity and the study of ethnic identity must be placed. From the proposed ethnic self-emplacement perspective, I have examined those issues related to the multiplicity of identities and the process of ethnic differentiation, leaving others to future clarification. This analysis has led to the following observations:

1. In recognition of the multiplicity of social identities which includes ethnic identity, future study of social identity (particularly ethnic identity) needs to adopt a configurational approach, which explicitly accommodates itself to the configuration of constituent identities,

2. A clearer conception of operative identities and the situational triggers of each identity is needed to help us better understand the interrelationship among constituent identities;

3. The nature and consequences of ethnic identity are shaped by whether it is self-initiated or externally imposed; hence, the source of differentiation deserves due attention as a powerful determinant,

4. Ethnic differentiations are effected by markers and sustained by

symbols: yet, relatively little is known on the range of potential markers and the dynamics of ethnic symbolism,

    5. Ethnic differentiation takes place against the swirl of social devaluation, economic struggle, and political power inequity. Since contextual specifics of ethnic differentiation determine the consequences of ethnic identity, ideologically based apprehension and enthusiasm would better be substituted by efforts to enhance our understanding of the dynamics of ethnic differentiation.

NOTES

    1. For ethnic politics prior to the 1960s, there is the classic work by Gerson (1964); and a good coverage of the 1960s is to be found in Weed, 1973, chapters 6, 7, and 8 in particular.

    2. For a comprehensive, historical treatment, see John Higham's *Send these to me: Jews and other immigrants in urban America* (1975).

    3. For exemplary novels, see Adamic (1935, 1942), Gambino (1974), Thomas (1968), and Kessler-Harris (1979); for citizen testimonies, see U. S. Commission on Civil Rights (1980); for autobiographical recollections, D'Antonio (1975), Moskos (1977), and Vecoli (1974).

    4. For exemplary selections, see *The Menorah Treasury: Harvest of half a century* (Schwarz, 1964).

    5. For a comprehensive account of ethnicity and literature, see Sollors (1980). Though confined to Jewish writers, Guttmann (1971) provides an in-depth analysis of the theme. For an incisive discussion of Cahan, see Higham (1975, pp. 88–101). For Yezierska, *The open cage: An Anzia Yezierska collection* (Kessler-Harris, 1979) would be a vivid testament. Adamic has been too long overlooked by students of ethnicity, but a recent workshop on his writings (held at the University of Minnesota, 1981) may create an atmosphere to reappraise his contribution. In the meantime, some of his books may serve to reflect his life-long interest in ethnicity— *Grandsons: A story of American lives* (1935), *From many lands* (1940), *What is your name?* (1942), and *Nation of nations* (1944).

    6. For ethnic conflict in the Arab world, see Young, 1976, pp. 373–427, and for discussion of ethnicity-related conflict in an international context, see Esman, 1977, and Said & Simmons, 1976.

    7. The guiding notion, it would be recalled, is that while the first generation immigrants were preoccupied with the immediate problems of survival and subsistence, the second generation (i.e., immigrants' offspring) had to undergo enormous strain as it attempted to balance the competing, often conflicting, influences of the ethnic family background and the "Americanization" forces operating outside its homes, particularly in public schools. The strain of this balancing attempt often has led the second generation to rejecting parents and what is embodied by their family ethnic milieu. The third generation, on the other hand, was eager to seek its heritage and restore a sense of continuity, because it was comfortable and confident in its Americanness and hence no longer haunted by a feeling of shame over its ethnic heritage.

    8. For example, after endorsing subjective awareness as the key definiens of ethnic identity in the early part of his book *Ethnic identity in American society*, Dashefsky (1976) slips into using ethnic identity as synonymous with ethnic group in a later chapter entitled "Does ethnic identity matter?" On the other hand, the core stratum is regarded as so pervasive and deep-seated that it may be even inaccessible to and unfathomable by ordinary queries. A direct

quote from Erikson may be appropriate here: "But the core of that unification called identity is at best 'preconscious,' that is accessible only to musings at moments of special awareness . . . . Mostly it is 'unconscious' and even repressed" (1967, p. 233). In *Poverty, ethnic identity, and health care* (Bullough & Bullough, 1972), one can replace ethnic identity with ethnic group without any loss in meaning. This usage is not an isolated event: some view ethnic identity as "simply a label or sorting device" (Devereux, 1975, pp. 48–49).

9. These 65 studies were located from a search of 19 prominent social science journals (in some cases going as far back as 1945), and they all deal with some aspect of ethnicity. Note that ethnicity and ethnic identity are used interchangeably not only in Isajiw (1974), but in others as well (e.g., Gordon, 1964; Sandberg, 1974).

10. For a brief but useful comment on the significance of this basic striving, see Pettigrew, 1978, p. 3.

11. In this connection, see Condie & Christiansen, 1977, who take afro wigs and hair models, bleaching cremes, and hair straighteners as changing symbols of black identity and chronicle the rise and fall in the frequency of their commercial advertisement in *Ebony* magazine.

12. Markers and symbols could be epiphenomenal characteristics like accent and body gesture or core elements of ethnic culture. See Smolicz, 1981, for elaboration of how core cultural elements may serve as symbols of ethnic identity.

13. Various chapters in *Ethnic encounters: Identities and contexts* (Hicks & Leis, 1977) are pertinent here. In particular, see the chapter by Schiller on the emergence of Haitian identity among Haitian immigrants in New York, Friedlander on West Bengalese and caste, and Kertzer on Italians and political allegiance.

14. The Ethnic Identity Questionnaire has 50 items. Some of the exemplary content-based items are: I especially like Japanese foods; I enjoy Japanese movies; I prefer attending an all-Japanese church; I am not too spontaneous and casual with people; I usually participate in mixed group discussions; an older brother's decision is to be respected more than that of a younger brother.

Chapter 10

ADAPTIVE CONFLICT AND ADJUSTIVE COPING: PSYCHOCULTURAL APPROACHES TO ETHNIC IDENTITY

George A. De Vos

A DUALISTIC APPROACH: ADAPTIVE AND ADJUSTIVE DETERMINANTS

In my own work with ethnic identity and minority status I have been attempting to reconcile as complementary two basic approaches many social scientists see as alternative or conflicting. I find the ultimate theoretical task of psychological anthropology and social psychology to be identical—whatever the immediate differences in research strategies and specialized interests—namely, a dualist interpretation of social behavior as determined both by social structure and by personality structure.

In discussing my approach to ethnicity I shall not refer to the extensive literature in social psychology or discussions of the concepts of social self which have been variously described by Sarbin and others (Erikson, 1964; Goffman, 1959; Hyman & Singer, 1968; Pettigrew, 1964; Sarbin, 1968d, 1969; Sarbin & Allen, 1968–1969; Sarbin & Scheibe, 1980). In this chapter I shall merely affirm that an ethnic identity is one of a variety of emphases in a social self. Elsewhere (De Vos & Romanucci-Ross, 1975) I have defined ethnic identity as a past-oriented form of social belonging in contrast to present or future-oriented forms of definitions of the self. Others have approached "ethnicity" from a more sociological perspective (e.g., Glazer & Moynihan, 1970, 1975). In a psychocultural approach I have emphasized both the "expressive" as well as the "instrumental" usages of ethnic

This chapter was prepared while the author was in Europe as a Visiting Professor with the Centre Richet d'Etude des Dysfonctions de l'Adaptation, University of Paris V and with the Kath. Universitet de Leuven, Belgium.

identity. It cannot be understood solely as an instrumentally oriented attempt to adapt socially. Adjustive personality (intraindividual) variables underlie the expressive needs that become represented in ethnic behavior.

In the first section of this chapter my emphasis is on social structural problems and issue of "status" related to ethnic identity. The latter part of the chapter concerns itself with the concept of coping, again, as related to ethnic identity.

In a dualist approach it is necessary to differentiate between the concepts "adaptation" and "adjustment." As I use these terms, adaptation refers to the vicissitudes of one's relationship to social groups; adjustment refers to vicissitudes of internal psychological structures (cf. De Vos, 1974; 1976c). The self, an "emic" concept, is inherently part of human consciousness. Adaptation is experienced in the self. It refers to how the individual assesses his/her getting along with others or how he/she assesses the achievement of his/her goals. A study of coping mechanisms refers to the adjustive structures underlying the experience of the social world. They comprise the ego, an "etic" concept related to these operating psychological processes which are not necessarily experienced subjectively. In effect, problems of adjustment are usually experienced only when there is a self-conscious awareness of inner rigidities or incapacities, i.e., "maladjustment," rather than when the ego is functioning appropriately and automatically in an adaptive manner.

Sarbin and Scheibe (1980) note how the self is located in a general social structure. A social structure is, in one perspective, a network of ascribed and attained social roles that changes during the life span of the individual. An individual locates himself in this system through an inferential process—a continual process of knowing who one is in reference to the others with whom one interacts. I employ a similar model, but with stronger emphasis on the inherent conflict over role models and status ascriptions that occurs in complex societies. Such conflicts are even more compounded in multiethnic class–stratified social structures as well as in societies having a caste separation (De Vos, 1965a, 1966, 1967, 1969, 1976b, 1980c, 1982; De Vos & Wagatsuma, 1966, 1969).

Although adaptation in minority socialization is an important topic, here I want also to emphasize the adjustive aspects of identity in relation to personality mechanisms involved in internalization. Much as I would agree with Sarbin's role theory approach stemming from his understanding of the social self, I question the apparently exclusive emphasis on the continuing force of status ascription. Further, I call attention to problems related to understanding why social ascription imposed from the outside becomes *selectively* effective in helping individuals within given ethnic groups answer "Who am I?" The reader will readily perceive that the contentions that follow are not contradictory to Sarbin's main theoretical development. They do, however, flow from a dualist perspective and they attempt to bridge the social structural theory of social self and a psychocultural perspective in understanding ethnicity as it may be influenced by defensive or self-protective coping mechanisms. In this respect, it is most specifically related to problems of internalization which have been an issue in social theory from the time of Durkheim and his introduction of the concept of collective representations in sociology. Later, George Herbert Mead (1934) attempted better to delineate the development of the "I" and the "me" as the internalization of social experience. This approach out of the social interactionist tradition is complementary to Freud's usage of the concept of superego in psychoanalytic theory.

At issue in examining ethnic identity in either or both a sociological or more strictly psychoanalytic context as well as in Witkin's theories of social differentiation (1967, 1969, 1978; Witkin & Berry, 1975; Witkin et al., 1974) and in the concept of accommodation as advanced by Piaget (1966, 1968) is how internalization of social norms operates differently among various ethnic groups depending on cultural-historical circumstances as well as individual vicissitudes. I shall touch more on this issue later in my discussion of different coping strategies utilized by those who tend to become defensively ethnic as opposed to those who become socially mobile.

IDENTITY: PAST, PRESENT, OR FUTURE ORIENTED?

In another study (De Vos & Romanucci-Ross, 1975) I discussed how on a social structural level ethnic divisions in a society are less socially accommodative than lineage, class, or caste forms of social groupings. Continuing ethnicity implies by its very nature a system of beliefs about social belonging emphasizing a *past* origin different from the society in which one has been allocated a *present* minority status. Ethnicity can be a continual source of competition if not a direct conflict since there is no necessary final allegiance to a society on the basis of one's common origin (De Vos, 1972, 1980c). Ethnic groups do not readily accommodate to a fixed and disadvantaged position within a stratified system. Their disadvantaged position may be based on a previous defeat, conquest, or forced assimilation (De Vos, 1977). Internal processes involved in an ethnic identity must be differentiated from supposed psychological traits ascribed to a minority by the majority.

As I shall argue subsequently, alternative personality patterns are indeed involved in the rigid, even reactive, maintenance of past-oriented ethnic identity in contrast to other patterns more conducive to social mobility even in situations of discrimination, in which, nevertheless, one changes the focus of one's identity to the present or future rather than maintaining a past orientation.

Attempted changes in identity orientation may be in the direction of either new present-oriented occupational role definitions of the social self, or more future-oriented revolutionary definitions of wished-for social change in which social roles may be reorganized by radical changes of social structure (see De Vos & Romanucci-Ross, 1975).

On a psychological level, in some groups but not in others (De Vos, 1978), a defensive past-oriented social identity is selectively maintained by emphasizing a defensive cognitive style excluding threatening new cognitive accommodations. For example, a traditional Polish peasant thrust into new social circumstances may seem defensively dull or unwilling to learn middle-class urban norms. Such a coping style differs from that found among those who individually or even in groups are less "blocked" when they seek to find new modes of adapting economically or socially in situations of change. Those who change their identity orientation must be adjustively more ready to practice some form of what is usually perceived as upward social mobility. For example, the more cognitively flexible ambitious children of immigrants into the United States could more quickly emulate the white Protestant majority in speech patterns, if not completely in thought.

An alternative to forming enclaves within an ethnic group by maintaining a past-oriented identity, or to facile changing of behavioral patterns, is the chronic lack of resolution of inner conflict over one's true self, a condition leading to what has been cogently described by Erikson (1964, 1968b) as "diffuseness" in identity. Such an adjustive pattern is frequently found during an adolescent transition period but is not limited to adolescence. For example, a Londoner from Wales may not be able to resolve whether one is "Welsh" or "English" until later in life. How these three alternative patterns are related specifically to selective saliency in internally structured coping mechanisms is discussed in the latter section of this chapter.

By its very nature, a salient ethnic identity puts heavier emphasis on contrastiveness as a mode of social identity, often as a reaction to social discrimination. It emphasizes past separateness. Although not always made explicit, the separateness is perceived as flowing from differences in basic moral or religious principles from the majority or from other groups. Members of a class- or caste-segregated society appear to handle conflict in ways different from those of an ethnically separated society. Conflicts and dissension resulting from social inequities can be toned down by some form of ideological or shared religious appeal emphasizing social unity (De Vos, 1976c). For example, French nationalism since the revolution of 1789 has been based on the present-oriented concept of citizenship, which has helped to marshal a unified patriotic allegiance in a continuing socially stratified society. Despite this emphasis on citizenship, regional dissension has continued among the ethnic Bretons, the Corsicans, and the various inhabitants of the "Occitain" south. Ethnic militancy has become strong in such specific groups as the Muslim Algerians and black Martiniquans who have been facing "racial" discrimination and are perceived as less "assimilable" than immigrant Catholic Portuguese. As another example, Yugoslavia is a multiethnic state with ethnic divergences that continue old political and religious animosities and that continually threaten to tear the fabric of a unified government.

In such multiethnic situations a historical sense of diversity remains available as a point of reference. Ethnic pluralism implies social and political complexity. There is likely to be less stability as a result of resistance in complying with the perceived *external* dominance of centralized government. The awareness of differences can outweigh possible communalities among members of different social strata. What is percived as exploitation by outsiders, or by a relatively successful alien minority, is more bitterly resented than when the supposed exploiters are considered belonging to the same "people" (i.e., Nazi Germany's delusional persecution by "economically exploitative Jews"). Or, a reinforced memory of a possible past, hoped-for political independence (i.e., Armenians in Turkey), can continue to be part of a sense of a present social self defined in ethnic terms.

In order to maintain one's valued identity a person may forego an openness to new experiences. Further development toward psychological differentiation may be too challenging when it demands some release from a previous narrower form of social identity. Coming in contact with wider circles of social experience is experienced as a challenge and may be beyond the immediate integrative capacity of an individual. Difficulty in language learning in Belgian children compared with Dutch children is an example. Walloons "cannot" learn Flemish and Flemings "cannot" learn French. The Dutch, more secure in their identity, readily learn any foreign language that is expedient for them. The Flemish bear hatred toward the French-oriented Walloons for having been degraded and reduced to secondary citizenship during a period when French speakers were accorded economic and political ascendancy.

A defensive rigidified maintenance of a past-oriented social self then becomes apparent. Selectivity in "taking in" experiences starts very early. On the level of psychological structure, therefore, a "selective permeability" of experiences, may differ in intensity in maintaining a past ethnic identity compared with assuming other alternative or overlapping forms of social identity.

Patterns of social expectancy maintain ethnic separateness in situations of social contact that involve political domination existing through several generations in many proximate regional communities in Europe. One learns early who one is because one is imprinted early with linguistic or other "emblems" important to the integrity and continuity of one's group or to its pride and collective affirmation. Alternative imprints do not "take" as easily. There is less penetration or accommodation since these later experiences might be in conflict with already developing patterns that are involved in group maintenance.

Even where there is almost total linguistic acculturation in a specific ethnic group such as the Irish, where much of the substance of a previous culture is by and large lost, "Irish" intonational patterns in speaking English emblematically remain to mark one's identity. One maintains some symbolic usage of language as a mark of allegiance, even when the total substance of one's linguistic heritage is in danger of being lost. "Black English" is a mark of allegiance in the United States used both instrumentally and expressively. It can be part of personality constriction for some or part of adaptive social maneuvering for others.

ETHNIC COMMITMENT IN SOCIAL IDENTITY

One measure of a social identity is a sense of relative commitment to past, present, or future in situations of conflict in possible roles. In this perspective a social identity is manifest in a number of alternative priorities. Ethnicity is only one form of social commitment that may be operative in given individuals in given circumstances. A sense of social belonging that transcends the immediate self can be located on two dimensions. It can be located on one of roughly six levels of increasing generality from individual to more widely inclusive group identity; at the same time it can be more intensively concerned with a present, past, or future time reference. Ethnicity is characterized by being a group specific, past-oriented emphasis in the sense of selfhood (see Figure 10.1).

A person whose sense of self—hence social commitment—is present oriented can emphasize most specifically involvement in his present family of procreation or even the class in which his occupational role is located. He may also regard as most important his loyalty as a citizen. Even more generally, some individuals may give priority to a present-oriented identity that transcends any political community.

However, for others, none of these present-oriented social identities, specific or general, may be considered sufficient or satisfactory. The individual, therefore, may devalue his present identity orientation in the name of new possible allegiances or attributes to be realized only in the future. Such a future orientation again may be of increasing levels of

Figure 10.1. The Dimensions of Priorities in Social Belonging Defining the Self

←TEMPORAL ORIENTATION OF IDENTITY→

	PAST	PRESENT	FUTURE
1.	"Human" origins	Common humanity	Internationalism or a universalistic religious ideology or political movement
2.	Ethnic identity (Racial, ethnic-cultural, territorial, linguistic, esthetic, religious, economic)	Loyalty to the state, citizenship, contemporary dominant ideology	Dreams of aggrandizement of one's society
3.	Kingroup ascription	Class or caste loyalties	Competitive class mobility
4.	Familial pride or affirmation of prestige of family of orientation; family occupational ascription	Family of procreation; achievement of family	Family mobility or passing
5.	Parental ascriptions or specific progenitor or identity with mentor or master of a craft	Individual occupational attainment or present oriented social role	Individual "passing" or social mobility into a desired role
6.	Specific human model for the self; independent or "role" attainments	"Self" as distinct from social roles	Personal salvation, internal "self" development through discipline or therapeutic procedure

(left margin, vertical) INCREASING LEVELS OF GENERALITY →

generality. On a very specific level, one may begin an idiosyncratic search for future internal self "development" through disciplinary practices, educative means, or therapeutic regimes. Acute discontent with the present in society may remain completely specific or a person may strive in levels of increasing generality for change in present social status or the status of one's family, or change in the relative class status of one's social or occupational group. One can become committed to a more general revolutionary change in society by joining an ideological or religious movement. In these latter instances commitment is sometimes symbolized by a rebirth of initiation actually conducted as a rite into a new group as an affirmation of new allegiance and new collective purpose (Sarbin & Adler, 1971).

Dissatisfaction with the present can also be symbolized by a recommitment to a past form of social belonging—again in singular or general terms. There are those who emphasize privileged lineage, e.g., the elite quadron or octaroon families of New Orleans, or the deposed royalty of France. What is more common, however, and is the subject of our discourse, is selfhood through ethnic allegiance (e.g., the third generation Algerians in France and the third generation Koreans in Japan). For some, past ethnicity and present citizenship are seen as congruent (e.g., the Japanese or the "true" Germans of Hitler's Germany). For others they may be polarized into forms of internal tension and divided loyalty (e.g., the Northern Irish, the Ukrainians of the Soviet Union, the Kurds and Armenians of Turkey). A wide range of internal tensions between past, present, and future commitments in loyalty are possible.

As Sarbin and Scheibe (1980) have discussed there are also numerous complexities between ascribed and attained status positions. When present-oriented status positions are more or less unsatisfactory, one may seek to take individual or group means to change status ascription as well as seek attainment of a new status. A particular occupation, for example, that of teacher or of social worker, may be ascribed a status within the society which the members find inappropriate. Once a person attains an occupation, he or she can seek to change its socially accorded status collectively, e.g., through union activities or legislation, or the individual may decide instead to change his occupational role. As Sarbin and Scheibe point out, it is no easy matter to change an ascribed status marked by birth. However, in a large complex society in which one's origins can be masked and one's background disguised so as to "pass" and assume a nonethnic identity (e.g., name changes such as Battenberg to Montbatten, and the Bank of Italy to the Bank of America; in some cases individuals are forced to change, e.g., the wholesale conversion of Jews in Spain in the fifteenth century). Much can be said about the complexity of the issues related to a "self" involved in situations of passing (De Vos, 1977). The novelist has done more with these issues than the social scientist.

"Passing" has become a political as well as social issue for many selfconscious groups. Whereas in some groups members would be allowed to pass were they capable of doing so, today should an individual seek advantage by passing, members of his own group would expose him. This tendency to sanction those who seek individual advantage is noticeable specifically among Mexican-Americans, black groups in the United States, and among the Koreans in Japan. At present in the latter group there is great ambivalence about changing one's name to Japanese. Increasingly popular athletes and entertainers are "coming out of the closet" but many remain disguised to avoid offending their public. Militant Koreans are less tolerant of such expediency.

Looked at in a comparative anthropological perspective, ethnicity has variable salience in different societies. For example, the concepts of citizenship, ethnicity, and "race" for most Japanese are equivalent. This general social perception makes for great difficulty for the minority Koreans who are in effect treated as racially inferior. This form of implicit racism in Japanese society stems from the concept of genetic uniqueness and the fact that the Japanese continue the illusion that they are ethnically homogeneous. This ethnicity, therefore, is based on implicit racial as well as cultural concepts. This "racial" concept helps explain the maintenance of caste segregation in Japanese society. The burakumin or former outcastes are considered of alien origin and biologically inferior. These pseudo-scientific rationalizations have superseded concepts of ritual impurity which were operative in the past (De Vos, 1966).

If we turn to India, a society that is directly structured on a traditional caste conceptualization of hierarchy, we find that ethnicity and class play less salient roles, although concepts of social class are becoming increasingly important. In India, the ordination of society in respect to purity is still much in force and ethnically dissimilar groups have been assimilated by conceptualizing them somewhere within the "caste" framework of the society.

Turning to Europe we find, generally speaking, that the concept of class has been an overriding one in the definition of status. Marxist theory of social structure continues to be employed in explaining social and economic conduct. It is much easier for a European worker to understand his social position in class terms than it is for a Japanese worker, for example, or even an American worker. What is very apparent among Europeans is the effects of class on social acceptability. This has in the past cut across national lines and ethnic lines as well. However, more recently the regionalism related to specific ethnic enclaves has again reasserted itself and is becoming a counterforce to class concepts. For example, in France, the Breton ethnic movement in the past was dominated by "rightists," who were even pro-German in their hatred for the central government. Most recently, both in Brittany and in the Southern Occitain area around Toulouse, it is members of the Communist Party who play down their concept of an international class struggle and are favoring the cause of oppressed ethnic minorities and advocate linguistic as well as economic autonomy for these regions of France. Ethnicity has become so powerful as a social unifier that leftist politicians who in the past affirmed future-oriented forms of international communism are in some instances readapting their political strategy to take advantage of past ethnic resentments.

In the United States one can note similarly that class explanations of exploitation have less appeal among racial minorities who, as in the case of American blacks are much too aware of segregation practiced between persons of supposedly similar class affiliation. To escape from the caste definitions of the past, black militants have come to use ethnic rather than class concepts in political mobilization. Ethnic concepts are much more readily available given the multiethnic awareness of American society. Since ethnicity does not of itself define individuals negatively in a stratified society, American blacks have found it advantageous to compete effectively as a group within the American social structure by affirming an ethnic rather than a class solidarity. Theoretically, therefore, one must see the saliency of an "ethnic" past orientation differing with cultural and historical circumstances.

CHANGING OR MAINTAINING STATUS

The contribution of ethnically oriented peer reference groups in the development of social self-identity is complex, as is the relation of peer reference group to the process of internalization (De Vos, 1978, 1980a, 1982). It differs with the degree to which the family has failed to serve as the locus for emotional support or satisfaction. In ethnic situations, one can point to the difference between the compensatory use of the peer group as a refuge from unsatisfactory family relationships and the adaptive use of the peer group with respect to acquiring a social identity different from that of one's parents. The degree of family cohesion is an important factor in the choice of a given peer group among the alternatives available (De Vos, 1982).

Ethnic allegiance can be used in a combative way, forcing changes in social ascription. However, the adaptations attempted by those whose ethnically defined status positions disadvantage them socially are not always that amenable to conscious choice. Individuals from different backgrounds with different cultural patterns are subject to differential socialization experiences (De Vos & Wagatsuma, 1966, pp. 228ff). Their early socialization may conduce some proportionate number toward the utilization of coping mechanisms in a self–protective manner which results in maladaptive social responses, a topic to which I now turn.

COGNITIVE STYLES RELATED TO MAINTENANCE OR CHANGE OF ETHNIC IDENTITY

It is useful to discuss (De Vos, 1980a, 1982) some of the cross-cultural and minority group implications of both the Piagetian theories of cognitive development (cf. Dasen, 1972; Price-Williams, 1975; Ramirez & Price-Williams, 1974) and the psychological differentiation theory of Witkin and his associates (Witkin et al., 1974; Witkin & Berry, 1975). The heart of both theories is an emphasis on "maturation" or progression of cognitive development. Cultural relativists are uncomfortable with development concepts that include a physiologically based progression since they tend to see differences in cognitive styles simply as alternative forms of situational adaptation and do not wish to consider whether there is a structurally based adjustive progression from less to more differentiated forms of intellectual response. They fail to discriminate between the socially *adaptive* use of style of thought, such as the concrete forms of thought used to solve navigational problems among the Polynesians (Gladwin & Sturtevant, 1962), and the psychological maturation of *adjustive* structures of thought that are inherently sequential, such as the development of abstract thought in literate societies (cf. Piaget, 1927, who discusses the acquisition of an "objective" position in causal reasoning supplanting "realism" in children's thought).

I can identify three basic styles of coping mechanisms. Hardly anyone will deny the existence of various so-called defense mechanisms or coping mechanisms in human behavior. These mechanisms may be divided into roughly three ordering sequences. I believe it is useful to regard the human ego as operating analogously to biological cells. The basic functions are: intake, exclusion (that is, a boundary protection in contact), and expulsion. At the earliest stage of ego development we find these three basic mechanisms at work. In their most primitive form they have been defined as "introjection," "denial," and "projection." Traces of these basic mechanisms persist in almost unmodified forms in adult behavior in every culture. For the most part, the earlier forms of these mechanisms become transmuted through a process of differentiation in an interactive balance with one another. The persistence of the primitive forms in imbalanced, maladjustive, and rigidified ways contribute to unwanted conduct. In some societies, such unwanted conduct is diagnosed as mental illness. One must stress the fact that diagnosis is usually attempted when unwanted conduct interferes with social functioning rather than when cognitive malfunctioning is unobtrusive and does not cause some manifest social disturbance.

CONTRASTIVE OR EXPULSIVE THOUGHT

Frequently noted in the social science literature, such unwanted conduct is not particularly illuminated by the use of a medical-psychiatric frame of reference. In some groups, socially approved thought utilizing projection is almost universal. That is, either individually or collectively, there is an external expulsion of undesirable thoughts or behavior that becomes more readily perceived as evident outside the self or outside the group. Group identity is very often based, partially at least, on an ability to perceive others in a contrasting pejorative sense; for example, among many American Indians other groups are "nonpeople." Others are negatively evaluated in reference to traits that may be equally present in one's own group (Germans see Jews as concerned with money). The mechanism of projection is widespread in human society. However, as theoretically conceived it is sometimes not sufficiently related to other transmutations, for example, status maintenance by the use of displacement. In displacement, problems internal to a group are perceived as characteristics of a vulnerable lower status or ethnic group as well as an outside enemy, for example, lower status white southerners who see blacks as ignorant and dirty. Such objects of displacement are often subject to ethnic and racial scapegoating and other related social phenomena (De Vos & Wagatsuma, 1966, chapter 18).

The traditional view of projection fails to give sufficient weight to the connection between projection and a personal or collective need to represent power and control as internal experiences. A particular culture can emphasize a style of ego development that expects a member to seek individual mastery and to perceive self-control as an internal process. This projective emphasis in the use of "mechanisms of defense" can lead to problem-solving behavior in which the individual is self-reliant rather than passively dependent on others to resolve one's problems. The individual takes the initiative in the manipulation of the social as well as material environment.

Projection in its earlier forms is first related to the earliest sense of omnipotence. Its partial continuance protects the individual against the experience of utter helplessness. In its later transmutations it can finally lead to the attainment of objective, analytic, logical thought as a basic mode of coping with and controlling the environment. The primary adjustive progression is a growing capacity to use thinking (i.e., problem solving) as a means of internal control as well as external control.

The early maturational phases of thought processes related to control are involved in prelogical, magical thinking (Piaget, 1927, 1932) or primary process thinking. Magical thought is prevalent in literally every society, including so-called modern ones. Magical thought arises from assigning causality on the basis of contiguity and similarity.

Magical forms of precausality differ from early introjective thought processes concerned with intention or with emotional states in which power is experienced in fusion with external beings in coping through introjection of the outside. One is initially not separate, but part of. When separation comes to be experienced, power must be sought from external intentional willful beings. Such external, often personalized, force, with which one seeks engulfment—reattachment—or which one seeks to "ingest" symbolically in communion, is found in religious (as opposed to magical) representations cross-culturally.

Anthropologists sometimes distinguish between the intentionality of power in "religion" and the mechanical precausal operation of power in "magic" (Malinowski, 1948). The mechanical precausality found in magical thinking is in its earlier stages of coping confounded with the instrumental use of power in thought and language originating within an individual. This is opposite to ingestive coping wherein there is a "religious" direct experience of helplessness and incompleteness in relation to outside powerful intentional beings. In use of inclusive coping the person expresses hoped-for adherence in an effort to incorporate power from outside sources by a process of introjection, or conversely, to share in power by being absorbed within a larger entity. Illustratively, Jean Rouch, the French ethnographic filmmaker, made a powerful documentary on an African "new religion," which sprang up in Ghana before the end of the British colonial regime. In this film a group in a communal feast dismembers a dog sacrifice, ingesting its power in trance. They become deified representations of British power—the viceroy, the general, the train engineer, and so forth. These individuals in their daily lives are powerless. They have observed with incomplete understanding the exercise of power by aliens governing them. Then too the Christian sacrament of the Mass, symbolically represents ingesting the body and blood of Christ in Holy Communion. This was used as a symbol by the submerged people who espoused Christianity at the time of the Roman Empire and used Christian beliefs to bring about a universalist future-oriented social revolution that transcended particular ethnic loyalties.

"Contrastive" coping is related to two forms of observable conduct. First, the individual can show signs of "grandiosity" emphasizing one's omnipotence or the ultimate omnipotence of one's group (a belief in a sense of internal power which is not supported by the "facts"). Second, there can be "delusions" of persecution in which internal destructive feeling states are perceived externally as a sense of threat to one's integrity, which must be maintained by more emphasis on defensive control (i.e., delusions concerning Jewish or Communist conspiracies).

In some cultures, the disciplined use of logical classification or formal analysis may only rarely be attained since the training for these potentials is lacking. However, anxious suspiciousness may continue to characterize social relations. One finds contrastiveness emphasized, even institutionalized, in the prelogical processes that continue to operate within such a society. Schwartz (1976), for example, describes the "paranoid ethos" of Melanesian societies. In such societies, in terms used by George Herbert Mead, the "me" is saliently experienced as "different from" others, whether the individual achieves a higher level of formal cognitive operations or not.

Looked at in a social framework such highly internalized individuals are at times quite capable of individual adaptive social mobility behind their ethnicity. They do not use the social group attachments as a reference of self-evaluation and are free to join other groupings in an instrumental fashion (e.g., "successful New Yorkers" who in origin come from either the large Jewish, Irish, or Italian ethnic minorities in the city). They act instrumentally without taking the subjective feelings of self or others into account (e.g., Anglo children as compared with Mexican-American or Mexican children) (Madsen, 1967; Madsen & Shapira, 1973). A relative incapacity to sense the emotional consequences of instrumental action may be observed. It is in this respect that there may develop some internal maladjustment but attain external adaptation: a competitive, results-oriented social system rewards intellectual competence at the same time devaluing harmony and receptivity in human relationships.

INTRASEPTIVE THOUGHT

In some discussions, "empathy" is regarded as a mature development arising from the contrastive mechanisms that begin as projection. This is not so. Empathy is related to another developmental series starting with introjection which transmutes progressively into identification and culminates in more mature forms of social group involvement. The processes of "taking in" or intraception of experiences remains part of consciousness of self in society.

The development of such a sequence starting with introjection is not widely discussed in the social science literature. One must distinguish stages in the coping mechanisms involved in taking in experiences in the progressive differentiation of cognitive schemata and the resultant "accommodation" by which the schemata of "belonging" are altered by the experiences taken in. In thinking of the social "self" as a schema one must distinguish also between a relatively ready receptivity which allows experiences to occur to a consciously developing social self, and the relative permanence of accommodation that may alter the self toward a more differentiated definition. This distinction must be kept in mind in understanding the progressive operation of an introjective mechanism as an essential operation of a developing ego structure. All experiences taken in do not result in an identification that alters the resulting concept of self. Social internalization starts with the earliest experiences before there is any separation of me and not me. Only progressively are some developing precepts located permanently inside and others outside. What is introjected may be experienced "inside" but it may not become a permanent part of the self. For example, one may become facile at imitation, like the comedian Danny Kaye being a Dane or a Russian, without any stable identification of thought, feeling, or behavior becoming a permanent attribute of the self. This is the nature of "play." One may feel an ethnic role without permanently becoming it. Only progressively in a balanced progression between coping mechanisms do experiences lead to permanent accommodations and limitations. One may imitate another more desired ethnic identity without assuming it permanently for oneself.

Sensitivity to and the taking in of social feelings also allows one to "identify" with others without the necessity of becoming the other. There is a progressive maturation of "taking in" toward mature self control in empathy and compassion.

The social internalization and accommodation that includes aspects of one's ethnic identity begins with the earliest phase of ego development. A self-consciousness develops out of internal experiences. But some experiences may continue to be a form of play resulting in no further change in self-concept or the development of the social self-identity. The adult individual, who becomes part of a specific ethnic entity, goes through a progressive development of a relative sensitivity in the taking-in of social feelings. Some feelings are excluded as disharmonious or threatening. Other feelings evolve progressively into empathy and compassion, which can safely be extended to others not of one's group.

The mechanism of introception from early on emphasizes first fusion, then identification, and later, similarity and closeness without becoming totally "identified." There is a development of the sympathetic recognition of experiences as going on within other individuals and in turn knowledge of the similarity of experience with others.

In the most primitive level of introceptive coping there is as yet no complete separation of self from the outside so that external stimuli are experienced internally. A very important aspect of such early introceptive experience is that power is experienced as personalized, that is, it is related to intentional attitudes and that consequently precausality also can be personalized. A sense of separation brings about a sense of helplessness well described by Freud as separation anxiety. One assuages this by "belonging" (de Grazia, 1948). There is early confusion and shifting saliency between projective mechanical precausality and personalized introceptive precausality. Self-consciousness develops out of a recognition internally of the continuous interrelationship between inner feelings and feelings of others in the social environment. One remains part of a family, later a group, possibly an ethnic group. In Piagetian terms, certain internal conceptual or perceptual schemata are continually open to accommodate to new personalized experiences that are part of oneself during the period when the self is not completely separable from outside beings of power. In seeking to assuage "belonging" in a multiethnic situation, one must contend with a richness of potential alternatives that somehow must be selected out.

What is sometimes characteristic of individualistic societies emphasizing personal autonomy is that there is less saliency for the sense of belonging. That is to say, there is less maturation in the sense of being part of as well as being different from others. A well-balanced socialized self is continually experiencing how it is related to the social environment. Hence the mechanism of introjection at each stage has to do with the social development of this sense of belonging. This continual, progressively differentiated taking-in of social attitudes is emphasized in Sarbin and Scheibe's chapter of this volume.

On a cognitive level, processes comprising internalization can be related to perception of similarity and ultimately to emphasis on forms of synthetic or creative thought. These processes are involved centrally in religious experiences and the recognition of poetic relationships, whereas the "contrastive" projective mechanisms previously discussed emphasize analysis and distanced or objective thought.

In the first stage of introjection the early self cannot be readily distinguished from the outside. One finds residues of this type of experience cross-culturally in reports of mystical experiences and ecstatic states, sometimes cultivated deliberately by religious cults or brought about by the use of psychedelic drugs. Such experiences are found in so-called acute schizophrenic episodes in which a person expresses concern over cosmic events experienced as taking place within the self.

In Piaget's heteronomous dependent stage of social development the mechanism of introjection is transmuted through a variety of problems that occur before a stable identification takes place. When the developing ego structure is properly balanced, social directives are being gradually internalized as a more permanent part of the self so that there is less need for immediate external sanctioning to guide behavior.

A balance is necessary in the transmutation of exclusion, expulsion, and introception. When imbalanced too far in the direction of too ready, continually new introceptions, consistent forms of identification do not take place as readily. There are psychodynamic reasons for such problems to occur that we cannot discuss here. Suffice it to say that it may have to do in some instances with the limiting implications of a stable identification. When a stable type of identification that defines one's relationship with others remains incomplete, one finds, alternatively, problems of alienation or loss of a sense of investment in others. Conversely, some individuals seeking to attain a sense of belonging may submit themselves temporarily or permanently to a leader or belief system that gives them regulation. Erich Fromm in his volume, *Escape From Freedom* (1968), discusses such a sequence of anomie and diffusion in Germans prior to the Nazi "ethnic affirmation" of Adolf Hitler. This external submission to authority is necessary because a sense of inner regulation is found to be relatively missing in situations of social anomie.

Individuals suffering a sense of malaise in this respect also may seek to guide their action through imitation. To use Reisman, Glazer & Denney's (1950) term, they have an "other-directed" nonstabilized superego, which necessitates continued use of an outside reference group. Peer-oriented forms of belonging become a viable solution.

To extend Erikson's term, ethnic identity *diffusion* occurs as part of an experience of internal conflict over inconsistent or contrastive directives or purposes. As discussed by Witkin, there are basic differences in given cultural traditions in the degree to which some individuals are socialized to depend on the internalization of directives, while others are socialized toward the continual use of the outside society for clues to guide behavior. Definitions of morality or values can remain external and depend on continual sanctioning by outside authorities in order to give direction to individuals. In situations of social stratification this "outside" authority can be resisted by joining a deviant reference group. Through much of their history Sicilians have formed groups covertly resisting official authority as outside and alien (Finley, 1968). Looked at in Piagetian terms there is a "heteronomous" period in which the mechanism of imitation is prominent. Imitation depends upon continual use of an immediate reference group, in contemporary American society, most often an ethnic subgroup. In this transitional use of imitation there is no fixed accommodation to internal stabilized schemata that later can come to comprise a secure social identity.

In identity diffusion the situation is somewhat different. The adult individual lacks a capacity to find focus or commitment. He may become isolated from others. He remains incapable of selecting, especially in a multiethnic situation, a satisfactory but limited identity out of the variety of alternative possibilities. He lacks consistent goals or purposes that serve as stable foci for the self as part of a complex society in which he must find specific commitment. This state may be briefly experienced, limited to adolescence, or it may become a chronic condition leading sometimes to a more permanent sense of alienation.

The adult use of internalizaton is in balance with the other basic mechanisms leading to some maintenance of consistency and contrast. When an individual develops a stable concept of self and is capable of some detachment he is more capable of perceiving outside events without assigning the attribution that the events are taking place only in direct reference to the self. That is to say, the more mature individual can distinguish between compassion and empathy for others and the internal experience of an event as a necessary part of the self. Nevertheless, a continuing sense of social belonging depends upon the social sensitivity of individuals for each other. The mature individual, therefore, maintains as part of his or herself a sense of social belonging and group commitment. At the same time, he or she recognizes the interdependence of the self with other parts of a total social system. There is controlled involvement in events. Ideally one can arrive at a satisfactory balance between synthetic and analytic thought, between compassion and detachment, between moral social concerns and scientific objectivity. These concerns will be found in how an ethnic identity is maintained and with what degree of saliency.

EXCLUSION MECHANISMS IN MAINTENANCE OF THE SELF

Let us now turn to the third basic form of coping mechanism, which I have discussed in reference to my concept of "selective permeability" (De Vos, 1978). These processes of exclusion prevent entry of inconsistent or threatening material into the developing ego. The mechanism of denial in its primitive form directly excludes forms of external reality that would disturb a vulnerable inner consistency.

This same mechanism evolves into selective permeability (De Vos & Wagatsuma, 1966) during the heteronomous phase of social development. With the development of the social self the exclusion of external stimuli becomes highly selective. What is allowed to enter must conform to a defensively held sense of social identity. When this sense of identity becomes very narrowly and defensively defined one observes problems of constrictive nonlearning as I have illustrated in respect to Hawaiians, Mexican Americans, and American Indians (De Vos, 1980a, 1982).

In this mode of ego boundary maintenance, early denial is later transformed into the general mechanism of repression that is used to ward off threat from one's own unconscious impulses. It is, in this aspect, the converse to the use of contrastive mechanisms in "isolation" or "intellectualization" wherein affect is sacrificed to controlled thought. Conversely, in utilizing the exclusion mechanism too rigidly in selective permeability to new experience, cognitive growth is sacrificed to defend one's self against the experience of disruptive thoughts. Affectively laden ego-alien dissonant experiences are automatically avoided or are prevented from entering consciousness.

This form of coping appears as "dissociation" and is sometimes manifested culturally in religious rites or institutions utilizing trance or mind-altering drugs. It may also appear in what are perceived to be pathological in so-called "culture-bound syndromes." The individual, in the context of his social group, can utilize an altered state of consciousness in order to gain some indirect expression in ritual of those social inconsistencies not appropriate to his stable, rigidly defined social roles. Such dissociation is very widely expressed in religious ceremonies such as the Peyote Cult, or Southern snake handling groups in the United States (LaBarre, 1938, 1962). Most societies utilize some forms of trance state or "possession" experience.

The more mature transformation of this mechanism of exclusion is manifest in an adult capacity for concentration and focus in the definition of social role. Individuals come to define themselves with relative degrees of consistency in their occupational, family, or other role commitments and are able for the sake of efficiency of action to exclude what would be disruptive or distracting social or personal proclivities.

PATTERNS OF SOCIAL CONFORMITY OR DEVIANCY

Differences in cognitive styles are related to the conditions under which social norms are internalized and therefore result in different patterns of social conformity or deviancy. They may continue to be perceived as externally enforced or they come to be related in one fashion or another to a capacity to sense guilt in respect to one's social behavior. The three basic emphases in coping as just discussed can be conceptually superimposed on these alternative directions to form a grid related to social conformity.

In considering ethnic minority patterns one must include some theoretical issues related to social conformity or social deviancy as they are defined internally or experienced in reference to the social self. There are alternative theoretical approaches found in this present volume that emphasize how social definitions of role behavior influence self concepts. On the other hand, one must also consider psychodynamic theories explaining degrees of rigidified internalization. I believe some systematic attention to differences in emphasis in coping mechanisms cross-culturally will help us understand why certain individuals at given levels of ego development may or may not be relatively susceptible to social definitions in applying to themselves either positive or negative concepts referring to their behavior as part of a multiethnic society.

Some individuals may be more vulnerable than others to social attitudes defining or "labeling" them as conforming or delinquent. Individuals from certain ethnic or minority groups may be more influenced than others by negative definitions of their group in assessing themselves. The Japanese in the United States were relatively independent of negative social definitions attributed to them in comparisons with more socially vulnerable groups (De Vos, 1978).

In understanding why some experiences do not "take" for individuals in given ethnic groups, let us briefly consider delinquent behavior. I have found a correspondence cross-culturally between the status of debased minorities such as Koreans and Burakumin in Japan, blacks and Mexican Americans in the United States, and southern Italians in northern Italian cities (De Vos, 1978, 1980b). I have also found selectivity of those who become delinquent in the eyes of the community dependent heavily on such factors as internal family cohesion, which may or may not be related to a cultural tradition. I infer that it is the youth of given groups that manifest high field dependence in cognitive functions that show more susceptibility to delinquency. How does this relate to alternative personality patterns?

As I view modern writings related to alienation, I perceive that Durkheim's contentions of how deviancy or suicide are related ultimately to loosening social cohesion are valid in a statistical sense. Incidence of delinquent behavior in youth is certainly another manifestation of some lack of overall social cohesiveness. It is not amiss to note a direct relationship between a high delinquency rate and the fact that in our society, 40 percent of black youths have no satisfactory social role, are unemployed, and have no grounds for optimism that their social conditions will improve.

On the other hand, the very strong relationship of these two social observations does not negate the importance of psychodynamic variables to be considered in the selectivity of delinquency in given social circumstances. In my comparative work in Italy and Japan (De Vos, 1980b) I have found in both instances, in a controlled comparison of a small number of families, that despite cultural differences and other social variables there is in each instance a notable lack of family cohesion experienced directly in those who become delinquent in contrast to members of ethnic minorities from similar circumstances who do not become delinquent. Here the measure of outer social cohesion is relative to its influence internally in particular families but not in others.

When one lives in a given social environment from infancy, one thinks with the conceptual tools available as suggested by Durkheim's concept of collective representations. But one also learns to comprehend one's inner state and the meaning of one's social attitudes in terms learned from one's primary family, and only then from one's immediate peers. One's readiness to act in a conforming or in a deviant manner with regard to the social norms of the majority differs both with one's minority status and with family cohesiveness. In some groups and some families the vicissitudes of socialization are more apt to produce, when they are detrimental, "neurotic" individuals, as in the American white or black middle class (Hollingshead & Redlich, 1958). Whereas in other groups such as lower-class Puerto Ricans in New York or lower-class ghetto blacks (De Vos, 1978), where there is already collective resentment of social authority, one is more apt to find manifest acts of social deviancy such as delinquency. Following Durkheim's concept of anomie, Merton (1957) pointed out that such groups will develop alternative modes of achievement, modes considered by the majority as criminal. Apart from that, there are on an individual, psychological level social attitudes about external authority, which in some cases derive from problems of internalization that must be examined as directly related to family socialization.

Individuals structurally incapable of anticipation of the social consequences of their behavior to themselves and others may be regarded as in the extreme position related to "openness" of experience. Individuals with high levels of imitative role playing as well as cognitive facility may be considered "psychopathic" when they practice forms of socially fraudulent behavior with little compunction as to their effect on others. In some, the capacity for fraud or fraudulent role playing is coolly instrumental. However, in others, one finds a deep expressive need to deceive and betray trust by being a fraud.

Some individuals, regardless of their relative level of cognitive constriction of field dependence, manifest a negatively perceived view of external authority and what would be considered a relative lack of internalization or a potential for guilt as a constraint on behavior. The sense of potential self-destructiveness attendant upon possible internalization of social directives may be difficult in many of these individuals. One finds among ethnic minorities (e.g., Sicilians in northern Italy or Koreans in Japan) that give evidence of these forms of socially deviant behavior there is strong present or past sense of resentment toward the majority culture, and therefore a form of justification of behavior. Should the justification of this resentment be challenged, it creates severe problems about the necessity of internalizing negative self-perceptions that are felt to be destructive. Individuals are free to act destructively toward others without automatic constraint operating to prevent their behavior so long as they have some inner justification for the appropriateness of destructive behavior toward hated groups and their dominant authorities. In situations of strong ethnic resentment there is a compounding of problems about social deviancy between the sense of group resentment and individual psychological features of personality.

A number of problems of internal malaise related to internalization have been noted in abnormal psychology and diagnosed as "narcissistic character disorders." This concept is useful in understanding the inability of some individuals to reach a sense of social and personal commitment in their relationships with others in a modern, multiethnic society. Suffice it to state that the inability to commit oneself to another person or to a fixed sense of belonging depends on an internal resolution of who one is, when open alternatives exist. One has to have some sense of a cohesive social core for the accommodative change involved in a stable identification that more selectively limits relationships to others. If one continuously absorbs alternative experiences that do not adhere, there remains a continual hunger for new ones. There is a psychological impasse particularly noted in some individuals who have narcissistic problems that result from the early period when one has to detach oneself gradually from maternal envelopment. These conceptions are useful in understanding the sense of alienation and ultimate suicide found in some Japanese authors in a modernizing Japan in contact with western alternatives (cf. De Vos, 1972, chapter 17) or Koreans residing in a socially discriminating Japan who find it is expected that they become deviant.

It is difficult for some highly sensitive, alienated Japanese to achieve any sense of social adherence. In many instances they have had some contact with western culture and found this contact challenging to their own ethnic identity. Some other Japanese, conversely, continue to commit themselves so completely that they cannot distinguish self from social role (De Vos, 1972, chapter 17).

Robert Lifton (1970) has cogently described the prevalence of "protean" individuals in modern societies such as the multiethnic United States. These are individuals who are extremely sensitive to social currents. They are flexibly responsive to various complex nuances in their social relationships. Like chameleons they change color with circumstances. Their experiences make no permanent accommodative dent that causes a stabilization of the inner self-identity.

In many such individuals the hunger for new experiences remains insatiable. The "aliments of experience," as Piaget once described them, in the early stages of the formation of conceptual schemata do not stick to the ribs of any permanent identity. Such highly sensitive people are often found in the arts. They can, in modern settings, express a type of intense social malaise. Therefore, they reflect a society in transition that has no unified concept of where it is going.

In some cases this malaise comes to the attention of the psychiatric profession. Psychiatrists have difficulty dealing with individuals of this sort since they do not fit the more traditional categories of neurosis or psychosis as they have been understood. They are therefore often termed "borderline" although their ego structures are well differentiated and in no danger of collapse. What they are suffering is another form of the problem which Erik Erikson has well documented as identity diffusion when it occurs as part of adolescent transition.

Related specifically to multiethnic situations, one finds that such individuals cannot commit themselves to any satisfactory form of social or ethnic identity that would allow them either to gain social satisfaction in some sense of social self, or, not finding the alternative satisfactions in the present, to find a way of losing oneself at least to some degree in ideology defining future human goals.

In my study of the Japanese I have reported that the more alienated authors (De Vos, 1973, chapter 18) who had come in contact with Western literature such as Sōseki or Mishima have not been able to find some religious solace on conversion to a religious system as has occurred in some of their Western counterparts such as Graham Greene or Evelyn Waugh.

Highly differentiated intellectuals who suffer a profound existential malaise, whatever their class or ethnic background, are cognitively far removed from field dependent minority youth who show poor school performance. These are, indeed, the extremes of a cognitive continuum. On the constrictive end of this continuum one finds the use of denial and repression and an exclusion of experiences that would challenge one's ethnic identity. In the other direction one finds the extremes of those sensitive to past or present social experience. External stimuli are taken in quickly. While the cognitively constrictive defend themselves from new experiences, those excessively open feel continually devastated by social alternatives. Authors such as Cesare Pavese, James Joyce, D. H. Lawrence, or James Baldwin exemplify such malaise (De Vos, 1978).

Looked at anthropologically there are numerous cultures that institutionalize forms of dissociation, which permit the more socially constricted individual in subordinate social roles to behave in alternative roles forbidden during a fully conscious state, as in voodoo behavior in Haiti (Metraux, 1946, 1959, 1960). They can realize certain potential only under trance conditions—be they the adaptation of opposite sex roles as described by Bateson in his germinal book *Naven* (1936) or by becoming powerful European officials in the African religion documented in the film on an African religion "Les Maitres Foux" as mentioned above. In this film low-status Africans in trance become possessed by powerful British officials experienced from afar during the colonial period.

There are also the extreme conditions of introjection found in mystical, ecstatic, or psychedelic experiences such as those produced by LSD, in which ego boundaries are more or less dissolved and the external is experienced consciously as taking place within the self.

In both instances these states are transitory. Neither ecstasy nor trance can be maintained. Note that there is a difference between them. Ecstasy is conscious. The self is present. In a dissociated trance the self is absent. The search for psychedelic "experience" is found in "antinomian" individuals in periods of social transition as described by Nathan Adler (1968). There is in seeking the ecstatic a desire to break the boundaries and inhibitions of ordinary roles or identities. This contrasts with the trance which occurs in seeking for liberation in a more constrictive traditional society. In a traditional setting, the self cannot participate in a conscious state in any serious break in rigidly prescribed roles or social identities.

Cognitively constrictive individuals may not be satisfied with limited roles but remain defensively "ethnic" or low in social status. They can only extend themselves under conditions where ordinary self cannot bear witness, as in trance. Conversely, individuals seeking psychedelic experiences are often not satisfied with the narrow ethnic or other social self-definitions given them by their immediate group. They seek to expand beyond previous definitions toward some hoped-for development of internal sensibility. In some individuals a continuing desire for fusion exists. They seek some form of continual, diffusively realized contact that makes them feel part of an entity rather than alone. They experience a need to merge with others. One can point to the apparently anomalous case of individuals seeking ecstatic liberation within the regulation of an external system. Cases of this type are like the anomic pre-Hitler Germans mentioned above (Fromm, 1968), finding no internal structures that permit true autonomy or self-controlled, limited social participation. They bind themselves sometimes to a cult figure, or continually seek expression in ritualistic behavior that makes them officially part of a group.

Some can have experiences of excess that frighten them, which lead to an alternative groping toward some strict religiously or ethnically defined regimen. For example, some young Jews embrace a form of rigid orthodoxy as a means of redefining the self after an attempted antinomian break. Others, resentful of their more liberal parents, seek orthodoxy as a resolution of an inner incapacity to achieve comfort in relative autonomy. The recent Iranian revolution gives evidence to similar trends toward religious nationalist identity in middle-class Iranian youth.

I can only mention here another dimension of psychoanalytic understanding of internalization. It has to do with the relative danger of libidinal or aggressive thoughts, or the danger of behavior as related to thought. Some socially deviant persons cannot afford to internalize in a satisfactory manner due to the self-destructive implication that internalization would entail (cf. the Korean youthful suicide discussed by Sasaki & Wagatsuma, 1981).

One can look at a variety of adaptive or maladaptive possibilities in which ethnic identity becomes salient. Some individuals who may rigidly internalize (such as a Flemish nationalist) may use an ethnic identity in a hostile contrastive way. On the other hand, a Fleming such as Jacques Brel who wishes to escape his ethnicity (De Vos, 1979) may be individualistically self-oriented and socially mobile and resent that others "claim" him ethnically. Some cognitively constricted ghetto youth (Pettigrew, 1964) employ narrow defensive forms of ethnic identity. Blacks who can internalize middle-class goals are marked sometimes by a so-called neurotic condition of affective constriction, and by the other defensive maneuvers as the black patients studied in therapy by Ovesey (Kardiner & Ovesey, 1962). Black adopted children of socially mobile white American parents suffer with problems of identity diffuseness, which make any stable satisfactory use of identity as a social resolution relatively difficult.

In this rather complex and dense presentation I have tried to demonstrate that there has been insufficient integration between psychological theory and research related to coping mechanisms, on the one hand, and social role theory, on the other. Basically the "me" as defined by George Herbert Mead (1934) has three components. As related to my typology the intraceptive "me" is experienced in one aspect as a part of society. On the other hand, it is experienced contrastively in the need to differentiate self from others. Third, the "me" is also experienced in a need for internal harmony and consistency. The three primitive mechanisms of introjection, projection, and denial are transmutable by socialization processes into mutually balanced mature social experiences of the self. Out of introception emerge empathy and compassion; out of exclusion a capacity for focus and concentration in pursuit of one's social roles, and out of contrast an equally salient capacity for objectivity in problem solving and intellectual mastery. The line of inquiry taken by Witkin, Piaget, and others has pointed up a need to explore systematically some of the basic problems of socialization related to the process of internalization as related to social structure as well as to personality structure.

One can surmise from this chapter that if it suffers from any imbalance it is because it is more an attempt to synthesize seemingly contrasting psychological and sociological theories, than it is an attempt to analyze their differences. Let us hope that my too metaphoric and intraceptive use of social concepts may, at least, be stimulating—the better to balance our collective purposes as social scientists—to analyze, synthesize, and bring about internal consistency in social theory, one outcome of which would be a clear understanding of ethnic identity.

PART IV
SOCIAL IDENTITY AND
EMPLOYMENT

Concepts that are successfully employed to describe and explain social phenomena seldom remain static. It is expected that unanswered questions and unaddressed problems will become the focus for extensions and elaborations. So it is with social identity. Drawing their inspiration from literary sources, the three chapters in this section extend the usefulness of the social identity model, making contact with such belletristic notions as the narratory principle, emplotment, self-narrative, and polyphony.

In parsing the fundamental identity question "Who am I?" one is forced to a semiotic exploration of the first-person singular pronoun. Not the first to try to penetrate the meanings of "I," Mancuso and Sarbin employ the "narratory principle" to guide their analysis. They argue that human beings are inveterate storymakers and storytellers. They propose that "I" is the storyteller, "me" is not coterminous with "I," rather "me" is a narrative figure in a story, such as hero, villain, or fool. The actions of the figure in the self-narrative are guided by a plot structure. Human actions, in order to be understood, must be organized into patterns, into plots. Emplotment is the process of organizing discrete actions into a meaningful story. Support for the narratory principle is drawn, in part, from current empirical work in cognitive science.

The contribution of the Gergens is in the same genre. They demonstrate the utility of the concept of self-narrative in understanding identity. Self-narratives serve the same functions for individuals as historical narratives do for societies and civilizations. Neither type of narrative has inherent directive properties but is constantly being reconstructed in the context of action. Self-narratives and historical narratives serve to justify or to criticize social acts.

The Gergens offer a taxonomy for the emplotment of self-narratives. They describe plots of stability, plots that are progressive, and plots that are regressive. The types cross over traditional literary categories. A convincing argument is made for including the notion of reciprocity for storymakers. Other persons serve as narrative figures in one's self-narrative; at the same time one becomes a figure in the self-narratives of others. This reciprocity feature supports a "sense of collective reality."

If the formulation of social identity had but one merit, it would be the concern for the complexities of human conduct. Most of the chapters in this collection propose concepts and methods that confront complexity. Human beings are seldom situated so that only a single role enactment need be accounted for. Multiple statuses are the rule—the enactment of corresponding roles may create conflict and contradiction. In his contribution, Rosenberg draws upon Shakespeare's *Macbeth* to illustrate the complex nature of identity, and coins a metaphor that sensitizes us to complexity: polyphony. Not only do we all speak in many voices, but so do reciprocal others. The events leading to the ultimate destiny of tragic heroes are, in principle, no different from those of ordinary mortals. Only by recognizing the complexity of human interaction—that each of us speaks in more than one voice—can we do justice to a robust understanding of social actions.

Chapter 11

THE SELF-NARRATIVE IN THE ENACTMENT OF ROLES

James C. Mancuso and Theodore R. Sarbin

Who is it that can tell me who I am?

King Lear I iv 237

I'll never be such a gosling to obey instinct
But stand as if a man were author of himself,
And knew no other kin.

Coriolanus V iii 34

Social identity is one of a family of terms that includes self-concept, phenomenal self, social self, ideal self, etc. In the theory of social identity advanced by Sarbin and Scheibe (1980), self is the superordinate concept, the socius being subordinate. The social identity question "Who am I?" is but one of a set of recurring self questions that demand answers.

We propose to engage in an analysis of the formation of conceptions subsumed under the general heading "self." The guiding metaphor for our analysis is the "narratory principle" (Sarbin, 1981, 1982). In the appropriate place, we shall describe how storymaking and storytelling are apt metaphors to communicate about self and its grammatical relatives "I" and "me."

In this introductory section, we describe briefly the basis for positing the narratory principle as a fundamental guide to human thought and action. Then we turn to applying the narratory principle to self, indicating that self-narratives are created and told in much the same way as stories about historical figures, fictional characters, and fabled animals. Among other things, we show how the storytelling metaphor tacitly guided other commentators on the self, including James and Mead.

In order to explore the epistemic side of self-narration, we examine contemporary work in memory and judgment. The correspondence of cognitive theorists' macrostructure with the narrativist plot structure is noted. We describe several pertinent studies on text processing that lend support to the silent operation of the narratory principle. Using the findings of cognitive research, we apply the narratory principle to the self.

We present data and argument to support the notion that "the I" and "the me" (expressions developed by James and Mead, among others) are features of a theory of self-narrative. "The I" is the narrator, the agent, the organizer; "the me" is the actor, the player, the performer. The results of applying the narrative metaphor direct us to stating the requirements for a theory of personality. Finally, we discuss the place of emotions in self-narratives, making use of the observation that the conduct generally labeled "emotion" is aptly described as a transitory social role.

THE NARRATORY PRINCIPLE

We employ the narratory principle as an overarching conception to account for the silent organizing and patterning of ecological events. In our view, the narratory principle embraces a variety of conceptions coined by psychologists to explain perceptual organization, such as combination rules, integrating hypotheses, organizing principles, macrostructure, and heuristics. These conceptions are used to account for a primary observation: people organize chaotic, meaningless sensory inputs into meaningful patterns or structures. The narratory principle gives warrant to "meanings" as the appropriate subject matter for students of thought and action.

The underlying assumption in employing the narrative as a root metaphor is: human beings think, perceive, imagine, and dream according to a narrative structure. Given two or three sensory inputs, a human being will organize them into a story, or, at least, the framework of a story. When one probes into the ordered or patterned perceptual response, it becomes immediately apparent that a plot is imposed on the disparate inputs. The construction and use of plots, herein called emplotment, is the central feature of the narratory principle.

Whether dealing with the perception of geometrical figures, the ordering of humorous cartoons, or the understanding of historical events, human beings try to emplot unorganized data into a coherent story. For example, for the organization of historical events, it has been demonstrated that historians with different aesthetic preferences organize the same data according to one rather than another class of emplotments. Comedy, tragedy, romance, and satire provided the form of emplotment for each of the leading historians of nineteenth-century Europe (White, 1973). The actions of individuals and groups (the raw data for social scientists) by themselves do not lead to comprehension, implication, and evaluation. Only when the raw data are placed in the context of a plot structure does the possibility exist for establishing a coherent account.

A number of experiments give strong support to the concept of the narratory principle. Michotte (1963) presented his subjects with a visual display that included two or more colored rectangles in motion. Under control of the experimenter were the moving figures' speed, direction, and distance traveled. For certain patterns of movement, the observers would attribute causality to the rectangles. For example, if rectangle A stopped after moving toward rectangle B, and if rectangle B then began to move, the observers would say that B got out of A's way. The observers' descriptions are interesting. "It is as if A's approach frightened B away." "It is as if A in touching B induced an electric current which set B going." "The arrival of A by the side of B acts as a sort of signal for B to G." Some of the displays produced comical effects and induced laughter.

The experiments make clear that the meaningless movements of the rectangles were assigned meaning through imposing a narrative form. The observers' reports reflect the use of miniature plots. Laughter was a response when the observers' emplotted the actions of the rectangles as narrative figures in a human comedy.

Another experiment (Heider, 1958) is even more supportive of the hypothesis that people are ready to use the idiom of the narrative to make sense of meaningless movements of geometrical figures. A short motion picture film recorded the movements of three geometrical figures at various speeds and in various directions. A large triangle, a small triangle, and a circle moved in a bounded field. Observers reported the movements of the figures as human action; the figures were reported as characters in dramatic encounters. The observers' reports were not about triangles and circles in physical motion, but about people engaged in human actions according to recognizable plot structures.

These experiments demonstrate a universally recognized fact: that stimulus inputs become organized into a pattern, the form of the pattern being influenced by previously acquired knowledge. The patterns, we believe, are likely to be expressed through the construction of a narrative plot. The organizing principle, emplotment, directs the assignment of meaning to the meaningless stimulus inputs.

Support for the narratory principle may be uncovered in the history of humanity. Storytelling has been a pervasive human activity at least since the time of the Homeric epics. It is supported by the oral tradition, still a vital force in socialization and enculturation. From ancient times to the present, parables, fables, and myths have been employed to guide moral conduct. Storytelling is universally practiced to enlighten and to entertain. A special class of stories, myths of origin and creation, have been (and continue to be) employed to illuminate cosmological questions.

A moment's reflection will convince the reader that the narratory principle is at the heart of human conduct. Consider any slice of life. We experience our fantasies and daydreams as stories. The rituals of daily life are put together to tell a story, as is the pageantry of ceremonial occasions. Our dreams are experienced and narrated as stories, sometimes with mythic colorings. Even survival may depend on the talent to employ the narratory principle. In a world of meanings, survival is problematic if the person cannot construct and interpret narratives about interweaving lives.

The equating of narrating and knowing has some support from philological analyses. "Know" and "narrate" have a common origin in the Indo-European *gna*. To know and to narrate are intimately related human actions. Current usage would place the two conceptions on a dimension of public–private: knowing is a more private action than narrating.

THE NARRATIVE METAPHOR
AND THEORIES OF SELF

The foregoing is a sketch of the narrative as a root metaphor for understanding human thought and action. With this sketch as a background, we turn specifically to theories of self.

Perhaps more than any other, symbolic interactionist theories of self hold a valued place in discussions of identity. The central conception of these theories is "that one's self concept is a reflection of one's perceptions about how one appears to others" (Shrauger & Schoeneman, 1979, p. 549). A close examination of the writings about the term "self-concept" reveals that the intended reference is the epistemic placement of self within judgment dimensions such as trait scales or other kinds of attributional measures.

A theory of self-development involves far more than a person's ability merely to locate himself along judgment dimensions. A fuller theoretical statement includes the observation that people develop a "first-order" self–concept as well as the kinds of "second-order" self-concepts (self-as-objects) employed in the studies reviewed by Shrauger and Schoeneman.

We develop our essay from a statement taken from an earlier theory of self-development. "The self as I is seen as an *inference*, a high-order inference or cognitive structure, which develops as a result of and consists of lower-order inferences (or reference schemata) which are here called empirical selves" (Sarbin, 1952, p. 19). In this essay, we advance and support the proposition that people conceptualize the first order self, the I, by treating self, metaphorically and literally, as a storyteller.

The history of personality theory is replete with efforts to elaborate and to maintain the utility of notions about self, notions that tacitly make use of the storyteller metaphor. Our objective is to make explicit the observation that the narratory principle underlies the fashioning of theories of self-development.

THE INFERENCE THAT THE I IS A STORYTELLER

Formal theorists as well as naive theorists of the self have made use of the metaphor of the storyteller. G. H. Mead (1925), who is credited with having revolutionized theories of self, wrote:

> We can talk to ourselves, and this we do in the inner form of what we call thought. We are in possession of selves just insofar as we can and do take the attitudes of others toward ourselves and respond to these attitudes. . . . We assume the generalized attitude of the group, in the censor that stands as the door of our imagery and inner conversations, and in the *affirmation of the laws and axioms of the universe of discourse.* (Mead, 1925, p. 272, italics added)

The metaphor of the storyteller is immediately apparent. Two first person we's are involved. One we takes the attitude of others toward the second we. The primary I (the singular of Mead's we) prepares a text for action by assigning roles to those who belong to our society, the roles forming second-order I's or, more grammatically, me's. I, in addition, submits the story to the censor (read literary or drama critic). By comparisons with past events, the censor "predicts" the social response that the elements of the story will evoke. The censor "pretests" the pretexts for action.

William James, another scholar who took a contextualist view of self, also implicitly incorporated the storyteller and the censor into his theory of self.

> . . . That something which at every moment goes out and knowingly appropriates the *Me* of the past and discards the non-me as foreign, is it not a permanent abiding principle of spiritual activity identical with itself wherever found? That it is such a principle is the reigning doctrine both of philosophy and commonsense, and yet reflection finds it difficult to justify the idea. If there were no passing states of consciousness, then indeed we might suppose an abiding principle, absolutely one with itself, to be the ceaseless thinker within us. But [yesterday's states of consciousness and today's states of consciousness] have a functional identity for both know the same objects and so far as the bygone me is one of those objects they

react upon it in an identical way, greeting it and calling it *mine*, and opposing it to all things they know. (James, 1892, p. 202)

James was apparently unconcerned whether his readers would recognize a "something" that "goes out and *knowingly* appropriates" the second-order me's of the past. Additionally, the censor—who also appears to have the power of knowing that which is me or mine—reacts to the storyteller's constructions! "In its widest sense, however, *a man's Me is the sum total of all he can call his*, not only his body, and his psychic powers, but his clothes . . . " (p. 177). The storyteller, the self, for James, identifies a particular psychic power as "mine," and "my state of consciousness" advises me of the "truth" of that call.

Mead and James, after all, were writing about self in the common sense as well as in the formal sense. As all writers must, James and Mead interacted with their respective readerships and tacitly strove to evoke certain imagery, believing that their references to I and We would evoke the reader's storyteller metaphor. Readers would "know" the subject of their discourse and would "know" the laws and axioms that describe the functions of storytelling selves. These writers, like any of us who can engage in sociality, knew that human beings carry out their missions in a context of constant social activities that are often perplexing, contradictory, ambiguous, and confusing, a condition that helps generate the self-as-storyteller.

James helped to redirect thinking about self-conceptualization. As a pragmatist and contextualist, he rejected the prevailing formistic conceptions of self as "a permanent abiding principle of spiritual activity."[1] James promoted the idea that we learn to categorize our second-order selves (self as object) by noticing the judgments of those around us, particularly as they relate to categorizing the "material me" and its extensions. Other twentieth-century theorists, Mead and Cooley among them, influenced by mechanistic and contextualist metaphysics, also rejected formist conceptions of a priori selves linked to submerged theological entities.

Together these thinkers moved several steps toward making explicit that which scholars of behavior had generously treated implicitly. They were at the borderline of breaking out of the kind of conceptual trap by which behavior scientists had taken for granted such concepts as "personality traits," "innate intelligence," and "insanity." Just as a long line of scholars had failed to recognize that these concepts had undergone a metaphor-to-myth transformation, so James did not recognize that preformed selves depended on an unmarked metaphor—the metaphor of self as the storyteller who reads out the labels that nature has attached to each person's inborn, behavior-guiding traits. By saying "*a man's Me is all he can call his,* not only his body, and his psychic powers, but . . . ," James tacitly introduced "self" ("he")—the storyteller who "calls" the choreography. Taking "he" as a known entity, James failed to recognize that "he" stands as a pronoun for the metaphoric storyteller. Had James undressed the metaphor, the course of the development of conceptions of self might have taken the direction of recognizing the importance of storytelling in human thought and action.

Self in Theories of Persons

James followed an ancient tradition when he took for granted this particular metaphor-turned-myth. In modern translations of Homer we find Achilles telling his mother that he would not return to his homeland, "since my *thumos* (the spirit; the source of impulse) does not bid me live or exist among men unless Hector first is struck by my spear and loses his life" (Iliad, XVIII, 90f). Each time that a person (ordinary or scholarly) says, "I expect that . . ." or "I hope that . . ." or "I wish that . . ." or "I fear that . . ." he indicates that, in his conceptual network, the I has composed a plot that is supposed to produce a particular outcome; not unlike the case of Achilles' *thumos* laying out his plot of action.

Adkin's (1970) description of Plato's conception of *psyche* demonstrates Plato's effort to elaborate the narrator metaphor. Plato divided the *psyche* into three parts (in the *Republic*): the *logistikon*, by which *psyche* calculates and reasons; the *epithumetikon*, that with which it loves, hungers, thirsts, and so forth; and the *thumoeides*, the spirited aspect which, among other things, is the source of anger at injustice. The *epithumetikon* is unruly; and, unlike the *thumoeides*, does not follow the rules of the *logistikon*. When spirit and desire become unruly the *logistikon* cannot contemplate the essence of the universe. A logical plan for action cannot be composed by the self; the storyteller cannot take full account of the platonic essences or class categories in constructing a plot. Under these conditions, scripts for self-enactments, then, would be illogical and chaotic.

It was not difficult for Saint Paul to graft Old Testament views of man's basic sinfulness onto Plato's conceptions of the narrator, and to establish a view of self that has dominated Western thought for nearly 2,000 years. In Paul's version, self constantly struggled for control of the storymaking and storytelling process. Throughout life self is antagonized by flesh (pseudonym: Passion), the source of human evil.

The passions, like the *epithumetikon*, take over reason. Bercovitch (1975) documents an extreme form of the views that grew out of Paul's early Christian personality theory. The Puritans in America, to be pure and to deserve their deliverance to their new land of Canaan, raised their struggle against their sinfulness to the level of an internecine war—a war of "a Puritan Sisyphus, driven by self-loathing to Christ and forced back to himself by the recognition that his labors are an assertion of what he loathes" (p. 19). If a Puritan engaging in this struggle were to prepare an inappropriate plot or plan for action, he would have to construct the plot by turning to his personal faith, and incorporate a recognition of Christ's power against the anti-Christ. The latter figure, embodied in flesh, diverts self from the way of salvation. Faith would guide dramatic action, and the Puritan would find direction in overcoming the basic human evil, which constantly seeks its expression in behavior.

Psychoanalysis and the Self

Trilling (1972) explored the bases for the concern about self-expression that became evident in the seventeenth century, contemporaneously with the burgeoning of the New World Puritan concern about self. He shows the relationship between the development of personality theory and the effort to maintain the self-as-storyteller metaphor. Trilling notes that in the eighteenth-century novelists became concerned with the matter of sincerity. Could a person be taken to be sincere? What were a person's obligations to be sincere? Society, as represented by those with whom one interacts, disapproved of insincerity. In other terms, people expect others to demonstrate personal sincerity by enacting self-composed scripts that show sequential consistency between acts, claims, avowals, and other verbalizations. Subplots that conflicted with one another made for an improper or unconvincing story. Against this demand for consistency, sincerity became a virtue. The problems of insincerity were compounded when the storyteller "read reviews," that is, observed the reactions of others to his enacted tale, and then agreed that the figure in the narrative, the second order self, had acted inconsistently.

After tracing out the literary history of the ideas of sincerity and authenticity, Trilling notes the relationship between personality theory and the storyteller metaphor. He proposes that the growth of psychoanalysis—a theory which purports to expose inauthenticity—is related to the modern disenchantment with narration. " . . . psychoanalysis is a science which is based upon narration, upon telling. Its principle of explanation consists in getting the story told—somehow, anyhow—in order to discover how it begins" (p. 140).

Trilling, correctly showing that psychoanalysis is implicitly concerned with narration, contributes to our understanding that Freud's theory, while adhering to the narrator metaphor, held out the promise of helping one to discover the "true" beginning of the story. Psychoanalytic processes purported to lead to the reality (libidinal instinct) for which the story's events substituted, and to help a person come to terms with his own deplorable inauthenticity. Freud's theory is viewed as an effort to provide biologically meaningful, if pessimistic, explanations of the internal narrator (the ego, the I) that fails to adhere to the rules that bind a storyteller. The metaphor of self-as-storyteller was preserved by utilizing the "libidinal energy" metaphor. Like Plato's *epithumetikon*, Freud's unbridled libido could intrude to confound the storyteller.

The preceding observation highlights the point that Freud and Plato both subscribed implicitly to the metaphor of the narrator. Both developed similar resolutions to problems that evolved from their efforts to apply the interlocked premises within their knowledge networks relating to the self-as-storyteller. As they resolved these problems they publicly communicated their basically similar conclusions. Freud's communications were well received by a growing, mechanistic behavior science movement; and he was credited with "discovering" the unconscious forces. Freud's work authenticated the procedures by which psychological practitioners worked to lead patients to uncover the source of the whole story. That is, by psychoanalytic technique a healer could reveal that another character in the story, the libido, lurked continuously in the dark shadows to lure the enacted selves into neurotic performances, many of which bore the taint of sexuality. The twentieth-century patient sought help from a modern, medically trained doctor to discover the presence of this updated version of Plato's allegorical character, the *epithumetikon*—the source of unruly passions.

We note that the process of constructing abstracted schematics involving a figure such as *epithumetikon* or libido is not unlike the creation of Bunyonesque allegory. Characters or places are invented, as abstractions, to account for the turns in the story plot. Psychoanalysts, unlike Bunyon, can assume the status of scientists because their narrative figures are masked as "energies" rather than animistic or spiritistic entities. Further, they promised to reveal the story's beginnings; which is to say, they have promised to uncover the mainspring of human action.

Radical Mechanism and Self

After the middle of the twentieth century, mechanistic psychologists (behaviorists) had provided the foundation for a personality theory that purported to eliminate those remnants of formism and vitalism contained in psychoanalytic and trait-oriented theories. Significantly, one can readily detect the failure of mechanistic principles when one tries to apply them to discussions of self. Bowers (1973) focused on this failure. He was responding to Mischel's (1968) advocacy of situationism. "While trait and state theories search for consistencies in people's behavior across situations, social behavior theory seeks order and regularity in the form of general rules that relate environmental changes to behavior changes" (p. 150). "Behavior depends on stimulus situations and is specific to the situation" (p. 177). Bowers (1973) notes that if one adopted the mechanistic features of this variant of behaviorism, he would find "individual differences in behavior within the same situation as something of an embarrassment—to be conceptualized as a result of past experience or simply as error variance" (p. 318). He goes forward and then makes a statement that mechanists find unassimilable: " . . . situations are as much a function of the *person* as the person's behavior is a function of the situation" (p. 327, emphasis added). In this sentence the italicized person is easily taken to be self-as-storyteller. By introducing the storyteller a theorist removes the acting selves—the me's—from being under the exclusive control of the environment. Choice is ascribed to Self. Mechanists hold to a preconception that the cosmos *is* a mass of events that are causally interconnected by forces. In this cosmology a cause temporally precedes an effect. To propose that Self is an agent, a cause of action, is to contravene a basic proposition in mechanist cosmology. To say that self is a cause leaves unfinished the task of mechanistically explaining the cause of self.

It is no surprise, then, that mechanists have argued to demonstrate the invalidity of the concept of self-as-author, as creator of scripts. Reinforcement, as an energy concept, can better explain that which appears to be self-choice. "An organism can be reinforced by—can be made to 'choose'—almost any given state of affairs" (Skinner, 1956, p. 1065).

But, as Bowers has noted, mechanism at its best is embarrassed by the appearance of responses that differ from those which had been reinforced in a particular situation. For example, Bandura and Walters (1963), in their influential exposition of a mechanistic personality theory say:

> In all cultures there are social demands, customs, and taboos that require a member to exhibit self-control . . . . In conforming to these [social demands], the child has often to relinquish behavior that has previously led to immediate and direct reinforcement and to replace this by responses that are less efficient for obtaining immediate reinforcement for the agent. Thus, even the basic socialization processes involve the acquisition of a certain degree of self-control and the observing of social prohibitions and requirements. (p. 165)

In this quotation the term *child*, like the term *person* in the quotation from Bowers, stands in place of the term self-as-author. The child (self) may, somehow, "relinquish" a behavior that had previously been attached, by reinforcement, to a particular stimulus situation. The problem for the mechanist, at this point, is to describe this relinquishment while adhering to mechanistic principles.

Bandura (1977), in a considered effort to go beyond mechanistic, behavior-explaining principles, retrieved the narrator metaphor and gave the storyteller the power of calculating expectations.

> An efficacy expectation is the conviction that one can successfully execute the behavior required to produce the outcomes. Outcomes and efficacy expectations are differentiated, because individuals can believe that a particular course of action will produce certain outcomes, but if they entertain serious doubts about whether they can perform the necessary activities such information does not influence their behavior.
> . . . The strength of people's convictions in their own effectiveness is likely to affect whether they will even try to cope with given situations. (p. 193)

In this quotation, the terms *individuals*, *they* (in the phrase "if they entertain serious doubts"), and *people* stand in for self. Self is convinced, Bandura appears to say, that one of the second-order selves can produce or cannot produce particular outcomes, thus self can predict the course of a story in which the second-order self might become the protagonist. If self has a positive "efficacy expectation," the self-as-actor "tries to cope with the situation." Bandura is not explicit about "who" determines that one's self is capable.

As noted above, we observe that the network of concepts that are used to view the first-order self is that network that is used to describe a storyteller. As an illustration, we can recognize that we are talking about people's conceptual networks. We can then reformulate Bandura's statement, as follows: A person believes that his/her self, as author, has knowledge about the effectiveness of the second–order self (self as narrative figure). The composition of a particular plot (beginning, protagonist, means, goals, outcomes, etc.), then, depends on self's efficacy expectations. We now turn to considerations about the conceptual network surrounding self.

THE STRUCTURE OF SELF-NARRATIVE

In that people conceptualize the first-order self, I, as a storyteller, they will think about the construction of plots for second-order selves, me's, in the same terms that they think about narrative construction in general. This argument is built on the basic assumption that epistemic processes are constructive. That is, all input is organized by the knower, then stored in memory. This organizing takes place in a context that includes epistemic networks already represented and stored by the person.

Macrostructure, Plot Structure

In the narrativist vocabulary, the author of one's self-narrative constructs characters, figures, and roles to meet the requirements of his/her story. Macbeth, for example, authors no less than 17 second-order selves, such as warrior, murderer, husband, philosopher, etc. (see Rosenberg, this volume).

The observation that people continuously reconstruct selves, me's, can be profitably interpreted as memory processing. Some contemporary investigators have described the restructuring of events (including selves) with the help of a model that emphasizes semantic networks: that is, patterns of meaning (Collins & Loftus, 1975; Collins & Quillian, 1972a, b).

Recent experimental work on cognition makes use of categories that are parallel, if not isomorphic, to the categories that illuminate storytelling. The language of cognitive science, derived from spatial and mechanical metaphors, conveys a message similar to the description of storymaking and storytelling.

We cannot review in this chapter the considerable progress in the study of prose processing (see, for example, Fredricksen, 1977; Kintsch, 1977; Mandler & Johnson, 1977; Rumelhart, 1975; Thorndyke, 1977; van Dijk, 1977). A critical review of this work would make clear that people carry about an extended, tacitly applied knowledge network about the ways in which stories are emplotted. As indicated in our introduction, it appears obvious that in the course of their experience with stories people develop and use anticipatory schemata or plot structures to make sense of potential nonsense. People bring to an incipient story a previously learned catalog of plots, which is then used to comprehend and to encode the currently perceived text.

Stories are constructed in the same manner as are sentences. The emplotment of a story parallels the ordering of a proper syntactical sequence. Novelists, poets, and historians have long recognized that people search out narrative dependencies, such as cause and effect relationships, goal seeking, connections, and conflict resolution, and these expectancies guide the comprehension of discourse. Further, since anticipatory schemata, such as plots, scripts, and themes, actually facilitate comprehension, memory and recall are enhanced. The ability to relate new information to an existing structure influences initial storage and subsequent retrieval from long-term memory.

Comtemporary research is accumulating to support the notion that people take "macropropositions" to their reading of textual materials.

These macropropositions, which follow from the person's implicit theory of how stories are emplotted, allow inferences to be built from the propositions that are directly cued in the language of the text. Such tacitly constructed inferences provide summary structure to the text in the form of abstract frames or scripts. As a result, the gist of a story is easily recalled by cueing the abstract frame (that is, the plot) along the specific cues that fit the frame for the narrative under discussion.

Given that experience with storytelling provides a basis for acquiring and using plot structures, we would expect emplotment strategies of individuals to reflect cultural differences. Tannen (1980) explored differences in macrostructure by comparing stories told by Greek women to stories told by American women. American women, among other things, more regularly acted as if they were engaged in a memory experiment. Greek women were more clearly bent on telling a story that followed a personally chosen theme. As a result, American women reported more extraneous detail, whereas Greek women tended to report only that detail which helped to develop the theme they had chosen to follow. The Greek women more often constructed causal inferences based on human motives, whereas American women used concrete, empirical cause–effect links.

Tannen's data illustrate the consequences of differential cultural exposure to storytelling style. She suggests that the Greek culture continues to be heavily influenced by the oral tradition, as described by Olson (1977), whereas the American style reflects the kind of systematic, conventionalized storytelling strategies that are promoted by the Western European literate tradition. Olson notes, for example, that the literate tradition has promoted the conception of singular, direct, empirically demonstrable causal linkages.

To recapitulate, one's reading or listening to a narrative is guided, facilitated, and organized by one's anticipations of the plot sequence. If a person's experiences have led to the development of a catalog of plots—a narrative grammar—that allows for anticipating and organizing the sequence of a prose passage, he/she can more readily process, store, and then recall the story's contents. There is evidence that one develops plot structures as one develops any epistemic category and that the actions of other persons in one's social mileu facilitate the development of one or another kind of plot structure.

Macrostructure and Self-Defining Scripts

The foregoing digest is preliminary to a discussion of self-narrative and the place of first and second-order selves, I's and me's. It seems clear that people interpret occurrences in ways that correspond to their knowledge network relative to the macrostructure of stories. A self-narrative must, like any other narrative have at least a beginning, a middle, and ending, or, at least, the sense of an ending (Kermode, 1967). Causal linkages are to be specified as simple categorical connections or computed calculations of probabilities of achieving ends. As noted before, personality theorists have been engaged in efforts to lay out socially validated theories concerning the operation of Self. Under this kind of analysis some personality theories can easily be seen as Bunyonesque allegories. Some allegorical theories, like psychoanalysis, are taken to be major scientific advances. They appear to explain mysteries that cannot be easily subsumed by more general, socially validated, naive theoretical views of the storyteller who is skilled in manipulation of the details of plot structures. Such allegorical explanation accounts for the fallibility of storytellers (the intrusion of Plato's *epithumetikon* or Freud's libido) while retaining general macrostructural principles.

Constructing Second-Order Selves

The symbolic interactionist perspective on self, as noted before, focuses on the ways in which a person validates his/her self-enactments. In the foregoing text we have advanced the proposition that the first-order self-concept, *I*, self-as-storyteller, is a construction that persons develop for use in understanding the creation of self-narratives. The protagonists in these self-narratives are selves-as-objects, that is, second-order selves. In explaining their own ongoing self presentations, people act as if they hold the belief that self-as-storyteller (the I) has authored a script to guide role enactments as heroes, villains, fools, or whatever.

Our prescription for a personality theory must include the source of self-defining action. A theory of persons should specify the acquisition, retention, and functioning of the epistemic networks that a person employs in the processing of stimuli associated with his/her own role enactments, that is, the defining actions for his/her second-order selves.

Whereas the foregoing discussion has focused on a commonplace epistemic network relative to self-as-organizer, a theoretical framework for discussing the construing of on-the-spot second-order selves (me's) is available. Mancuso and Ceely (1980) analyzed the construction of second-order scripts in the current technical language of memory-process functioning. From a constructivist/contextualist orientation, they supported the utility of the concept of schema in discussions of memory processes. Each part of a person's stream of conduct is then seen to be a reconstruction of a self-standard—a self-defining construction—by which the person anticipates the subsequent sensory input.

Mancuso and Ceely borrow heavily from the concepts elaborated by Rumelhart, Lindsey, and Norman (1972), Rumelhart and Ortony (1977), and Collins and Loftus (1975). Rumelhart and his associates focus on the idea of embedding of representational units within a person's memory system. These writers distinguish between the representation and storage of abstract as against specific information. They use the term, schema, as a counterpart to our terms, self-standard and self-construction. In their discussion schemata refer to the data structures that represent the abstract, or generic, constructions that can be retrieved from long-term memory.

The notion of embedded schemata designates hierarchically ordered generic, person-describing attributes or properties. For example, in the self-defining proposition, "I am a 'hostile' person," hostile designates a generic subschema; that is, a schema subsumed by a superordinate such as "socially bad." Additional subschemata that might be embedded in a person's superordinate socially bad–socially good schema would be evasive, inconsiderate, slovenly, and so forth, not all of which holds the same criteriality in delineating the socially bad prototype.

In an action situation the narrator self creates a self-as-object to meet the requirements of a plot. Selves or actors are constructed from a stored representation of schema and its subsumed subschemata. The subschemata involved constitute variable slots that are filled during the (re)construction process.

It is not without interest that Rumelhart and Ortony (1977) draw a parallel between self-defining schemata and a play in which "the internal structure of the schemata correspond to the script of the play" (p. 101). Scripts and plays are categories of the humanities, the home of literature and narrative emplotment. Among others turning to humanistic studies for descriptive categories Abelson (1975), Schank (1975a, 1975b), and Schank and Abelson (1977) clearly adopt a storytelling mode. They focus on episodic memory, that is, memory organized around one's involved role enactments (Tulving, 1972). The unit chosen to represent this specific or contextually bound information in memory is the episode, corresponding to an event or action sequence in which self-as-object is a narrative figure.

Abelson and Schank also describe a generalization process in memory organization, represented by the grouping of contextually similar episodes. Features or properties common to the different episodes may then be identified and organized. The resulting semantic or generic memory structure is a script that, like a general narrative plot can include variable slots (character descriptions) corresponding to the range of instances contained in the various input episodes subsumed by the respective scripts.

Variability and Stability of Second-Order Selves

A large problem looms over this discussion. At several points we have referred to variable slots in generic schemata. In this story about the working of memory, an assumption is held that these variable slots may be filled with generic subschemata, or with feature- and property-defining subschemata. For example, a person might instantiate self-as-object with the generic schema anger. Rather than fill the slot that describes "vocal characteristics" with loud and high pitched, the slot is filled with normal volume, slowly, and deliberately enunciated. This concept of variable slots is crucial in a discussion of self, for it is by this concept that one accounts for variation in role enactment across situations that might be said to be similar. A person might enact an anger script, but, depending on context (with employer, with teenage son, with lover) the enactment will vary. His "me's," second-order selves, are not replicates. Schemata that represent the features of selves and the relational linkages that unite these properties within generic schemata are posited as the elements of storage. These subschemata are, metaphorically, "plugged into" the generic schemata— the macrostructures or plot structures that are retrieved to guide the memory processing involved in the reconstruction of self as hero, self as bystander, self as victim, or other second-order selves. We face the question, What influences the selection of the subschemata (subplots) that are plugged into the variable slots?

This problem's importance is reflected in, among other things, the attention given it by contemporary investigators (Collins & Loftus, 1975; McClelland & Rumelhart, 1981). These essays rely on quasi neurological language, e.g., spread of activation, inhibition, facilitation, and so on. The concepts marked by these terms are congruent with current knowledge regarding neurological functioning. As such, they are especially appealing to behavior scientists. To us, these concepts are metaphors that help to describe how details are fitted into generic plot structures. More specifically, these sometimes opaque metaphors describe the ways in which a self fills in the subplots that are retrieved to create second-order selves.

It would not serve our purposes here to iterate the arguments to support one or another of the conceptions applied by cognitive theorists to discussing how the variable slots are filled. Suffice it to say that current work in cognition makes use of an assumption that is also central to story construction. McClelland and Rumelhart (1981) put it well. " . . . we assume that 'top-down' or 'conceptually driven' processes work simultaneously and in conjunction with 'bottom-up' or 'data driven' processing to provide a sort of multiplicity of constraints that jointly determine what we perceive. Thus, for example, we assume that knowledge about words of the language interacts with the incoming featural information in co-determining the nature and time course of the perception of the letters in the word" (pp. 377–378).

In the narrativist language, the assumption would be expressed as follows. Knowledge about plot structures and scripts for particular role enactments interact with incoming information about role location, role demands, etc. It is the simultaneous "top-down" and "bottom-up" process that co–determines the nature and the temporal sequence of the actions of the self as narrative figure. For example, once the script for angry person has been activated, the contents of the script may vary, but the interplay of input and plot will jointly determine whether or not the actor will holler, threaten physical harm, use abusive epithets, etc.

Attending to the Storyteller

When a person completes a script, such as the angry-person script, that script becomes the framework for the self-standard (Carver & Scheier, 1981), or the reference signal (Powers, 1973, 1978) against which input is constantly monitored. We assume, also, that the script generated contains an action component (Weimer, 1977). The actions (performance, role enactments) are carried out in anticipation of changes in the ecology. The target for the angry-person script is expected to react by apologizing, by withdrawal, by reciprocal anger, etc.

These scripts, taken as standard definitions, simultaneously become "top-down" conceptualizations that must integrate the subsequent bursts of sensory input. And, in this way, the self-standards are anticipations of the ensuing input about self. This use of "anticipation" is consistent with the fundamental postulate of George Kelly's personal construct theory (1955) (Mancuso & Adams-Webber, 1982). At those times when the filled-in script, i.e., the self-standard, fails to integrate ecological input, the person may be described as experiencing epistemic strain (strain in knowing) (Sarbin & Mancuso, 1980, p. 196). Intense psychological effort is then mobilized to derive new, potentially confirmable hypotheses. People have no difficulty in recognizing these situations of problematic anticipation. Script building—the setting of self-standards—happens on the spot to anticipate the next moves of self and others.

Reconsidering the Storyteller Metaphor

This effort to consider self within the framework of concepts from current work on cognitive processes does not take us a great distance from the self-as-storyteller metaphor. By accepting the propositions explicitly and implicitly embodied in the above discourse, we would view all psychological activity as a matter of processing sensory input through a system by which that input evokes schemata, categories, plots, etc. (Note that we, with less than exemplary agility, have avoided serious questions about how that system was set in place. We have, however, presented results of investigations that support the basic proposition that experience, particularly with cultural factors, does shape a person's epistemic system.) Any principle which describes input processing is applicable to the creation and development of second-order selves. Whether in the language of cognition or of narration, schemata or plots make sense of events. The schema or plot that integrates the input is simultaneously an anticipation.

When events in the world fail to match the world as anticipated, epistemic strain is experienced, a condition that brings the construing process "on to attention." Ordinarily, the storyteller modifies the narrative to optimize epistemic strain.

In this account of self, the anticipation is the expected outcome for the story. Paradoxically, the beginning of the story stands in as the end of the story. Like any story, the meaning of events within the action becomes fully apparent only when the ending is told. The self-narrative is no exception. There are the plots, there are the roles to be played, the feedback from other actors, the modification of action and/or plot, and the sense of an ending (Kermode, 1967). The organizing facet of personality, the self-as-narrator, is continuously engaged in the preparation of scripts that will allow confirmation of the initial descriptions applied to the narrative figures whose actions operate on the feedback-producing environment.

This organizing function comes to attention at those points in the enactment of a script when the audience (the environment) fails to validate the appropriateness of the action sequences. At this point, the catalog of text-processing plots is retrieved and another plot is employed. The self, the referent for the I, now looks like a storyteller who creates narratives that have appropriate beginnings, protagonists, antagonists, cause-and-effect sequences, goals, consequences, and so forth. Like all storytellers, the goal of the creator of the self-narrative is to produce a coherent story. The criterion of coherence, of course, is variable from person to person and from time to time. Because of space limitations, we cannot enter into a discussion of the aesthetics of narratives, self or other. Suffice it to say that the criteria for a coherent story are not recondite (Sarbin, 1981, 1982; Sutton-Smith, 1979, 1980).

An Example: Emotions and Self-Narrative

When a person behaves as if he were angry, it can be explained in a variety of ways. A careful look at some explanations will, however, reveal the reliance on the self-as-storyteller metaphor. One actor, reflecting his use of the metaphor might say, "He made me angry. I lost control and I let him have it. I hope I taught him a lesson." An application of the framework developed in this essay would lead us to transmute this statement into "That man's actions put me (second-order self) into a state of anger. My storyteller lost control, and my second-order self carried out actions that are a part of the anger state. The self as storyteller had calculated that the self as actor would probably succeed in halting that man's actions." In this translation, however, anger appears to come from outside the storyteller. Anger pushes aside the self and takes over the person's conduct. As in Plato's and as in Freud's theory, an emotion is taken to be an intrusion into the smooth unfolding of a story.

Averill (1979, 1980a, 1980b) presents a series of propositions in which anger itself is a scripted story. Anger, like any other emotion, is a transitory social role. Anger would not be taken to be outside the storyteller. The transitory social role labeled anger would be called forth and would become the script for the self as actor. It has, however, become commonplace, through thousands of years of experience, to treat anger as a passion. Averill carefully analyzes the history and current usage of emotion as passion, and proposes that this long history helps to account for the entrenchment and extensive validation of the authenticity of the script.

The idea of an anger script meshes well with our previous discussion of self-categorization and nested schemata. Indeed, the subschema for passion becomes central to this view of anger as a transitory social role. We would begin, as one begins to discuss any epistemic process, by assuming that a person will use the anger script when he/she faces a particular set of events. As Averill points out

> the classification of 'typical' instigations to anger is no simple matter . . . . One source of difficulty has been the tendency to focus on the specific kinds of incidents which arouse anger, . . . as opposed to the manner in which such incidents are evaluated by the individuals involved. For example, is the [anger-inducing] interruption (criticism, etc.) considered justified, or could it have been avoided with a little care and foresight? (p. 48)

When people introspect with regard to the instigation of anger they usually refer to some kind of unjustified or avoidable harm.

To discuss the beginning of anger, we remind the reader that the ending of the story is always implicated in the story's construction. In other words, when a particular plot is activated to make sense of occurrences, the ending of the story is set, and action is conducted toward obtaining environment–induced feedback that validates the ending.

This process usually proceeds without coming on attention. It is when the process fails—and anger scriptings frequently fail—that the person tries to introspect his construction of the input. At this point the person's storytelling macrostructure is clearly exemplified in the introspected cognitive activity. The plot calls for insertion of beginnings, causes, consequences, and so forth. In the introspection, causes are supplied, and in the cultures with which we are familiar unjustified harm becomes the causal nexus.

In the example above, the ending of the story is "teaching him (the target of the anger) a lesson." The variable slots in the story macrostructure are filled in with action-guiding subschemata that can produce a reaction in the target, and that reaction might be, among other things, subsequent restraint or expressions directed toward the self as actor.

The variable slots in the anger script might contain "steady, cold, precise enunciation of the actor's objection"; or, "loud, high pitched vocalizations"; or, "quavering voice, suggesting intense holding back of violent action" or, indeed "violent action." We would agree with Averill that one feature of the anger script is rarely variable, the attribution of the emotion to a class of events called passions. In the societies with which we are familiar, the generic schema for anger invariably contains the subschema labeled passion. To be under the influence of a passion is to be out of control. The very idea of passion is a subplot in the overall emplotment of emotional reactions.

From this perspective, then, that which Freud and Plato took to be an intruder into the storyteller's activity is but another instance of the storyteller's choice of roles. In other words, in certain contexts the narrator's purposes are achieved by assigning to the second order self, the me, the transitory social role of anger. Averill provides a suitable conclusion to this discussion of anger as a transitory social role. The term anger is applicable to "a socially constituted response which helps to regulate interpersonal relations through the threat of retaliation for perceived wrongs, and which is interpreted as a passion rather than as an action so as not to violate the general cultural prescription against deliberately harming another" (p. 71). In short, many people are not willing to believe that they would compose a story in which the second-order self, self-as-actor, would engage in mean or cruel conduct. For these people the anger script can be called up. It then appears to the world and to the author that the metaphoric storyteller had been overpowered, overwhelmed by the intrusion of passion.

Denouement

To tell this story we have made use of high-level abstractions, not unlike the employment of allegorical figures. The moral of the story, however, is commonplace to human psychological activity. In the context that human beings are inveterate storytellers, we have tried to show that people act as authors of self-narratives. Not only are they the authors and dramatists but also the narrative figures and actors. We have reviewed some of the current work on memory and judgment processes to relate the storyteller metaphor to current psychological work.

The implications of these views are easily stretched to include other commonplace matters. In other work (Sarbin & Mancuso, 1980) we have discussed the ways in which the verdict of schizophrenia is declared on persons who fail to develop and to maintain validated self-concepts. In that discussion our focus was on the failure of selves as narrative figures—second-order selves. We now would need to consider thoroughly the consequences of developing and using an unconventional concept of first-order self. What happens when one believes that his life story is created by his master-mind psychology professor, or by an all powerful diety, or by a computer that floats in outer space? Why does such an individual become a candidate for phenothiazine treatment, while a person who believes that his life is guided by an internal storyteller does not so readily reach that candidacy? What happens when a person believes that he/she has authored inconsistent stories about the same narrative figure? Does psychotherapy help people to answer questions such as: Is it legitimate for the self (as author) to assign self-as-actor to the class socially good, when the self-as-actor performs an assertively angry script? Is such valuation consistent with being assigned to the class, socially bad, when self-as-actor performs a hostile anger script? Is psychotherapy a course in drama or literary criticism?

NOTE

1. The terms contextualist and formist are drawn from Pepper's (1942) root metaphor analysis of metaphysical positions. The place of formistic, mechanistic, and contextualistic paradigms in behavior sciences is discussed explicitly in Mancuso (1977), Sarbin (1977), and Sarbin and Mancuso (1980).

Chapter 12

NARRATIVES OF THE SELF

Kenneth J. Gergen and Mary M. Gergen

Man is always a storyteller! He lives surrounded by his and others' myths.
With them he sees everything in his life, no matter what befalls him. And
he seeks to live his life as though he were telling it. (Sartre)

Traditionally inquiry into self-conception has been concerned with
states of being, that is, with the individual as a stabilized entity. The
research concern has been essentially triadic. It has first entailed the
development of a wide variety of measuring instruments designed to tap the
structure, content, and evaluative underpinning of the individual's self-
conception at a given time. Second, it has focused on various factors that
could figure in the determination and alteration of the individual's conception of self. Finally it has been occupied with the effects of a given
configuration of self-conception on subsequent activity. Thus, for example,
researchers have developed instruments for assessing self-esteem, have
examined a range of formative influences, and explored the behavioral
implications of possessing various levels of self-esteem. Yet, in spite of the
many insights generated in this traditional orientation to self, it is important
to recognize its limitations. In doing so, we may become sensitized to
significant lacunae in theoretical development. It is just such limitations in
the traditional orientation that set the stage for the present undertaking.

Work on the present chapter was facilitated by a grant from the National Science
Foundation (#7809393) and the working facilities at Heidelberg University so graciously
provided by Carl F. Graumen. We wish also to express our appreciation to the following
friends whose self-narratives gave us inspiration for this chapter: Winston J. Churchill,
Deborah Curtiss, Emil Liebman, Harvey S. Miller, and Dagmar Westrick.

Traditional research on self-conception is earmarked by two widely prevailing characteristics: such research tends to be both *mechanistic* and *synchronic*. It is mechanistic in its assumption of an internal structure governed in mechanical fashion by external inputs, and it is synchronic in its concern with the causes and effects of the individual's characterization of him or herself at a given moment. Thus the individual is generally imbued with a structure of self-descriptions (concepts, schemata, prototypes) that remains stabilized until subjected to external influences from the social surroundings. While revealing in certain respects, such orienting assumptions are myopic in others. First, they ignore the individual's capacity to shape actively the configuration of self-conception. They deny the potential of the individual for reflexive reconstruction of self-understanding. Needed then is attention to the ways in which the individual actively constructs his or her view of self, not as a pawn to social inputs, but as a constructive agent in social life. Second, the traditional views fail to appreciate the individual's understanding of him or herself as a historically emerging being. It may be argued that one's view of self in a given moment is fundamentally nonsensical unless it can be linked in some fashion with his or her past. Suddenly and momentarily to see oneself as "fat," "poetic," or "male," for example, might seem mere whimsy unless such concepts could be attached to a temporal context revealing their genesis. How did it come about that such terms are being employed in the present context? The fact that people believe they possess identities fundamentally depends on their capacity to relate fragmentary occurrences across temporal boundaries. The present analysis, specifically concerned with the individual's active construction of personal history, is thus *reflexive* and *diachronic*. It is concerned with states of active becoming as opposed to passive being.

We shall employ the term "self-narrative" to refer to the individual's account of the relationship among self-relevant events across time. In developing a self-narrative the individual attempts to establish coherent connections among life events (Cohler, 1979; Kohli, 1981). Rather than seeing one's life as simply "one damned thing after another," the individual attempts to understand life events as systematically related. They are rendered intelligible by locating them in a sequence or "unfolding process" (de Waele & Harré, 1979). One's present identity is thus not a sudden and mysterious event, but a sensible result of a life story. As Bettelheim (1976) has argued, such creations of narrative order may be essential in giving one's life a sense of meaning and direction.[1]

It is the purpose of the present chapter to open consideration of the manner in which people construct narratives for the self. Our analysis is divided into two parts. First we shall consider narrative forms, in both their temporal and dramatic aspects. The attempt in this case will be to develop a means of characterizing forms of narrative. Using this analysis as grounding we can turn to the relationship of self-narratives to social interaction. Although self-narratives are possessed by individuals, their genesis and sustenance may be viewed as fundamentally social. The function of differing narrative forms along with their construction in social interaction will be of particular concern.

Before embarking on this analysis a word must be said about the relationship between the concept of self-narrative and related theoretical notions. In particular, the concept of self-narrative bears an affinity with a variety of constructs falling generally within the domains of rule-role and dramaturgical theory. However, there are significant distinctions. The concepts of rule (Harré & Secord, 1972), role prescription (Sarbin & Allen, 1968–1969), interaction ritual (Goffman, 1974), and scripts (Schank & Abelson, 1977) have all been employed in dealing with the psychological basis for sequences of action across time. Further, in each case, theorists have generally assumed an autonomous base for human action. In these respects such terms are similar to the concept of self-narrative. However, unlike the latter concept, theorists in each of these cases have tended to assign governing or directive functions to the various structures. That is, the individual is said to consult or interrogate the relevant rule, role prescription, ritual understanding, or script for indications of proper or appropriate conduct. The individual thus carries with him or her a psychological template relevant to interaction sequences, and assesses the propriety of his or her behavior in accord with the template. In contrast, we view the self-narrative as possessing no inherent directive capabilities. Rather, it may be viewed as a construction undergoing continuous alteration as interaction progresses. The individual in this case does not consult the narrative for information.[2] Rather, the self-narrative is a linguistic implement constructed and reconstructed by people in relationships, and employed in relationships to sustain, enhance, or impede various actions. In this sense, self–narratives function much as histories within the society more generally. Histories do not in themselves have directive capacities. They are symbolic systems used for such social purposes as justification, criticism, and social solidification.

DIMENSIONS OF NARRATIVE FORM

Man, in a word, has no nature; what he has is . . . history. (Ortega y Gasset)

To argue that individuals attempt to knit their life events into coherent sequences is to open the door to a variety of interesting and important issues. What functions do self-narratives play in the life of the individual; can self-narratives be distinguished in terms of their functional as opposed to dysfunctional capacities; what are the origins of self-narratives; and what relationship do such narratives bear to social life more generally? Inquiry into such issues depends importantly on the existence of a differentiated vocabulary of narrative form. Without distinctions among narrative forms theoretical explorations of these various issues may remain shallow or constrained. Although a full elaboration of narrative form is beyond the scope of this chapter, our later discussion of the social context of narrative will benefit from consideration of two major aspects of form: the temporal and the dramatic.

TEMPORAL FORM IN SELF-NARRATIVE

One essential aspect of narrative is the capacity to generate directionality among events; that is, to structure the events in such a way that they move over time in an orderly way toward a given end.[3] Our initial question concerning this temporal aspect of narrative concerns that of variations in form. On what grounds can one distinguish among forms of temporal sequence? There are few available resources on which to draw in answering this question. The most extensive accounts of variations in narrative form are found in the analysis of drama and literature. In his analysis of mythical forms, for example, Northrup Frye (1957) argues that there are four basic forms of narrative, each of which is rooted in the human experience with nature and most particularly with the evolution of the seasons. Thus, the experience of spring and the uprising of nature gives rise to the comedy. In the classic tradition comedy typically involves a challenge or threat, which is overcome to yield a happy ending. A comedy need not be humorous. It is, rather, similar to what is now popularly called a melodrama. Problematic situations develop and are overcome. In contrast, the free and calm of summer days give inspiration to the romance as a dramatic form. The romance in this case consists of a series of episodes in which the major protagonist experiences challenges or threats and in each case emerges victorious. The romance need not be concerned with attraction between people. During the autumn, when one experiences the contrast between the life of summer and the death of coming winter, the tragic form is born; and in winter, with one's increasing awareness of unrealized expectancies and the death of dreams, irony and satire become relevant expressive forms.

Joseph Campbell's (1949) analysis of primitive myth is helpful. As he proposes, there is one central "monomyth" from which a myriad of variations have been drawn in primitive mythology. The monomyth, rooted in unconscious psychodynamics, concerns the hero who has been able to overcome personal and historical limitations to reach a transcendent understanding of the human condition. For Campbell, heroic narratives in their many local guises serve vital functions of psychic education. For our purposes, we see that the monomyth carries a form similar to that of the comedy–melodrama. That is, negative events (trials, terrors, tribulations) are followed by a positive outcome (enlightenment).

These discussions enable us to shift to a more abstract perspective. What is common to the sequential shift we find in the tragedy, the comedy–melodrama, the romantic saga, and the monomyth are shifts in the evaluative character of events over time. Essentially, we seem to be confronted with alterations in a primary dimension of human experience, the evaluative (cf. Gordon, 1968, 1976; Osgood, Suci & Tannenbaum, 1957; Wells & Marwell, 1976). That is, in linking experiences the dramatist appears to establish directionality along a good–bad dimension. Or, as Alasdair MacIntyre (1977) has put it, "Narrative requires an evaluative framework in which good or bad character helps to produce unfortunate or happy outcomes" (p. 456). Do such alterations have a counterpart in the person's attempt to understand his or her cross-time trajectory? It would appear so, as attested to by such common queries as: "Am I improving?" "Is my life happier now?" "Are my abilities declining?" " Am I maintaining the high standards I once committed myself to?" or "Am I growing as a person?" To answer such questions the individual selects discrete incidents or images occurring across time and links them through evaluative comparison (cf. Hankiss, 1981; Labor & Waletzky, 1967).

Given what appears to be a fundamental means of generating coherence and direction over time, we can proceed more formally to consider the problem of narrative types. At the most rudimentary level we may isolate three forms of narrative. The first may be described as a stability narrative, that is, a narrative that links incidents, images, or concepts in such a way that the individual remains essentially unchanged with respect to evaluative position. As depicted in Figure 12-1, we also see that the stability narrative could be struck at any level along the evaluative continuum. At the upper end of the continuum the individual might conclude, for example, "I am still as attractive as I used to be," or at the lower end, "I continue to be haunted by feelings of failure." As can also be seen, each of these narrative summaries possesses inherent implications for the future. That is, they furnish an indication or anticipation of forthcoming events. In the former case the individual might conclude that he or she will continue to be attractive for the foreseeable future and, in the latter, that feelings of failure will persist regardless of circumstance.

This rudimentary narrative may be contrasted with two others of similar simplicity. The individual may link together experiences in such a way that either increments or decrements characterize movement along the evaluative dimension over time. In the former case we may speak of *progressive*, and in the latter *regressive*, narratives (see Figure 12-2). For

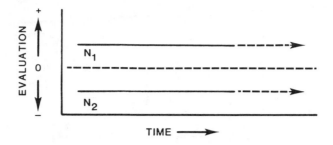

Figure 12.1. Positive (N_1) and Negative (N_2) Stability Narratives

example, the individual might be engaged in a progressive narrative with the surmise, "I am really learning to overcome my shyness and be more open and friendly with people," or a regressive narrative with the thought. "I can't seem to control the events in my life anymore." Directionality is also implied in each of these narratives with the former anticipating further increments and the latter further decrements.

As should be clear, these three narrative forms, stability, progressive, and regressive, exhaust the fundamental options for the direction of movement in evaluative space. As such they may be considered rudimentary bases for other more complex variants. Theoretically one may envision a potential infinity of variations on these rudimentary forms. However, for reasons of social utility, aesthetic desirability, and cognitive capability, the culture may limit itself to a truncated repertoire of possibilities. Among this limited set we may place the tragic narrative, which in the present framework would adopt the structure depicted in Figure 12-3. The tragedy, in this sense, would tell the story of the rapid downfall of one who had achieved high position. A progressive narrative is thus followed by a rapid regressive narrative. In this sense of comedy-melodrama is the reverse of the tragedy: A regressive narrative is followed by a progressive narrative.

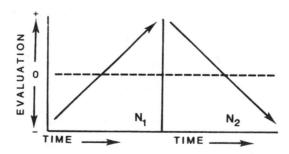

Figure 12.2. Progressive (N_1) and Regressive (N_2) Narratives

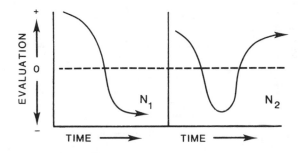

Figure 12.3. Tragic (N_1) and Comedy-Melodrama (N_2) Narratives

Life events become increasingly problematic until the denouement, whereupon happiness is rapidly restored to the major protagonists. Further, if a progressive narrative is followed by a stability narrative (see Figure 12-4), we have what is commonly known as the happily-ever-after myth, which is widely adopted in traditional courtship. And we also recognize the romantic saga as a series of progressive-regressive phases. In this case, for example, the individual may see his or her past as a continuous array of battles against the powers of darkness.

Before considering a second aspect of narrative form two matters deserve brief attention. First, as should be apparent from this discussion, narrative forms are in no way to be construed as objective reflections of one's personal life. The individual should be able to use virtually any form to account for his or her life history. Particular narratives may be implied by the manner in which one evaluates the events entering into the narrative construction. However, events themselves do not contain inherent valuational properties. Such properties must be attributed, and the attributions are contained within the particular constructions one makes of the events. Whether any given event is good or bad depends on the framework one

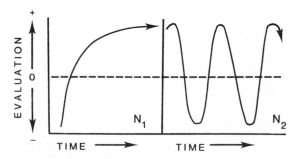

Figure 12.4. "Happily-Ever-After" (N_1) and Romantic Saga (N_2) Narratives

employs for understanding, and the potential array of frameworks for rendering events intelligible is without apparent limit.[4]

Second, although many illustrations of these narrative forms can be found in the arts, this is not simultaneously to accept the enticing but problematic view that life accounts are merely reconstituted forms of art. To be sure, from children's fairytales to television serials, from primitive religious myths to the most sophisticated novel, the narratives outlined thus far recur with great regularity. And, one can scarcely imagine that those who are frequently exposed to such forms could remain unaffected by them. Bettelheim's (1976) analysis of the profound effects of fairytales in the life of the developing child is quite compelling in this respect. Yet, at the same time such forms are not necessarily the inventions of autonomous story-tellers, witchdoctors, or literary craftsmen. Such individuals are also members of their culture and can scarcely remain unaffected by the narrative forms that are already imbedded therein.[5] Life and art are thus interdependent. However, that similar narrative forms may be found over many historical periods and differing contexts suggests that their fundamental genesis may be furnished by the requisites of human interaction. We shall return to this issue in treating the social utility of narrative forms.

DRAMATIC ENGAGEMENT IN NARRATIVE FORM

We now see how coherence among events may be produced through evaluative contrasts. However, we have said little about one of the most phenomenologically salient aspects of narrative form: the capacity to create feelings of drama or emotion. We may refer to this aspect of narrative form in terms of dramatic engagement. In the same way that theatrical productions vary in their capacity to arouse and compel an audience, so may the individual's selection of narrative vary in its capacity to generate or reduce dramatic tension in one's life. How are we to understand the elements giving rise to these variations in emotional engagement? Of course, dramatic engagement cannot be separated entirely from the content of a given narrative. Yet, segmented events in themselves appear limited in their capacity to sustain engagement. For example, a film depicting the continuous, random juxtaposition of startling events (a gunshot, a sword waving, a horse jumping a wall, a low-flying aircraft) would soon produce tedium. It is the relationship among events, not the events themselves, that seems chiefly responsible for sustaining dramatic engagement, and a theory of narrative form is essentially concerned with such relationships. What characteristics of narrative form are necessary, then, to generate dramatic engagement?

At this preliminary juncture, one must again look at the dramatic arts as a source of insight. In this case, it is of initial interest that one can scarcely locate a theatrical exemplar of the three rudimentary narratives proposed above. A drama in which all events were evaluatively equivalent (stability narrative) would scarcely be considered drama. Further, a steady but moderate enhancement (progressive) or decrement (regressive narrative) in a protagonist's life conditions would also seem to produce ennui. At the same time, it is also interesting to observe that the tragic narrative depicted in Figure 12-3 bears a strong resemblance to the simpler, but unarousing regressive narrative (Figure 12-2). How does the tragic narrative, with its consistently powerful dramatic impact, differ from the more rudimentary regressive narrative? Two characteristics seem particularly significant. First, we note that the relative decline in events is far less rapid in the prototypical regressive narrative than it is in the case of the tragic narrative. Whereas the former is characterized by moderate decline over time, the latter organized events in such a way that decline is precipitous. In this light one may conjecture that the rapidity with which events deteriorate in such classic tragedies as *Antigone*, *Oedipus Rex*, and *Romeo and Juliet* may be essential to their dramatic impact. More generally, it may be suggested that the rate of change, or more formally the acceleration of the narrative slope, constitutes one of the chief components of what is here termed dramatic engagement.

A second major component is also suggested by the contrast between the regressive and the tragic narratives. In the former case (see Figure 12-2) there is unidirectionality in the slope line whereas in the tragic narrative (Figure 12-3) we find a progressive narrative (sometimes implied) followed by a regressive narrative. It would appear to be this "turn of events," or more precisely the change in the evaluative relationship among events, that contributes to a high degree of dramatic engagement. It is when the individual who has attained high goals, has reached the apex of ecstasy, or has at last discovered life's guiding principle, is brought low that drama is created. In more formal terms, the alteration in narrative slope may be considered a second major component of dramatic engagement.

When we consider both alteration in and acceleration of narrative slope as basic components of dramatic engagement, we are led to a more general conclusion. Both of these components are similar in one respect: they both point to some aspect of phenomenal change as a basis of dramatic tension. Acceleration and alteration in slope may be viewed as two realizations of this more fundamental experience.

MACRO-, MICRO- AND MULTIPLES IN NARRATIVE FORM

> My characters are conglomorations of past and present stages of civilizations, bits from books and newspapers, scraps of humanity, rags and tatters of fine clothing, patched together as is the human soul. (Strindberg)

Thus far we have attempted to outline a number of rudimentary narrative forms, along with some of their more common derivatives, and to open discussion on differences in dramatic impact. We must now turn our attention more directly to the operation of narrative forms in daily life. This account will have two aspects. In the first instance we may consider the normal capacities with which the individual enters social relationships, and in the second, the function and development of narratives in interpersonal encounters. In inquiring into personal capacities it is important to appreciate the individual's exposure to a milieu of multiple narratives. Normal socialization will typically offer the individual exposure to a wide variety of narrative forms, from the rudimentary to the complex. Thus, the individual typically enters relationships with a potential for employing any of a wide number of forms. In the same way an experienced skier approaches a steep incline with a variety of techniques for effective descent or a teacher confronts a class with a variety of means for effective communication, so the individual can usually construct the relationship among life experiences in a variety of ways. At a minimum, effective socialization should equip the person to interpret life events as constancies, as improvements, or as decrements. And, with little additional training, the individual should develop the capacity to envision his or her life as tragedy, comedy–melodrama, or a romantic epic.

Not only do people enter social relationships with a variety of narratives at their disposal, but, in principle, there are no temporal parameters within which events must be related through narratives. That is, one may attempt to relate events occurring over vast periods of time, or determine the relationship among events within a brief period. One may find it possible to see his or her life as part of an historical movement commencing centuries ago, or as originating in early adolescence. At the same time, the individual may choose to describe as a comedy–melodrama that which has unfolded as friends select their positions at the dinner table. We may use the terms "macro" and "micro" to refer to the hypothetical or idealized ends of the temporal continuum within which events are related. Macronarratives refer to those events spanning broad periods of time while micronarratives relate events within brief durations.[6] The historian typically excels in the macronarrative, while the comedian who relies on sight gags may be the master of the micronarrative.

Given the capacity to relate events within different temporal perspectives, it becomes apparent that people often engage in the construction of nested narratives, or narratives within narratives.[7] Thus, they may come to see themselves as part of a long cultural history, but nested within this narrative they may possess an independent account of their development since childhood, and within this account establish a separate portrayal of their life as a professional, or the development of their image within the few preceding moments. A man may view himself as bearing the contemporary standard for a race that has struggled for centuries so that he may live (a progressive narrative) and at the same time see himself as one who was long favored by his parents only to disappoint them with increasing frequency as he grew older (the tragic narrative), and simultaneously see how he managed to rekindle the waning ardor of a woman friend on a given evening (the comedy–melodrama).

The concepts of nested narratives raises a variety of interesting issues. To what extent may we anticipate coherence among nested narratives? As Ortega y Gasset (1941) has argued in his analysis of historical systems, "the plurality of beliefs on which an individual, or people, or an age is grounded never possesses a completely logical articulation" (p. 166). Yet, on the basis of the wide range of social psychological work on cognitive consistency, one might anticipate a general tendency for people to strive for consistency among nested narratives. There are also many social advantages to "having one's stories agree." To the extent that consistency among narratives is sought, macronarratives acquire preeminent importance. Such narratives seem to lay the foundations within which other narratives are constructed. One's account of an evening with a friend would not seem to dictate one's account of one's life history; however, one's life history does constitute grounds for understanding the trajectory of the evening. To extrapolate, it may be ventured that those people with an extensive background in the history of their culture or subculture, or with an elaborated sense of their place in history, may possess more coherence among narratives than those with a superficial sense of their historical position. Or, placed in a different light, people from a young culture or nation may experience a greater sense of freedom of momentary action than those from cultures of nations with a long and prominent historical narrative. The former may experience a lesser degree of strain to behave in a way that is coherent with the past.

THE SOCIAL UTILITY OF NARRATIVE FORM

> Think of the tools in a tool-box: there is a hammer, pliers, a screw-driver, a rule, a glue-pot, glue, nails and screws. The functions of words are as diverse as the functions of these objects. (Wittgenstein)

Having outlined a range of narrative forms within the common repertoire, we are in a position to inquire more directly into the relationship between self-narratives and social interaction. This analysis can proceed in two parts. First, we can examine the social origins of various narrative forms. We can then turn to the manner in which such narratives are molded within social interaction. In the first case, we have seen that although a variety of narrative forms are potentially available to people, the individual usually relies on a delimited subset. We may advance our understanding of why we do not find an infinity of formulations if we consider functional needs within organized society. The viability of complex social institutions, large or small, benefits from the widespread capability of its members to employ a circumscribed range of narrative forms. This is to argue that a major source for narrative form resides in the social sphere and particularly within the requirements for adequate social functioning.

Consider first the primitive narrative of self-stability. Although generally void of dramatic value, the capacity of people to identify them-selves as stable units has vast utility within a culture. One's capacity to act functionally within society depends largely on the degree of its social stability. If others' conduct shifted randomly from one moment to the next one would be rendered helpless. There would be little way of knowing how to achieve any goal (including sustaining life) that depended on others' actions. Thus, much effort is expended by people in establishing recurring or stabilized patterns of conduct, and ensuring through various sanctions that they are maintained. This broad societal demand for stability of conduct finds its functional counterpart in the ready accessibility of the stability narrative on the personal level. Negotiating social life successfully requires that the individual is capable of making him or herself intelligible as an enduring, integral, or coherent identity. For example, in certain political arenas, it may be of great functional value to present oneself as a "born Southerner, raised in the South, married in the South, and part of its future." Or, on the more personal level, to be able to show how one's love, parental commitment, honesty, moral ideals, and so on have been unfailing over time, even when their outward appearances have seemed more variable, may be of exceptional importance in retaining ongoing relations. In most relationships of importance, people wish to know that others "are what they seem," which is to say that certain characteristics are enduring across time. One major means for rendering such assurances is through the construction of stability narratives.

It is important to note at this point a major way in which the present analysis conflicts with more traditional accounts of personal identity. Theorists such as Prescott Lecky, Erik Erikson, Carl Rogers, and Seymour Epstein have all viewed personal identity as something akin to an achieved condition of the mind. The mature individual, on this account, is one who has "found," "crystallized," or "realized" a firm sense of self or personal identity. In general this condition is viewed as a highly positive outcome, and once achieved, variance or inconsistency in one's conduct may be minimized. However, from the present vantage point, the individual does not arrive at a stabilized state of mind. Rather, he or she develops the capacity for understanding him or herself in this manner and to com-municate this understanding creditably to others. One does not acquire a state of "true self" but a potential for communicating that such a state is possessed.

This latter position becomes fortified when we turn to the social functions of the progressive narrative. On a general level there would appear not only a pervasive need for stability but also a contrasting need for change. Given that any action has both positive and negative consequences according to some standard, and assuming that positive consequences are to be preferred over negative, it follows that an improved or enhanced quality of any action may be desired. In this way people can see themselves, their world and their relations as possessing the potential for positive change. They can see their poor condition as subject to alleviation, and life as promising brighter horizons. For many people indeed this hope furnishes a chief motivational source. Careers are selected, sacrifices endured and many personal pleasures (including one's most intimate relations) are sacrificed in the belief that a progressive narrative can be achieved. And, it is clearly of great functional value to be able to construct such narratives for others. For example, a political leader may wish to argue that although the economy was depressed when he or she took office, it has shown steady improvement. Or, on a personal level, the success of many relationships depends importantly on the ability of the participants to demonstrate how their undesirable characteristics have diminished over time—even if they appear to be continuing undaunted. In effect, the general investment in positive change is best expressed through a narrative that demonstrates the ascending relationship among events over time.

As should be evident from this analysis, one must be prepared in most relationships to render an account of oneself as both inherently stable, and yet, in a state of positive change. Functioning viably in a relationship often depends on one's ability to show that one has always been the same, and will continue to be so, and yet, contrapuntally to show how one is continuing to improve. One must be reliable but demonstrate progress; one must be changing but maintain a stable character. Achieving such diverse ends is primarily a matter of negotiating the meaning of events in relationship to each other. Thus, with sufficient skill one and the same event may figure in both a stability and a progressive narrative. For example, graduation from medical school may be used as evidence that one has always been intelligent, and at the same time demonstrate that one is on route to high professional status.

Can a case be made for the generalized social value of regressive narratives? Inasmuch as increments of one kind are tantamount to decrements of another, the necessary counterpart of the progressive narrative in the first case is the regressive narrative in the second. In order for one's nation to gain hegemony in world politics it may be necessary to interpret the power of other nations as declining. An increase in feelings of community safety may depend on one's assessment of a decline in juvenile crime. And, on the more personal level, one's account of self as increasing in maturity of judgment, on the one hand, may entail the contrary perception of a reduction in youthful impetuosity on the other. In effect, regressive narratives are logically tied to the creation of progressive narratives.

One may object to this argument: although regressive narratives serve as the logical inverse of the progressive, they are not genuine regressions according to the evaluative criteria proposed above. That is, regressive relations are derived, but the evaluative connotation in such cases is positive as opposed to negative. Can a case be made for regressive narratives in which the evaluative experience is a negative one? What needs might be served by seeing the world or oneself as in a state of degeneracy? At least one compelling answer to this question is furnished by taking account of the common effects of regressive narratives. In particular, when people are informed of steadily worsening conditions they often attempt to compensate. They strive to offset or reverse the decline through enhanced activity. Through intensification of effort, they attempt to turn a potential tragedy into a comedy. Regressive narratives furnish an important means, then, of motivating people toward achievement of positive ends. This means is employed on a national level when a government demonstrates that the steady decline in the balance of payments can be offset only with a grass-roots commitment to purchasing locally-manufactured products. The same technique may be employed by the individual in attempting to bolster his or her enthusiasm for a given product. Otherwise wishing to avoid effortful activity, people goad themselves into action by bringing to mind a regressive narrative.

In sum, we see that the development of certain rudimentary narrative forms is favored by functional needs within the society. Stability narratives are favored by the common desire for the social world to appear orderly and predictable; progressive narratives offer the opportunity for people to see themselves and their environment as capable of improvement; and regressive narratives are not only entailed logically by the development of progressive narratives, but have an important motivational function in their own right. Given a social basis for a variety of narrative forms within the individual's repertoire, we turn finally to the manner in which specific narratives are constructed in ongoing relations.

THE SOCIAL NEGOTIATION OF NARRATIVE

> Composition of action as plot . . . depends on the consensual and generative relationships of individuals. (Burns)

Narrative construction can never be entirely a private matter. In the reliance on a symbol system for relating or connecting events one is engaging in an implicit social act. A concept acquires status as a symbol by virtue of its communicative capacity; that is, its position within a meaning system is shared by at least one other person. A movement of the hand is not a symbol, for example, unless it has the capacity to be understood by at least one other person. Thus, in understanding the relationship among events in one's life, one relies on symbols that inherently imply an audience. Further, not all symbols imply the same audience; personal narratives that have communicative value for certain audiences will be opaque to others. Over and above this definitional linkage of narratives to the social sphere, the social basis of narrative construction is amplified in two additional processes: public realization and articulation. Each will be treated in turn.

As apparent in the preceding discussion of the motivational properties of regressive narratives, narrative constructions frequently have behavioral implications. To maintain that one has always been an honest person (stability narrative) suggests that one will avoid temptation when it is subsequently encountered. To construct one's past in such a way that one has overcome increasingly greater obstacles to achievement (progressive narrative) suggests that one should treat oneself with a certain degree of respect. Or, to see oneself as losing one's abilities because of increasing age (regressive narrative) is to suggest that one should attempt to accomplish less. Most importantly for present purposes, as these behavioral implications are realized in action they become subject to social evaluation. Others can accept or reject such actions; they will find them credible or misleading. And, to the extent that such actions are rejected or found improper, doubt is cast upon the relevant narrative construction. If others express doubt about one's honesty, suggest that one's pride is unmerited, or find one's reduction in activity unwarranted, revisions are invited in the narrative construction relevant to such actions. Thus, as narratives are realized in the public arena, they become subject to social molding.[10]

As the individual's actions encounter varying degrees of approbation, the process of articulation comes to play a prominent role. That is, it becomes increasingly necessary for the individual to articulate the implicit narrative line in such a way that the actions in question become intelligible and thus acceptable. If faced with others who doubt one's honesty, one can demonstrate how his or her previous actions have been without blemish. Or, one can try to convince others of the validity of the progressive narrative by legitimizing one's pride, or the regressive narrative by justifying one's diminished activities. In effect, whether a given narrative can be maintained depends importantly on the individual's ability to negotiate successfully with others concerning the meaning of events in relationship with each other (cf. de Waele & Harré, 1979).

Active negotiation over narrative form is especially invited under circumstances in which the individual is asked to justify his or her behavior, that is, when one has acted disagreeably with respect to common frames of understanding. However, the process of social negotiation need not be solely a public one. People appear generally to avoid the threat of direct negotiation by taking prior account of the public intelligibility of their actions. They select in advance actions that can be justified on the basis of an intelligible or publicly acceptable narrative. In this sense, the bulk of the negotiation process is anticipatory or implicit; it takes place with an imaginary audience prior to the moment of action. People take into account others' perspectives and the likelihood of their actions being accepted prior to acting. In this way most human interaction proceeds unproblematically.

RECIPROCITY AND GUILT IN NARRATIVE FORMATION

> My experience cannot directly become your experience . . . . Yet, nevertheless, something passes from me to you . . . . This something is not the experience as experienced, but its meaning. (Ricoeur)

The social generation of narrative construction does not terminate with the negotiation process in its implicit and explicit forms. An additional facet of narrative construction throws its interactive basis into vivid relief. Thus far we have spoken of narratives as if solely concerned with the temporal trajectory of the protagonist alone. This conception must now be expanded. The incidents woven into a narrative are not only the actions of the single individual but interactions with others. Others' actions contribute vitally to the events to be linked in narrative sequence. For example, in justifying his continuing honesty, the individual may point to an instance in which another person has tempted him; to illustrate one's achievement may depend on showing how another person was vanquished in a particular competition; in arguing that one has lost capabilities he or she may point to the alacrity with which a younger person performed a particular task. In all cases, the action of the other enters as an integral part of one's own actions. In this sense, narrative constructions typically require a supporting cast. The implications of this fact are broad indeed.[11]

First, in the same manner that the individual feels that he or she has priority in self-definition, others also feel themselves to have primary jurisdiction over the definition of their own actions. Thus, one's understanding of the supporting role played by another cannot easily proceed without the acquiescence of the other. If others are not willing to accede to their assigned parts then one can ill afford to rely on their actions within a narrative. If another fails to see his or her actions as "offering temptation," the actor may be unable to conclude that he or she has displayed honesty; if the other can show how he or she was not really vanquished in a given competition the actor can scarcely use the episode as a stepping stone in a progressive narrative; if the younger person can demonstrate that his or her alacrity was only an apparent one, far overestimating true abilities, then the actor can ill afford to weave the incident into a regressive narrative.

This reliance on others' definition of their actions places the actor in a precarious position. As we have seen, people possess a variety of narrative forms ranging over various periods of time and which stand in various relations to each other in terms of nesting. At the same time members of a supporting cast may choose at any point to reconstruct their actions in opposing ways. Thus, an actor's success in sustaining any given narrative is fundamentally dependent on others' willingness to play out certain parts in relationship to the actor. In Wilhelm Schapp's (1976) terms, each of us is knitted into others' historical constructions, as they are into ours.

This delicate interdependence of constructed narratives suggests that a fundamental aspect of social life is a reciprocity in the negotiation of meaning. Because one's narrative constructions can be maintained only so long as others play their proper supporting roles, and in turn because one is required by others to play supporting roles in their constructions, the moment any participant chooses to renege, he or she threatens the array of interdependent constructions. For example, an adolescent may reveal to his mother that he believes she has been a very bad mother, thus potentially destroying her continuing self-narrative as a "good mother." Yet, at the same time, the son risks his mother's reply that she always felt his character was so inferior that he never merited her love. His continuing narrative is thus thrown into jeopardy. A lover may announce that she has begun to feel her male partner no longer interests her as he once did, thus potentially crushing his stability narrative; however, she does so at the peril of his replying that he has long been bored with her, and happy to be relieved of his lover's role. In such instances the parties in the relationship each pull out their supporting roles, and the result is a full degeneration of the narratives to which they contribute.[12]

It would appear that most relationships are not under the immediate threat of mutual withdrawal. In part this is because many people are content with existing reciprocity. There is little to gain in abandoning the support roles that, in turn, also serve one's own constructions. However, there are three additional mechanisms that may insulate members of a relationship from quixotic resignations, and the resulting "collapse of reality." Reciprocity is protected first by the incorporation of others' narratives into one's own. That is, the other's self-construction and one's place in the supporting cast are integrated into one's own self-narrative. Thus people do not merely rely on the supporting roles that others play but come to believe in others' beliefs in these roles. One may not only see his or her mate playing a supporting role as "loving helper" in one's upward route to success, but also comes to believe that the other possesses a private narrative in which this role has a major place. The attempt is thus not only to weave into one's own narrative others' actions, but their underlying narrative constructions as well. The individual thus shelters his or her own constructions by including within them the constructions of others.[13]

A second means of protecting oneself from ontological abandonment is to engage in an objectification of the relationship thus shifting concern to the history of this emergent entity. Rather than each individual seeing him or herself as an independent entity requiring support, individuals may decide that together they create a new entity—that of the relationship itself. Once objectified ("We have a relationship") the participants can shift to the simpler task of negotiating one narrative rather than two. Rather than concerning themselves with such issues as whether each individually is "growing as a person," for example, they can negotiate about the trajectory of the mutually created relationship. "Is our marriage failing?" "Is the team's desire to win growing stronger?" or "What is happening to the morale of this organization?" are all relevant questions to ask once the relationship has become objectified and the relevant narrative created.[14]

Finally, one cannot underestimate the power of guilt in maintaining reciprocity in narrative construction. Guilt can be invoked when one party of an interdependent unit accuses another of falling short of his or her history, of failing to live up to the narrative that has been agreed upon as objective. The feeling of guilt is the emotional counterpart of perceiving a threat both to one's sense of reality and to the other's continuing support. Thus, such comments as "and all along I thought you were an honest person!" "I have supported you all this time because I thought you had real ambition, but now . . . " or "you said you were my close friend, but no friend could ever . . . " all imply that the accused has failed in playing out a part that was implied by a previous narrative construction. The accused is thus faced with the threat of a joint loss, first of being able to rely on the construction itself (e.g., "I am an honest person, ambitious, a friend . . . "), and second, of relying on the continuation of the supporting cast member. A common reaction to such accusations is *restorative negotiation* in which the accused person attempts to demonstrate the falsity of the accusations. Thus, by employing periodic challenges to the validity of the others' narratives, members of a relationship can ensure that collective or reciprocal agreements are maintained over extended periods of time.[15]

NOTES

1. The self-narrative need not be a verbal construction. Although verbalization may be common, a sense of narrative may be imbedded in a more basic experience of fittingness or directionality among events. Dialogue is necessary neither for an appreciation of the propriety with which scenes fit together nor a sense of mounting tension, climax, and denouement. Similarly, jazz musicians may possess an understanding of how one improvised segment of a piece fits with its immediate antecedents, although analytic tools are incapable of precisely rendering the relationship.

2. Although a full critique of the concept of role, rule, or script as a directive device is beyond the scope of this chapter, it is important to note that they are subject to most of the weaknesses inherent in concepts of mental structure. For a more complete analysis see Gergen (in press).

3. As Applebee (1978) maintains, the mature narrative requires the elaboration of a center or core situation; shifts in sequential events thus clarify, extend, or modify new aspects of the central theme. As illustrated in a variety of developmental studies (cf. Applebee, 1978; Pitcher & Prelinger, 1963; Vygotsky, 1962), the ability to construct narratives of this form does not typically emerge in the child until the age of five to six years.

4. For amplification, see Gergen, 1980.

5. As Rubin and Wolf (1979) demonstrate, for example, children rely on social roles to which they are exposed to develop narrative roles in makebelieve.

6. See, for example, Albert and Kessler's (1978) analysis of the structure of endings in encounters.

7. See also Feldman's (1979) analysis of nested identities.

8. As the present treatment indicates, the facts of one's life do not dictate narrative form; one employs a narrative form to order the interpretation of life events. For a discussion of relativity in constructing events themselves see Gergen (1982).

9. It may also be proposed that regressive narratives can sometimes serve as justificatory devices for inaction. By demonstrating how one has been forced by an unfolding series of events into a poor position, one can continue to enjoy the case of inactivity (e.g., "I have grown too old to take up skiing"; "I have been through such agonies that I deserve a rest").

10. As should be evident, the present analysis favors what Sutton–Smith (1979) has termed the dialogic account of narrative construction (Levitt, 1978; McDowell, 1975; Stewart, 1978; Watson, 1972) rather than the monologic orientation (Mandler & Johnson, 1977; Stein, 1978; Sutton-Smith, 1979). That is, it views narratives as emergents from social rather than intrapsychic processes.

11. See also Sarbin's (1980) analysis of hypnosis as a process requiring participants to agree to assigned roles in relationship to each other.

12. As MacIntyre (1979) has described, when interpretive support systems drop away, the resulting "epistemological crisis" must be resolved by developing a new narrative "which enables the agent to understand *both* how he or she could intelligibly have held his or her original beliefs *and* how he or she could have been so drastically misled by them. The narrative in terms of which he or she first understood and ordered experiences is itself made into the subject of an enlarged narrative" (p. 455).

13. Relevant is Cicourel's (1970) concept of "reciprocity of perspectives," referring to the common assumption that each person would have the same experience if they were to change places. Thoroughgoing reciprocity would lead to full mutuality of narrative incorporation.

14. One may not always agree to join another's attempt to objectify a relationship. See, for example, Harré's (1977) discussion of the way in which people are often trapped by others' use of the term "we." As Ellen Berscheid has pointed out in a personal communication, one essential basis for joining in an objectification of relationship is trust. One must believe in the

others' resources to sustain a given construction of "we" across time and situation. People may also resist joining in the objectification of relationship because they fail to see how the future may enable them to generate a history. If creating narratives gives one's life meaning and direction, then one may limit relationships to those with whom histories may be jointly constructed.

15. For a compelling account of the weaving of narratives within the culture at large (including the scientific culture), along with a discussion of the social bonding capacities of such narratives see Nieburg (1981). Inasmuch as historical accounts typically employ the narrative as an ordering device (cf. Danto, 1965; Gallie, 1964; White, 1965) inquiry is invited into the societal functions of historiography.

Chapter 13

A METAPHOR FOR THE IDENTITY OF TRAGIC HEROES

Marvin Rosenberg

The complex protagonists of great tragic drama guard the secrets of their personality almost as obstinately as do complex humans. These immortal imagined figures are designed to accentuate the mystery of the self and its experience. Into their few hours of stage identity is compressed a range of traits, passions, and violent behavior that most mortals will not in a lifetime begin to experience—but that almost all mortals recognize from secret fantasies. The tragic heroes and heroines show to their worlds the many strained faces suited to their surface obligations, while at various covert and silent levels, they must wonder, agonize, and curse at the crises they are made to confront, at the cruel human condition they inhabit, at the forces known and guessed that control that condition. There is no escape: the playwright-god impels his protagonists into an uncertain, ambiguous world, relentlessly driving them to the boundaries of sanity, then of life, testing their personalities to exhaustion (Rosenberg, 1980).

So in their brief fictive lives, under the obligations of the compressed roles they are "born" with, achieve, and have thrust upon them, they are at various times kind, cruel, happy, anguished, open, crafty, loving, hating, hopeful, hopeless—in fact they experience, in extremes, the recognizable character dialectics native to mortality. The great tragic figures do not only experience their passions successively: often—again mirroring the complexity of mortality—they are *simultaneously* impelled to kindness and cruelty, loving and hating (as in Hamlet's "nunnery" scene with Ophelia). One passion or a cluster of passions may seem momentarily to dominate the character's behavior, but what the character represses (and sometimes reveals in soliloquy or gesture) may be more significant than the overt action (Rosenberg, 1958).

To suggest the intricate, dynamic complexity of this kind of tragic characterization, with its multiplicity of often contradictory roles, drives, impulses, and traits, I have proposed the metaphor: *polyphony* (Rosenberg, 1978). A tragic character composition has these tones—or voices—in it: some harmonious, some dissonant, some nuclear, some peripheral grace notes. The combinations of tones are perceived in mixed chords that change as the character's complexities shift and develop. Only very rarely does a tragic hero get to sound a pure, sweet note of uncomplicated joy: perhaps Romeo at the moment his love is accepted, Othello embracing Desdemona on the Cyprus quay—though even then muted discords murmur in the polyphonic implications of language and dramatic context; most often the distinctive melody of tragedy is dissonance.

The polyphony metaphor allows not only for the chording of a character's core identity, but also for its mobility. Thus, a major note of benevolence in the complex of King Lear's impulses in his first scene, as he asks his daughters to compete in loving him, quickly gives way, when his youngest disappoints him, to a dissonance of dismay and then a thunder drum of anger—and underneath all, such repressed cries as a yearning for love, the pain of rejection, the self-hurt of rejecting, the apprehension that he may lose control of his wits. The metaphor has application to human experience: we sometimes in one or other of our roles move to a clear, lyric note of creative self-realization in love, play, work, transcendence; yet often other, darker voices—doubt, anxiety, anger, lust, self-concern—may begin to counterpoint a willed state of harmony and, rising to fortissimo, overwhelm it. In life, the shifting combinations of notes often form successive, evanescent chords, but only rarely with such compressed staccatos as with a tragic hero, whose various roles and character qualities, fiercely challenged by the immediacy and variety of catastrophic circumstance and continuous threats to the self's stability, struggle for emergency resolution.

We try, by stretching our powers of empathy, to know the doomed characters of tragedy in the full multiplicity of their identities. But here a special kind of Heisenberg principle operates. Each observer who attempts to inhabit the self of an open-ended dramatic personality brings to the identification a different set of rooted attitudes and perspectives that must color the character perception. Hamlet, for instance, has notoriously become a kind of projective test for his interpreters. Some of us, as readers or actors, identifying (and identifying with) our Prince, have found him (us) at the lyrical end of the spectrum: a sweet young man, noble, gentle, even impeccable (we may cut or ignore some of Shakespear's lines to sustain the desired harmonic). Some at the other extreme perceive a wholly discordant Hamlet—cruel, hateful, even evil (here we are more likely distantly to identify, rather identify with).

We may all read the same text, but manage to hear different notes dominating the character's polyphony. Then many of the subtle undertones between the two extremes noted above may be lost to us, we hear only the voices we are prepared to hear—as sometimes in life we listen selectively to the polyphonies of companions. Shakespeare's characters are particularly susceptible to this partial identification because of the tremendous concentration in them of recognizable human qualities.

Consider Macbeth—and the differing voices perceived in him. Some idea of the multiplicity of human traits that Shakespeare packed into the character may be gauged from a collection of hundreds of descriptives— many contradictory—used to identify him by scholar-critics and reviewers of performances. These descriptives are drawn from every page of a catalog of trait names.[1]

No fixed personality inventory could be developed from even a synthesis of these descriptives, because at any one moment Macbeth's combinations of voices will be in transition, as his center adapts surfaces to meet the crises beating on him from within and without. The shifting of voices reciprocates partly with the many roles voiced in Macbeth: warrior, courtier, kinsman, husband, lover, poet, philosopher, player, host, murderer, hypocrite, liar, king, tyrant, traitor, sorcerer. He is most single, most innocent of counterpoint, as the warrior concentrated on killing for his country. In an ultimate realization of his physical identity he has defeated a dangerous invader, dispatched a traitor, and saved his king from deposition, the kingdom from oppression. But even in his initial moment of triumph as the pure heroic fighting man, some sense of his social, courtier's self will be felt by the actor—or imagining reader—to intermix in his mind: not only with notes of personal glory, but also of the praise of his peers and his king, of possible elevation to a new thanedom—and perhaps already a faint whisper of the crown itself if his royal kinsman should die.

Macbeth's marital roles, of husband and lover, reflect an established— even romantic—base; but they cannot now be disentangled from his social involvements and his dreams of the future. Only the flint of his loved wife, and her partnership with him in ambition, could strike in him enough of a fire to act the traitor-murderer; but from now on he will fuel it himself. In Shakespeare, as in life, characters change as new roles require altered scripts: Macbeth finds himself playing parts he could only have fantasized in the beginning, and he starts performing the motions, and speaking the lines, of king, liar, hypocrite, tyrant. Through it all the old voices of the initial Macbeth—warrior, poet, philosopher, husband, lover—are heard, but no longer grasping at innocence, now only at despair.

As with Shakespeare's other tragic heroes, Macbeth's complex identity contains the best and worst of resonances we regard as "human." The actor—or reader—who would empathize with such an identity must imagine flexibly enough to allow a flow of voices that will sound all the essential notes in the whole, in a very intricate interplay: for, as in life, a dramatic character is partly shaped by the actions and reactions of others in close personal and social relationship. These others sound complex polyphonies of their own, occasionally for the moment harmonizing with the hero—but, in tragedy, only for the moment. The best of the others are tactlessly dissonant, as with Desdemona and Cordelia, while the worst (Iago, Edmund) suffer a harsh inner discordance that they seek to visit on the hero—whose psyche will inevitably become, as Ophelia says of Hamlet, "Like sweet bells jangled, out of tune and harsh."

So we see Macbeth's polyphony vibrating to the vectors of social and personal forces about him. At first, he seems in harmony: he has won a great battle, he is returning from it to the adulation of his peers who will reinforce his present lofty status. But first, curious, ambiguous female figures—disharmonious voices—intercept him, and resonate on the dark strings within him. These old haglike "witches," (surrogate mothers?) so tempt him with images of replacing an old king (father figure?) that he is almost unstrung physically. But an even more dangerous female awaits him at home—his wife, so ambitious for him and herself, and as wife-mother so ready to conspire with him to destroy the old man that she calls on murderous supernatural spirits to arm her resolve. Yet she has been a loving wife, who must try—and in the event, fail—to extinguish her innate compassion. Her polyphony is also complex, as may be discerned from her many differing critical descriptives, numbering in the hundreds.[2]

For the first three acts, and briefly at the end, she magnetizes MacBeth's actions, even when his energy is diffused into his nonmarital roles; she is largely defined by her relationship to him, though she too must accommodate herself to urgent social demands. Life usually provides some pauses between the crucial moments when the pressure of circumstance wounds and shapes mortals, not so in *Macbeth*, where, even more than in most tragedies, time and emergency relentlessly sculpt the strength and weaknesses of the main characters. Macbeth feels his Lady bound to him by love, and she does provide the support and strength he needs when he seems, midway, broken by his hallucinations; she, to move him to murderous ambition, derides his manliness, so cruelly she has been interpreted as castrating him; finally she, who seemed at first strongest, is the one who gives way and deteriorates as his crimes invite him to do worse. As the words describing her suggest, she, like Macbeth, in her waking and sleeping hours is touched with glimpses of the best and worst of the human condition: sometimes fearless, sometimes shattered; tender, tough; coldly rational, helplessly irrational; adult, childlike; hopeful, despairing.

Shakespeare's interweaving of the two character polyphonies manifests his genius for sensing the dynamics of personality interaction. As in life, husband and wife, each, has an individual identity—and here each shifts and deforms under pressures exerted by the other. Both sometimes disclose themselves, but both also retreat behind masks from each other as well as the world. Each may at one time seem the instigator of criminal action, but we (they?) cannot easily tell which is the manipulated, which the manipulator. Macbeth brings from Duncan's camp a vision of the ill-won kingship, then seems to back away from it until she urges him on: some actors have emphasized this as a device to procure the external compulsion Macbeth needed to proceed. Lady Macbeth, in turn, senses this impulse, but imperfectly, disastrously for both. She has some idea of Macbeth's strengths and weaknesses, but only from what he has been, not what he will be. This is also true of herself: she is as deceived in her own capacity for remorseless violence as she is in her estimate of his essential "milk of human kindness." She too pursues a greedy vision until the reality of it sickens her—and sickens her the more as she realizes what her urgings have done to her husband. In these experiences they transcend their particular hierarchical social world, with its special temptations to upward mobility. If we cannot ourselves know the excitement of killing for kingship, we can still share vicariously the urgency to rise to the highest of social stations, if need be, over parent, sibling, indeed any obstacle in the way. And we can be haunted by the thought of the price exacted for unholy ambition. So we are prepared to hear the multiple voices in the queen-murderess' polyphony change radically in key from those of the Lady-wife, as also those of the noble thane turned king-murderer.

The two character complexes are made up of such polar extremes that only Shakespeare's genius—or life itself—could produce plausible interacting personalities from them. The dialectic could hardly be stretched further.

Observe how actors portraying Macbeth have been described in terms of his polarities. The list below represents reviewers' comments on Macbeth as portrayed by different actors:

> Richly furnished with good, fatally susceptible to evil.... Magnificently great in passion, ambition, imaginative capacity to feel: also poor, vain, cruel, treacherous, snatching ruthlessly over friend and kinsman.... Soaring imagination, heroic courage, animal cunning, instinctive nobility, and craven hypocrisy... brutal enough to kill, noble enough to feel conscience.... Innately ambitious, religiously humane.... Brave in battle, quaking in imagination.... Capacity for remorse equal to his capacity for ambition.... Lofty ambitions, deep, dark desires, kind affections, treacherous disloyalty.... The milk of human kindness and bloodthirstiness comingled... in action a monster, in language a poet, in feelings the greatest of sufferers.... The most sentimental of butchers... victim as well as malefactor.... Ferocious warrior, sensitive

poet, the fear of the haunted, murderer, dreamer, doer, tyrant, sniveller, warrior, philosopher, Shelley-Himmler, Hamlet-Fortinbras-Claudius. (Rosenberg, 1978)

The opposites in Lady Macbeth's polyphonic performances have been similarly noted by reviewers and critics:

> So slight and luscious in appearance, so fervent in speech, so ruthless in scorn for her husband's wavering, yet withal so truly his devoted help-meet. . . . Murderess, yes; fiend of cruelty, yes; yet woman through and through . . . . A woman whose sun rises and sets in her husband, against whose absorbing love for her "man" no moral scruples, no feminine tenderness, no mental weaknesses would weigh for a moment. . . . She loved him passionately, and in her own tigress fashion, tenderly . . . . Her humanity is visible every moment . . . . Pride and rage, vengeance and despair, melancholy and weariness of the heart struggle passionately. (Rosenberg, 1978)

Inevitably, when two such complex personalities meet in tragedy—or in life—and their reciprocating impulses have an occasion to fuse in murderous aggression, terrible inward and outer pressures scrape and hammer at their identities. But unlike life, where personalities must stand or fall on the qualities and possibilities they are given to live with or change, in drama their very natures and their fates may be arbitrarily amputated. The deeds and attributes of living individuals cannot be edited, by hindsight, once the moving finger has written; but the words that shape dramatic characters survive only by the permission of actors, and directors, and expurgators—who themselves are often submissive to the wills of their audiences. And audiences are at the mercy of strange cultural and aesthetic impulses. Shakespeare's characters in particular have suffered from this. Whole cultures have tuned out significant notes in his polyphonies in favor of simplified chordal arrangements easier on ears fearful of his uncompromising sounding of the depths as well as the heights of the human diapason. This has been painfully true of Macbeth and his Lady: one measure of how very complex they are is to contrast what Shakespeare wrote with the truncated identities left when social, critical, and theatrical censorship muffled or silenced the resonances of what Macbeth called the "deep and dark desires." So tragic characters, like people, are sometimes shaped—sometimes distorted—by social pressure.

In the Restoration theatre, some 50 years after Shakespeare died, the taste for popular, undemanding entertainment was already corrupting *Macbeth* (and others of Shakespeare's plays). The witches, meant to be such sinister tempters to Macbeth, now multiplied and became a pretty singing, dancing corps to entertain King Charles' frothy society. The "weird sisters" would be degraded, for a century and a half, into stereotyped, broom-sticked creatures of comedy, unqualified to ensnare a tragic hero.

Some other way had to be found to lure Macbeth, initially a figure of nobility and conscience, toward regicide. This was especially necessary in eighteenth-century theatre, when the emerging image of the tragic hero was of a man of sensibility; a sentimental gentleman who, if he did do wrong, hardly meant to, and suffered touching remorse. To make Macbeth fit this image, deep notes in his polyphony had to be softened or silenced. For instance, the terrible murder, ordered by him, of Macduff's wife and child, was excised, so audiences were relieved of any visual evidence of his brutality. In the same way, Macbeth was not allowed to kill the young soldier who challenged him in the final battle. Not only were these essential tones in the complex muted for the sake of "poetic justice"; a final speech was put into his last lines, a mealy-mouthed confession of shame and remorse wholly uncharacteristic of the character—as if a Beethoven symphony were adulterated with an ending from a Tin Pan Alley ballad.

The model for this aborted characterization, the famous actor David Garrick, was far and away the most popular interpreter of the role in his time. Only rarely was he criticized, as in this scolding from a judicious correspondent properly offended:

> You almost everywhere discovered dejectedness of mind . . . more grief than horror . . . heart-heavings, melancholy countenance, and slack carriage of body. The sorrowful face and lowly gestures of a penitent which have ever a wan and pitiful look . . . quite incompatible with the character.

But this was the Macbeth Garrick's audiences evidently wanted—sensitive, pathetic, wife-driven.

Garrick's Lady, Hannah Pritchard, was particularly fitted to dominate her man. She was taller than he—a famous contemporary picture of the two after Duncan's murder shows him teetering indecisively, fearfully, while she, towering grim and purposeful, almost smiling, coolly quiets him with a finger to her lips. He has carried the daggers from the murder scene, and is afraid to return them; she seizes them, according to an eyewitness

> from the remorseful and irresolute Macbeth, despising the agitation of a mind unaccustomed to guilt, and alarmed at this terror of conscience, presenting a picture of the most consummate intrepidity of mischief.

When Macbeth tried to resist her first incitements to murder, "her whole ambitious soul came forth in fury to her face, and sat in terror there." When Macbeth was frightened by Banquo's bloody ghost during the banquet scene, she seized his arm with "angry and reproving looks . . . and assumed a look of such anger and terror as cannot be surpassed." She was famous for her display of callousness, her "mind insensible to compunction," her "horrible force of implacable cruelty."

Why should the eighteenth century require such reductive distortions of the playwright's insights into personality? Ostensibly it was to bring him closer to "proper" principles of drama: for example, a gentleman soldier should not be an out-and-out villain, and decorum required that if such a man did do something to deserve to die, he must acknowledge his sins. Decorum was then another face for the censorship of those words and ideas, including many relating to the sexual act, threatening to the Puritan morality developing in Europe, as the middle class grew. So the word "whore," so casually used by Shakespeare and his contemporaries (and ours), would disappear from the stage in the mid-eighteenth century, and remain censored until well into the twentieth. So *Macbeth*'s Porter scene, with its earthy language and action, would also disappear from the stage. Of course the superficial denial of overt references to sexuality, or the denial of dark and deep desires, did not eliminate what was repressed; covert satisfactions would be achieved in other ways. We half-create the images we perceive of characters—or people; the eye of the beholder edits with unspoken instructions from our deepest levels. The critics and actors who saw Lady Macbeth as so fierce may have been abetting a need that later psychological critics would identify in the role.

Perhaps she satisfied the fantasy of the archetypally dangerous female, in the guise of the bad mother, who joined with her son to kill the father, and resume dominance. The weird sisters can be interpreted as variants of this image: half-masculinized women—Banquo sees them with beards on their chins—malign to men. The terrible female figure drives the victimized man to fateful acts that destroy him; then, for her awful guilt, she must herself disintegrate. So, as Shakespeare created her, Lady Macbeth has been seen as satisfying unconscious impulses (one critic suggests that we *want* her to incite Macbeth to kill the father figure) and also as paying the penalty for her crime. In the eighteenth century, as she took the major guilt to herself, the remorseful Macbeth, dwindling into an honorable murderer, could escape with a relative innocence undisturbing to spectators, while she could rise to an almost Satan-like malevolence (so she was often called "fiend") that distanced her beyond the empathy that audiences would normally experience, thus becoming accomplices in her guilty humanity.

Fortunately, as the nineteenth century wore on, artists of the theatre began to insist on voicing the repressed notes in Macbeth and his Lady. Macbeth's murderous impulses were allowed him; the witches came back in their more sinister form, and Macbeth could once again vibrate to their uncanny influences. By the late nineteenth century, as psychologists generally became more interested in more inward complexities of humanity that had for so long been the province of art and literature, the theatre gave a place to Macbeth's insecurities, his deep fantasies, and his irrational urgencies; and touches of what were then called "neurasthenic" began to shadow his introspections, his marital relationships, his violence.

Filling out the equation, Lady Macbeth would be allowed to be a loving wife as well as an inciter to murder; the tendernesses which Shakespeare reveals, then represses, in her early moments, but that erupt more fully in her haunted sleepwalk, were allowed to be sounded even under her overtly savage moments. By the end of the nineteenth century, Sarah Bernhardt was stressing the Lady's sensual as well as emotional attachment to her Macbeth, and the erotic note in their polyphonies would be more and more openly heard in the 1900s. Actresses discovered basic insecurities in the Lady also; they accentuated her strain when summoning unseen evils to her aid, and sometimes her deterioration could be seen to begin even before the murder that she encouraged had taken place.

Drama functions to arouse spectators—emotionally, intellectually, spiritually, and physically. Given that a drama's components are under artistic control, the more complexly they reflect human experience, the more widely and intensely they excite reactions in our response repertories. Complex dramatic characters—like complex people—being made of a multitude of notes struck from the keyboard of the human condition, rouse vibrations in the many corresponding strings—conscious and hidden—of spectators. A welcome duty of the student of Shakespeare's tragedy—in parallel with that of the student of life itself—is a dedication to developing the utmost possible sensitivity to the myriad voices of humanity that are sounded in tragic character. The sounds are sometimes surds, unvoiced: we must listen to subtext as well as text, to the implications of gesture, of grimace, of silence, to the unspoken—even unspeakable—that lies beneath speech.

"Nothing human is alien to me," said the playwright Terence; the immortal tragic characters lead us to perceive, if we will attend, how much of the sad music of humanity is scored in us.

NOTES

1. Abandoned, abject, absent, abrupt, abstracted, affectionate, aghast, agitated, agonized, almost godlike, almost superhuman, amazed, ambitious, amiable, apathy, appalling, apprehensive, atheist, athlete in evil, authority, awe-inspiring, awesome. Badgered, barbarian, barbaric, beast, betrayed, bewildered, bitter, bloodthirsty, bloody, bluff, bold, bombastic, brainsick, bravery, brawny, broken, brooding, brutalizing, brute, bullies, buoyant, burly, butcher. Callous, catlike, charisma, charm, cheerful, chivalric, clairvoyant, clarity of vision, coarsening, commanding, complex, compulsive, confused, conscience, conscientious, consternation, contemplative, contrition, convulsive, cornered, corrupted, courageous, court-

liness, coward, crafty, credulous, cruel, cunning. Damned, dangerous, daring, dark, dauntless, decisive, defender, defiant, degenerates, degraded, defection, delicate in perception, deserted, desolate, despairing, desperate, despondent, determined, disappointed, disgust, dishevelled, disillusionment, distempered, distracted, distraught, divided, divinely human, dominating, dreamer, driven, dutiful, dwarfed. Earthy, emotional, endurance, energy, envy, excitable, expressive, extraordinary, evil. Faltering, farouche, fatalist, ferocious, ferocity, fervor, feverish, fierce, finely strung, flawed, forlorn, frank, frantic, frightened, furious, furtive. Gallant, gangster, generous, genial, gentleness, gibbering, gladiator, gloomy, goaded, goodness, graciousness, grandeur, granite, great, greed, grief, grim, growing, gullible. Haggard, half-crazed, half-hypnotized, hallucinating, harrowed, harshness, hasty, hated, haughty, haunted, headlong, heartless, heartrending, henpecked, hero, heroic, hesitant, hollow, homicidal, honorable, hopeless, human, humanity, humankindness, hypocritical, hysteric. Imaginative, impatient, impenitent, imperial, imperious, impetuous, impulsive, indomitable, infuriated, ingratiating, instability, instinctive, intelligent, intrepidity, introspective, introvert, irresolute, irresolution, irritable, isolated. Jealous, just. Kindness. Lachrymose, lion, listlessness, lofty, loved, loving, loyal, lying, lyrical. Mad, magnanimous, magnificent, majestic, malevolent, maniacal, malicious, manliness, manly, massive, materialist, melancholy, menacing, mercurial, mighty, monster, moody, morally triumphant, morally defective, morbid, mournful, murderous, muscular. Narcissism, nervous, nimblewitted, noble, nobleman, nonplussed. Observant, oppressed, optimistic, overwhelmed, overwrought. Passionate, paternal, pathetic, pathos, patriot, pensive, perplexed, petulant, philosophical, pious, pitiable, poetic, powerful, preoccupied, pride, primitive, prudent. Rapt, rash, rational, rationalizing, ravaged, raving, reckless, rectitude, refined, reflective, reluctant, remorse, remorseful, remote, repentant, reserved, resolute, savage, scheming, secretive, self-aware, selfish, self-regarding, self-torturing, semi-barbaric, sensitive, sensitivity, sentimentalist, sexual, shame, shamefaced, shifty, shivering, shrinks, shuddering, sickened, simple, sinister, sin-laden, smug, solitary, sombre, splendid, stalwart, stateliness, stern, stormy, strong, strongly sexual, stultified, stupefaction, subdued, sublime, subtle, suffering, suggestible, suicidal, sulky, sullen, superstitious, suspicious, sweet. Temperamental, temperate, tempest-haunted, tempestuous, tender, terrified, thoughtful, tigerish, timid, timorous, tired, tormented, torn, tortured, touching, traitor, trapped, treacherous, troubled, turbulent, tyrannical. Unbridled, uncertain, undecided, underdog, uneasy, ungovernable, unregretful, unscrupulous, unstrung, untamed, untruthful, unwhimpering, unyielding, usurper, uxorious. Vain, valiant, vehement, vicious, victorious, vigorous, vindictive, violent, virtuous, visionary, vital, (incandescent) vitality, voluptuous, vulnerable. Wanton, warlike, warrior, weak, weary, wicked, wild, wise, wistful, withering, worn, worried, wretched.

2. Acquiescent, admirable, affectionate, agitated, agonized, alarmed, alluring, ambitious, amiable, anguished, appalling, ardent, asp-like, authoritative, awe-inspiring. Baleful, barbarian, beautiful, benign, bird–like, broken, buoyant. Calculating, callous, captivating, caressing, cerebrant, charming, chilling, Cleopatra-like, clever, clinging, coaxing, cobra-like, cold, commanding, competitive, compulsive, confident, consoling, contemptuous, convulsive, coquettish, courageous, cowardly, cruel, cunning. Delilah-like, daring, dark, dauntless, delicate, demented, demoniac, depraved, depressed, dessicated, desolate, despairing, determined, devoted, dignified, disdainful, dishevelled, domestic, domineering, dreamy. Eager, eerie, enchanting, energetic, enthusiastic, Eve-like, exalted, excited, exhausted, exotic, explosive, exuberant. Faithful, fascinating, fatalistic, feline, feminine, ferocious, fervent, fierce, fiery, firm, flattering, flinty, fluctuant, forcible, fragile, frail, frenzied, full-blooded, furious. Gaunt, gentle, ghastly, glad, glamorous, glassy-eyed, glittering, gracious, grand, grim. Haggard, harsh, hateful, haughty, headstrong, heart-stricken, highstrung, hopeless, horrible, horror-stricken, hospitable, human, hurried, hypocritical. Imperative, imperial, imperious, impetuous, implacable, impulsive, incantatory, indomitable, inhuman strength, inner

strength, insidious, insulting, intelligent, intense. Keen. *La Belle Dame Sans Merci*, lovable, loves, loving, loyal. Magnanimous, magnetic, magnificient, majestic, malevolent, malignant, managing, mannish, massive, masterful, materialistic, maternal, melancholy, melodious, merciless, mettlesome, miserable, mournful, moving. Nervous, neurotic, noble. Pallid, passionate, pathetic, petty, petulant, piteous, pitiful, plaintive, poignant, possessive, potent, powerful, practical, presence of mind, prophetic, proud. Rapacious, rapid, realistic, reckless, regal, relentless, remorseful, resolute, resourceful, restrained, rich, rigorous, ruthless. Saccharine, savage, scornful, secret, seductive, self-possessed, self-restrained, sensitive, sensual, serpentine, severe, sexual, sharp-tongued, she-cat, sincere, sinister, sinuous, soft, soothing, sorrowful, spectral, spiteful, spontaneous, splendid, staring-eyed, stately, statuesque, steely, stern, stimulating, stoical, stolid, strident, strong, subtle, suffering, sulphurous, sweet. Taunting, tearful, tender, terrible, terrified, testy, tigerish, tigress-like, tormented, torn, tortured, touching, touch of vulgarity, treacherous, triumphant, troubled, turbulent. Unbalanced, uncompromising, undaunted, unflinching, unimaginative, unnatural, unscrupulous, unselfish, unswerving. Vehement, vibrant, vigorous, virginal, vital, vivid, vixenish. Wan, warm, watchful, wheedling, wifely, wild, will, witch-like, womanly, worn, wracked. Youthful.

PART V
THEORETICAL PERSPECTIVES
ON SOCIAL IDENTITY

Every psychological conception has limitations, and social identity is no exception to this rule. This final group of three essays provides a set of somewhat different perspectives on the identity problem. While the precise sense in which social identity is used varies from chapter to chapter, the major effect of this section is to demonstrate the relation of our key conception to a variety of other topics in contemporary psychology. Juhasz argues that is is useful to distinguish social identity from its neighbors, human and personal identity. Miller discusses the conception of self as it has evolved in psychological theory and as it is viewed by current cognitive theories, particularly in connection with the question of defining an identity as abnormal or pathological. Hogan and Cheek argue that the problem of identity is larger than the problem of social identity, which they see as primarily that form of identity having to do with conformity to conventional social roles.

In their own way, each of these essays attempts to place the problem of social identity in larger psychological context. Juhasz chooses to explore in his essay the unfashionable notion there is such a thing as human nature. His position is opposed both to the existentialist/relativist position of modern social science and to the innate difference doctrine of apologists for racism. Rather, Juhasz takes the position that such classical antinomies as Appollonian versus Dionysian, or fire versus water, or earth versus air, or origin versus source express fundamental human characteristics, out of which social identity emerges. Similarly, he argues that personal identity and social identity are distinct—and this because persons are not individually substitutable. There is only one Joseph Juhasz, whereas individuals within social roles are substitutable—there are many editors or dentists. Juhasz notes that the boundaries or edges of human and personal identity are blurred and subject to negotiation. What is human, what is not; what is "me" and what is not—these are matters for disputation and redefinition. But Juhasz insists that the centers of human, social, and personal identity are quite well fixed, despite the fuzzing about adjacent edges. His essay constitutes an elaboration and expansion of components of identity, which the social identity model places at the extreme granted end of the continuum. As such, it touches upon matters of the most profound significance for the valuation of identity—human, social, and personal.

Miller likewise accepts some universals in conceptions of self and identity. He observes that self-reflection is a universal that may be inferred from language. Self-enhancement is also seen as a universal motivational principle, while this is often obscured because of the presence of other motivational principles at the same time. Even so, the content of self and identity are seen, after Mead and Cooley, to be products of learning. In Juhasz's terms, one's personal identity develops out of a universal genetic background of human identity.

Miller emphasizes the significance of the requirements of effective social functioning for the maintenance of self-esteem and, later in his essay, for the question of how pathological identities develop. Human society depends on differentiation of function and interpersonal predictability for survival. If an individual acts in such a way as to impede the smooth functioning of the group, then the person loses esteem and might be said to be exhibiting abnormal symptoms. The modern conceptions of scripts and schemas are employed to advance this argument. Individuals develop schemas and scripts as a way of regulating their participation in conventional social interactions. On occasion, deficiencies in identity come about because of improper social training, resulting in inappropriate scripts. Or problems can emerge because of dissociations of subidentities and tendencies for defenses to produce cognitive distortions. Social controls then effectively degrade the offending person, with concomitant attempts either to segregate the person or place the person in a therapeutic or correctional environment. Miller's argument here is fully consistent with the conception of social identity transvaluation presented in Chapter One.

Hogan and Cheek employ the term social identity in a more restricted sense than that which is detailed in Chapter One. The advantage of their approach is that is produces a clear distinction between two modes of describing psychological maturity—one of which entails conformity to the requirements of social roles, and the other (more psychological) form of maturity that requires autonomy from external norms as a proof of authenticity. Their discussion revolves on the distinction between inner controls and outer controls, with the suggestion that this venerable distinction within personality theory must be incorporated into contemporary identity theory. Hogan and Cheek review recent research on self-presentation and self-monitoring in connection with the inner-outer distinction. The result is a clarification of the importance of inner and outer controls for various psychological consequences—individual adaptability, growth, and moral development. The same distinction is found in research on locus control and on field dependence. Hogan and Cheek present some of their own empirical work on personal versus social identities. They find support for the view that the most psychologically mature individuals are not those with the most autonomous identities, as some theories of moral development suppose. Rather the most mature are those whose identities integrate the competing demands of autonomy and conformity to social standards. An optimal identity for Hogan and Cheek is one that is both social and autonomous. Though the terminology is different, this is parallel to the assertion in Chapter One that the optimal psychological condition is one in which the individual enjoys both the implicit gift of respect as well as the wages of social esteem.

Chapter 14

SOCIAL IDENTITY IN THE CONTEXT OF HUMAN AND PERSONAL IDENTITY

Joseph B. Juhasz

The focus of this book, social identity, derives its clarity in part from the relations to its conceptual neighbors: human identity and individual identity. On the one side, social identity is adjacent to human identity. Human identity, or as it is more commonly known, human nature, is the ground from which our social identities are carved by our interactions with other human beings.

On its other side, social identity is adjacent to individual identity. Our individual identity is the unique, individual sense of self that we have all our lives, despite enormous changes in identity through time or space. In this sense our individual identity is one aspect of our identity that transcends, connects, and gives substance to our multiple and ever-changing social identities.

Both these conceptual neighbors of social identity—human and individual identity—are more enduring than the shifting, dynamic social identities for which they are the context. This chapter is addressed to the task of understanding some of the connections between social, human, and individual identity. In this way we hope to understand some features of the changes in social identities as they occur in the context of an enduring human nature and personal identity.

I am deeply indebted to T. R. Sarbin and Larry Goldberg for their help in the preparation of earlier drafts of this chapter.

THE FUNCTIONS OF IDENTITY

To begin to understand the fundamental relationships between human, social, and individual identity, it is helpful to point out the questions to which matters of identity provide answers. This is a way of specifying the functions served in the lives of human beings by the different components of their identity.

When explicitly or implicitly we are confronted with the question: "Is this a human being?" or "Am I a human being?" we are addressing matters of human identity. Questions of the sort: "Is this my mother?" "Am I the father of this child?" "Is this my boss?" "Are we all freemasons?" "Is he an Arab?" and so forth have to do with matters of social identity. They presuppose an affirmative answer to the first question relating to human identity—without an affirmative answer to the first question the second set of questions is meaningless.

"Is this Mom?" "Is this Jenny?" "Is this Mike?" "Am I myself—or have I been bewitched?" are questions that have to do with matters of personal identity. They do not identify social roles or statuses but rather specific individuals. Mother can be replaced by another individual. Bosses come and go. I know that I am different from situation to situation in my many roles. But Mom, Jenny, Mike, and my inner sense of Me transcends such changes. The capacity to occupy social roles is a prerequisite to having a personal identity. Yet the converse is also true. A person must have an individual identity before we let him or her occupy a social role. Thus, the connection between social and individual identity does not have the simple hierarchy that relates human and social identity.

These three classes of questions have in common the epistemic process whereby issues of identity provide answers to questions of recognition. Human identity shows recognition of membership in the species. Social identity shows recognition of pertinent categories into which the species can be sorted. Individual identity has to do with the recognition of the same person despite multiple memberships in many categories. Despite the relative dynamism of social as against human and individual identity, all three types of questions concern themselves primarily with constancies. The principal function of identities for human beings, then, is to provide for constancy amid change and for persistence among transformation. In this process human and personal identities serve as anchors for the relational changes charted by social identities.

WHO IS HUMAN?

A motion picture title like *Tarzan the Ape Man* is enticing, in part, because it plays with the borderline that divides men from apes—that determines who counts and who does not count as human. It titillates our interest in matters of human identity.

Is Eichmann's behavior in Hungary in part explicable (though not excusable) by stating that he had an erroneous definition of "human being?" That he did not accord the status of "human" to Jews, Gypsies, and other "inferiors?" Such questions are also intriguing because they arouse our interest in the dividing line between humans and nonhumans.

Or consider this statement about a Vietnam veteran: "His feeling toward mankind is that they are worthless. He has absolutely no regard for human life. If he saw a human and a dog standing in the road . . . I think he would sooner save the dog" (Eicher, 1981). Once again there is an intriguing element of confusion here about the boundaries of the concept human (the difference between humans and dogs)—and the behaviors and attitudes that are implied by such confusion.

Issues having to do with the beginning and end of human life (and its implications for abortion, artificial life support systems in hospitals, capital punishment, and like matters) are very much in public consciousness at the moment. Such issues also have to do with the definition of "human being" and illustrate its importance in everyday affairs.

These issues, and numerous others we have not explicitly considered, demonstrate some important things about the concept of human nature, of human identity. In the first place we see that who constitutes a human being is not itself a context-free or ahistorical phenomenon. Definitions of humanity vary from place to place and time to time and from person to person within similar contexts. And this contingency of definitions of human being, itself demonstrates the important fact that human identity and social identity are inextricably intertwined concepts.

The attribution of humanity to another being is not a process that takes place outside a social and cultural context. In this sense to say that another is human—or to say that one is human—is related to social identity for it involves the identification of that person as a member of the group "humans."

What we note as we examine the shifts in definition of who constitutes a human being is that the "edges" of humanity are open to negotiation. The edges respond to political, economic, religious, or environmental pressures. The borderlines are continually tested and explored. This exploration, in its turn, continually blurs the dividing line between social and human identity. This organic connection between social and human identity is a reciprocal one. Shifting definitions from either source can affect the other in a continual process of redefinitions and shifting categorizations.

Yet, the very looseness of the edges of the definition of "human" reinforces an equally important fact about human identity. Underlying any specific definition of human to be found in any given historical context is a center that is itself all the more solid because its edges are blurred and shifting. The center of the concept is essentially timeless, culture free, and nonnegotiable. A somewhat oversimplified but essentially correct way of identifying that center is to say that it is the biological underpinning of human identity. Human identity indicates that we are members of the same species: we are able to produce fruitful offspring and perpetuate the race.

It has long been recognized by psychologists that the maintenance both of the family and of the successful dominance of oppressed groups depends on strong taboos against intermarriage and cohabitation. The taboo against incest can be considered as an extension of the self into the family. The taboo against miscegenation on the contrary is a denial of human kinship with oppressed social groups. These taboos use cultural means to obscure the biological reality of racial identity with those psychologically nearest and most distant from self—with members of the family and of despised "subhuman" groups. Here, again, the intertwining of social and human identity becomes manifest in spite of the strength and reality of the underlying human nature.

Biologically speaking, it is a given fact that the long-range survival of the human species will be in part dependent on our ability to perceive potential mates correctly. Any culture that too radically alters this substratum obviously tempts biological suicide.

The essential humanity that derives from species identity only evolves in biological time. Such changes are not visible to the experiences of one or even of several life-spans—and thus for the purposes of experience, species-humanity is both timeless and culture free. In contrast, the social roles from which we derive our social identities are continually open to redefinition in cultural time—between and sometimes even within generations. Yet, as we have said, the edges of that essential humanity are continually being negotiated and renegotiated between adjoining, competing, and interacting social groups and segments of society.

Earlier we said that to equate the center of the concept of human identity with a biological substratum is something of an oversimplification. To be sure, culturally imposed mating preferences will in time affect the gene pool. Thus, in evolutionary time, the edges of what we say constitutes human nature, our version of human nature, begin to influence the very thing being talked about. In that sense human nature is both what it is (the "truly" timeless element) and what we say it is (the historical factor). It should nevertheless be emphasized that this particular organic connection only works in evolutionary time and has no effect either on human or social identity as we encounter it.

Our theories, myths, religious beliefs—our true stories about human nature—affect the horizons, the edges of humanity. In this way there is a drift in one direction or another—an evolution of human nature.

The true stories themselves—the myths, theories, religious beliefs—

which surround the core of the concept of human nature are open to change and interpretation. The question of what all those with whom we can successfully mate have in common has as its answer a truth with which we must struggle, a truth we must constantly reconstruct—just like any other truth. Historical circumstances, including the invention of devices such as computers, which mimic activities previously thought to be in the human province exclusively, place constant strain on such efforts. As past interpretations wear in, they wear out as well. These interpretations become part of the background with which future interpreters have to work.

We can therefore expect that the true story about what is human nature—the true story about human identity—will be found in its essentials in the most enduring of ancient theories, myths, and religious beliefs about anthropogenesis and about the kinship of human beings. One test of the truths of such stories is their endurance and their tendency to be essentially culture free.

We also know that in each time and place these theories, myths, and beliefs about human nature will have to be interpreted to be meaningful in their circumstances. As social, economic, ecological, and political conditions change, the myths, theories, and beliefs require interpretation and reinterpretation.

Finally, we have seen that the stories themselves will drift over evolutionary time. The reinterpretations in their subtle changes and colorings produce the invisible and miniscule changes that in the long term provide for such drifts.

Our task in specifying the connections between human and social identity then becomes, in part, that of identifying the mythical ground of human nature in a way that is understandable to our generation. In this way we show some of the sources of the vocabulary of social identities with which our culture fleshes out interpersonal intercourse.

IS THERE HUMAN NATURE?

"Identifying the mythical ground of human nature" sounds like both an impossible and an unfashionable task. At least two extremely influential traditions of our time deny the reality of any kind of human nature or human identity. On the one side, existential theories in philosophy (Husserl, 1965; Lawrence & O'Connor, 1967; Sartre, 1947, 1963a) and their psychological and phenomenological analogs (Berger & Luckmann, 1966; May, 1961; Shütz, 1962, 1964, 1966) simply assert that human nature is simply what we say it is. From this perspective human nature is an aspect of social identity, pure and simple. It is the most basic of our ascribed roles.

On the other side, "biological" theories attempt to divide the human race into meaningful subspecies. Coon (1962) asserted separate evolution of the main races of humanity—a claimed biological estrangement among the races that has a long history before and after his influential and historic work.

Between them, the existentialist and the biological positions leave little conceptual space and less fashion for digging up the outmoded concept of human nature, as we are attempting to do. For between them, these two positions claim the strong intellectual and affective loyalty of the vast majority of social scientists. The burden of proof for showing the utility of the concept of human identity will be on us.

Existentialist Traditions

The root of the existential view that there is not an identifiable human nature is the belief that human beings are free to choose their "essence" (Sartre, 1956). A useful oversimplification of this would be that the horizons of what it means to be human are only limited by our imagination (Sartre, 1963 b). Our limits are set by our imagination because human imagination is a function of circumstances of political and historical context (Gurvitch, 1971).

It is easy to see the power that the existentialist position has over the convictions of social scientists. Strong beliefs about a fixed human nature characterize traditional, feudalistic, preindustrial societies. In these societies the majority of social roles are ascribed, the majority of statuses are conferred for life. The belief in a fixed human nature seems to be appropriate only to such societies in which sentiments, character, temperament, or traits can be seen as unchanging entities that reside primarily in a person's ancestry—his or her "breeding" (Wirth, 1938, 1956).

As society changes from feudal to industrial underpinnings, havoc is wrought in the concept of fixed sentiments, character, temperament, and traits (Ellul, 1964; Gerth & Mills, 1953). As psychological trait theories are discredited in the industrial society, it is natural to sweep away with them their conceptual superordinate—the belief in a fixed human nature or human identity.

The existentialist tradition, then, arises from the startled experience of persons with rapidly changing characters, with temperament changes that reflect their surroundings, with traits that are context specific, and with sentiments that are subject to education (Flaubert, 1898). The existentialist tradition accounts for these phenomena by placing the context of causation for such changes in the social milieu, on the one hand, or inside the person changing, on the other. Either way, it denies the reality of any kind of underlying, unalterable human identity.

The existentialist viewpoint shows that for most human beings temperament reflects the mood of one's company. It shows that traits are lasting as long as they are useful, functional, adaptive. It shows socialization to be the process in which sentiments are refined, polished, and shaped to their socially intended use. Adolescence, a concept invented to account for some of the role transformations of industrial society, comes to the foreground in existentialist analyses of identity. From the existentialist viewpoint the storms and stresses of adolescence are particularly important in shaping the sentiments of the adult person (Allport, 1955; Erikson, 1950; Mead, 1934).

The person who is a mere product of his or her circumstances represents the masses in the existential analysis. Against the masses of persons who passively accept their alotted social roles stand the existential heroes (Sartre, 1961). Like Mark Twain's *Mysterious Stranger* (1913), the philosopher, the scientist, and the psychologist can transcend the fate of being a pawn pushed about by the transcendental players. These heroes rise above their own culture. To rise above the culture means, in this instance, the ability to see that other humans' actions are only meaningful in their own cultural milieu—in existential terms, to rise above culture is to gain the insights of cultural relativism, nonethnocentrism, or nonanthropocentrism.

The existentialist analysis cuts with a two-edged sword. It categorizes human beings into two classes: the ignorant and slave, and the learned and free. The ignorant slaves are mere products of their culture—immersed in it—rationalizers rather than rational animals. The few who are free and knowing, those belonging to the special culture of the culture-free social scientist philosopher, transcend their ready-made social identities and are free to forge their own definitions of who they are. They are able to reason without having to rationalize.

The liberating effect of the discovery of cultural relativism is primarily the product of the work of Franz Boas (1911, 1940) and his pupils (Benedict, 1934; Mead, 1928). These anthropologists destroyed the traditional concept of human nature. Prior to their work, social scientists believed with Darwin (1871) that rationality represented the unique evolutionary excellence of the human species. By laying bare the original sin of ethnocentrism, Boas and his pupils revolutionized the social sciences. They revealed the run-of-the-mill human as a rationalizing rather than a reasoning creature—constantly involved in explaining away the difficulties raised by the closed system of their own culture categories. Only the elect social scientist was seen as a person freed from these biases of rationalizing.

The existentialists' complex view of a dual human nature created the presently dominant relativist view, according to which each culture or subculture is free to define human nature in its own terms. This position assumes that each culture, mired in its own world, defines what or who is human according to its own needs. Relativist anthropologists like to point to the killing of parents, of young offspring, and other outlandish behavior. These serve as examples of the wide variation between definitions of human being as they vary from culture to culture. (Haring, 1949; Harris, 1974; Sargent & Smith, 1949).

On the other side is the enlightened social scientist. This person is able to discern that the one regularity among human beings is the freedom to choose their own identity, as long as they can put their culture beyond them (Mannheim, 1936). This is due to the supposed fact that once one's horizons have widened, a person is free to choose one's culture. This extends all the way to the freedom to join the international culture of social scientists. Being a participant observer, a field worker, the social scientist goes through the pretense of being one of the masses all the while maintaining the integrity of the reasoning scientist (Kluckhohn, 1962; Kluckhohn & Murray, 1949).

If Darwinism produced a passive election by evolution as the savior from the fallen human condition, the relativists produced a salvation by works, by process, by education, and by enlightenment. This self-righteous idea of salvation by education must have seemed as truth itself to the tiny band of intellectuals who originally espoused the relativist position.

We have taken this much space to expound the existentialist position, because it tends to be the starting point from which contemporary revulsion against a concept of a human nature proceeds. It is critical to understand the strengths and weaknesses of the existentialist position for elucidating the concept of human nature and its relation to the role system of social identity.

The principal strength of the existentialist position lies in its correct insight into the plasticity of human identity. Its principal weakness is that it tends to push that insight too far—all the way to denying that there is anything solid for the plasticity to work from.

One way to understand the overextension of relativism by those who would deny any kind of human identity, is to understand the irony of that extremist position. The relativist position of the existentialist thinkers is destroyed by its unwitting irony. It is only the "superiority" of Western science—its objectivity, its decenteredness, its reversibility, its wealth, its privilege, its political and economic access to other cultures—that makes the very perception of the phenomenon of ethnocentrism possible. The freedom to choose between cultures is a privilege of the well-educated, blasé, mobile Western scientist.

The very assertion of objectivity by the scientist in the face of the attributed "superstition" of lesser folk lays bare the unstated assumption of the scientist that the other humans lack the objectivity he possesses. The position that arrogates objectivity to science alone is so certain of its unassailable superiority as to be unaware of the vanity of its position. This viewpoint is an ironic one, because it means the opposite of what it says. It says "all cultures are equal." It means "all cultures are equal in being inferior to the special subculture of which I am a member." While saying "I am equal and free" it alludes "you are inferior and a slave."

Even at its best the writings of such contemporary master relativists as Goffman (1961, 1974), Szasz (1961, 1976), or the Braginskys show their patronizing belief that the lesser creatures whose lives they are investigating and describing are happier in their unrealized thrall to the dictates of their culture or subculture. There is a bittersweet feeling here of a loss of innocence through which the freedom of the existentialist hero is obtained (Hesse, 1929). Underlying the assumption of no human nature embedded in the existentialist position, lies the unexpressed belief that the scientist alone possesses true human nature. This tragic-but-true human nature is the ability to transcent ideology (Sampson, 1981). The idea is that in transcending their cultural milieu scientist-heroes lose their innocence and take on the tragic burden of consciousness (Zimmer, 1944).

The Behaviorist Parallel

The behaviorist position represents an interesting parallel to that of the existentialists and phenomenologists. Like the existentialists, the behaviorists represent the behavioral scientist as the exception to the rule of general ignorance, superstition, and rationalizing. Like the existentialists as well, they hold that for the average person there is no human nature. Such an individual is a pawn of the environment.

From Watson's assertions about the malleability of human nature (1928) to the recent past (Rachlin, 1970; Skinner, 1971), behaviorists have taken an extreme environmentalist position. According to this stance, identity is a function of one's circumstances—pure and simple. It is only the behaviorist who has the insight to see that the rest of humanity are in the thrall of culture—a culture that can be changed at will by the clever and beneficent scientist.

Watson, in his final role as an executive at the J. Walter Thompson advertising agency, or Skinner (1948) in his Frazier alter ego, then turn the knowledgeable behavioral scientist into a kind of *deus ex machina*. The scientists alone know how to manipulate the rest of us as pawns of our environment.

Watson in his career and Skinner in his imagination both left academia. More consistent than the existentialists, they saw the implication of their position regarding the unreasoning ignorance of the masses. Ultimately, their hero is not the philosopher-king of Sartre, but the opinion molder, the advertiser, the propagandist, the political, economic, psychological thought technologist.

Yet, the black irony of the behaviorist position destroys itself in much the same way as the subtle irony of the existentialist. Both require a priestly class of leaders, of Grand Inquisitors, who keep the truth from the masses (for their own good). This truth is that truth can set you free (Dostoevski, 1927).

The existentialist and behaviorist views trace back to ancient, esoteric and recondite myths. These myths identify the human quest with the rare discovery by the elect that we are all gods *in potentia* (Corbin, 1969, 1977; Tolstoy, 1894). According to this story the hidden potential of human beings is obscured by the current horizon of ignorance, the veil of seeming, the burden of illusion (Maslow, 1971; Moustakas, 1956; Suzuki, 1959).

While the vision of potential divinity is a highly attractive one, it flies in the face of direct experience. At its root this story fails to take account of the fact that whatever is divine about humans is too well hidden to make much of a difference. Certainly the secret is all too well kept by the wars, tortures, and other horrors that are constantly besetting us. For our purposes, the final test of the value of this view relates to its possible uses. I can say with absolute certainty that the horizons of seeming, ignorance, and illusion have me and all possible readers of this chapter sufficiently in their grip that new revelations about human potential will no doubt come well after any possible use of these words has passed.

On a less cosmic level, we can assert that if human nature is some ascribed role, as the existentialists and the behaviorists would have it, then the truth of that proposition is untestable. It is a proposition that destroys itself in the making. If we are pawns then it lies beyond the power of self–discovery for us to find out that we are pawns. For us to be able to discover our pawnhood we *all* have to be something more than pawns—not just some small coterie of the elect. If we are all more than pawns, then there is something above and beyond culture—a human nature—that we all share.

Relativism, which was a natural outgrowth of the expansion of the sphere of achieved roles in an industrial society, led to excessive claims about the malleability of human nature. Time has come to reassess the relationships between social identity and human identity—the one relatively malleable, the other relatively stable over long periods of time.

Biologically Based Theories

Competing for the allegiance of social scientists with the existentialist and behaviorist viewpoints are the biologically based theories of those who would deny the common humanity of the race. These biologically based theories identify different lines of descent for present social, racial, national, kinship, or other social groups.

At the time of the European explorations, theories of a different line of descent to Australian, African, and American aborigines abounded. Josiah Priest's *Bible Defense of Slavery* (1852) was perhaps the last of these explicitly theologically based arguments. Priest considered slavery the just punishment meted out to the Negro race for the sin of their ancestor, Ham. Ham was the murderer of Noah. According to Priest, the patricide of Ham split the human race—and since that time Negroes have occupied their less-than-human position.

From the writing of dc Gobineau (1853–1855) to the present, theories of evolution have been proposed which assign innate racial differences to human groups. For de Gobineau, for example, the black race represented passion and was the source of lyricism and the artistic temperament. The yellows represented order, utility, and mediocrity. The whites are representatives of reason and honor.

When investigators looked within the white race, they found parallel differences. De Gobineau identified the Aryans as representatives of reason and honor. The Teutons were said to be the purest descendants of the Aryans. De Gobineau's three-way classification was thoroughly worked out for the Europeans in the writings of Chamberlain (1899), Woltmann (1903), and Günther (1923, 1927). These all agreed that the proper classification was that of Nordics, Alpines, and Mediterraneans. Here the Nordics were the superwhites. The Alpines proto-yellows, and the Mediterraneans proto-Negroes.

Both the classifications of the world's races and the races of Europe achieved great scientific, popular, and political currency. American immigration policies were changed, in part, through Madison Grant's (1916) well-known version of the tripartite classification of Europeans.

These efforts, in effect, depended on evolutionary versions of a human family tree that assigned separate lines of descent to the races of the human species. Many such family trees were produced, among which the more important were those of Osborn (1918), Smith (1929), and Warden (1932). The physical anthropologist Klaatsch (1923) carried this line of argument the furthest by explicitly associating gorillas, orangutangs, and chimpanzees with the ancestors of the Negroid, Mongoloid, and Caucasoid races, respectively.

The best-known revival of the human family tree concept was the one proposed by Carleton Coon in 1962. Coon's theory is that *homo erectus* evolved into *homo sapiens* not once but five times, each of which was widely separated from the other both in time and space. The first to evolve, according to this theory, were the ancestors of the Caucasians, and the last to evolve were the ancestors of the Negroes. According to Hirsch (1981) the positions of such contemporaries as Shockley (1966), Jensen (1969, 1980), and Herrnstein (1973) can be traced to the influence of Coon's theory.

We categorized the relativism of the existentialist–behaviorist theories as reflections of mobile societies. From such a perspective the biologically based theories could be construed as reactions against mobility. They may be fueled by fear of interaction with strangers. Such interactions have of course been taking place at an unprecedented pace both between Europeans and non-Europeans and within European societies. It is not fanciful to imagine that fears of sexual interactions with strangers might have been especially strong (Putnam, 1961). Such intermixing (outbreeding) could be seen as quite threatening to the social stability of one's own group—to one's own social status within that group (Mannoni, 1956; Marine, 1969).

But that very horror of intermarriage, of miscegenation, underlying the racial theories, gives the lie to their claim that there is no common humanity that unites all of us. From the biological viewpoint the fatal attraction of the "lower" races for the members of the "higher" races is the proof of the long-term viability of such supposed "cross breeding." If evolution works, and if the hypothesis of racial superiority difference is correct, we have nothing to fear, for biological mechanisms will assure the eventual decline of the less fit and their eventual replacement by the superior stock.

In fact if one looks at the writings of the racialists—even to the present—one is struck by the explicit or implicit supposition that biological selection has ceased to operate within the human race (e.g., Eysenck, 1971). In places one gets the impression that the writer assumes that selection is working in reverse (Jensen, 1980). But, if that is the case, one must assume that the evolution of the races is itself a questionable proposition. The racialists cannot have it both ways any more than the extreme relativists/environmentalists can have it both ways. The extreme nativism of the racialists suffers from self-contradiction, precisely as the extreme environmentalism of the relativists had. It is interesting to note that both in their rhetoric and in their content there are fascinating analogies between the positions of the biologically based theories and of contemporary conservative parties. There are similar analogies between the existentialist/behaviorist positions and contemporary liberal parties.

The racialists' position does in fact suffer from an ethnocentrism that is striking and pervasive. Yet, the extreme relativists go too far in denying any limits placed by inheritance on human potential. We are not really free to choose our own nature—if for no other reason than that there are genuine biological constraints on it. The truth in the biologically based theories is that biological necessity unites human beings far beyond the accidents of culture.

This long examination of contemporary views that would deny the utility of the concept of human nature or human identity leads to the conclusion that both theories are erroneous. The concept of identity can only sensibly be approached from an understanding of the underlying stability of human nature from which social identities can be formed—but by which social identities are circumscribed.

THE MYTHOLOGICAL BASIS OF HUMAN IDENTITY

The Story of Adam and Eve

We have said earlier that to begin a reinterpretation of human nature we must turn to stories of anthropogenesis. Our examination of contemporary views and their antecedents has shown us that there is truth in the statement that human nature is unitary and also more than unitary—that we have a common humanity and a potential for difference, which is part and parcel of that common humanity. Further, the anthropological theories have shown that we should not search for the differences in a racialist fashion. All of these qualifications point to the Adam and Eve story—common ancestors—as embodying a powerful metaphor for understanding the basis of the human condition.

The consistency across cultures with which theories of anthropogenesis have identified a common ancestor pair has been shown by Frazer (1907–1915), W. Juhasz (1943), Jung (1968, 1970), and Levi-Strauss (1969a, 1969b, 1973) among others. Here again, Adam and Eve stand as examples of an important theme.

It is my belief that to understand the bases of human nature and its relation to social identity we must return to the structural properties of myths, such as the Adam and Eve myth. In a sense this is a search for "human universals" as undertaken by Jungian psychology (Barthes, 1967; Harré, 1980; Jung, 1966, 1971) and structuralism (Culler, 1975; Derrida, 1972; Katz, 1976; Piaget, 1971; Slobin, 1971).

In the case of identity I do not believe that we can find either a common "grammar" or a common "vocabulary" (Alexander, Ishikawa & Silverstein, 1977; Juhasz, 1981) of humanity. Humans share no common set of rules nor a common set of elements. Such searches tend to ethnocentrism or false generalization. I believe that Jung (1971) was essentially correct in searching for human identity in *attitudes* that are structurally embedded in all personalities. In understanding the potential of such a structural analysis we can begin a search of commonly used oppositions to describe the Adam and Eve duality/unity. The Adam and Eve story here serves as an emblem for traditionally conceived sets of oppositions, which, in their unity, describe the bases of the human personality—human identity.

At its best, the Adam and Eve story suggests that human beings can be understood to arise from an archetypal ground of relation to the Father or Mother, respectively. There is strong implication of gender identification of these two poles—and certainly human beings, from a biological perspective, need some clear gender identification. But to identify mythical figures like Adam and Eve literally with their corresponding gender is unfaithful to the multivalence and ambiguity of myths. It is a beginning toward the understanding of such mythical concepts to say that they can be thought to represent the limits of potential within which and among which human beings in general and any single human being in particular, can vary.

Each person has a "home" within such a range of possibilities—and this home is not unrelated to his/her gender identity. One way of picturing the task of a life, of a group, or of a society, is to say that it involves the exploration of possibilities away from home—to clarify both the home and its surround, to give one a sense both of place and space (Suzuki, 1964). Home is place, the bounded and the safe. Surround is space, the boundless and the venturesome (Tuan, 1977). To describe human nature, then, is to lay out the boundaries of possibility within which human lives act: it is to begin to label the attitudes with which human beings relate to each other in the specifics of social roles—social identities.

Mother and Father

The Adam and Eve story points out that there are certain biological/social characteristics that all humans possess. They proceed from and experience a father and a mother. They have the potential to be either mothers or fathers but not both. If mothers, they have the potential of bearing further fathers- and mothers-to-be. If fathers, they have the potential for impregnation—an act conceptually and biologically but not experientially associated with parenthood (Barthes, 1970).

Psychologically, in terms of identity, the critical feature of these universals of biology and experience is the fact that motherhood is an experiential given, while fatherhod has to be discovered. Fatherhood is an inference. It is the range and type of experiences between the given and the inferred that defines human nature or human identity. This range and type of experience has been described and studied under a host of labels—some few of which we will examine here, as a start toward a contemporary reinterpretation of human identity.

Such a reexamination is timely, if for no other reason, because past interpretations have had a distinctly sexist bias—they proceeded strictly from the father's perspective. Worse, they identified "good" with the perspective of the father, and bad, with that of the mother (Freud, 1964). Certainly one of the more important historical events of the past 50 years or so is the emergence of some objectivity toward the valuation of the characteristics of father and mother (Daly, 1978).

RULES AND SOCIAL IDENTITY

As we trace out the labels that have become associated with the father/mother distinction, we see that they provide opportunities for rules with which expectations about conduct can be specified. It is these rules, which are organically connectable to the fundamental attitudes, that provide for the connection between human and social identity. It is not unlikely that these rules can be construed as role expectations that are variously attached to different kinds of ascribed or achieved roles (Sarbin & Allen, 1968–1969; Sarbin & Juhasz, 1981).

For the purposes of illustration and exploration, we shall show how each of the attitudes archetypically associated with the father/mother distinction can be related to current interpretations of the ascribed role, mother. The role "mother" of course, like all other roles, emerges from human identity. But it has a special place in these and among these roles since it is at the point of direct emergence of interconnection between human and social identity.

While the fundamental attitudes associated with human identity are essentially timeless, it is our view that the rules at any time and place associated with those attitudes define the fundamental features of social identity, and are relatively transient (Peters, 1958). We shall then focus on interpretations of the mother role in North American, Anglo culture at the present time. The repertoire of such rules, like rules of grammar, are within the competencies of all of us—although like rules of grammar, verbalizing them is difficult (Fodor, 1968). Once verbalized, they can be matched against the intuitions of one or all members of the community who are willing to do so in good faith (Searle, 1969). Thus "rules" of behavior, like rules of grammar, are not validated in surveys, or by the cognoscenti, or committees of sages, but rather by the general consensus that they embody current practice in a given segment of the community (Harré, 1980; Mates, 1964).

ONTOLOGICAL AND EPISTEMOLOGICAL THEMES IN HUMAN IDENTITY

Certain themes or attitudes archetypically associated with the father/mother distinction are given in the nature of the distinction itself. These themes form one cluster of attitudes to help us understand human identity. Such "given" themes are ontological: they relate to the very *being* of humanity.

Other themes or attitudes that have come to be associated with the father/mother distinction are universally inferred from the ontology of fatherhood/motherhood. These themes form a second cluster of attitudes with which we can clarify the concept of human identity. Such "inferred" themes are epistemological: they have to do with the range and ability of human beings to know their own condition.

In discussing the manifestations of the mythological bases of human identity, we shall use these clusterings of the basic themes as our outline. One could probably find numberless themes emerging from the basic experience of our humanity—and perhaps one day someone shall begin to collect them all. For our purposes we have taken prominent, historically significant examples, that show the extent of such themes and their clustering around the "given" and the "inferred."

Having their basis in the given side of human experience are such themes as Dionysian–Apollonian, Sky–Earth, Fire–Water, and Ancestor–Source. Among the important fundamental attitudes that are inferred from the human condition—and that have to do with our ability to infer—are: concrete–abstract, representation–presentation, disjunctive–conjunctive, and outlining–penumbration. We shall examine these dimensions in a little detail in the sections following, and attempt to relate the current concept of the role "mother" to them.

MANIFESTATIONS OF THE MYTHOLOGICAL BASES OF HUMAN IDENTITY

Ontological Themes

1. Dionysian–Apollonian

Through Rohde (1925), Nietzsche (1968), and Benedict (1934) come the contemporary interpretations of these terms. It is a given of human experience to associate oneself and one's actions with the rational and ordered or the orgiastic and emotional side of life. All our actions and experiences are ranged in this dimension. The dimension can, without exaggeration, be considered as the ontological basis of human identity.

Yet the distinction between Dionysius and Apollo in their approaches to life is a "symbolic" one, rich in implications, which takes place in the context of human activities, human history, and human meaning systems. It is not as if we did not in a profound way share the use of these dimensions with other creatures—with the rest of creation. Human beings are not simply "animal plus" (White, Juhasz & Wilson, 1973). Rather, the ability to operate within this dimension is what allows us to recognize ourselves and others as fellow human beings from a psychological perspective. The dimension—emerging from the archetypal energy arising between father and mother—provides the tension within which human acts gain their historical and personal meanings (Foucault, 1972).

Many would agree that this contemporary identification of the tension between mother and father with two male gods is inappropriate to our circumstances (Chesler, 1972). It is at least partially true that using these masculine gods is inappropriate. This situation reflects the strange emergence of our mythological understanding from a patriarchal context. Yet, in its mythological origins, the association is not totally inappropriate either.

Apollo's role in the Eumenides (Aeschylus, 1953) as champion of a rationalistic ethics is in line with this contemporary interpretation. As related to us, Apollo's rationalism in the Eumenides was explicitly based upon the supremacy of the father over the mother. This witnesses at once the great age and the explicit sexism of the identification of the Apollonian with the male gender rather than the psychological ontology of the condition of the father.

Certainly some would argue that Apollo's opposite number should be Demeter, Cybele, or some other mother god. Yet, the role of Dionysius in the mysteries makes him a passable stand-in (Kerenyi, 1977).

In their mythical character, Apollo and Dionysius both reveal a far more rounded, and richly evolved character than a simple modern identification of the Dionysian with the mother and the Apollonian with the father would have it. Apollo's ability to foresee the future is insightful. In accomplishing her designs through Dionysius, her son, the Great Mother reveals the paradoxical outcomes of the sensuality of birth-giving labor (Graves, 1948). Apollo intuits alogically; Dionysius carries out the rational designs of his mother.

How does the quality of being able to perceive the world and to act in it within the Dionysian–Apollonian distinction map onto the current social role of mother? In her public performance as mother, a contemporary interpreter of this role is expected to provide day-to-day emotional sustenance and shelter. She is almost like a nurse to those under her charge.

The direct, spontaneous, unplanned outpouring of supportive emotional provisions is her hallmark.

There is often a taboo against experiencing the orgiastic elements of sustenance giving. The current relaxation of this taboo during childbirth and nursing is strong witness to the change in valuation associated with motherly attitudes. The full experience of Dionysian ecstasy is now almost expected rather than tolerated in the literal nursing of infant care. It has even come to be acceptable in the ecstasy of birth giving—an experience previously anesthetized out of consciousness.

In the sense of this revision, the social identity of mother—unlike her mythical/human identity—has undergone change within our own generation. The far-reaching implications of such a change are perhaps just now beginning to be understood. Not the least of these implications is the question of how such changes will affect male–female and mother–child relationships.

We have seen in this initial example how the archetypal father/mother relationship becomes manifest in a dimension of human identity: Dionysian–Apollonian. We have also provided one example of how such dimensions of human identity map onto social roles.

2. Sky–Earth

Even more ancient than the identification of the father with Apollo and the mother with Dionysius, is the sky–earth distinction. Father is sky; mother is earth. These are old concepts, drawn from ancient cosmology, and part of the ontological givens of human experience. To be human is to have one's home in the sky or on the earth—and to be able to experience the polarity of being attached to those two homes.

The adjectives "airy" and "earthy," in their contemporary usage, in fact, preserve many of the meanings traditionally associated with this dimension. The most obvious connotations of airy are lofty and illusory (Aristophanes, 1970). The sky-father is difficult to find—and when found, is difficult to apprehend. The father is elevated and powerful. He is something like a Kafka (1937) father.

The most obvious connotations of earthy are practical and gross (Gorky, 1923). The combination practical-gross unites the qualities of concreteness—one of the epistemological qualities of mother—with the ontological, Dionysian, gross. This combination is both intriguing and absorbing (Gorky, 1921; Hillman, 1979).

Air is the space in which Apollo moves. Earth is the dwelling place of Dionysius. Apollo ventures forth from earth in the morning to return to it at night—to rest. Sun meets earth at the horizon. Earth is the stable home from which we venture—to which we return (Zimmer, 1956).

This is another dimension undergoing dramatic change in its current interpretation in the actual role of mother. Traditionally, in Western society, the interpretation had to do with the role of father as law giver and the role of mother as law enforcer and interpreter (Bernard, 1981). Today, the mother is still expected to be down-to-earth, but what down-to-earth is and how it is valued have undergone change.

It is not mother's earth biology that stands out in contemporary interpretations. Nor do we see much of the earth mother of the 1960s any more (Anonymous, 1974). Rather, today's earthiness involves the ability to reach common-sense decisions and conclusions not marred by overconcern with either rationalization or rhetoric. In this sense it is highly valued without necessarily being patronized. Earthiness is becoming a quality as appealing to males as females.

3. Fire–Water

This distinction between the dry-and-hot and the moist-and-cool also comes from ancient cosmology. Fire reaches from the earth toward the sky. It is an earthy emblem or token of the sun. Water flows always closer and closer to the center. It comes from the sky, reaching for the earth. As rain, or as snow, it is something that comes from the sky to give life to earth.

These characteristics of fire and water enrich our understanding of sky and earth. Both fire and water and sky and earth line up with father and mother respectively—but the complementariness of the characteristics show their search for a union with one another. In this sense they demonstrate not so much a dichotomy as a resolving tension between the poles of these continua.

Fire is said to be humanity's first and greatest invention—the use of fire is often used as hallmark of the species. It was "stolen from the gods." Water, on the other hand is often considered female: the source of life (Morgan, 1973) rather than an invention of living humans. We particularly associate the ocean—the mother and goal of all waters—with femaleness—with the mother. Much could be written of Poseidon's complex relationship with Demeter in the mysteries (Kerenyi, 1977). Suffice it to say that the union of water and earth forms clay—the archetypal stuff of pots, bricks, idols, and Adam.

Fire and water as emblems of Adam and Eve—as our sources of invention and of life—show us another range of possibilities that we have open to us as humans. This, too, is an ontological theme, flowing from the direct experience of our humanity. The mythological concepts of earth, air, water, and fire form a most important complex in this ontological view of our common humanity. Water and fire, most importantly, serve to unite earth and air. Water and earth make clay, which when heated in the fire and dried in the air gives us pottery and other sorts of utilitanda, images, and idols.

The aspect of the current interpretation of the social role mother that most directly relates to water has to do with "dissolution of differences." Water, in this sense, can also be thought of as softening the often stubborn earthiness of dry, barren visions of the mother figure. Compare, for example, the Empress in the Tarot, who is pregnant, with the High Priestess, who is severely virginal as the solemn keeper of the heavenly law (Cavendish, 1975).

Mother partakes of the archetypal water in the sense that she is close to the processes which dissolve and mediate differences. Mother is seen as forgiver, peacemaker, confidante, comforter, and resolver of conflicts.

Water as the "universal solvent," as that which seeks the center, as the gravitationally stable—these are the characteristics that contemporary interpretations particularly emphasize. Mother, more than anything else, in her social identity, is expected to take the lead in averting psychological and physical conflicts. She is supposed to emphasize similarities over differences, she is to bring quiet to the storms of passion (Woolf, 1925).

This quieting, smoothing role is not an antiemotional one. It is rather that the contemporary mother is expected to be grounded enough in her own emotions to salve and cool down the fire of those less able to control themselves. This is not a denial of her Dionysian roots, but rather a rounding out of her Dionysian excesses. The heat of Apollo is a dry and furious heat. The frenzy of the Bacchante, on the other hand, is moist and organic (Kerenyi, 1977). This is the difference between the psychological fire of the father (a means of division), and the psychological water of the mother (which is a means of union, which washes away differences, which cleanses the earth, and puts out fire) (Corbin, 1964).

The mother's uniting function, in her social as well as her archetypal identity, is evident in her primary responsibility for the next generation of fathers as well as mothers. She must offer to sons as well as daughters an atmosphere of calm. She must do this in an even-handed way. This is not Apollonian rule making. It is the desire and tendency, at least in public, when enacting her social role, to erase differences, reduce conflicts, ease tensions, and lessen the strain of transitions. Thus, the "watery" quality of general human identity is translated to visible role demands of social identity.

4. Ancestor—Source

On its face, these two terms are a fairly accurate statement of the difference between father and mother in the profane and literal as well as the mythical and figurative sense. Father is an ancestor. It is possible—even in a matrilineal society—to trace a line of descent to him (Levi-Strauss, 1969a). Mother, on the other hand, is the direct source of life—even in the most extreme of patriarchal societies. Mother is the one from whom—in the most ontological of senses—we separate ourselves at birth. The ontological reality of parenthood sets up circumstances by which we return to the ancestor—having made a voyage of discovery (Suzuki, 1964). We ventured from a place of safety—from mother—after an act of separation and differentiation.

To take this argument a step further is to say that the distinction between ancestor and source is the distinction between the mediate as against the immediate and direct cause. It can be thought of as a distinction between probabilistic and deterministic kinds of relationships (Brunswik, 1949, 1950). The ancestor represents mediate cause which is indirect and therefore probabilistic in nature. It can be thought of as causation through the agency of another. The source is a direct and material cause.

Ontogenetically it is a fascinating and important fact that our birth is hidden from us in memory. Some imperative of ontogenesis hides the innocence of childhood from the sophisticated adult. It has been proposed that it is the very discovery of mediation, of the sophistication of knowing how to use detached signifiers (Piaget & Inhelder, 1971) that blots out the memory of the infant's innocent paradise. In any case the result of the childhood amnesia is that for human beings all knowledge is mediate—we experience degrees of mediation (Sarbin & Bailey, 1966). As humans we deal with the ontological given of direct experience; as adults we are alienated from immediacy by the very tensions between mother and father, between the ontological and the epistemological that define our humanity.

In her Dionysian aspect, mother as interpreted by and in our culture, is a source of sustenance and nourishment. She provides a tactile, even sensual connection with the mythologically unknowable source. In this aspect as source she is the "home base"—the place to which we can always return for unquestioning acceptance. The place from which the human venture begins. In this guise, the "role demand" is that she provide unquestioning haven for her children.

Epistemological Themes

1. Concrete-Abstract

Certainly one fundamental dichotomy for humans to cope with is the one between concrete and abstract ways of dealing with problems. If we accept the fact that the character of Eve is given, while that of Adam is mediate and has to be inferred, we can understand the classic association of concrete with the female and of abstract with the male. Concrete is the given, the specific, the direct, the experienced. Abstract is generalization from specifics to classes, from experience to theory.

Whether our approach to the world and ourselves is concrete or abstract, the distinction itself has to do with our ability and tendency to infer. This inferring tendency and ability in its own turn derives from the Dionysian–Apollonian positions that we are able to take. The ontological givens of the father/mother, Adam/Eve condition give rise to epistemic concerns with concrete or abstract approaches to phenomena. In this sense dimensions such as concrete-abstract are "derivative" and stand in complementary opposition to ontological themes such as Dionysian–Apollonian.

We recognize one another as human, then, in part by inferring or perceiving ourselves as acting in a space in which the abstract–concrete dimension is meaningful (von Bertalanffy, 1967). As with the other dimensions these are not diacritica of being human in the sense that they split us off from the rest of creation. Rather they mark us as human in that their realization in the specific human contexts of social life relate to our social and personal identities. The development of the abstract–concrete dimension is nevertheless an achievement of humans—an aspect of human evolution. In this sense it is a powerful manifestation of the Adam/Eve, mother/father archetype.

But how do we recognize, on the basis of the abstract-concrete attitude, someone such as a mother in contemporary North American Anglo culture? In public situations, the mother is expected to take the lead in dealing with specific problems, guidance issues, matters of daily routine, etc., of the child. She is expected to "consult" the father on matters of "policy." The day-to-day administration of these policies is the province of the mother.

This rule establishes a set of relationships that in their own turn allow us to recognize mothers. These relationships are between mothers and children and mothers and fathers. All things being equal, the one dealing with the daily routines of policy concretizing is liable to be the mother. This expectation—the beginnings of a social identity—is in its own turn related to the fundamental attitude: concrete–abstract. In the case of the mother, the connection is to the concrete—for mothers are expected to find their home in concreteness—just as Eve has her home there.

2. Representation–Presentation

At its center, this is a distinction between the talker and the doer. Directness in this sense is doing—and being indirect is associated with talking. Of course, talking is a kind of doing—or part of some doing (Austin, 1962; Searle, 1969). Yet there are important distinctions between the two.

To put it simply, the difference is between something that refers as compared to something that simply is (Juhasz, 1976a, 1981). This distinction is that between referential and nonrepresentational activity (Langer, 1942). The dimension itself shows that human beings are capable of both—but that each of us has a "home" where activity is the most comfortable in this dimension (Lacan, 1968).

If concrete–abstract attitudes can be seen as arising from and being related to the Dionysian–Apollonian distinction, then the representation-presentation theme can be thought to have a similar relation to the theme of Sky–Earth. The ontology of Sky and Earth suggests the very directness and indirectness that define presentation and representation. Presentation and representation can be thought of, then, as epistemological analogs of Earth and Sky, respectively.

Many human activities and products are representational in that they speak to that which is already known and articulated—and refer to it in some manner. Many other human activities and products do not refer to anything at all. They *are* or *become*, but they do not *refer*. Such activities, processes, or products are presentational.

These complementary processes of presentation and representation have their projection into the contemporary role of mother. Artaud (1958), Foucault (1970), Derrida (1972), Tafuri (1980), and a host of others have characterized the contemporary condition as one in which a chasm has arisen between words and actions. Here, mother as uniter, stands for a reconciliation between words and actions. She is an opponent of lie and artifice. Her magic is sympathetic, not incantational (Middleton, 1967; Shotter, 1979).

Mother is the teacher of language. But she teaches the corpus of the language and corrects errors. She is not expected to teach grammar—in fact she is expected not to teach grammar—as that occupation is set aside for "experts" (Bruner, Oliver & Greenfield, 1966; Nelson, 1980). Mother offers an example, mother must set an example. Nothing is further from mother than to say "do as I say—not as I do" (Roberts, 1971). Her actions speak louder than her words. She is required to exhibit, rather than to expound or explain virtue.

3. Disjunctive–Conjunctive

There is a kind of logic that works by a principle of either/or—a logic in which the principle of the excluded middle works. There is another kind of logic that operates on the principle of the both/and. Here there is no law of contradiction. The former of these could be called a disjunctive and the latter a conjunctive principle. Human beings perceive themselves in a world of possibilities between adhering to one or another of these principles.

As an epistemological theme, the disjunctive and conjunctive logics are related to the ontological dimension Fire–Water. Fire divides and water unites in a sense analogous to the logic by distinction, which is disjunctive, and the logic of similarities, which is conjunctive.

The distinction between disjunctive and conjunctive reasoning is one of the bases of Freudian psychology. The complex relationships between conscious and unconscious thought and primary and secondary process thought cannot be discussed here. But both of those dichotomies can without too great an exaggeration be characterized as revolving around the issue of the power and realm of disjunctive versus conjunctive thought (Freud, 1953, 1957, 1963). Much of psychological thought since the time of Freud has been directed at understanding these relationships. One essential problem that is increasingly recognized is the strong sexist and ethnocentric bias with which Freud and his contemporaries approached this problem (Juhasz, 1977).

For contemporaries such as Ogilvy (1977) and Hillman (1972) this is the dimension on which human nature primarily operates. In this interpretation disjunctive thought is a primary quality of monotheism and conjunctive thought that of polytheism (Jung & Kerenyi, 1949). In a mythological sense the struggle between these "two principles of mental functioning" has to do with the disjunction's commitment to the "one" and conjunction's to the "many" (Freud, 1955). A particularly oppressive fact about our culture is our association of polytheism—the ability to tolerate competing and mutually exclusive principles—with paganism. It is almost a given, though that the either/or attitude will be less tolerant than the both/and. For father, either/or is the key to fatherhood. For mother both/and are conceivable. Patriarchal societies tend toward monotheism—and the attendant narrow-mindedness that is endemic to it (Freud, 1964).

To say that the contemporary mother is "polytheistic" is only to say that she is bedeviled by significantly more incompatible role damands than is the contemporary father. In responding to two or more "musts" that are mutually incompatible one must achieve both/and thinking—one must know how to serve two or more masters.

The classic conflicting role demands facing mothers is that as women they are expected to be "less than human" while as mothers they are expected to be more than competent.

4. Outlining–Penumbration

This is the last distinction we shall consider. It speaks to two distinct ways in which form may be generated. Any form can be established either by defining the outline of the edges of the form, or it can be established by showing how it reflects and absorbs light, by shading, gradation, chromaticity, movement, rhythm, and tempo.

The dimension outlining–penumbration is the epistemological analog of the ontological distinction Ancestor–Source. Forming an object by penumbration involves an attempt to render the "immediate" play of light and dark, reflection and shade. While penumbration strives for the direct "sensation" of light and dark, outlining strives for the achievement of "perception" through the separation and disjoining of object and space (Klee, 1953).

In defining the edges we give boundaries. These boundaries give plasticity to the whole and set it apart from the empty space surrounding it. This gives us figure and ground, object and void (Hofstadter, 1980).

If we think of the object as a reflector, or source of light, we sculpt as it were not the "object" but the void itself. This, too, establishes the dialog between object and space, self and other—but the concern is for the center not the boundary—for the materiality not the surround.

The human identity characteristics that parallel the above approaches to making things are contrasting ways of distinguishing between the self and others. The father sculpts, whittles with a knife. The mother plays with the elusive, equivocal, juxtapositioning of light and shade, valley and promontory, plain and defile.

In this eighth and last dimension that we are considering, then, we celebrate the ability of humans to "sculpt" or define themselves in fundamentally different ways. These two modes of creation are *ex materia* and *ex nihilo*. We create ourselves—as well as the forms around us—by outlining (subtraction) and by penumbration (congealment). These two ways can be both antagonistic and complementary. In a sense they refer to the interplay of fantasy with physical form in the creation of our surroundings (Juhasz, 1976b).

The notion of penumbration ties to the complementary role demands on mothers in two specific ways: on the one hand it has to do with the "centeredness" of the mother, on the other it has to do with her "softness." By centeredness we mean a concern for essentials and an ability to intuitively hit the nail on the head when dealing with practical problems. In this way her concerns are with the center, with the essentials, rather than with the periphery or the boundaries.

Forming by light and shade rather than outlining also gives objects a "soft" character. This softness comes from a lack of concern with boundaries, and means an ability to give in to pressure—a kind of passive ability to absorb before having to react. In everyday affairs this means an ability to control by indirection, by responding obliquely, by working from a sense of reserve (in both senses of that term). Mothers recognize one another, and can be recognized by this interesting combination of centeredness and softness.

THE RELATION OF HUMAN TO SOCIAL IDENTITY

We have seen, from our attempt to outline the relation of the social role "mother" to the dimensions of human nature that arise from the Adam and Eve dichotomy that current role models involve interpretations of the basic dimensions of human nature (Shotter, 1979). It is beyond the scope of this chapter to enter into the outlining of a great number of social roles and their relation to these fundamental dimensions of human nature. What is elementary about the process is our ability at any time or place to orient ourselves to our basic humanity by the script of demands and expectations that defines our social role and makes up our social identity.

We conceptualize "human nature" as a basic attitude complex. In a given epoch, a given social complex can derive specific expectations from these basic attitudes. Any human being has the capacity to occupy a place along each of these dimensions of human nature. But more importantly, to be human is the ability to experience many places along these dimensions. Equally important is the concept of each person's specific "home"—the most comfortable and natural place along the dimensions.

Our general humanity, our human identity, *is* the total of these capacities. The poles of the capacities have a "masculine" or "feminine" function or identity. These relate to our characteristic stance *vis à vis* ourselves and the world. But in its essence the "masculine" and "feminine" functions give a relationship on the mythical plane to our ancestors, to Adam and Eve.

Our relation to ourselves, the world, our mythical ancestors, is of course related to our life experiences. In this sense, the existentialists and behaviorists are right in pointing out that our human nature is acquired over time. The underlying human nature—the range of possibilities—has the breadth and the ambiguity of interpretations that makes humans the subtle, supple, and adaptable creatures that they are.

Human identity involves our competences as human beings. It provides the opportunities for the specific skills and performances that we produce under specific circumstances. Human nature provides the wherewithal of social identity. The competences of human nature establish our limits and define our horizons. These limits and horizons are exciting, because in evolutionary time they change. Within a specific life span they delimit and state possibilities.

HUMAN IDENTITY, SOCIAL IDENTITY, PERSONAL IDENTITY

We have provided a sketch outline of the general possibilities we have as human beings—an outline of human identity. We have also showed how each individual is faced at any time and place with a host of (often conflicting) role damands. Our personal identity is related both to the human and the social identity we possess.

Personal identity is related to human identity. Each person has a specific constellation of "homes" on each of the "dimensions" of human identity. Each of us is related to Adam and Eve in a unique constellation of their ancestral characteristics.

Personal identity is also related to social identity. Our personal identity involves a refashioning and rewriting of societal roles and performances. The social identity which we refashion to our personal identity will bear the stamp of our persnal constellation of human identity. In this respect there is an interaction effect between social and human identity in the formation of a personal identity.

Social Identity and Personal Identity

We know that no two mothers respond to the demands of their role performances in exactly the same way. One of the reasons for this is that as humans develop a genuine personal identity, they learn to deviate in specific and predictable ways from the societal standards that define what, for example, a mother is. It is because of these deviations from a standard that a person can not only be recognized as mother, but as *this* specific mother as well.

In effect what we are talking about here is an evolution of a personal style with which an individual carries out the host of social roles he or she is called upon to enact. This personal style of role enactment will, in a person with a cohesive personal identity, cut across the social roles, and form a meaningful context.

It is not for us here to outline the differences between "sane" role interpretation and "insane" or "criminal" deviance (Sarbin & Juhasz, 1975, 1981). Suffice it to say, that in normal role interpretation there is always a measure of departure from expectations. Even within the departures from the expectations of a single role, these variations form a cohesive whole. It is in fact these cohesive departures from the norm within and between roles that in their sum keep a society's or a group's role from atrophying. Conversely, a group or society that does not allow for a personal style in the carrying out of its roles is one that will not be able to meet internal or external challenges effectively.

Over generations the role demands and expectations themselves change. The very changes in a role like "mother," as interpreted in North America, came in part from the independent performances of many mothers. As more women nurse their babies in public, have their birthing in the home, and work as competent professionals, the societal expectations of how mothers do behave, and ought to behave, change (Laslett, 1972).

This specific person, this specific mother, then, is recognizable from the way she relates to the role of mother. She has developed her specific way of exploiting the systematic indeterminancy (Katz, 1976) of the role system. This systematic indeterminancy is in its own turn a function of the richness of the archetypal human nature underlying it.

Human Identity and Personal Identity

In my human nature itself, I am not just any human being—I am this particular human being. I am this human being not simply because I possess a potential for occupying a position on a number of dimensions that define my ancestral inheritance. I am this specific human being because I have a specific legacy on all of these dimensions. This human being, this I, this Joseph Juhasz, has a set of homes: he is more closely related to earth than air, to Apollo than Dionysius, to water than fire, to outlines than penumbrations—and so on. This is *my* personal nature. This personal nature, in its interaction with my social identity, makes me more fit for some social roles than others.

The study of lives reveals that as their life histories unfold, people sample, explore, and develop aspects of their "human potential" that are away from their "home" on each dimension (Binswanger, 1963). In fact, part of what we mean by a differentiated personal identity—by a true personal style—is the level of success in exploring the sum total of such a "human potential" (Laing, 1967; Singer, 1973). But, finally, to achieve a rounded personal identity one must gain confidence in the center of his or her personality. We must learn to act from our specific set of "homes" (Jacobi, 1973).

The tragedy of many life histories comes from a lack of venturesomeness away from the initial set of "homes" in which we find comfort. Equally many tragedies can be traced from the homeless feeling of the "man without qualities" (Musil, 1953) of the "protean man" (Lifton, 1968), the man with the existential anguish of he who has no home at all (Mishima, 1968). Such people have had their human nature taken away from them by the illusion of freedom provided by a mobile society (Tafuri, 1976).

UNIVERSAL STYLE, HISTORICAL STYLE, PERSONAL STYLE

We have been examining the relations among that which all human beings have in common, that which specific persons belonging to groups have in common, and that which makes the individual human unique (Wollheim, 1979). This involves a search, first of all, for universal patterns of human experience. These universal patterns are related to our common inheritance, to our common ancestorhood, to a set of "parents"—to the fundamental patterns of human relationship that transcent culture, time, and place. This is the universal style of a human being.

The universal patterns are not manifest. What are manifest are patterns of interbehaving in a given time and place. This observable patterning of human interactions is the manifestation of an abstraction: the role system. The role system provides the historical style that is a given society's interpretation of the archetypal patterns of human relationships.

While the universal patterns change only with biological evolution, the role patterns are subject to cultural change. Thus, in individual experience, the universal patterns are timeless and given, while the social patterns are contingent and at times even arbitrary.

A personal identity is a life process. It develops from a person's specific affinity to the range of possibilities provided by the universal givens of human existence. It develops equally from the specific ascribed and achieved roles that have tested the suppleness of that inheritance. Personal style, personal interpretation, is then a factor of both universal and historical styles of being human. It is finally the source of dynamism and change on both the universal and the historical level. For it is only convincing deviation from that which is expected that can provide impetus for change and growth in human relationships.

SUMMARY

Social identity, as a concept and as an empirical reality in our lives, is anchored in our human and personal identity. By human identity is meant the enduring human nature that allows us to recognize one another as members of the same species. To assert that there is a human nature goes against two important contemporary traditions. On the one hand the existentialists, behaviorists, and cultural relativists assert that human nature is an illusion. According to these theorists, human nature is whatever we say it is. On the other hand biologically based theories attempt to identify subspecies of humanity who trace their ancestry to separate forebears. According to these, human nature varies according to race.

In fact, it would not even be possible to have social identities if an enduring and essentially unchangeable human nature that takes in all of humanity were not operating in the background. Similarly, our social roles, the components of our social identities, could not exist in a stable society were not our individual personal identities there to transcend the changes in role demands that move us from one occasion to the next.

What defines the human condition is the potential for experiencing the multiple practical and spiritual implications of the philogenic and onto-genic consequences of the difference between motherhood and fatherhood. These psychological consequences are experienced ontologically and epistemologically in numerous ways, of which we considered eight important dimensions. Among ontological dimensins we looked at Dionysian--Apollonian, Sky–Earth, Fire–Water, and Ancestor–Source. Among epistemological dimensions we examined concrete–abstract, presentation–representation, disjunction–conjunction, and outlining–penumbration.

Social role demands emerge from current interpretations of such dimensions for a given social role. As an example, we considered the contemporary, North American, Anglo interpretation of the social role: mother. We saw how such a social role is related to and determined by the fundamental dimensions of human identity.

A personal identity emerges from the departures from role expectations that an individual carves out from current societal definitions. In their coherent and consistent rendering, they become a personal style with which a person carries out his or her opportunities and obligations. Personal identity likewise develops as one gains deeper understanding of his or her characteristic "home" on each dimension of human identity. A life can be seen as the systematic exploration of possibilities of human and social identity away from the unique set of "home places" that each person has. In the exploration, the person with the strong individual identity gains deeper understanding of and facility with the anchoring home places of his or her social and human identity.

Chapter 15

SELF, SYMPTOM, AND SOCIAL CONTROL

Daniel R. Miller

This chapter is devoted to rethinking a conception of self previously proposed by the writer (Miller, 1963). Interpersonal and societal implications of the construct have been expanded, and its operations reinterpreted in cognitive terms. Specifically, it is proposed that self-as-object is an organization of those attributes of the individual's social relationships that have consequences for the society's welfare, and that it is a primary means whereby the society achieves control over its citizens. Self-as-agent is interpreted as a set of schemas that organizes perception, communication, judgment, and action with others. A concluding section illustrates possible values of the proposed system by applying it to some refractory problems in psychopathology.

PROPERTIES OF SELF

Most issues about the self were identified by the beginning of this century. There are four general kinds.

Universality and Sameness

Is the concept of self necessary? If it did not exist, would it have to be invented? The universality of the concept suggests that everyone must be identified. Anything that matters in a society—be it object, force, natural

The author is very appreciative of the helpful comments of Sharon Armstrong, George Sobelman, Elliott Jaques, and Karl Scheibe.

process, or person—is given a label so it can be recognized by people whose welfare it affects. The term self is one such label. The fact that every society refers to its citizens by names and pronouns indicates how important their identities must be to the implementation of certain societal functions.

Possible keys to the significance of self and identity are provided by their etymologies. "Self" is derived from a Latin stem, *se*, which connotes sameness, and is used to emphasize that a reference was being made to a particular object. Common to the terms "identity" and "identify" is the stem, "iden," derived from the Latin *idem* meaning "the same." Self and identity, then, imply that the object is the same at different times and in different settings. It has also been suggested (*Oxford English Dictionary*, 1971) that the work identity is derived from the Latin *id ens*, or "that being," which signifies that the object has an essence that remains the same over time, even though it keeps changing. In other words, a man is the same being as an adult that he was as a child, even though he keeps maturing.

Meaning

Many theorists regard the self as a point of reference for interpreting social meanings. Unlike the rest of the world it has special properties, such as sensations, intentions, and feelings. Although these resemble the properties of other selves, their actual experience is unique to oneself. This uniqueness is exemplified by the fact that I have two sensations when I touch a part of my body, but only one when I touch anything else.

Each person has a name that identifies him to those who know him and to himself. The name is far more than a label. It usually provides clues about properties as varied as sex, ethnicity, religion, generation, race, and social status, even one's possible values and styles of behavior. Tentatively acting on those clues during a first encounter, we are often gratified to find that they facilitate our making a successful social contact.

Commenting on the universality of personal pronouns, which are substitutes for names, Boas (1938) notes that terms like "I" and "thou" are linguistic means of distinguishing between one's self, the person being addressed, and the object of conversation. Pronouns also reveal additional information of considerable social significance: whether the referent is singular or plural (I, we), human or nonhuman (he, it), masculine or feminine (he, she), the agent or object of action (he, him), and whether the action is reflexive (ourselves). Finally, the possessive form (hers) can refer to a plethora of attributes, such as possessions, responsibilities, psychological states, and physical characteristics. Unlike names, which tend to be denotative, personal pronouns can connote virtually everything associated with a person. It is not surprising, then, that the word "self," which is so connotative, is derived from a pronoun.

Self as Object and Its Evaluation

The self is not a given; it must be learned. The very young child is aware of a body, feelings, and wishes, but it is years before he refers to them verbally by a possessive pronoun. He is even aware of other people as entities before he is aware of having a self. In fact, it is through his cognizance of others' concepts and values, particularly as expressed in adults' sanctions of his behavior, that he begins to have a self. As Mead (1934) puts it, " . . . the individual experiences himself as such, not directly but only indirectly, from the particular standpoints of others."

Once an object is discriminated, it is evaluated at the same time that it is perceived. With self-consciousness, the child and others hold him responsible for acting and expressing himself within limits defined by the common norms. He becomes an object to himself by internalizing the attitudes of others within the groups to which he belongs. From then on, he evaluates himself in ways that reflect how others judge and treat him.

Standards of self-judgment vary with the individual's stage of development. The first foci of socialization, the bodily functions, form the nucleus of self-as-object. The initial training provides the child with information about the nature of adults, their conceptions of his functions, and the norms of certain social relationships. The intense pleasures and pains associated with success and failure in meeting the parents' standards create the foundations of values that are used in judgments of the self.

Self-As-Agent and Monitoring

In addition to being responsive to others, each of us is autonomous: we initiate activities, pursue goals, control impulses, choose from among possible acts, accept or reject social pressures, even change ourselves. Once the self is differentiated, it can be used for an autonomous activity that transforms all social relationships: the sensing of others' reactions during an encounter. Mutual monitoring is at the heart of interpersonal communication. As conceived by both psychoanalysts (Klein, 1952) and sociologists (Mead, 1934), monitoring is achieved primarily by putting oneself in the place of the other participant in the relationship. This process entails a projection to the other person of what we would feel if we were in his place, and then an identification with him.

THE SOCIAL CONTEXT

Quite a number of the attributes of self have been listed thus far. It is a social product that has to be learned; it identifies the individual as being the same at different times; its names and identifying pronouns signify membership in social categories such as gender, generation, and ethnicity; it is a primary vehicle for understanding others during social interaction; it is the object evaluated by each group when it judges its members' behavior; it is internalized so that each member of the group sees himself from the standpoint of the group; it is presumed to be the agency of autonomous action.

At first the list seems heterogeneous, but consideration of its contents reveals some common denominators. First, in the course of participating in the activities of various groups, each person develops a sense of self and a feeling of responsibility for those of its attributes that are of consequence to the other members. Second, the group constantly evaluates each member's self, fitting its judgments to what might be expected of a person with his traits at his stage of social development. Third, meeting their standards requires skill in monitoring others' reactions as a basis for coordinating one's behavior with theirs. Fourth, the attributes of self with which the group is most concerned pertain to autonomous and reflexive behavior with other group members and bearing on the common welfare. Each member is expected to show understanding, self-control, and a sense of responsibility.

These themes convey the overall impression that the group uses the evaluation of self as a means of setting limits on its members' behavior. For the control to be effective, each member must be socialized so he is impelled to earn the group's approbation by maximal contributions to its goals. At a minimum, it is necessary that the member have a sufficient need for the group's acceptance to avoid violating their standards of acceptable behavior.

As used here, the term "group" refers to any collectivity—family, employing organization, or informal network. It is through collective behavior that the total society gets its work done. Functionally, a society is like a colony of coral polyps. Just as the individual members of such a colony cannot prosper except as part of a collective physiological system, the individual human cannot prosper except as part of the collective social system. Humans thrive only if the society can continually carry on requisite functions, such as recruitment of its citizens for purpose of reproduction, the production and distribution of scarce goods, and the protection of citizens from sources of harm both within and outside the community.

Such activities are inherently interpersonal, a fact that is reflected in the names of social positions. If there are offspring there must be parents; if there are buyers there must be sellers. Everyone's participation in these reciprocal activities is evaluated in terms of its import for the group's welfare. Acts that are viewed as being directly or potentially damaging to functions required for the society's survival—acts such as those prohibited by the Ten Commandments—are considered immoral. Moral values are usually weighted heavily in a group's evaluations of its members' selves.

The significance of self, then, is best understood in the context of people carrying on the interpersonal activities that implement the requisite functions of the social "colony." The attainment of common goals requires constant attention to mutual perception, and the coordinated judgment and regulation of self and other.

Social control is achieved by means of the citizens' anticipated and actual evaluations, which, through their effects on the judgments of selves, by both group and individual, reinforce conformity to the values of group and community. Hence the processes entailed in social interaction and evaluation both validate the self of each participant and serve as the agency by which the community imposes constraints on its members. Experiences in social relationships thus create an organization of self that enables the individual to be a productive member of society.

TYPES OF IDENTITY

Empirical self, self-as-agent, self-awareness, social selves, looking-glass-self, presented self—the variety of concepts suggests that the term self is a generic one which subsumes a number of different topics, such as self-deception, the nature of guilt, the connection between consciousness and reality, and the difference between "me" and "I." In this chapter concepts related to self have already been invoked in considering the additional topics of social control, communication, and social motivation.

Clarity in formulating pertinent questions requires a differentiation among the different selves and parts of selves. At this point the term "identity" is substituted for the generic term "self," which has many surplus meanings, some of which are alien to what is being discussed in this chapter. The term "self" is retained, but used in a restricted sense. As noted earlier, identity has two connotations: it is a pattern of observable or inferable attributes that identifies a person to himself or to others, and it refers to a socially labeled, enduring object that is frequently evaluated by the person and others in the group.

Clarity about the meaning of identity requires that it be differentiated from social role, a concept with which it is often confused. In a group, the role of each member is defined by others' expectations and norms concerning his behavior. The expectations are similar for two people with the same role, but the identities of each are as unique as their fingerprints. To define someone's role, one studies the pressures exerted by the others; Rommetveit (1955) refers to them as "role-sending." Identity refers to someone's conception of what a particular person is like, not to others' expectations of the person. Role and identity are related in that the norms of a role establish many of the standards by which the identity is judged. In order for a son to be accepted by his family, his identity—what he is like— cannot deviate too much from his social role—what he is expected to be like. A marked discrepancy between role and identity usually creates pressure on the individual to change his identity.

As used here, identity is labeled with respect to object and identifier. Identifiers can be a public or the individual himself. The pictures that neighbors, tradesmen, and teachers have of a family, for example, are its public identities for those groups. The picture that its members share about themselves is their self-identity. Similarly, every person in the family has numerous public identities, each referring to the way he is viewed by a particular group; and a self-identity, a private conception of what he is like.

Always concerned about the adequacy of each member's contributions to its goals, the group judges the worth of his public identity on the dimension of public esteem. The family, in other words, has conceptions both of what the father is like and how good a father he is. Correspondingly, each person judges the worth of his self-identity on a dimension of self-esteem.

Since identity is a creation of our experiences with others, it is often assumed that self-esteem is determined by others' judgments. In Cooley's description of the "looking-glass self" (1902), for example, he postulates a sequence of three events: " . . . the imagination of our appearance to the other person, the imagination of his judgment of that appearance, and some sort of self-feeling, such as pride or mortification." He begins, then, with the presumption that each member of the group has what is called here an objective public identity and an objective public esteem, the term "objective" referring to how the group actually thinks. Learning about these from the ways in which others treat him, the individual develops a subjective public identity and a subjective public esteem, the term "subjective" referring to the fact that these are his impressions, and not necessarily the group's actual conceptions. Finally, Cooley postulates that these determine self-identity and self-esteem.

In this account, the individual is portrayed as a pliant object of social pressures rather than an autonomous self-as-agent, who can reject information that is inconsistent with his self-identity. James (1890) has observed that everyone picks a "truest, strongest, deepest self . . . on which to stake his salvation," and which he cultivates for much of his life. This is the internal picture of what he is like, and which guides his perceptions, judgments, communications, and actions in all reciprocal activity. When his public's conception of him deviates markedly from that internal picture, he may be inclined to dismiss them even if their judgment places a higher value on that self than he himself does. Accepting their version would require too radical a change in a structure that takes years to develop.

STRUCTURE OF IDENTITY

The significance of identity has been attributed to its functions as an agency of social control and the maintenance of social ralationships. Common to both is the individual's participation in the judgments of public and self-esteem. An understanding of the processes of evaluation requires a preliminary description of the topography of identity.

Structurally, an identity may be diagrammed as a circle consisting of three regions. At the center is a concentric core, the "real me," with traits that interact with those in the other regions. To Symonds (1951), the components of the core are "formed earliest, lie closest to the center of the personality, and hence are the most difficult to change." Examples are body image, gender, and deeply ingrained personality traits that are evident no matter what the person does.

The remainder of the circle representing identity is divided into segments, like pieces of pie, each representing a subidentity (Miller, 1963). These are parts of identity that are organized with respect to the primary relationships in one's life. One can have subidentities as mother, accountant, tourist, or saint. An adult male has a public subidentity for each of the publics to whom any of his relationships is of consequence, publics such as his family, his colleagues, and his friends. The structure of each subidentity is delimited by the pressures of role, the person's capacities, and the attributes of others in complementary positions. A person's subidentities tend to interact when they enter into relationships within the same social context. Within the family, for example, a woman's attributes as sister and daughter affect her characteristics as mother.

Each participant adjusts to role pressures by dividing the subidentity into a persona (Jung, 1953), or presented region of the subidentity, and a sequestered, private one. This division, or splitting, permits the participant to use the segment of subidentity that implements the common goals, and to contain the segment that might interfere with the activity. Splitting enhances the common endeavor when based on an understanding of the mutual goals, an appreciation of another's needs, and a sensitivity to relevant standards of behavior. It may damage the common endeavor when it is organized with respect to internal pressures unrelated to the participants' goals.

APPRAISAL OF IDENTITY

People picture the attributes of an identity as locations on dimensions. A dimension is a set of alternative attributes which have a common referent and constitute a linear scale. Most people conceive of a trait as located on a segment of a dimension rather than on a precise point. Being regarded as a coward, for example, places a person in the lowest segment of the dimension labeled as courage. An identity consists of many kinds of socially significant attributes, but a large proportion of the dimensions pertain to attributes of action. It is actions that have the greatest effect on the welfare of others, so it is actions about which groups are most concerned and for which people are held most responsible.

A group assigns specific values to each segment of a dimension. At a minimum, there is a threshold dividing the dimension into acceptable and unacceptable segments. Often, attributes in the acceptable range are dichotomized into satisfactory and desirable categories. Appraisal of identity depends on the salience, or weighting, of the dimension in addition to an individual's location and the value placed on it. The weighting is determined by the significance of the dimension with reference to the group's goals. In the appraisal of a teacher's public esteem, for example, theoretical sophistication is more salient than taste in clothes. The more salient a dimension, the more the change of a member's location affects his public esteem.

Moral dimensions are very salient to all groups. According to Miller and Swanson (1958), moral dimensions pertain to deliberate acts that affect the welfare of the community or one of its subgroups. Poisoning a reservoir is immoral because it is deliberate and threatens the community. Compulsive overeating is not immoral because it is beyond the eater's control and is damaging only to that individual. It is proposed, then, that a member's public esteem varies with his standing on a dimension weighted by the value the group places on his location and the salience of the dimension.

Analogous to salience, self-involvement is the weighting of a dimension in accordance with the individual's values. To the extent that he is identified with the group in which he is participating, his self-involvement approximates the salience of the dimension for the other members. But they represent one of a large number of possible reference groups (Hyman, 1942) with which the individual feels identified and whose norms he uses in judging the adequacy of his identity. Using a group for a frame of reference does not necessarily mean that he is a member, that he feels positively about them, or that they are even real.

Reference groups free us from the tyranny of the immediate social context. They provide us with many frames of reference that we can use to select, modify, or reject the norms of the actual group in which we are participating. The nature and significance of the resultant autonomy are considered in further detail in the next section.

SCHEMAS AND SCRIPTS

Identity is a cultural artifact; it is socially defined and then internalized. As exemplified by subcategories, such as group identity and objective public esteem, it is a set of interrelated cognitive constructs. For half a century the predilections of many social scientists for operationism, environmentalism, and physiological models of motivation have led them to dismiss cognitive constructs as reifications. Identity as a cognitive construct was particularly unacceptable to people who often dismissed it as an unexplained force within, but independent of, the person, and a source of behavior different from motives. In recent years, an increasing number of investigators have been studying cognitive structures—called maps, templates, or schemas—that throw further light on the functions of identity. Psychologists seem to be settling on the term schema, which was used by Piaget (1926) and Bartlett (1932).

Neisser (1976) defines schemas as cognitive structures that are "internal to the perceiver, modifiable by experience, and somehow specific to what is being perceived." To make sense of the world, we process perceived information by means of schemas. We also use them as plans for directing action, and as patterns of action. Unlike some structural concepts, schemas are subject to constant change. They determine the directions of exploration that make new information available, and are, in turn, modified by that information.

Identity which, as already noted, represents a set of social constructs, may be viewed as an organization of interrelated schemas, cognitive patterns for interpreting events and acting on the basis of the interpretations (Rogers, 1951; Sarbin, 1968b). One basis for such interpretations and actions is provided by the "internal society" (Klein, 1958), which is a cognitive organization of relationships with people and groups who have been most significant in our lives. This living record of salient events from the past provides the bases for schemas which are activated by associated events in the present, and which enable us to interpret such events and to act appropriately.

Traditional descriptions of the internal world (Freud, 1947; Hyman, 1942) tend to concentrate on its objects, and to play down the parts of identity to which they are connected and the nature of relationships between identity and object. Mead emphasizes that the identity is meaningful only in the context of an irreducible interpersonal unit consisting of two people, each engaged in action with the other as object, and both experiencing complex emotions as they strive to attain their goals. The perception of such a unit can vary from concrete visual images, such as a mother spanking her refractory child for attacking his brother, to relatively abstract constructs, such as shyness with the opposite sex, or even a symbol such as a mandala.

The aforegoing illustrates some advantages that schemas have over static, intrapersonal constructs such as mental retardation, oral fixation, and factor loadings. First, they keep changing as a function of a new information. Second, if a problem can be phrased in cognitive terms, there is no difficulty in describing associations between the properties of individuals or social relationships in either dynamic or static terms. Third, they lend themselves to an analysis of the temporal properties of relationships.

Social scientists generally eschew temporal analysis, favoring spatial metaphors that freeze the descriptions of events at specific points in time. Indeed, it is often assumed that a valid index of a personal trait would reveal a constancy that is independent of any spatiotemporal context. Native intelligence is one instance of an attribute that is presumed to be unchanging. So are many of the characteristics formed during the first years of life, and which are emphasized in the psychoanalytic literature.

The detailed analysis of spatial and temporal variables has suffered an undeserved neglect, despite their importance for the understanding of social relationships. In their desire to develop general theory that is applicable to all forms of life, psychologists have tended to favor abstract, atomistic constructs, and to neglect some of the promising leads contained in systems such as Tolman's cognitive map (1948), Lewin's life space (1948), Barker's social setting (1960), and Jaques' time span (1976). There is only a trickle of research on temporal variables, which are so fundamental to the coordination of the participant's activities in social encounters. The sequence of acts, their timing, and the adjustment of behavior to changing social forces are a few of the issues that affect the participants' success in attaining their goals.

A number of promising temporal units have been proposed for purposes of analyzing social interaction. Murray's interpersonal proceeding (1959) and Barker and Wright's action circuit (1954) both pertain to a sequence consisting of an initiation of action by one person followed by another's response. Miller's chain of reaction (1961) and Thibaut and Kelley's behavior sequence (1959) refer to acts in succession that are directed to the attainment of goals. Barker and Wright's episode (1955) is a temporal unit of social interaction that mediates trains of action, has direction with respect to goals, and is identified in terms of setting and issues at the point of termination.

Schemas are particularly suited to temporal analysis. Once an episode begins, it activates schemas of past events, which are experienced in spatiotemporal terms, as though an internal film were being projected into the current visual field. It is in this way that categories of schemas are used to organize the current event cognitively. The projection is also experienced internally, so that there is a continual reliving of emotionally laden incidents from the past, particularly ones that are connected with vivid incidents and problematic relationships.

Projection of schemas from the storeroom of the internal world of identity enables the participant in a relationship to put himself in the position of another and to behave in a manner that is appropriate to the common activity. The process is thus basic to social communication.

A major contribution to temporal analysis is the script (Abelson, 1973; Schank & Abelson, 1977): " . . . a hypothesized cognitive structure which, when activated, organizes comprehension of event-based situations" (Abelson, 1980). Conceived as a special type of schema, the script is a grouping of inferences about the potential occurrence of a set of events. The occurrence of one of the events in the set creates the expectation that others in the set will also occur. Of particular relevance to social relationships is the "strong" script (Abelson, 1980), which was implied in the metaphor, used earlier, of the self-as-agent projecting films of earlier encounters. The strong script includes anticipations about the order of associated events, which can vary from sequences that must be followed rigidly to complex structures that offer many options, allow for correction when unforeseen interferences occur, and permit the intermixture of other kinds of activities.

Investigators have not been sufficiently consistent in their conceptions of schemas and their attributes, and it is necessary to propose some arbitrary definitions. To this end, it is proposed that a schema be visualized as a cone-shaped solid. A line between the tip and the center of the circle at the broad end defines the temporal dimension. Points near the narrow end of the temporal dimensions are close to the time when the schema originated; points near the broad end are closer to the present. The progressive increase in diameter indicates that with time, the cognitive organization is increasingly differentiated. A slice across any location on the temporal line yields a circle within which the cognitive map at that point in time may be defined. A strong script is a sequence on the temporal dimension of components from different cognitive maps. In what follows, the term schema is used in the generic sense; it refers to the entire cone or cognitive organization, thus subsuming cognitive maps and scripts.

PUBLIC ESTEEM AND DEFENSE

Esteem is a fundamental schema used in the evaluation of identity. In their judgments of esteem, people tend to divide it into three segments: a high level that anyone would welcome, an acceptable level for which most people are willing to settle, and an unacceptable one that is so low that it interferes with participation in social relationships. In different societies, the methods of achieving at least the threshold of acceptable esteem are as diverse as burning blankets and committing hara-kiri, but no one questions the universality or the motivating force of the drive.

During an encounter, each participant presents an identity on the assumption that it will be honored, that the initiation of acts consistent with the presented identity will elicit a partner's complementary responses consistent with the common endeavor. Such acceptance signifies that the level of public esteem is acceptable, and consequently, tends to validate the self-identity. Each participant knows that he is judged in terms of his capacity to keep the mutual activity viable, his manifestations of responsibility, and the goodness of his intentions (Pepitone, 1958). Each is held accountable as an agent of his actions because he is presumed to have attained reflective self-evaluation, the capacity to anticipate others' desires, and the ability to control impulses the expression of which would be inimical to mutual goals (Taylor, 1977).

Any discrepancy between public and self-esteem signifies that the group is exerting pressure on the member to change the schemas that guide his judgments and actions in relationships with others. But the contents of communicated public identity are useful only if they are within "latitudes of acceptance" (Sherif & Hovaland, 1961), which are limits established by the schemas of self-identity.

There is abundant empirical evidence (Shrauger, 1975) of a universal inclination to alter cognitively any information about public and self-esteem that signifies a required change outside the latitude of acceptance. People are inclined to overestimate their successes and to ignore or diminish their failures (Zeller, 1950); to take credit for good performances when working in teams, but to blame their partners for poor performances (Johnston, 1967); to be attracted to others who provide them a pattern of improving relationships (Aronson & Linder, 1965); and to set goals that are not too hard to achieve so that improved later performances will add luster to public esteem (Jones & Berglas, 1978). When people are so ready to employ cognitive distortion even when threat to self-esteem is minimal, how much more likely are they to do so when attributes fundamental to self are threatened with devaluation (Greenwald, 1980)?

As used here, defense refers to the cognitive distortions that may be employed to maintain at least a minimally adequate evaluation of one's identity. Freud's definition of defense (1936)—"all the techniques of which the ego makes use in the conflicts which potentially lead to neurosis"—is too vague to be of practical use, but his clinical references suggest that defenses make the individual unaware of morally unacceptable impulses. Anna

Freud (1936) lists some functions of defenses, such as keeping "ideational representatives of repressed instincts" from becoming conscious, altering inappropriate strengths of needs, and preventing the awareness of unwelcome, uncontrollable events. Klein (1958) adds the function of splitting.

Miller and Swanson (1960) propose three criteria for identifying any defense: (1) indirect evidence, such as the contents of dreams and subliminal perception, indicates that an unacknowledged event has been perceived; (2) the individual is unaware of the event; (3) another percept is substituted for the original one. The type of defense is inferred from the nature of the substitute.

Defenses are employed when a threat to identity cannot be eliminated by ordinary problem solving. They are oversimplified schemas that maintain an acceptable level of self-esteem by means of self-deception. A reduction or simplification of cognitive dimensions creates distorted alternatives to realistic perception of the problem.

IDENTITY AND ABNORMALITY

Many systems have been proposed for classifying the different types of identity. If a system is to represent more than an arbitrary pigeonholing of concepts, it must be shown to generate answers to refractory problems in the field. In the remainder of the chapter, some of the principles pertaining to identity are applied to the definition of abnormality in order to derive answers to problems such as the establishment of criteria for defining symptoms, the goals of psychotherapy, and the bases of interpretation.

It would be difficult to overstate the social significance of being treated as abnormal. The type of diagnosis may determine whether a patient is held in a psychiatric ward against his will or allowed to retain his civil liberties, whether a felon is executed or held in psychiatric custody, and whether a child is allowed to go to a public school or is sent to a hospital for the mentally retarded. It is tragic for many of these people that such critical decisions vary with the "experts" biases; there is so much disagreement about criteria. Specialists do agree that abnormality is some kind of deviation from certain norms, but not about the kinds of norms or the types and amounts of deviation. A comparison of changes from the second to the third editions of the Diagnostic and Statistical Manual of the American Psychiatric Association (1980) provides vivid testimony of the uncertainty that professionals feel about the definitions of various symptoms and the criteria for deciding on the definitions.

The differences in viewpoints are not surprising when one considers that the same term, abnormality, is used in making assessments as varied as the advisability of hospitalization, legal responsibility, and intellectual deficit. Also assuring the inevitability of disagreement are the differential partialities of diagnosticians to physiological, psychological, and socio-logical frames of reference; to different schools of clinical theory; and to conceptions that locate pathology in the individual with handicapping symptoms, the family with disturbed relationships, the ecnomically de-teriorated community, and the nation with a political system that engenders genocide.

Many of the decisions about such moot issues are made for us if we begin with one fundamental premise about abnormality: like self, it is a social construct. Throughout history, every society has identified certain of its citizens as abnormal. Often the criteria for identification have been specific to the society, but, despite the diversity, there is a common core on which all societies agree, certainly in the cases of madness and depression, which is recognizable in biblical descriptions, the writings of the Middle Ages, and the psychiatric descriptions of the twentieth century. Moreover, societies have always applied the label of abnormality to individuals. Only in recent years have social scientists invoked it to describe social units such as family, community, and nation.

To understand the reasons why certain pathologies seem to be iden-tified universally, we begin, as in the case of self, with the society monitoring and judging the moral adequacy of its citizens' contributions to socially requisite activities. Various groups devise processes of socialization aimed at developing the capacities necessary to meet the minimal standards for engaging in such activities. Formally, family and school, for example, teach children to fear the consequences of violating basic norms, to judge themselves in terms of their performances, and to take pride in promoting the common welfare. Informally, such goals are achieved by the constant mutual evaluation of all citizens as they participate in their comercial, familial, and occupational activities.

Not everyone can meet even the minimal standards. Incapacities or deliberate violations can threaten the community. When that occurs, the individual's identity is invalidated so far as the implementation of the requisite activities is concerned. To protect other citizens, the violater may be isolated, reeducated, punished, or banished.

Deviants are readily divided into three types. Some violate the law, often for personal gain. They are the felons. If they know what they are doing and are doing it deliberately, they are legally responsible for their crime. Some lack the intellectual capacities to meet their social responsi-bilities. They are the mentally retarded. If they are sufficiently helpless, they may need shelter and special education. Some have psychogenic problems that interfere with their capacities to engage in social intercourse. The latter are the abnormal subjects that are of special interest here. The key to their difficulties is provided by the simple point that the activities that implement the society's goals arc all interpersonal.

We are now in a position to describe the conditions that lead a person to be considered abnormal. The label of abnormality is used when (1) a participant in an interpersonal activity behaves in a manner that interferes with the pair's attempts to attain its goals; (2) the interpersonal activity in which the pair is engaged can affect the society's welfare; (3) either or both participants, or the group of which they are members, think that the deviant person is deficient in judgment or self-control, so that he is not responsible for the handicapping behavior; (4) others with the power to make the authoritative judgment support the original impression.

The concept of abnormality is a judgment that a person is incapable of participating in a particular type of collective activity. It is meaningless, in other words, to classify Robinson Crusoe alone as either normal or abnormal. The label becomes meaningful once Friday appears on the scene and they start to do things together. However, this definition raises more questions than it answers. Which attributes create the problems? Under what conditions? What kinds of difficulties do they create? What are their possible causes?

Stress, in forms such as conflict, trauma, and low self-esteem, is usually invoked to explain the origins of abnormal behavior. Discrepancies leading to lowered esteem usually create the greatest personal stress when the involvement is high, and the individual can do nothing to change the offending attributes; he is not sufficiently intelligent or talented or physically coordinated to gain even the minimal approbation of the group. Equally stressful is stigmatization because of impulses or behavior that is universally condemned as immoral. Extreme examples are incest and child molestation.

Even though one is shunned by an important group, it is extremely difficult to shed even a discredited identity, the creation of which has required so much time and effort. Usually, an emotional part of the social isolate violently rejects the group's evaluation. This means, however, that he is cognitively out of step with the others. Even if he could find a member of the group who is willing to participate with him in some activity, their interaction would soon come to a confused halt because their differing conceptions of his identity would make it difficult for them to know how to behave with one another. People go to any lengths to prevent such a catastrophe.

ORIGINS OF DEFICIENCIES IN IDENTITY

Deficiencies in identity can be traced to three interrelated sources: inadequacies in social development, dissociations of subidentities, and predilections for defensive, cognitive distortions. These are now considered in turn.

The social psychological and clinical literatures are replete with accounts of developmental problems affecting identity. Some are developmental problems affecting identity. Some are developmental in that they are products of past crises that interfered with subsequent maturation. Others are the products of common conflicts that are hard to resolve with much success. Examples are Oedipal rivalry with a competitive parent, and envy of a favored sibling. It is difficult to ignore or to resolve such problems, which a child must endure for years. Plagued by a script that is the heritage of this type of relationship, the adult keeps replaying it in fantasy in a vain attempt to lay to rest the ghosts from the past. This preoccupation can interfere with one's ability to monitor events in the present, particularly when intense emotion is a salient feature of the script. It is consequently activated by episodes with similar affects, but that are not necessarily similar in other respects (Abelson, 1980) A script that is so overloaded with emotion becomes a Procrustean bed into which the current experience is fit by the necessary stretching or trimming of incompatible facts.

Usually such stressful relationships produce dissociated identities. In one such instance, a mother who is guilty about her lack of love for her daughter keeps giving her contradictory messages that express affection and aversion. Verbally, the mother praises the daughter and invites her to approach so she can be cuddled. But the mother's physical expressions clearly convey a warning to stay away. The daughter is ultimately dissociated into two segments: a passive one that is always seeking the unavailable, loving mother, and an autonomous one that keeps her distance from others unless she can control them.

Such scripts create no end of difficulties for others. In later years, the daughter's husband is likely to be confused by the oscillations between avoidance and domination, on one hand, and pleas for mothering, on the other. Such scripts are subject to continuing rumination because the infantile segment cannot relinquish the hope of reliving the past with more favorable results. Yet the woman cannot hope to reproduce her infantile relationship with a loving mother, if for no other reason than that the autonomous part of her dissociated identity is horrified at the prospect.

Divisions of identities may be categorized as either splits or dissociations. Splits of identities into segments are usually attributable to discontinuities in the relationships established in different settings or periods of development. Discontinuity is, of course, inevitable when the child goes from one stage of development to the next. The parents who are delighted by the passive appeals of a one-year-old are critical and anxious if he does not show more initiative a year later. Even within the same period, parents cannot help but be somewhat inconsistent. Such are the sources of the splits in subidentities that we all recognize when we attribute some action to the childish or the adolescent parts of ourselves. Splits tend not to interfere seriously with cognition.

Certain divisions of the self, for which the traditional label of dissociation is retained here, do create complications in the assessment of ongoing events. They originate in relationships with dissociated people who give multiple, inconsistent messages. A dissociation can last only as long as the two segments are separated by a barrier to awareness. But inability to recognize a part of oneself does not prevent it from being expressed; the lack of insight may actually facilitate the expression of the offending segment. The adult who, as a child, could never respond correctly to his mother's mixed messages may displace his hostility to other women and be honestly confused by their resentment.

DEFENSIVE SCHEMAS AND IDENTITY

If the different kinds of schemas employed by the self-identity were ordered in terms of veridicality or effectiveness in resolving personal difficulties, defenses would receive low rankings on both counts. They are typically invoked to resolve problems beyond the individual's rational resources, and they are employed primarily to deceive oneself about the facts that are threatening to one's identity. But self-deception is costly. Incorrect assumptions about a problem preclude rational solutions— if there are any. They also create special interpersonal handicaps. An explication of these costs requires the initial description of defenses as schemas.

Defenses can be categorized in terms of degree of complexity, scope of distortion, and problems to which they are applied. At the simple end of the dimension of complexity is the total obliteration of painful information. This only requires that the individual look away, go to sleep, faint, or withdraw from the setting. Slightly more complex are the processes that reduce the possible interpretations of an event to two alternatives, such as good–bad, pleasant–unpleasant, inside–outside, or successful–unsuccessful. Projection, for example, changes the experienced location of an event, usually an impulse, from inside to outside the bodily boundaries; denial transforms the evaluation of the event from bad to good.

Still more complex are the defenses of identity that confine the distortions to displacements along cognitive dimensions of the event. In the case of an aggressive impulse, for example, the wish can be shifted from a relative to a criminal on the dimension of possible objects thus eliminating the guilt connected with the original target. Fury can be replaced by impatience on the dimension of affects, and physical attack by criticism on the dimension of acts. Displacement on one or more dimensions can alter the total meaning of an impulse, even when the cognitive organization is otherwise unchanged.

Defenses with the same degree of complexity can also differ in the proportion of the cognitive map that is distorted. Fainting, for example, obliterates all of consciousness, while selective forgetting obliterates only part of it. Similarly, projections may be employed to disown so much of the self-identity that the sense of bodily boundaries is lost, or it can be restricted to a specific impulse.

Finally, most defenses are more applicable to certain problems than to others. Some, such as denial and displacement of an object, are most appropriate to the modification of understanding; others, such as undoing an act by a cancelling ritual or the prevention of an attack by turning it against oneself, are most suited to the modification of action.

ABNORMALITY AND THE SOCIAL ENCOUNTER

Developmental difficulties, dissociation, and defenses contribute to behavior that disrupts social intercourse. Just how this occurs is best illustrated when contrasted with adequate interpersonal functioning. Even a short, informal meeting of two acquaintances requires an impressive coordination of effort. The participants try to be alert to one another's feelings, which are conveyed by a multitude of verbal and nonverbal, logical and expressive messages. The shared information serves as feedback that helps them to coordinate the contents of their communication so that the integrated flow of behavior is directed toward the common goals. When they they differ on the apporpriate sequence of acts, they test one another's impressions until they arrive at a consensus.

Competence in monitoring the feelings of one's partner requires a reservoir of scripts to interpret ongoing events. Monitoring enables each participant to match his scripts with those of the partner and to coordinate his actions accordingly. The coordination, in turn, requires that he be able to join the partner in synchronizing the sequence of steps in the shared script, meanwhile conforming to social norms as complex and subtle as those pertaining to eye contact, physical distance, and areas of the body that may be touched. A complete description of such norms and their variations in terms of the setting, activity, and the other's gender, generation, and status (Birdwhistell, 1970) would be so complex as to make it seem miraculous that a pair of friends could perform even a simple task with any success. Yet, everyone participates in many such social events daily. If we could not, the society would perish.

In a viable encounter, there is an unmistakable spontaneity in the participants' contributions to the common stream of behavior. The spontaneity is the product of a delicate equilibrium in the stream of behavior. This equilibrium is easily destroyed when either participant is handicapped by developmental, dissociative, or defensive problems. Preoccupation with unresolved developmental problems, for example, tends to increase their influence on the perception of current events, which are consequently misinterpreted. The preoccupation with reminiscences of things past also interferes with the retrieval of other scripts more relevant to the present episode.

Dissociation, which sometimes causes an individual to oscillate between incompatible segments of a subidentity, disrupts the communication needed for reciprocal activity. Dissociation is also handicapping because it creates a fragmentation of mature subidentities into less differentiated ones that were established in earlier stages of development. As a result the individual is more self-centered and uncontrolled than before, and less sensitive to others' feelings and to appropriate standards of behavior. Such regression to earlier subidentities is often reinforced by the choice of a spouse with complementary attributes. Consequently, the marital pair can employ their childish subidentities to obtain illicit gratification by their collusive activities in the privacy of their home.

Regression also creates social difficulties because it increases the employment of the cognitive simplification of interpersonal events. A man whose use of dichotomous thinking causes him to deny his imperfections and to idealize his self is on a wavelength different from that of others who are less averse than he to acknowledging his deficiencies. His self-idealization may result in even more serious problems if it also creates a hypermanic excitement. In that event, he speaks and acts rapidly and erratically and exerts exceptional effort, thus precluding shared communication and synchronous activities.

These examples seem sufficient to illustrate how attributes of identity can interfere with the coordination and synchrony necessary to conduct interpersonal activities. A diagnosis of abnormality is made when the interference violates norms, primarily moral ones, that pertain to socially requisite functions, and is caused by an incapacity to engage in the required reciprocal behavior. This definition of abnormality rules out political deviants, midgets, eccentrics, felons, drug addicts, and the mentally defective. Membership in some of these categories obviously signifies that the individuals are creating serious social difficulties, but is is not a sufficient condition for the deviants to be considered abnormal.

The association between identity and abnormality suggests answers to other clinical problems, in addition to the establishment of criteria for recognizing symptoms. Most specialists, for example, feel that therapy should have positive goals, not only the elimination of symptoms. On first consideration, some of the goals that have been proposed, such as trust, the ability to work, and sexual potency, seem heterogeneous and arbitrary. Yet they are all types of interpersonal competence, the lack of which contributes to an individual being labeled as abnormal. The examples pertain to the competence needed to implement societal requisites in social, occupational, and sexual relationships, respectively. The improvement of such capacities is the primary goal of therapy. It follows that interpretation in psychotherapy should be focused on the attributes of identity that hinder the use of these capacities. The therapist makes an interpretation, in other words, when the patient's comments or behavior provide evidence of such attributes.

Instead of abnormality, topics such as the organization of social motivation, the origins of shame and guilt, and the sources of consistency in behavior, could have been used to illustrate the theoretical significance of identity. Behavior that seems inconsistent, for example, when interpreted with reference to social pressures or the strengths of motivations may become comprehensible when the schemas of identity are included in the analysis. The striking proliferation of imaginative theoretical (Mischel, 1977) and empirical (Wegner & Wallacher, 1980) papers during the 1970s justifies some optimism that, despite the anxieties that some psychologists continue to experience about the philosophical status of identity, it is a subject that is coming of age.

Chapter 16

IDENTITY, AUTHENTICITY, AND MATURITY

Robert Hogan and Jonathan M. Cheek

The purpose of this chapter is to clarify the concept of social identity by suggesting that it is only a portion of a larger concept, that identity means more than social identity. We try to show this in three ways. Through historical argument, we suggest that social identity reflects only one portion of the "inner-outer" metaphor—a distinction traditionally of great importance in social psychology—and that both portions of the metaphor are necessary for understanding identity. Using psychological argument, we suggest that social identity is rooted in personality development and is therefore only one aspect of the larger process of identity negotiation. Finally, by empirical argument, we show that social identity refers to a discrete personological syndrome and cannot, therefore, encompass identity in all its aspects.

Within the context of clarifying the concept of identity, we make four additional points that are worthy of mention in themselves. First, we wish to dramatize the importance of the inner–outer metaphor in personality and social psychology. Second, we show that this metaphor does not reflect a bipolar dimension but rather implies independent elements. Third, we argue that any adequate conception of identity and psychological maturity must include both sides of the inner–outer metaphor. Finally, we try to show that principled nonconformity, despite its popularity in social psychology, is not in itself equivalent to maturity.

Before we begin, however, it will be useful to define our key terms— social identity, authenticity, alienation, and maturity. Following Sarbin (1954) and Sarbin and Allen (1968–1969), a social role is defined as an organized set of behaviors that belongs to an identifiable position or status in one's family or community. Social identity is therefore a function of having a particular status in one's group, and thus having something to do in that group. As Sarbin and Allen remark, " . . . identity is built up from inter-actions with the occupants of complementary statuses" so that " . . . one's social identity is an effect of role enactment. . . . Social identity [is] a part process of the self, representing those cognitions arising from placement in the social ecology" (1968–1969, p. 550). Once again, then, social identity is a function of the social roles one plays in one's group. This definition implies, on the one hand, that social identity is socially bestowed, it reflects the roles one is allowed (by others) to play. On the other hand it implies that social identity is a sum, over time, of the roles one has played; it is therefore composed of elements which may vary in the degree to which they are integrated.

The foregoing definition of identity comes from sociological theory. It is rooted in a long tradition of social thought going back at least to G.W. F. Hegel (1770–1831) (cf. Hogan, 1976, pp. 128–144), a tradition that takes a very particular viewpoint on the relationship between the individual and society—namely, that individuals are the creatures of social and historical forces beyond their control. Existentialist philosophy, as developed by S. Kierkegaard (1813–1855) and F. Nietzsche (1844–1900), takes strong exception to this Hegelian thesis. The existentialists oppose the concept of social identity with the notion of authenticity. For the existentialists, to the degree that one's identity is defined by external sources, one surrenders control over his or her life, and is no longer responsible for his or her actions. Authenticity for the existentialists is defined by two themes. First, one must strive for self-knowledge; one must become aware of the reasons for one's actions. Persons whose identities merely reflect the social roles they are allowed or forced to play are usually unaware of the reasons for their actions (cf. Hogan, 1976) and are, therefore, inauthentic. Second, by achieving self-knowledge, one is able to (and should) define one's identity for oneself. Self-awareness and self-definition are the defining features of authenticity. People who are self-aware and define their own identities are authentic and autonomous.

The existentialists propose a definition of role that is quite different from Sarbin's—namely, a course of action, a style of life that one chooses in the full light of self-consciousness. Autonomous or authentic people define their roles for themselves. To the degree that they play social or organiza-tional roles, they do so with role distance; they understand that these roles are, in a deep sense, alien and external.

It should be clear that social identity and authenticity are opposite notions. With the concepts of social identity and authenticity in mind, we can now define alienation. People who are alienated are persons who, on the one hand, are estranged from the normal patterns of social interaction in their social groups; they have no roles to play. At the same time, these persons are estranged from themselves *and* from society, and both aspects of alienation are important for our definition. That is, alienation means psychological estrangement from oneself and other people.

Finally, the notions of social identity and authenticity contain competing visions of psychosocial maturity. From the perspective of social identity, maturity is a function of one's social roles, the interrelationship among these roles, and one's involvement in them. Other things being equal, the more roles, the more interrelated they are, and the more involvement, the more mature will the actor be. From the perspective of authenticity, the social identity view is wrong in every respect. Here maturity is a function of self-awareness, of playing one's organizational or social roles with detachment and role distance, and of being committed only to one's personally defined values and roles, freely and self-consciously chosen. The social identity version of maturity prevails in sociology and anthropology, the authenticity/autonomy version is found in modern psychology.

THE INNER–OUTER METAPHOR

The inner–outer metaphor is a protean concept in personality and social psychology although this seems not widely appreciated. The purpose of this section is to dramatize this theme by describing several of its manifestations in modern psychology. Specifically, we will discuss some of the ways in which the inner–outer metaphor has been conceptualized and assessed. This will illuminate the issue of whether inward and outward orientations represent bipolar ends of a single dimension or are two distinct, orthogonal dimensions. We conclude this section by examining the implications of the inner–outer metaphor for the psychology of identity.

The broadest example of the inner–outer metaphor occurs in the definition of personality itself. Allport (1937) described 50 meanings of the term personality. His list included examples from theology, law, sociology, and philosophy as well as psychology. In spite of the diversity of these definitions, MacKinnon (1944) concluded that two basic themes capture the essence of what is meant by personality. These themes are described in German by the words *Persönlichkeit* and *Personalität*. The first, *Persönlichkeit*, is personality defined by outward appearances and the distinctive impression that one makes on others. This definition reflects the derivation of the term personality from the Latin word *persona*, the mask worn by an actor to signify his role in a play. Sociologists and social psychologists tend to think of personality in terms of such public images.

Personality in the sense of *Personalität* refers to the inner nature or substance of man, to the essential core of our being. This definition emphasizes the deep, enduring, and often innate structures within an individual whose existence can only be inferred. Psychoanalytic and humanistic approaches to personality typically focus on such inner psychological states and processes rather than on external behavior. Although inward and outward orientations (e.g., *Persönlichkeit* versus *Personalität*) to the study of personality often appear as competing viewpoints, it is clear that any convincing theory of personality must deal with both aspects of human nature (Hogan, 1976).

Regardless of disagreements among social scientists about the definition of personality, it seems obvious that individuals do differ in their sensitivity to inner and outer sources of influence on their social behavior. Sociologists (e.g., Riesman, Glazer & Denny, 1950) describe "inner-directed" people as being guided by a "psychological gyroscope" of internalized values implanted early in life, whereas "other-directed" types are guided by the expectations of the people around them.

The first attempt to measure these two concepts resulted in some people being classified as *both* inner directed and other directed. In response to this apparently paradoxical result, Sofer (1961) constructed a forced-choice questionnaire to assess inner- versus other-directed values. Collins, Martin, Ashmore, and Ross (1973) suggest, however, that forcing these two value orientations into a single bipolar dimension may be a serious mistake. Their factor analysis of relevant personality items yielded independent dimensions of inner- and other-directedness; they concluded that, in addition to the two expected character types, "some respondents seemed free from all types of constraints and others were controlled by both of the mechanisms discussed by Riesman" (Collins et al., 1973). These findings suggest that Riesman's approach to the inner–outer metaphor may encompass two separate dimensions (i.e., inner direction and other direction) on which individuals may differ, rather than a single, bipolar dimension.

A related interpretation of the inner–outer metaphor is found in Snyder's (1974) efforts to assess individual differences in the way people manage self–presentations in social situations. According to Snyder (1979), high scorers on his Self-Monitoring Scale use social cues to guide their behavior, whereas low scorers rely on internal information, such as their emotions and attitudes, for cues to appropriate behavior. Thus a high self-monitoring individual presumably uses impression management tactics to express situationally appropriate behavior (e.g., Goffman, 1956); a low self-monitoring individual, on the other hand, presumably acts in accordance with his or her enduring self-image or "true self."

Snyder's hypothesis assumes that self-monitoring represents a single dimension, with high scorers having an outward, and low scorers having an inward orientation. Here again, however, the psychometric evidence fails to support a bipolar conceptualization. Two-factor analytic studies indicate that the Self-Monitoring Scale is composed of at least three relatively independent dimensions (Briggs, Cheek & Buss, 1980; Gabrenya & Arkin, 1980). Moreover, self-monitoring seems to be related positively to measures of a social or outward orientation but *not* negatively to measures of a personal or inward orientation (Cheek & Briggs, 1981). This indicates that a low score on the Self–Monitoring Scale reflects only the absence of an outward orientation rather than the presence of an inward orientation, a conclusion consistent with the view of Collins et al. (1973) that inner direction and other direction are in fact two independent personality dimensions.

In typologies of personality structure the inner–outer metaphor is usually represented by the introversion–extraversion distinction. Jung (1923) defined introversion as the inward turning of psychic energy (libido) and extraversion as turning it outward. The habitual and predominant emphasis of one or the other of these two psychological attitudes results in introverted and extraverted types of people. Jung believed that the dominant attitude, either introversion or extraversion, is expressed in different ways depending on the superiority of one of the rational functions, thinking or feelings, and of the irrational functions, sensing or intuiting. Although H. J. Eysenck rejects the specifics of Jung's complex theory of psychological types, he agrees that introversion–extraversion is a fundamental dimension in the structure of personality (Eysenck & Eysenck, 1969). Eysenck views introversion and extraversion as composites of the traits of sociability, impulsiveness, activity, liveliness, and liking excitement; someone with high scores on all five traits is a pure extraverted type, and someone with low scores on them is a pure introverted type.

Both Jung's and Eysenck's conceptualizations have led to the development of measures to assess individual differences in introversion and extraversion (Eysenck & Eysenck, 1968; Myers, 1962). Subsequent research confirms that various traits make up the introversion–extraversion dimension and that they can be measured separately by distinct subscales, but there is considerable disagreement about whether a single typological classification or several trait scores provide a better conceptualization (Carrigan, 1960; Eaves & Eysenck, 1975; Howarth & Browne, 1972). Although a broad bipolar introversion–extraversion scale may be useful in some situations, for research purposes construct and predictive validity are enhanced by using separate internally consistent measures that focus on single personality attributes (Horst, 1966; Nunnally, 1978).

Hogan (1975a) describes moral development in terms of two dimensions—rule attunement and social sensitivity—that also reflect the inner–outer metaphor. Rule attunement concerns accommodating oneself to adult authority in early childhood, which accommodation results in an internalized set of moral guidelines. Social sensitivity concerns accommodating oneself to the expectations of one's extended family and peer group in later childhood; this accommodation leads to a set of external moral guidelines. Individual differences in the outcome of these two processes are assessed by means of the Socialization and Empathy scales of the California Psychological Inventory (Gough, 1975). Combinations of scores on these two scales produces a typology much like that depicted in Figure 16.1. Moreover, the two scales, and presumably the tendencies they reflect, are uncorrelated.

Psychological analyses of the self use the inner–outer metaphor to distinguish aspects of self-awareness. William James (1890) defined the spiritual self as the perception of one's inner or subjective processes; this is contrasted with the social self, the recognition one receives from others. Recently, personality scales have been constructed to assess individual differences in the tendency to focus attention on the private, internal aspects of the self and on its public, external aspects (Fenigstein, Scheier & Buss, 1975). People who have high scores on the Private Self-Consciousness Scale tend to be more self-reflective and more aware of their feelings and attitudes than persons with low scores; people who have high scores on the Public Self-Consciousness Scale tend to pay more attention to their appearance and to be more concerned about what others think of them than do persons with low scores. These two dimensions are relatively independent, so that people may score high on one, both, or neither of the scales used to assess them (individuals who are neither publicly nor privately self-conscious presumably direct their attention toward the physical and social environment that surrounds them—see Buss, 1980, for a complete presentation of

Figure 16–1. The Structure of Identity

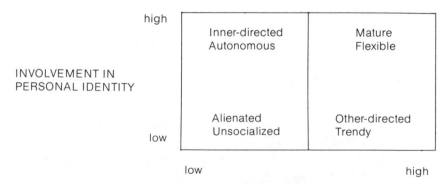

self-consciousness theory). A related approach to understanding the self assumes that people differ in terms of how they define or locate their real selves; some view their private, inner selves as being most "true" and closest to their natural impulses while others regard their social or institutionally defined selves as being the most significant part of their self-conceptions (Broughton, 1981; Ichheiser, 1970; Sanford, 1956; Turner, 1976). In terms of the inner–outer metaphor, then, the domain of the self may be divided into two separate components: private and public.

We have now reviewed several ways in which the inner–outer metaphor is reflected in definitions of personality, orientations to the social world, personality types and traits, cognitive styles, beliefs, and self-conceptions. In most cases the measures that define aspects of the inner–outer metaphor have been found to form two relatively independent dimensions rather than a single bipolar continuum. We conclude this section by pointing out that this theme is also important for understanding identity. Miller (1963) noted that the term identity has two distinguishable connotations: the first is identity as a social label, which he called public identity; the second is the private conception of self and feelings of continuity, or self-identity. As we mentioned in the introduction, sociologists define identity almost exclusively in social terms: "identity is socially bestowed, socially sustained, and socially transformed" (Berger, 1963, p. 98). Psychologists such as Jung (1957) and Maslow (1961), on the other hand, believed that people are most authentically themselves and most consistent with their real identity when experiencing a deep sense of personal uniqueness. Thus the structure of identity seems to contain two central dimensions: personal (internal) and social (external) aspects of identity.

The relationship between these two aspects of identity is a matter of some disagreement. Sampson (1978) argues that individuals find their most important characteristics in either the internal or the external environment and that, depending on their "environmental orientation," the process of identity mastery will be focused on one or the other of these two areas. In contrast, Erikson (1956, 1968a) described psychosocial identity as a synthesis of individual and collective aspects of identity; he emphasized the importance of balancing the individual's personal needs with the opportunities and requirements of the social world in achieving mature identity. From this perspective, personal and social aspects of identity may properly be regarded as dialectical rather than diametrical opposites. We will present some evidence bearing on the issue of how the aspects of identity are in fact related in a later section of the chapter. Next, however, we consider how identity develops, because we believe that the balance or conflict between personal and social aspects of identity plays an important role in the process of identity achievement (cf. Bourne, 1978; Marcia, 1976).

THE DEVELOPMENT OF IDENTITY

In this section we describe the development of identity from the view point of a particular theory of personality. This perspective, called socio-analytic theory (Hogan, 1982), is a blend of role theory (Mead, 1934; Sarbin, 1954) and evolutionary biology, along the lines suggested by Campbell (1965, 1975). The major assumptions of the theory are that *homo sapiens* evolved as a group living, culture-bearing animal, and that as a result, much social behavior is rooted in this early evolutionary experience. For example, social groups will be organized into roles as defined by the division of labor within the group. Moreover, the stability and coherence of the group is assured by the fact that people need attention and approval, but within a structured and predictable context. People are, as a result, compelled to interact, but their interactions are always to some degree ritualized. The ritualized nature of interaction varies from highly informal to highly formal depending on the context, but *every* interaction, regardless of how seemingly trivial, has a surprisingly precise structure. The division of labor within groups, and the ritualized nature of social interaction, make role playing (and the related phenomenon of self-presentation) constituent, biologically mandated features of human nature.

As Mead (1934) and others argue, roles are the primary vehicles for social interaction; while acting within our roles we can interact; outside our roles we have little to say to one another. Roles, then, are also units of socialization—the more roles we can play, the more effectively we can take part in the life of our family, tribe, community, or culture. Within a socioanalytic perspective it is possible to talk about both the phylogenesis and the ontogenesis of role behavior. About the phylogenesis we can offer only a few speculative observations; concerning the ontogenesis, we can speak more confidently. The two processes are linked by a common theme—how people behave in an interpersonal context reflects what they must do, in the larger context of their lives, to survive.

The Phylogenesis of Role Behavior

Homo sapiens probably evolved as the pack-hunting primate in the African Savannah (Lee & DeVore, 1968). Consequently, *homo sapiens* shares a number of characteristics with the other pack-hunting animals (e.g., lions, wolves, hyenas, and hunting dogs). For our purposes, the most important of these is the division of labor within each group. Particular physical and psychological endowments cause individuals to self-select into particular tasks—scout, leader, able-bodied hunter, etc. The specialized contribution an individual made to the survival of a pack must have been a source of status, preferential treatment, and identity in the primordial hunting group.

The role structure of an early hominid horde was probably more differentiated and complex than a modern chimpanzee troup. And the role structure of a modern organizational and bureaucratic unit is a linear descendent of the division of labor in the early hominid hunting band.

We would like to highlight two points about these speculations regarding the phylogenesis of role behavior. First, it is a standard notion of sociological theory that occupational roles are a source (if not *the* source) of people's identities. Second, Holland (1973) shows that there are clear personological correlates of people's vocational preferences. Holland goes on to develop a valid and reliable measure of identity based on the patterning of a person's vocational interests (Holland, Gottfredson & Power, 1980). Thus, occupational roles and vocational interests provide a way to both conceptualize and assess identity.

The Ontogenesis of Role Behavior

Social interaction depends on role enactment to the extent that little meaningful interaction takes place outside of our roles. Over time and for various reasons we develop self-images, idealized views of ourselves that we would like others to believe. These self-images, which are intended to maximize the amount of social approval we receive and minimize the opprobrium we must endure, initiate and guide our role performances (typified forms of self-presentation) *vis à vis* others. For sociologists, role playing is the source of one's self-image. We are suggesting, on the contrary, that people's self-images are the source of their role performances, although the consequences of these role performances may feed back into their self-images.

Garvey and Hogan (1973) show that children as young as three years are surprisingly sophisticated concerning how to do social interaction, and that their interactions always begin with children adopting conventional and rather stylized public self-images (e.g., mommy and baby, Batman and Robin, etc.). It seems, then, that people know how to interact through the make-believe process of image and role adoption from a very early age. The critical developmental questions concern what self-images children adopt and where they come from. As we suggested earlier, this depends on the structure of the social relationships in which a child is involved, as well as on the temperament of the child. From this perspective, identity develops in reference group terms in a manner consistent with Erikson's definition— while acting in a way that is most acceptable to oneself, one is simultaneously most valuable to the significant others in one's life.

Following Emler and Hogan (1981), we suggest that personality development passes through three broad stages, each typified by a qualitatively different set of control relationships. The first stage, which lasts from birth to about five years, is characterized by what Piaget (1932) called "unilateral constraint." From birth, children are locked into a set of authoritarian relationships, and their survival as well as their ability to acquire language and other fundamental aspects of culture depends on their making an appropriate accommodation to adult authority. Interactions with adults during this early stage are oriented toward pleasing them, in order to insure their attention and care. The roles children are allowed to play, or the kinds of self-presentation in which they are allowed to engage, are quite circumscribed, and largely dictated by adults. Obviously children will vary in the degree to which they are willing to comply with adult authority, and parents will vary in terms of the quality and quantity of care they are willing or able to provide their infant children (Bell, 1968; Buss, 1980). Across children, then, the outcome of this first developmental stage is quite variable. Some children will be strongly bound to their parents and their parents' evaluative standards, to the self-images and role performances derived from this first stage. At the opposite extreme, other children will be alienated from and conflicted by the evaluative standards with which they had to comply during this first part of life.

It must not be thought that the phase of unilateral constraint is necessarily an unpleasant experience. On the contrary, there is good reason to believe that it is an exceptionally pleasant and reassuring period in human development, a phase whose restoration people may even long for well into adulthood. It is, of course, a commonplace of psychoanalytic theory that people actually fear freedom and need authoritarian domination (Freud, 1950; Fromm, 1968). But we also know from years of developmental research (cf. Baumrind, 1971; Becker, 1964) that children who are raised in warm and restrictive homes are mature, well adjusted, and self-confident. They make an easy and effortless accommodation to adult authority, they deeply internalize adult values, and they remain throughout childhood and adolescence adult oriented as opposed to peer oriented (cf. Bronfenbrenner, 1970). Children raised in homes that are warm and permissive, cold and restricted, or cold and permissive are, in increasing degrees, alienated from adult values.

The second stage of personality development, which lasts from around age five to late adolescence, is characterized by what Piaget calls "reciprocal cooperation." Among most of the higher primates and in every human society children, past a certain age, leave the exclusive care of the nuclear family and move into the peer group. This second stage of development consists largely of establishing a place in the peer group. During this period, according to Piaget and others (cf. Youniss, 1981), children discover how to cooperate—they "construct the method" of cooperation through mutual negotiation and discussion. Thereafter, the rules they

use to organize their play are also constructed by means of reciprocal cooperation and discussion. Survival and status in the peer group
depend on a child's ability to acquire the method of cooperation. It follows
that roles that children play, or the forms of self-presentation in which they
engage, are also negotiated with the other peers through the method of
cooperation. Obviously children vary considerably in the degree to which
they are willing or able to engage in the reciprocal given and take of peer
relations. Lieberman (1977) shows that the quality of the infant–mother
attachment relationship during the first phase of development is positively
associated with good peer relations in nursery school. Thus, children who
are alienated from their parents during early childhood may have trouble
integrating into the peer group. We also believe that parents who are
unusually warm, nurturant, and restrictive may bind their children too
closely to them. This results in a child who has deeply internalized
parental norms and values, who adjusts particularly well to authority, but
who is alienated from peer relations.

Piaget seems to imply that unilateral constraint is unpleasant; at the
same time, he presents a romantic picture of peer relations: young people,
freed from the totalitarian bondage of the first developmental stage, are
joined together initially by the reflex of symmetrical reciprocity, to develop
the method of cooperation and then construct a free and democratic union
of youth, typified by distributive justice and subjective conceptions of
responsibility. Piaget's claims notwithstanding, it must not be thought that
the phase of mutual cooperation is uniformly pleasant experience. On the
contrary, we would like to suggest that the opposite may be true. Children
tend to bully, exploit, and persecute one another more often than they
cooperate and reciprocate. The reader might reflect for a moment about his
or her life in elementary school. There the younger, smaller, or weaker child
rarely gets its turn on the swing, and is usually assigned the least desirable
role in peer games *unless* an adult intervenes and requires that the other
children "play fair." On the whole, then, children probably suffer a decline
in the quality of life when they leave the exclusive care of their family and
move into the peer group (cf. Joyce, 1928). Moreover, children vary widely
in the degree to which they successfully make the transition to peer
relations. Some never make it; they remain forever alienated from their peer
group, lonely misfits on the outside looking in. Others make the transition
easily and seamlessly. For still others, dealing with peers becomes the first
genuinely pleasant and rewarding set of interactions they have experienced.
This latter group, mildly alienated from adult authority, becomes peer
oriented rather than adult oriented (cf. Bronfenbrenner, 1970; Riesman et
al., 1950). Their reference group is the immediate social environment.

The third stage in personality development begins most earnestly when
a young person encounters the world of work and must make an accom-

modation to bureaucratic structures. The distinctive features of these structures are well known and need no elaboration here. In most cases, gaining and maintaining a job means filling a position in an organization. The requirements of the job and the criteria for successful perfrmance are normally independent of the wishes, expectations, and intensions of the incumbent.

Children begin learning to live in the bureaucracy when they enter school. The role of student and the criteria of successful performance are normally established without much consultation with the individual pupil. Successful adaptation to bureaucratic systems requires that, on the one hand, a person be able to accommodate to the requirements of abstract authority (as opposed to the personal authority of early childhood), normally by conforming to the requirements of an impersonal role, usually in the absence of immediate and continuing feedback or supervision. On the other hand, a person must be able to interact satisfactorily with his or her co-workers. Here, in the world of work, all the lessons of childhood come together. Occupational status and success depends on the skill with which one can play roles that are externally assigned while at the same time maintaining cordial relations with peers.

Differential experience during the different stages of development gives a characteristic patterning to adult personality and identity. We suggest the following four ideal types (see Figure 16.1). First, there are persons who closely identified with their parents and the roles they played as children. Secure in their values, inner directed, and somewhat asocial, their identities are largely constructed out of internal resources. Such persons are overrepresented among scholars, research scientists, writers, and intellectuals. A second ideal type are persons who identified with their peers and the roles they played during the school years. Affiliative, outgoing, enthusiastic, but somewhat superficial in their relations with others, these persons are keenly attuned to trends and social expectations. They are overrepresented among politicians, personnel specialists, salesmen, and management consultants. A third ideal type are persons who identified with neither parents nor peers. Truly alienated, whatever deeply held values and beliefs they may cherish are perfectly idiosyncratic and unrelated to the normative values of the larger culture. At the same time, however, these persons are alienated from the peer group; egocentric and perhaps narcissistic, they are insensitive to social expectations, ruthless and exploitive in dealing with others. Finally there are persons who can be labeled mature. Their maturity is a function of the manner in which they have integrated the lessons of development; they are both inner directed and outer directed, principled and socially sensitive.

In the language of socioanalytic theory, personality development during the first phase of life concerns the evolution of character structure;

the lessons that we learn from our parents are consolidated in the form of character structure and to a large degree make up our private identities. Personality development in the second phase of life concerns the evolution of role structure; role structure refers to the self-images we adopt and the self-presentational techniques we learn while negotiating our paths through the adolescent peer group. Role structure to a large degree forms our public identity.

The entire discussion of this section of the chapter can now be summarized in terms of a single diagram (see Figure 16.1).

SOME EVIDENCE

If, as we have suggested, the structure of identity can be analyzed into personal and social aspects, then it seems reasonable to expect that there will be marked individual differences in the relative importance or value that people place on these two aspects of identity. Moreover, we believe personal and social aspects of identity are independent or orthogonal dimensions, rather than the endpoints of a single bipolar dimension. Using a questionnaire developed by Sampson (1978), designed to measure individuals' orientation to either the internal or the external environment in defining their identity, Cheek and Briggs (1981) found that importance ratings on Internal and External Location of Identity scales had a slight positive correlation ($r = .19$) rather than a strong negative relationship as conventional wisdom would predict.

Drawing on that preliminary analysis, the present discussion shows first that Sampson's (1978) list of identity characteristics can be revised to form two scales with adequate psychometric properties. These scales can then be used to assess inner and outer aspects of identity. Second, we show that these scales assess two relatively independent dimensions—personal and social aspects of identity. Third, we demonstrate that individual differences on both personal and social aspects of identity have significant implications for social behavior. We selected the dimension of independence of judgment versus conformity as the critical variable for this demonstration.

Cheek and Briggs (1981) selected two sets of items from Sampson's (1978) list of 22 identity characteristics to form scales assessing personal and social aspects of identity. Starting with those 22 items, we reworded some, deleted some, and added others to construct two six-item scales that seemed better to represent the domains of personal and social identity. Each item is rated on a scale ranging from 1 (not at all important to my sense of who I am) to 5 (extremely important to my sense of who I am).

In our review of the inner–outer metaphor we discussed public and private self-consciousness as manifestations of inward and outward orientations toward the self. We decided to use the measures of these two dimensions here in order to obtain some evidence for the convergent and discriminant validity of the personal and social identity scales. Awareness of oneself as a social object is measured by the Public Self-Consciousness Scale of the Self–Consciousness Inventory (Fenigstein et al., 1975). Items on this scale include "I'm usually aware of my appearance" and "I'm concerned about what other people think of me." The Private Self-Consciousness Scale of the Self-Consciousness Inventory measures the disposition to attend to the internal or private aspects of the self. Typical items on this scale are "I reflect about myself a lot" and "I'm generally attentive to my inner feelings." Both the Public and Private Self-Consciousness scales have well-established reliability and validity (see Buss, 1980, for a review of the relevant research). The self-consciousnes items are rated on a scale that ranges from 1 (extremely uncharacteristic) to 5 (extremely characteristic).

Barron (1953) developed his Independence of Judgment Scale empirically, choosing items that differentiated "independents" from "yielders" in the Asch conformity situation. There were nine items that discriminated independence from yielding in the experiment at the .01 level and 13 items that discriminated at the .05 level. All of Barron's subjects were men; the validity of the scale for distinguishing nonconforming from conforming women was established in a subsequent experiment (Strickland & Crowne, 1962). Here we used all nine items that Barron found significant at the .01 level, and nine of the 13 items significant at the .05 level (i.e., those with the best psychometric characteristics) to form an 18-item version of the Independence of Judgment Scale. This scale was administered with the same instructions as the Self-Consciousness Inventory, and its alpha coefficient was .72, an acceptable level of internal consistency (Nunnally, 1978).

One hundred and fourteen students (76 men and 38 women) participated in our study as part of their course experience in introductory psychology. Each student completed a booklet of questionnaire items that contained the personality measures just described. All analyses were initially performed separately for each gender. The results for men and women were found to be highly similar, so the data were combined for presentation.

The correlation matrix of responses to the 12 identity items was factor analyzed using the PA2 routine in *Statistical Package for the Social Sciences* with oblique rotation (Nie, Hull, Jenkins, Steinbrenner & Bent, 1975). As the columns of Table 16.1 reveal, there appear to be two distinct factors—one each for personal and social aspects of identity. The eigenvalues for these factors were 2.7 and 2.0, respectively. All of the items loaded above .30 on their appropriate factor. Only one item loaded above .30 on the other

Table 16–1. Factor Analysis of Personal and Social Identity Items

	Factor pattern loadings	
A priori scale assignment	Personal	Social
Personal Identity[a]		
My personal values and moral standards	.54	−.08
My dreams and imagination	.49	.06
My intellectual ability	.44	.21
My emotions and feelings	.53	.17
My thoughts and ideas, the way my mind works	.78	−.04
My feelings of being unique and totally distinct from other people	.35	−.02
Social Identity[b]		
My popularity and attractiveness to other people	−.01	.44
Being a part of the many generations of my family	.08	.33
The ways I have of influencing and of affecting others	.04	.55
My physical features: my height, weight, shape of my body, etc.	−.01	.41
Memberships that I have in various groups	−.47	.54
My feeling of pride in my country, being proud to be an American citizen	.08	.49

Note. $n = 114$.

[a]The Personal Identity Scale had a mean of 23.8 and a standard deviation of 3.2.
[b]The Social Identity Scale had a mean of 17.1 and a standard deviation of 3.5.

factor: "Memberships that I have in various groups." The negative loading of this social item on the personal factor was the only sign of bipolarity in the entire pattern of loadings, and the factor pattern correlation between these two factors was a modest .12. On the basis of these results, we concluded that it was appropriate to form two separate scales from this set of items.

The items on the Personal Identity Scale had an average interitem correlation of .27, and the alpha coefficient for this six-item scale was .69. The average interitem correlation of the social items was .20, so that the six-item Social Identity Scale had an alpha of .60. The correlation between the two scales was .09, which reinforces our view that personal and social aspects of identity are relatively independent dimensions.

To examine the convergent and discriminant validity of the Personal and Social Identity scales, we correlated them with scores on the Private and Public Self-Consciousness scales. We expected to replicate the findings of Cheek and Briggs (1981) that importance ratings for personal identity characteristics would correlate more strongly with Private than with Public Self-Consciousness and that social identity importance ratings would correlate more strongly with Public than with Private Self-Consciousness. As the results presented in Table 16.2 reveal, these expectations were confirmed. In the present sample Private and Public Self-Consciousness were positively correlated ($r = .19$), as they usually are (Buss, 1980), but this did not detract from the convergent and discriminant relationships shown in Table 16.2.

Having established preliminary evidence for the reliability and validity of the Personal and Social Identity scales, we turn to the question of their possible implications for individual differences related to social behavior. We expected that people who placed a high value on personal aspects of identity and a low value on social aspects would express their internal orientation by having the highest scores on Barron's Independence of Judgment Scale. Conversely, people placing low value on personal identity and high value on social aspects of identity should show their other directedness by having the lowest scores on Barron's scale (i.e., be conformers or "yielders"). The two remaining combinations of identity values should result in intermediate scores.

To test these hypotheses, we divided the subjects into four groups using mean scores on the Personal and Social Identity scales: high personal –low social, high personal–high social, low personal–high social, and low personal–low social. Because these classification factors formed cells of unequal n's, we used a regression approach for 2×2 analysis of variance with Zonderman's (1979) Matrix Operation Program. The cell means for Independence of Judgment scores are presented in Table 16.3.

The analysis of variance yielded significant main effects for both Personal Identity, $F(1, 110) = 14.94$, $p < .001$, and Social Identity, $F(1, 110) = 21.82$, $p < .001$. These main effects were qualified by a personal by social identity interaction, $F(1, 110) = 5.19$, $p < .05$, indicating that it is the combination of these aspects of identity that provides the best interpretation of subjects' Independence of Judgment scores. Individual t tests revealed that high personal–low social subjects had Independence of

Table 16–2. Correlations between Aspects of Identity and Self-Consciousness

	Private self-consciousness	Public self-consciousness
Personal Identity	.34*	.13
Social Identity	.04	.30*

*$p < .001$.

Table 16–3. Cells Means for Independence of Judgment Scores

		Social Identity	
		Low	High
Personal Identity	High	63.7	54.8
	Low	56.0	52.9

Note. In the total sample of 114 subjects, scores on the 18-item version of the Independence of Judgment Scale ranged from 40 to 79, with a mean of 56.8 and a standard deviation of 7.6. The *n*'s per cell were: 27 high personal–low social, 23 high personal–high social, 37 low personal–low social, and 27 low personal–high social.

Judgment scores significantly higher than those of each of the other three groups (*t*'s of 4.38 to 6.46, *p*'s < .001). The contrasting low personal–high social subjects were also quite distinctive; their scores were significantly lower than those of the low personal–low social group. ($t(62) = 2.03$, $p < .05$) as well as being lower than those of the high personal–low social group just mentioned. These low personal–high social subjects also scored lower on Independence of Judgment than the high personal–high social group, but the difference, while in the expected direction, was not significant ($t(48) = 1.13$, $p < .30$). As expected, knowledge of both Personal Identity and Social Identity scores provided the best prediction of Independence of Judgment scores (Multiple $R = .54$).

A subgroup of 79 students who had completed the Personal and Social Identity questionnaire also rated themselves on a check list containing 49 adjective pairs that was developed by Hogan and Johnson (1981). These rating scales were designed to assess seven personality dimensions which, according to socioanalytic theory, explain individual differences in high-level accomplishment across most significant spheres of human activity (Hogan, 1982). Results for four of the seven dimensions are worth mentioning in the context of our discussion of identity. The first relevant scale is Adjustment; high scorers on adjustment have self-confidence and self-esteem, whereas low scorers are anxious and insecure. The second scale is Prudence; high scorers make an easy accommodation to authority, low scorers are careless and undependable. The third dimension is Likability; high scorers are warm, friendly, and pleasant, low scorers are cold and critical. The fourth dimension is Sociability; high scorers enjoy and seek interaction, low scorers prefer to be alone.

Looking now at Figure 16.1, those persons we characterized as mature and flexible (high-highs) received high scores for all four scales—Adjustment, Prudence, Likability, and Sociability. The group we described as other directed (low-high) differed from the other three groups primarily in terms of high Sociability—this group had the highest Sociability scores in the entire sample—and low Prudence, which is consistent with our view of this group as peer oriented rather than adult oriented. Turning next to the group labeled Alienated (low–lows), they were typified by low scores for Prudence and Sociability—reflecting alienation from both adults and peers. Finally, the group we labeled as Autonomous received low scores for Sociability, Likability, and Adjustment, and high scores for Prudence. This pattern of scores suggests Autonomous people are unsociable, mildly neurotic, critical, and have strongly internalized values. This sounds more like Captain Ahab or a Biblical patriarch than an image of psychosocial maturity, which is consistent with our argument that autonomy or principled nonconformity is not equivalent to maturity.

CONCLUSION

As a way of concluding this chapter, we would like to summarize the various points we have made. At the same time we will indicate which of these points we feel are empirically substantiated and which are theoretical claims for which we have offered no evidence.

Our first point is that the inner–outer metaphor is a central theme and therefore vital concern in social and personality psychology. It is a protean concept that continuously recurs, showing up in a surprising variety of places. The pervasiveness of this theme is interesting in itself, and a matter of historical record. It seems a little odd, however, that the various researchers who have worked on different facets of this metaphor rarely seem aware of how generic the theme is. Perhaps these lapses in awareness are inevitable in a discipline that regards any research over ten years old as ancient history.

Our second point is that the inner–outer metaphor is related to the problem of identity in a fundamental way. Sociologists are correct in their view that social identity is a major factor in the organization of each person's life and behavior. At the same time, however, existentialist writers capture an important psychological truth when they insist that private sources of identity are also significant factors in social behavior. Personal values and social roles are distinguishable influences on social behavior. Evidence for this can be found in papers by Cheek and Briggs (1981), Scheier (1980), Turner (1976), and others.

Third, the degree to which people are committed to one of these aspects of identity is essentially unrelated to their degree of commitment to the other. Internal aspects of identity are largely independent of external or social aspects of identity. Evidence for that is summarized in the immediately preceding section of this chapter. We regard this as one of the more important points raised in this chapter, and one that seems essentially beyond dispute.

Our fourth point is that the degree to which people are invested in these two aspects of identity varies widely across individuals. Moreover, this differential investment has important consequences for everyday social behavior. We make this point in a simplified way in Figure 16.1, and we present evidence for it in Tables 16.2 and 16.3.

Our fifth point is that people's differential investment in public and private sources of identity can be traced to characteristic features of their developmental experience. Parent-Oriented but introverted children are likely as adults to value most highly the personal aspects of their identity. Peer-oriented adolescents will, as adults, value the social aspects of their identity. Alienation is indicated by a lack of identity of either a personal or a social nature. Finally, maturity is a function of integrating the two primary sources of identity. These claims about the developmental sources of identity are largely conjecture.

Our last point is that, contrary to the prevailing currents of modern psychological thought (cf., Hogan & Emler, 1978), maturity does not mean simply being autonomous. Papers by Asch (1956), Milgram (1963), and Kohlberg (1963) imply that conformity is bad and that principled non-conformers are the preferred moral type of our times. A consideration of human cultural evolution and the process of socialization suggests, however, that the ideology of individualism and nonconformity that characterizes much of American social psychology is more a symptom of a sick society than an accurate reflection of human nature (Hogan, 1975b). But the question is not really one of conformity versus nonconformity, it is a question of who the reference group is to which one conforms (i.e., internalized values or the current social environment). Our account of personality development and our adjective checklist evidence support Erikson's view of maturity as a function of successfully integrating both the inner and outer sources of one's identity.

BIBLIOGRAPHY

Abelson, R. P. Structural analyses of belief systems. In R. Schank & K. Colby (Eds.), *Computer models of thought and language.* San Francisco: Freeman, 1973.

Abelson, R. P. Concepts for representing mundane reality in plans. In D. Bobrow & A. Collins (Eds.), *Representation and understanding: Studies in cognitive science.* New York: Academic Press, 1975, pp. 273–309.

Abelson, R. P. *The psychological status of the script concept.* New Haven: Yale University Cognitive Science Program, Cognitive science technical report No. 2; March, 1980.

Abramson, H. J. The religioethnic factor and the American experience: Another look at the three generations hypothesis. *Ethnicity,* 1975, *2,* 163–177.

Adamic, L. *Grandsons: A story of American lives.* New York: Harper & Brothers, 1935.

Adamic, L. *What is your name?* New York: Harper & Brothers, 1942.

Adburgham, A. *A Punch history of manners and modes, 1841–1940.* London: Hutchinson, 1961.

Adkins, A. W. H. *From one to the many and many to the one.* Ithaca: Cornell University Press, 1970.

Adler, Nathan. The Antinomian personality: The Hippie character type. *Psychiatry,* 1968, *31*(4), 325–338.

Adorno, T. W., Frenkel-Brunswik, E., Levinson, D. J., & Sanford, R. N. *The authoritarian personality.* New York: Harper, 1950.

Aeschylus. *The Eumenides.* In *The complete Greek tragedies,* Vol. 1. Chicago: University Press, 1953.

Albert, S. & Kessler, S. Ending social encounters. *Journal of Experimental Social Psychology,* 1978, *14,* 541–553.

Alexander, C., Ishikawa, S. & Silverstein, M. *A pattern language.* New York: Oxford University Press, 1977.

Alexander, F. The psychiatric aspects of war and peace. *American Journal of Sociology,* 1941, *46,* 504–520.

Allen, V. L. & Scheibe, K. E. The social context of conduct. *The psychological writings of T. R. Sarbin.* New York: Praeger, 1982.

Allen, V. L., & Wilder, D. A. Categorization, belief similarity, and intergroup discrimination. *Journal of Personality and Social Psychology,* 1975, *32,* 971–977.

Allport, F. The psychology of nationalism. *Harpers,* 1927, *55,* 291–301.

Allport, G. W. *Personality: A psychological interpretation.* New York: Holt, 1937.

Allport, G. *Becoming.* New Haven: Yale University Press, 1955.

Alter, R. Epitaph for a Jewish magazine: Notes on the *Menorah Journal. Commentary,* 1965, *39* (May), 51–55.

Alter, R. A fever of ethnicity. *Commentary,* 1972, *53* (June), 68–73.

Alvarez, A. *The savage god.* London: Weidenfeld & Nicolson, 1971.

American Psychiatric Association. *Diagnostic and statistical manual,* III. Washington, D.C.: American Psychiatric Association, 1980.

Amir, Y. Contact Hypothesis in ethnic relations *Psychological Bulletin,* 1969, *71,* 319–341.

Amir, Y. The role of intergroup contact in change of prejudice and ethnic relations. In P. A. Katz (Ed.), *Towards the elimination of racism.* New York: Pergamon Press, 1976.

Anonymous. People at Blue Mountain Ranch. *January thaw.* New York: Times Change Press, 1974.

Appel, K. E. Nationalism and sovereignty: A psychiatric view. *Journal of Abnormal and Social Psychology,* 1945, *40,* 355–362.

Applebee, A. N. *The child's concept of story.* Chicago: University of Chicago Press, 1978.

Aptheker, H. *American Negro slave revolts.* New York: Columbia University Press, 1943.

Arnold, M. B. *Emotion and Personality,* vol. 1. New York: Columbia University Press, 1960.

Aristophanes. *The clouds.* In *Plays.* New York: Oxford University Press, 1970.

Aronson, E. & Linder, D. Gain and loss of esteem as determinants of interpersonal attractiveness. *Journal of Experimental and Social Psychology,* 1965, *1,* 156–171.

Artaud, A. *The theater and its double.* New York: Grove Press, 1958.

Asch, S. Studies of independence and conformity. *Psychological Monographs,* 1956, *70,* (9, whole no. 416).

Audy, J. R. Man the lonely animal: Biological routes of loneliness. In J. Hartog, J. R. Audy, & Y. A. Cohen (Eds.), *The anatomy of loneliness.* New York: International Universities Press, 1980.

Austin, J. L. *How to do things with words.* Cambridge: Harvard University, 1962.

Averill, J. R. Anger. In H. Howe & R. Dienstbier (Eds.), *Nebraska symposium motivation.* Lincoln, Nebraska: University of Nebraska Press, 1979, pp. 1–80.

Averill, J. R. A constructivist view of emotion. In R. Plutchik & H. Kellerman (Eds.), *Theories of emotion.* New York: Academic Press, 1980a.

Averill, J. R. On the paucity of positive emotions. In K. Blankstein, P. Pliner & J. Polivy (Eds.), *Advances in the study of communication and effect,* vol. 6: *Assessment and modification of emotional behavior.* New York: Plenum, 1980b.

Backman, C. Explorations in psycho-ethics: The warranting of judgments. In R. Harré (Ed.), *Life sentences.* New York: Wiley, 1976.

Baker, C. *Ernest Hemingway: A life story.* New York: Bantam, 1969.

Bandura, A. Self-efficacy: Toward a unifying theory of behavioral change. *Psychological Review*, 1977, *84*, 191–215.

Bandura, A. & Walters, R. H. *Social learning and personality development.* New York: Holt, Rinehart & Winston, 1963.

Banks, J. A. *Prosperity and parenthood: A study of family planning among the Victorian middle classes.* London: Routledge and Kegan Paul, 1965.

Banks, J. A. & Banks, O. *Feminism and family planning in Victorian England.* Liverpool: Liverpool University Press, 1964.

Barker, R. G. Ecology and motivation. In M. R. Jones (Ed.), *Nebraska symposium on motivation.* Lincoln, Neb.: University of Nebraska Press, 1960, pp. 1–49.

Barker, R. G. & Wright, H. F. *Midwest and its children: The psychological effects of an American town.* New York: Harper & Row, 1955.

Barnard, H. C. *A history of English education: From 1760.* London: University Press, 1961.

Barron, F. Some personality correlates of independence and judgment. *Journal of Personality*, 1953, *21*, 287–297.

Barth, F. *Ethnic groups and boundaries.* Boston: Little, Brown, 1969.

Barthes, R. *Systeme de la mode.* Paris: Seuil, 1967.

Barthes, R. Masculin, feminin, neutre. In J. Puillon (Ed.), *Exchanges et communications: Melanges offers a Claude Levi-Strauss.* Mouton: The Hague, 1970, pp. 893–907.

Bartlett, F. C. *Remembering.* Cambridge, England: Cambridge University Press, 1932.

Bateson, G. *Naven.* London: Cambridge University Press, 1936.

Bauer, R. A. & Bauer, A. H. Day to day resistance to slavery. *Journal of Negro History*, 1942, *27*, 388–419.

Baumrind, D. Current patterns of parental authority. *Developmental Psychology*, 1971, *4*, 1–103.

Becker, W. C. Consequences of different kinds of parental discipline. In M. Hoffman & L. W. Hoffman (Eds.), *Review of child development research*, vol. 1. New York: Sage Foundation, 1964.

Bell, D. *The coming of post-industrial society.* New York: Basic Books, 1973.

Bell, D. Ethnicity and social change. In N. Glazer & D. P. Moynihan (Eds.), *Ethnicity: Theory and experience.* Cambridge, Mass.: Harvard University Press, 1975, pp. 141–174.

Bell, R. Q. A reinterpretation of the direction of effects in studies of socialization. *Psychological Review*, 1968, *75*, 81–95.

Belloc, B. R. P. *Essays on woman's work.* 2nd ed. London: Strahan, 1865.

Benedict, R. *Patterns of culture.* New York and Boston: Houghton Mifflin Co., 1934.

Bennis, W. G. & Slater, P. E. *The temporary society.* New York: Harper & Row, 1968.

Bercovitch, S. *The Putitan origins of the American self.* New Haven: Yale University Press, 1975.

Berger, B. M. The sociology of leisure. In E. O. Smigel (Ed.), *Work and leisure.* New Haven: College and University Press, 1963.

Berger, P. L. *Invitation to sociology.* Garden City, N.Y.: Doubleday & Co., Inc., 1963.

Berger, P. L. & Luckmann, T. *The social construction of reality.* New York: Doubleday, 1966.

Berlin, I. *Against the current.* New York: Penguin, 1982.

Bernard, J. The good-provider role: Its rise and fall. *American Psychologist,* 1981, *36,* 1–12.

Besht, I. *Keter Shem Tov* (Hebrew). Jerusalem: Rosen, 1975.

Bettelheim, B. *The informed heart.* Glencoe, Ill.: Free Press, 1960.

Bettelheim, B. *The uses of enchantment.* New York: Knopf, 1976.

Billig, M. & Tajfel, H. Social categorization and similarity in intergroup behavior. *European Journal of Social Psychology,* 1973, *3,* 27–52.

Binswanger, L. *Being-in-the-world.* New York: Basic Books, 1963.

Birdwhistell, R. L. *Kinesics and context: Essays on bodily motion communication.* Philadelphia: University of Pennsylvania Press, 1970.

Blu, K. I. Varieties of ethnic identity: Anglo-Saxons, Blacks, Indians and Jews in a Southern county. *Ethnicity,* 1977, *4,* 263–286.

Boas, F. *The mind of primitive man.* New York: The Macmillan Co., 1911.

Boas, F. *The mind of primitive man.* Rev. ed. New York: Macmillan, 1938.

Boas, F. *Race, language, and culture.* New York: The Macmillan Co., 1940.

Bonacich, E. The past, present, and future of split labor market theory. *Research in Race and Ethnic Relations,* 1979, *1,* 17–64.

Botkin, B. *Lay my burden down.* Chicago: University of Chicago Press, 1945.

Boulding, K. Science: Our common heritage. *Science,* 1980, *207,* 831–836.

Bourne, E. The state of research of ego identity: A review and appraisal. Part II. *Journal of Youth and Adolescence,* 1978, *7,* 371–392.

Bowers, K. S. Situationalism in psychology: An analysis and a critique. *Psychological Review,* 1973, *80,* 307–336.

Braginsky, B. M., & Braginsky, D. D. *Hansels and Gretels.* New York: Holt, Rinehart & Winston, 1974.

Brewer, M. B. In-group bias in the minimal intergroup situation: A cognitive–motivational analysis. *Psychological Bulletin,* 1979, *86,* 307–324.

Brewer, M. B. & Silver, M. In-group bias as a function of task characteristics. *European Journal of Social Psychology,* 1978, *8,* 393–400.

Briggs, S. R., Cheek, J. M. & Buss, A. H. An analysis of the self-monitoring scale. *Journal of Personality and Social Psychology,* 1980, *38,* 679–686.

Bronfenbrenner, U. *Two worlds of childhood.* New York: Sage Foundation, 1970.

Brontë, C. *Jane Eyre.* Boston: Houghton Mifflin, 1959.

Broughton, J. M. The divided self in adolescence. *Human Development,* 1981, *24,* 13–32.

Brown, R. *Social psychology.* New York: Free Press, 1965.

Bruner, J. S., Oliver, R. R. & Greenfield, P. M. *Studies in cognitive growth.* New York: John Wiley, 1966.

Brunswik, E. *Systematic design and representative design of psychological experiments.* Berkeley and Los Angeles: University of California, 1949.

Brunswik, E. The conceptual framework of psychology. In O. Neurath (Ed.), *International encyclopedia of unified science,* (vol. 1, no. 10). Chicago: University Press, 1950.

Buber, M. *Hassidism and modern man.* New York: Harper and Row, 1958.

Bullough, B. & Bullough, V. L. *Poverty, ethnic identity, and health care.* New York: Appleton-Century-Crofts, 1972.

Burns, E. *Theatricality: A study of convention in the theatre and in social life.* London: Longman, 1972.

Buss, A. H. *Self-consciousness and social anxiety.* San Francisco: Freeman, 1980.

Cade, J. B. Out of the mouths of ex-slaves. *Journal of Negro history,* 1935, *20,* 294–337.

Cameron, N. A. *The psychology of behavior disorders.* Boston: Houghton Mifflin, 1947.

Campbell, D. T. Ethnocentric and other altruistic motives. In D. Levine (Ed.), *Nebraska symposium on motivation: 1965.* Lincoln, Neb.: University of Nebraska Press, 1965.

Campbell, D. T. On the conflicts between biological and social evolution and between psychology and moral tradition. *American Psychologist,* 1975, *30,* 1103–1126.

Campbell, J. *The hero with a thousand faces.* New York: Meridian, 1956 (1st published in 1949).

Carrigan, P. M. Extraversion-introversion as a dimension of personality: A reappraisal. *Psychological Bulletin,* 1960, *57,* 329–360.

Carver, C. S. & Scheier, M. F. *Attention and self-regulation.* New York: Springer-Verlag, 1981.

Cassirer, E. *The myth of the state.* New Haven, Conn.: Yale University Press, 1946.

Catholic Dictionary. New York: P. J. Kennedy & Sons, 1885.

Cavendish, R. *The tarot.* New York: Harper & Row, 1975.

Chamberlain, H. S. *The foundations of the nineteenth century.* London and New York: John Lane, 1910. (First published, 1899.)

Chandler, M. J. Relativism and the problem of epistemological loneliness. *Human Development,* 1975, *18,* 171–180.

Cheek, J. M. & Briggs, S. R. Self-consciousness, self-monitoring, and aspects of identity. Paper presented at the meeting of the American Psychological Association, Los Angeles, CA, 1981.

Chesler, P. *Women and madness.* New York: Avon, 1972.

Cheung, L. M. *Modernization and ethnicity: The divergence model.* Unpublished doctoral dissertation, University of Maryland, 1979.

Choron, J. *Suicide.* New York: Charles Scribner's Sons, 1972.

Chorover, S. L. *From genesis to genocide.* Cambridge, Mass.: MIT Press, 1980.

Chun, K. T. The myth of Asian American success and its educational ramifications. *IRCD Bulletin,* 1980, *15*(1 & 2), 1–12.

Chun, K. T. & Harris, D. J. *Functional consequences of ethnic identity: Developmental phase.* Washington, D.C.: U. S. Commission on Civil Rights, Office of Research, December 7, 1977.

Chun, K. T. & Sarbin, T. R. An empirical study of "metaphor-to-myth transformation." *Philosophical Psychologist,* 1970, *4*(1), 16–24.

Cialdini, R. B., Borden, R. J., Thorne, A., Walker, M. A., Freeman, S. & Sloan, L. R. Basking in reflected glory: Three (football) field studies. *Journal of Personality and Social Psychology,* 1976, *34,* 366–375.

Cicourel, A. *The social organization of juvenile justice.* New York: Wiley, 1968.

Cicourel, A. V. Generative semantics and the structure of social interaction. *Proceedings of the conference on sociolinguistics: 1969.* Rome: Luigisturzo Institute, 1970.

Clark, K. B. *Prejudice and your child.* 2nd ed. Boston: Beacon Press, 1963.

Clark, K. B. The search for identity. *Ebony*, 1967, *22*, 39–42.

Clemmer, O. *The prison community.* New ed. New York: Holt, Rinehart & Winston, 1958.

Cloward, R. & Ohlin, L. Delinquency and opportunity. Glencoe, Ill.: Free Press, 1960.

Cloward, R. & Piven, F. F. *The politics of turmoil.* New York: Vintage Books, 1974.

Cobbe, F. P. *Life of Frances Power Cobbe by herself.* 2 vols. Boston: Houghton Mifflin, 1894.

Cohler, B. J. Personal narrative and life-course. Unpublished Manuscript. University of Chicago, 1979.

Collins, A. M. & Loftus, E. F. A spreading activation theory of semantic processing. *Psychological Review*, 1975, *82*, 407–428.

Collins, A. M. & Quillian, M. R. Experiments on semantic memory and language comprehension. In L. W. Gregg (Ed.), *Cognition and learning in memory.* New York: Wiley, 1972a, pp. 117–137.

Collins, A. M. & Quillian, M. R. How to make a language user. In E. Tulving & W. Donaldson (Eds.), *Organization of memory.* New York: Academic Press, 1972b, pp. 310–351.

Collins, B. E., Martin, J. C., Ashmore, R. D. & Ross, L. Some dimensions of the internal-external metaphor in theories of personality. *Journal of Personality*, 1973, *41*, 471–492.

Collins, W. *No name.* London: Smith, Elder & Co., 1865.

Collins, W. *Armadale: A novel.* New York: Harper, 1874.

Condie, J. S. & Christiansen, J. W. An indirect technique for the measurement of changes in Black identity. *Phylon*, 1977, *38*, 46–54.

Connor, W. Ethnonationalism in the First World: The present in historical perspective. In M. J. Esman (Ed.), *Ethnic conflict in the Western world.* Ithaca, N.Y.: Cornell University Press, 1977, pp. 19–45.

Cooley, C. H. *Human nature and the social order.* New York: Charles Scribner's Sons, 1902.

Coon, C. *The origin of the races.* New York, Knopf, 1962.

Corbin, H. Divine epiphany and spiritual birth in Ismailian Gnosis. In J. Campbell (Ed.), *Man and transformation.* New York: Pantheon, 1964, pp. 69–160.

Corbin, H. *Creative imagination in the Sufism of Ibn 'Arabi.* Princeton: University Press, 1969.

Corbin, H. *Spiritual body and celestial earth.* Princeton: University Press, 1977.

Craig, A. G. & Pitts, F. N. Suicide by physicians. *Diseases of the Nervous System*, 1968, *29*, 243–281.

Craik, D. M. *A woman's thoughts about women.* New York: Rudd & Carleton, 1861.

Culler, J. *Structuralist poetics.* Ithaca: Cornell University Press, 1975.

Curtis, S. J. *History of education in Great Britain.* London: University Tutorial Press, 1965.

Daly, M. *Gyn-ecology: The metaethics of radical feminism.* Boston: Beacon Press, 1978.

Danto, A. C. *Analytical philosophy of history.* Cambridge: Cambridge University Press, 1965.

D'Antonio, W. V. Confessions of a third-generation Italian American. *Society*, 1975, *13*, 57–63.

Darwin, C. *The descent of man.* London: John Murray, 1871.

Dasen, P. Cross-cultural Piagetian research: A summary. *Journal of Cross Cultural Psychology,* 1972, *3*(1), 23–39.

Dashefsky, A. Theoretical frameworks in the study of ethnic identity: Toward a social psychology of ethnicity. *Ethnicity,* 1975, *2*, 10–18.

Dashefsky, A. *Ethnic identity in American society.* Chicago: Rand McNally, 1976.

Davis, D. B. *The problem of slavery in Western culture.* Ithaca: Cornell University Press, 1966.

Davis, K. Mental hygiene and the class structure. *Psychiatry,* 1938, *1*, 55–65.

De Bow's Review, 1858, 25, 51.

Degler, C. N. Slavery in Brazil and the United States: An essay in comparative history. *American Historical Review,* 1970, *75*, 1004–1028.

de Gobineau, A. M. *Essai sur L'inegalite des races humaines.* 4 Vols. Paris: Firmin-Didiot freres, 1853–1855.

de Grazia, S. *The political community: A study of anomie.* Chicago: The University of Chicago Press, 1948.

DeMause, Lloyd. *Foundations of psychohistory.* New York: Creative Books, 1982.

Derrida, J. *La dissemination.* Paris: Seuil, 1972.

Devereux, G. Ethnic identity: Its logical foundations and its dysfunctions. In G. De Vos & L. Romanucci-Ross (Eds.), *Ethnic Identity: Cultural continuities and change.* Palo Alto, Cal.: Mayfield, 1975, pp. 42–70.

De Vos, G. A. Assimilation and social self identity in the Japanese former outcaste group. In M. B. Kantor (Ed.), *Mobility and mental health.* Springfield, Ill.: Charles Thomas, 1965a, chapter 3.

De Vos, G. A. Conflict, dominance and exploitation in human systems of social segregation: Some theoretical perspectives from the study of personality in culture. In A.V.S. de Reuck & J. Knight (Eds.), *Ciba Foundation Symposium on conflict in society.* London: J. & A. Churchill, 1966, pp. 60–81.

De Vos, G. A. Psychology of purity and pollution as related to social self–identity and caste. In A. V. S. de Reuck & J. Knight (Eds.), *Ciba Foundation Symposium on caste and race: Comparative approaches.* London: J. & A. churchill, 1967, pp. 292–315.

De Vos, G. A. Minority group identity. In J. C. Finney (Ed.), *Culture change, mental health, and poverty.* Lexington: University of Kentucky Press, 1969, pp. 81–96.

De Vos, G. A. Ethnic identity and social stratification. *Journal of race,* April, 1972.

De Vos, G. A. *Socializaton for achievement: Essays on the cultural psychology of the Japanese.* Berkeley: University of California Press, 1973.

De Vos, G. A. Cross-cultural studies of mental disorder: An anthropological perspective. In G. Caplan (Ed.), *American Handbook of Psychiatry,* vol. 3. New York: Basic Books, 1974.

De Vos, G. A. Distanciation et hierarchie: Caracteristiques psycho-culturelles de la stratification humaine. In R. Bastide, J. Poirier & F. Raveau (Eds.), *L'autre et l'ailleurs.* Paris: Berger Levrault, 1976b.

De Vos, G. A. The interrelationship of social and psychological structures in transcultural psychiatry. In W. P. Lebra (Ed.), *Culture-bound syndromes, ethnopsychiatry, and alternate therapies.* Honolulu, Hawaii: The University Press of Hawaii, 1976c.

De Vos, G. A. The passing of passing: Ethnic pluralism and the new ideal in American society. In G. J. De Renzo (Ed.), *We, the people*. Westport, Connecticut: Greenwood Press, Inc., 1977.

De Vos, G. A. Selective permeability and reference group sanctioning: Psycho-cultural continuities in role degradation. In M. Yinger (Ed.), *Major social issues— A multi community view*. New York: Free Press, 1978, pp. 9–24.

De Vos, G. A. Jacques Brel est mort. In *Kultuurleven*, 1979/4—May. Leuven, Belgium, 1979, pp. 307–320.

De Vos, G. A. Ethnic adaptation and minority status. *Journal of Cross Cultural Psychology*, 1980a, *11* (1), 101–124.

De Vos, G. A. Family, deviancy and minority status: A psychocultural perspective on social indices of deviant behavior. In G. Newman (Ed.), *Crime and deviance: A comparative perspective*. Beverly Hills: Sage Publications, 1980b, chapter 6.

De Vos, G. A. L'Identite ethnique et le statut de minorite. In P. Tapp (Ed.), *La production et l'affirmation de l'identite*. Universite de Toulouse: Toulouse, France, 1980c.

De Vos, G. A. Adaptive strategies in American minorities. In E. S. Jones & S. J. Korchin (Eds.), *Ethnicity and mental health*. New York: Holt, Rinehart & Winston, 1982.

De Vos, G. A. & Romanucci-Ross, L. *Ethnic identity: Cultural continuities and change*. Palo Alto: Mayfield, 1975.

De Vos, G. A. & Wagatsuma, H. *Japan's invisible race: Caste in culture and personality*. Berkeley: University of California Press, 1966.

De Vos, G. A. & Wagatsuma, H. Minority status and delinquency in Japan. In W. Caudill & T.Y. Lin (Eds.), *Mental health research in Asia and the Pacific*. Honolulu: East-West Center Press, 1969, pp. 352–357.

de Waele, J. P. & Harré, R. The personality of individuals. In R. Harré (Ed.), *Personality*. Oxford: Blackwell, 1976.

(The) disputed question. *The English Woman's Journal*, 1858, *1*(6), 361–367.

Doise, W., Csepely, G., Dann, H. D., Gouge, C., Larsen, K. & Ostell, A. An experimental investigation into the formation of intergroup representations. *European Journal of Social Psychology*, 1972, *2*, 202–204.

Dollard, J. *Caste and class in a Southern town*. 3rd ed. Garden City, NY: Doubleday, 1957.

Dostoevski, F. M. *The brothers Karamazov*. London: J. M. Dent & Sons, 1927.

Douglas, J. *The social meanings of suicide*. Princeton, NJ: Princeton University Press, 1967.

Dresner, S. H. *The Zaddik*. New York: Schocken, 1960.

Drew, B. *The refugee: or the narratives of fugitive slaves in Canada*. Boston: J. P. Jewett, 1856.

Dubnov, S. *Toldot Hachasidut* (Hebrew). Tel Aviv: Devir, 1975.

Dushkin, A. M. Character education and teaching processes. In L. Roth (Ed.), *Problems of Hebrew secondary education in Palestine*. Jerusalem: Rubin Mass, 1939.

Eastlake, E. *Vanity Fair, Jane Eyre*, and the *Governesses' Benevolent Institution*. *Quarterly Review*, 1848, *84*, 153–185.

Eaves, L. J. & Eysenck, H. J. The nature of extraversion: A genetical analysis. *Journal of Personality and Social Psychology*, 1975, *32*, 102–112.

Edwards, J. R. Ethnic identity and bilingual education. In H. Giles (Ed.), *Language: Ethnicity and intergroup relations*. New York: Academic Press, 1977, pp. 253–283.

Eicher, D. Veterans' wives are still fighting Vietnam war. *The Denver Post*, September 24, 1981, p. 1-C.

Ekehamman, B. Interactionism in personality from a historical perspective. *Psychological Bulletin*, 1974, *81*, 1026–1048.

Elkins, S. M. *Slavery: A problem in American institutional and intellectual life*. 2nd ed. Chicago and London: University of Chicago Press, 1968.

Ellis, S. S. *The wives of England: Their relative duties, domestic influence, and social obligations*. London: Fisher, 1843.

Ellul, J. *The technological society*. New York: Knopf, 1964.

Emler, N. P. & Hogan, R. Developing attitudes toward law and justice. In S. Brehm, S. Kassin, & F. X. Gibbons (Eds.), *Developmental social psychology, theory and research*. New York: Oxford University Press, 1981.

Enloe, C. H. *Ethnic conflict and political development*. Boston: Little, Brown, 1973.

Epstein, A. L. *Ethos and identity: Three stages in ethnicity*. London: Tavistock, 1978.

Erikson, E. H. *Childhood and society*. New York: W. W. Norton & Co., 1950.

Erikson, E. H. The problem of ego identity. *The Journal of the American Psychoanalytic Association*, 1956, *4*, 56–121.

Erikson, E. H. *Childhood and society*. New York: Norton, 1964.

Erikson, E. H. The concept of identity in race relations: Notes and queries. In T. Parsons & K. B. Clark (Eds.), *The Negro Americans*. Boston: Beacon Press, 1967, pp. 227–253.

Erikson, E. H. Identity, psychosocial. In D. L. Sills (Ed.), *International encyclopedia of the social sciences*, vol. 7. New York: The Macmillan Co., and The Free Press, 1968a.

Erikson, E. H. *Identity, youth and crisis*. New York: Norton, 1968b.

Erikson, E. H. *Ghandi's truth on the origins of militant nonresistance*. New York: Norton, 1969.

Esman, M. J. *Ethnic conflict in the Western world*. Ithaca, N.Y.: Cornell University Press, 1977.

Ewart, O. The attitudinal character of emotion. In M. B. Arnold (Ed.), *Feelings and emotions*. New York: Academic Press, 1970.

Eysenck, H. J. *Race, intelligence and education*. London: Temple Smith, 1971.

Eysenck, H. J. & Eysenck, S. B. *Manual: Eysenck Personality Inventory*. San Diego: Educational and Industrial Testing Service, 1968.

Eysenck, H. J. & Eysenck, S. B. *Personality structure and measurement*. London: Routledge and Kegan Paul, 1969.

Farmer's Register, 1837, 5, 32.

Faunce, W. A. *Problems of an industrial society*. New York: McGraw-Hill, 1968.

Feldman, S. D. Nested identities. In N. K. Dengin (Ed.), *Studies in symbolic interaction*, vol. 2. Greenwich, Conn.: JAI Press, 1979.

Female education in the middle classes. *The English Woman's Journal*, 1858, *1*(4) 217–227.

Fenigstein, A., Scheier, M. F. & Buss, A. H. Public and private self-consciousness:

Assessment and theory. *Journal of Consulting and Clinical Psychology*, 1975, *43*, 522–527.

Fessler, L. Psychology of nationalism. *Psychoanalytic Review*, 1941, *28*, 372–383.

Finley, M. *A history of Sicily*. New York: The Viking Press, 1968.

Fisk University Social Science Institute, *Unwritten history of slavery*. Nashville, Tennessee: Fisk University, 1945.

Flaubert, G. *Sentimental education*. London: H. S. Nichols, 1898.

Fodor, J. A. *Psychological explanatin: An introduction to the philosophy of psychology*. New York: Random House, 1968.

Foss, B. M. On taking sides. *Bulletin of the British Psychological Society*, 1974, *27*, 347–351.

Foucault, M. *The order of things*. New York: Random House, 1970.

Foucault, M. *The archeology of knowledge*. New York: Pantheon, 1972.

Francois, W. *Automation: Industrialization comes of age*. New York: Collier Books, 1967.

Frazer, J. G. *The golden bough*. (3rd ed., 12 vols.) London: Macmillan & Co., 1907–1915.

Frederickson, G. M. & Lasch, C. Resistance to slavery. *Civil War History*, 1967, *13*, 315–329.

Frederiksen, C. H. Semantic processing units in understanding text. In R. O. Freedle (Ed.), *Discourse production and comprehension*. Norwood, N.J.: Ablex, 1977, pp. 57–87.

Freud, A. *The ego and the mechanisms of defense*. New York: International Universities Press, 1936.

Freud, S. *The problems of anxiety*. New York: Norton, 1936.

Freud, S. *Totem and taboo*. New York: Norton, 1950. (First German edition, 1913.)

Freud, S. The interpretation of dreams. In J. Strachey (Ed.), *Complete psychological works*, vols. 4 & 5, 1953.

Freud, S. *Beyond the pleasure principle*. In J. Strachey (Ed.), *Complete Psychological Works*, vol. 18, 1955.

Freud, S. *Five lectures on psychoanalysis*. In J. Strachey (Ed.), *Complete Psychological Works*, vol. 11, 1957.

Freud, S. *Civilization and its discontents*. New York: Norton, 1962. (Originally published, 1930.)

Freud, S. *Introductory lectures on psychoanalysis*. In J. Strachey (Ed.), *Complete Psychological Works*, vols. 15 & 16, 1963.

Freud, S. *Moses and monotheism: An outline of psycho-analysis*. In J. Strachey (Ed.), *Complete Psychological Works*, vol. 23, 1964.

Freud, S. & Bullitt, W. C. *Thomas Woodrow Wilson, twenty-eighth president of the United States: A psychological study*. Boston: Houghton Mifflin, 1966.

Friedman, M. *Overcoming middle class rage*. Philadelphia: Westminster Press, 1971.

Fromm, E. *The sane society*. New York: Holt, Rinehart & Winston, 1955.

Fromm, E. *Escape from freedom*. New York: Avon, 1968.

Frye, N. *Anatomy of criticism*. Princeton, N.J.: Princeton University Press, 1957.

Gabrenya, W. K., Jr. & Arkin, R. A. Self-Monitoring scale: Factor structure and correlates. *Personality and Social Psychology Bulletin*, 1980, *6*, 13–22.

Gallie, W. B. *Philosophy and the historical understanding*. London: Chatto & Windus, 1964.

Gambino, R. *Blood of my blood: The dilemma of the Italian-Americans.* Garden City, N.Y.: Doubleday, 1974.

Garfinkel, H. Conditions of successful degradation ceremonies. *American Journal of Sociology*, 1956, *61*, 420–424.

Garvey, C. J. & Hogan, R. Social speech and social interaction: Egocentrism revisited. *Child Development*, 1973, *44*, 562–568.

Gendron, B. *Technology and the human condition.* New York: S. A. Martins Press, 1977.

Genovese, E. D. The legacy of slavery and the roots of black nationalism. *Studies on the Left*, 1966, *6*, 4–6.

Genovese, E. D. Rebelliousness and docility in the negro slave: A critique of the Elkins thesis. *Civil War History*, 1967, *13*, 314.

Genovese, E. D. American slaves and their history. *New York Review of Books*, December 3, 1970, 34–43.

George, A. L. & George, J. L. *Woodrow Wilson and Colonel House: A personality study.* New York: John Day, 1956.

Gergen, K. Social psychology or history. *Journal of Personality and Social Psychology*, 1973, *26*, 309–320.

Gergen, K. J. Toward intellectual audacity in social psychology. In R. Gilmour & S. Duck (Eds.), *The development of social psychology.* New York: Academic Press, 1980.

Gergen, K. J. *Toward transformation in social knowledge.* New York: Springer Verlag, 1982.

Gergen, K. J. Self theory: Impasse and evolution. In L. Berkowitz (Ed.), *Advances in experimental social psychology.* New York: Academic Press, in press.

Gergen, K. G. & Morawski, J. G. An alternative metatheory for social psychology. *Review of personality and Social Psychology*, 1980, *1*, 326–356.

Gerson, L. L. *The hyphenates in recent American politics and diplomacy.* Lawrence, Kansas: University of Kansas Press, 1964.

Gerth, H. & Mills, C. W. *Character and social structure.* New York: Harcourt, Brace & World, 1953.

Gerth, H. H. & Mills, C. W. *From Max Weber: Essays in sociology.* New York: Oxford University Press, 1958.

Gladwin, T. & Sturtevant, W. *Anthropology and human behavior.* Washington: Anthropological Society of Washington, 1962.

Glazer, B. C. & Strauss, A. L. *The discovery of grounded theory: Strategies for qualitative research.* Chicago: Aldine, 1967.

Glazer, N. Ethnicity and the schools. *Commentary*, 1974, *58*, 55–59.

Glazer, N. & Moynihan, D. P. *Beyond the melting pot.* (2nd ed.) Cambridge, Mass.: M.I.T., 1970.

Glazer, N. & Moynihan, D. P. Why ethnicity? *Commentary*, 1974, *58*, 33–39.

Glazer, N. & Moynihan, D. P. *Ethnicity: Theory and experience.* Cambridge, Mass.: Harvard, 1975.

Gleason, P. Confusion compounded: The melting pot in the 1960s and 1970s. *Ethnicity*, 1979, *6*, 10–20.

Goffman, E. *The presentation of self in everyday life.* Edinburgh, Scotland: University of Edinburgh Press, 1956.

Goffman, E. *The presentation of self in everyday life.* Garden City, N.Y.: Doubleday Publishers, 1959.

Goffman, E. *Asylums.* Chicago: Aldine, 1961.

Goffman, E. *Frame analysis.* New York: Harper, 1974.

Going a governessing. *The English Woman's Journal,* 1858, *1* (6), 396–404.

Goodall, J. Chimpanzees of the Gombe Stream Reserve. In I. DeVose (Ed.), *Primate behavior.* New York: Holt, Rinehard & Winston, 1965.

Gordimer, N. *Burger's daughter.* London: Jonathan Cape, 1979.

Gordon, C. Self conceptions: configuration of content. In C. Gordon & K. J. Gergen (Eds.), *The self in social interaction.* New York: Wiley, 1968, pp. 115–154.

Gordon, C. Development of evaluated role identities. In A. Inkeles, J. Coleman & N. Smelser (Eds.), *Annual Review of Sociology, Vol. 2.* Palo Alto, CA: Annual Reviews, 1976, pp. 405–434.

Gordon, M. M. *Assimilation in American life: The role of race, religion, and national origins.* New York: Oxford University Press, 1964.

Gordon, S. *Lonely in America.* New York: Simon & Schuster, 1976.

Gorky, M. *Mother.* New York: Appleton & Co., 1921.

Gorky, M. *The lower depths.* In O.M. Sayler (Ed.), *The Moscow Art Theatre series of Russian plays.* London: Brentano's, 1923.

Gosse, E. *Father and son: A study of two temperaments.* New York: Oxford University Press, 1934.

Gough, H. G. *Manual: The California psychological inventory.* (Rev. ed.) Palo Alto, CA: Consulting Psychologists Press, 1975.

Gove, F. L., Hughes, P., & Geerken, K. C. Playing dumb: A form of impression management with undesirable side effects. *Social Psychology Quarterly,* 1980, *43*, 89–102.

(The) governess; or, Politics in private life. London, 1836.

Governess life: Its trials, duties, and encouragements. London: Parker, 1849.

Governesses' Benevolent Institution. *Report of the Board of Management for 1851.* London: Edward West, 1852.

Grant, M. *The passing of the great race.* New York: C. Scribner's Sons, 1916.

Graves, R. *The white goddess.* London: Faber & Faber, 1948.

Greeley, A. M. *Why can't they be like us? Facts and fallacies about ethnic differences and group conflicts in America.* New York: American Jewish Committee, 1969.

Greenbaum, W. America in search of a new ideal: An essay on the rise of pluralism. *Harvard Educational Review,* 1974, *44*, 411–440.

Greenwald, A. G. The totalitarian ego: Fabrication and revision of personal history. *American Psychologist,* 1980, *33*, 603–618.

Grylls, R. G. *Queen's College, 1848–1948.* London: Routledge and Sons, 1948.

Guetzkow, H. Multiple loyalties: A theoretical approach to a problem in international organization. Pub. #4. Princeton: Center for Research in World Political Institutions, 1955.

Guiles, F. L. *Norma Jean: The life of Marilyn Monroe.* New York: Bantam, 1970.

Günther, H. F. K. *Rassenkunde des deutschen Volkes.* Munchen: J. F. Lehmann, 1923.

Günther, H. F. K. *The racial elements of European history.* London: Methuen & Co., 1927.

Gurvitch, P. *The social framework of knowledge.* New York: Harper & Row, 1971.

Guttmann, A. *The Jewish writer in America: Assimilation and the crisis of identity.* New York: Oxford University Press, 1971.

Haas-Hawkings, G. Intimacy as a moderating influence on the stress of loneliness in widowhood. *Essence,* 1978, *2*, 249–258.

Hall, C. S. & Lindzey, G. *Theories of personality*. New York: J. Wiley & Sons, 1957.

Hamilton, D. L. A cognitive-attributional analysis of stereotyping. In L. Berkowitz (Ed.), *Advances in experimental social psychology*, vol. 12. New York: Academic Press, 1979, pp. 53–84.

Handlin, O. *Truth in history*. Cambridge, Mass.: Belknap Press, 1979.

Hankiss, A. Ontologies of the self: On the mythological rearranging of one's history. In D. Bertaux (Ed.), *Biography and society*. Beverly Hills: Sage, 1981.

Hansen, M. The third generation in America. *Commentary*, 1952, *14*, 493–500.

Harding, V. Religion and resistance among ante-bellum Negroes, 1800–1860. In A. Meier & E. Rudwick (Eds.), *The making of black America*. New York: Knopf, 1969.

Hare, A. *The story of my life*. 6 vols. London: George Allen, 1869.

Haring, D. G. *Personal character and cultural milieu*. Syracuse: University Press, 1949.

Harré, R. Incorporation of a stranger. In R. Harré (Ed.), *Life sentences*. New York: Wiley, 1976.

Harré, R. The self in monodrama. In T. Mischel (Ed.), *The self: Psychological and philosophical issues*. Oxford: Blackwell, 1977.

Harré, R. *Social being: A theory for social psychology*. Totowa, N.J.: Littlefield Adams, 1980.

Harré, R. & Madden, E. H. *Causal powers: A theory of natural necessity*. Oxford: Blackwell, 1975.

Harré, R. & Secord, P. F. *The explanation of social behaviour*. Oxford: Blackwell, 1972.

Harris, M. *Patterns of race in America*. New York: Norton, 1964.

Harris, M. *Cows, pigs, wars, and witches: The riddles of culture*. New York: Random House, 1974.

Hartley, E. L. & Hartley, R. E. *Fundamentals of social psychology*. New York: Knopf, 1952.

Hartog, J., Audy, J. R. & Cohen, Y. A. *The anatomy of loneliness*. New York: International Universities Press, 1980.

Hayes, C. J. H. *Essays on nationalism*. New York: Macmillan, 1926.

Hecht, J. J. *The domestic servant class in eighteenth-century England*. London: Routledge and Kegan Paul, 1956.

Heider, F. *The psychology of interpersonal relations*. New York: Wiley, 1958.

Herberg, W. *Protestant, Catholic, Jew: An essay in American religious sociology*. Garden City, N.Y.: Anchor Books, 1960.

Herman, S. N. *Israelis and Jews: The continuity of an identity*. New York: Random House, 1970.

Herman, S. N. *Jewish identity: A social psychological perspective*. Beverly Hills, Calif.: Sage Publications, 1977.

Herrnstein, R. J. *I.Q. in the meritocracy*. Boston: Atlantic/Little Brown, 1973.

Herzog, E. *Psyche und tod*. Zurich and Stuttgart: Rascher, 1970.

Hesse, H. *Steppenwolf*. New York: H. Holt & Co., 1929.

Hicks, G. L. & Leis, P. E. *Ethnic encounters: Identities and contexts*. North Scituate, Mass.: Duxbury Press, 1977.

Higham, J. *Send these to me: Jews and other immigrants in urban America*. New York: Atheneum, 1975.

Hillman, J. *The myth of analysis*. Evanston, Ill.: Northwestern University Press, 1972.

Hillman, J. *The dream and the underworld*. New York: Harper & Row, 1979.

Himmelfarb, M. Plural establishment. *Commentary*, 1974, *58*, 69–73.

Hints to governesses, by one of themselves. London, 1856.

Hirsch, J. To "unfrock the charlatans." *Sage Race Relations Abstracts,* 1981, *6,* 1–66.

Hoare, L. *Hints for the improvement of early education.* 18th ed. London: Hatchard, 1872.

Hofstadter, D. R. *Godel, Escher, Bach.* New York: Random House, 1980.

Hogan, R. The structure of moral character and the explanation of moral action. *Journal of Youth and Adolescence,* 1975a, *4,* 1–15.

Hogan, R. Theoretical egocentrism and the problem of compliance. *American Psychologist,* 1975b, *30,* 533–540.

Hogan, R. *Personality theory: The personological tradition.* Englewood Cliffs: N.J.: Prentice-Hall, 1976.

Hogan, R. A socioanalytic theory of personality. In *The Nebraska symposium on motivation: 1982.* Lincoln, Neb.: University of Nebraska Press, 1982.

Hogan, R. & Emler, N. P. The biases in contemporary social psychology. *Social Research,* 1978, *45,* 478–534.

Hogan, R. & Johnson, J. A. The structure of personality. Paper presented at the meeting of the American Psychological Association, Los Angeles, CA, 1981.

Holland, J. L. *Making vocational choices.* Englewood Cliffs, N. J.: Prentice-Hall, 1973.

Holland, J. L., Gottfredson, D. C. & Power, P. G. Some diagnostic scales for research in decision making and personality: Identity, information, and barriers. *Journal of Personality and Social Psychology,* 1980, *39,* 1191–1200.

Hollingshead, A. & Redlich, R. C. *Social class and mental illness: A community study.* New York: John Wiley and Sons, Inc., 1958.

Horowitz, D. L. Ethnic identity. In N. Glazer & D. P. Moynihan (Eds.), *Ethnicity: Theory and experience.* Cambridge, Mass.: Harvard University Press, 1975, pp. 111–140.

Horst, P. *Psychological measurement and prediction.* Belmont, CA: Wadsworth Publishing, 1966.

(A) house of mercy. *The English Woman's Journal,* 1858, *1*(1), 13–27.

Howarth, E. & Browne, J. A. An item-factor-analysis of the Eysenck Personality Inventory. *British Journal of Social and Clinical Psychology,* 1972, *11,* 162–174.

Huizinga, J. *Homo ludens: A study of the play-element in culture.* London: Routledge and Paul, 1949.

Hunt, J. McV. Traditional personality theory in the light of recent evidence. *American Scientist,* 1965, *53,* 80–96.

Huntington, S. P. The change to change: Modernization, development and politics. *Comparative Politics,* 1971, *3*(3), 283–322.

Husserl, E. *Phenomenology and the crisis in philosophy.* New York: Harper Torchbooks, 1965.

Hyman, H. The psychology of status. *Archives of psychology,* No. 269, 1942.

Hyman, H. H. & Singer, E. (Eds.), *Readings in reference group theory and research.* New York: Free Press, 1968.

Ichheiser, G. *Appearances and realities.* San Francisco: Jossey-Bass, 1970.

Irwin, J. *The felon.* Englewood Cliffs, N.J.: Prentice-Hall, 1970.

Isaacs, H. R. The new pluralists. *Commentary,* 1972, *53* (3), 75–79.

Isaacs, H. R. *Idols of the tribe: Group identity and political change.* New York: Harper & Row, 1975.

Isajiw, W. W. Definitions of ethnicity. *Ethnicity,* 1974, *1,* 111–124.

Jacobi, J. *The psychology of C. G. Jung.* 8th ed. New Haven: Yale, 1973.

Jahoda, G. The development of children's ideas about country and nationality: I. The conceptual framework. *British Journal of Educational Psychology*, 1963, *33*, 47–61.

James, W. *The principles of psychology*, vol. 1. New York: Henry Holt & Co., 1890.

James, W. *Psychology: The briefer course.* New York: Henry Holt, 1892.

Jaques, E. *A general theory of bureaucracy.* New York: Halstead Press, 1976.

Jensen, A. R. How much can we boost IQ and scholastic achievement? *Harvard Educational Review*, 1969, *39*, 1–123.

Jensen, A. R. *Bias in mental testing.* New York: Free Press, 1980.

Johnston, W. A. Individual performance and self-evaluation in a simulated team. *Organizational Behavior and Human Performance*, 1967, *2*, 309–328.

Jones, E. E. & Berglas, S. Control of attributions about the self through self-handicapping strategies: The appeal of alcohol and the role of underachievement. *Personality and Social Psychology Bulletin*, 1978, *4*, 200–206.

Joyce, J. *A portrait of the artist as a young man.* New York: Modern Library, 1928.

Juhasz, J. B. Psychology of paradox and vice versa. *Psychological Reports*, 1976a, *39*, 911–914.

Juhasz, J. B. *Psychology and physical form.* Berkeley: College of Environmental Design, 1976b.

Juhasz, J. B. Some conceptual limits on reliability estimates of measures of imagining. *Perceptual and Motor Skills*, 1977, *44*, 1023–1031.

Juhasz, J. B. Christopher Alexander and the language of architecture. *Journal of Environmental Psychology*, 1981, in press.

Juhasz, W. *Megvaltas fele: Uj vallastortenet*, Budapest: Barkoczy, 1943.

Jung, C. G. *Psychological types.* New York: Harcourt, Brace, 1923.

Jung, C. G. *The development of personality.* New York: Pantheon, 1953.

Jung, C. G. *The undiscovered self.* New York: The New American Library, Inc., 1957.

Jung, C. G. *Two essays in analytical psychology.* In Collected Works, 7 (2nd ed.). Princeton: University Press, 1966.

Jung, C. G. *Psychology and alchemy.* In *Collected Works*, 12 (2nd ed.). Princeton: University Press, 1968.

Jung, C. G. *Mysterium conjunctionis.* In *Collected Works*, 14 (2nd ed.). Princeton: University Press, 1970.

Jung, C. G. *Psychological types.* In *Collected Works*, 6. Princeton: University Press, 1971.

Jung, C. G. & Kerenyi, K. *Essays on a science of mythology.* New York: Pantheon Books, 1949.

Kafka, F. *The trial*, London: Victor Gollancz, 1937.

Kagan, S. Field independence and conformity of rural Mexican and urban Anglo-American children. *Child Development*, 1974, *45*, 765–771.

Kagan, S. & Madsen, M. Cooperation and competition of Mexican-American and Anglo children of two ages under four instructional ages. *Developmental Psychology*, 1971, *5*, 32–39.

Kagan, S. & Madsen, M. Experimental analyses of cooperation and competition of Anglo-American and Mexican-American children. *Developmental Psychology*, 1972a, *6*, 49–59.

Kagan, S. & Madsen, M. Rivalry in Anglo-American and Mexican children of two ages. *Journal of Personality and Social Psychology*, 1972b, *24*, 214–220.

Kallen, H. M. *Culture and democracy in the United States: Studies in the group psychology of the American peoples.* New York: Boni & Liveright, 1924.

Kamm, J. *Hope deferred: Girls' education in English history.* London: Methuen, 1965.

Kanter, R. M. *Commitment and community.* Cambridge, Mass.: Harvard, 1972.

Kardiner, A. & Ovesey, L. *The mark of oppression.* New York: W. W. Norton and Company, 1962.

Katcher, A. & Katcher, J. The restructuring of behavior in a Messianic cult. In R. Engleman (Ed.), *Personality and social life.* New York: Random House, 1967.

Katz, F. E. *Structuralism in sociology.* Albany: SUNY Press, 1976

Kedourie, E. *Nationalism.* Rev. ed. New York: Praeger, 1961.

Kelly, G. A. *The psychology of personal constructs.* New York: W. W. Norton, 1955.

Kelman, H. C. Foreword. In S. N. Herman, *Jewish identity.* Beverly Hills, Calif.: Sage Publications, 1977, pp. 9–12.

Kemper, T. D. *A social interactional theory of emotions.* New York: Wiley, 1978.

Keniston, K. *The uncommitted.* New York: Harcourt, Brace & World, 1965.

Kennedy, R. J. R. Single or triple melting pot? *American Journal of Sociology*, 1944, *49*, 331–339.

Kerenyi, K. *Eleusis.* New York: Schocken Books, 1977.

Kerenyi, K. *The gods of the Greeks.* New York: Grove Press, 1980.

Kermode, F. *The sense of an ending.* New York: Oxford Univ. Press, 1967.

Kessler-Harris, A. *The open cage: An Anzia Yezierska collection.* New York: Persea Books, 1979.

Kintsch, W. On comprehending stories. In M. A. Just & P. A. Carpenter (Eds.), *Cognitive processes in comprehension.* Hillsdale, N.J.: Lawrence Erlbaum Associates, 1977, pp. 33–62.

Klaatsch, H. *The evolution and progress of mankind.* London: T. F. Unwin Ltd., 1923.

Klapp, O. E. *Collective search for identity.* New York: Holt, Rinehart and Winston, 1969.

Klee, P. *Pedagogical sketchbook.* New York: Praeger, 1953.

Klein, M. On the development of mental functioning. *International Journal of Psychoanalysis*, 1958, *39*, 84–90.

Klein, M. *Developments in psychoanalysis.* London: Hogarth, 1952.

Klineberg, O. *The human dimension in international relations.* New York: Holt, Rinehart and Winston, 1964.

Kluckhohn, C. *Culture and behavior.* New York: The Free Press, 1962.

Kluckhohn, C. & Murray, H. A. *Personality in nature, society, and culture.* New York: Knopf, 1949.

Kochman, T. "Rapping" in the black ghetto. *Transaction*, 1969, *6*, 26–34.

Kogon, E. *The theory and practice of hell.* New York: Berkley Publishing Co., 1950.

Kohlberg, L. The development of children's orientation toward a moral order. *Vita Humana*, 1963, *6*, 11–33.

Kohli, M. Biography: Account, text and method. In D. Bertaux (Ed.), *Biography and society.* Beverly Hills: Sage, 1981.

Kohn, H. *The age of nationalism.* New York: Harper, 1962.

Kosinski, J. *The painted bird.* Boston: Bantam, 1978.

LaBarre, W. *The Peyote cult.* New Haven: Yale University Press, 1938.

LaBarre, W. *They shall take up serpents: Psychology of the Southern snake handling cult.* Minneapolis: University of Minnesota Press, 1962.

Labor, W. & Waletzky, J. Narrative analysis: Oral versions of personal experience. In J. Helm (Ed.), *Essays on the verbal and visual arts.* San Francisco: American Ethnological Society, 1967.

Lacan, J. *The language of the self.* Baltimore: Johns Hopkins, 1968.

Laing, R. L. *The politics of experience.* New York: Pantheon, 1967.

Laird, J. D., & Berglas, S. Individual differences in the effects of engaging in counter-attitudinal behavior. *Journal of Personality,* 1975, *43,* 286–304.

Lane, A. *The debate over* Slavery: *Stanley Elkins and his critics.* Urbana, Ill.: University of Illinois Press, 1971.

Langbaum, R. *The mysteries of identity: A theme in modern literature.* New York: Oxford University Press, 1977.

Langer, S. K. *Philosophy in a new key.* Cambridge: Harvard University, 1942.

Lasch, C. *The culture of narcissism.* New York: W. W. Norton, 1979.

Laslett, P. *Household and family in past time.* Cambridge: University Press, 1972.

Lasswell, H. H. Must science serve political power? *American Psychologist,* 1970, *25,* 117–123.

Lawrence, N. & O'Connor, D. *Readings in existential phenomenology.* Englewood Cliffs, N.J.: Prentice-Hall, 1967.

Lazarus, R. S., Kaner, A. d. & Folkman, S. Emotions: A cognitive-phenomenological analysis. In R. Plutchik & H. Kellerman (Eds.), *Emotion: Theory, research and experience,* vol. 1. New York: Academic Press, 1980.

Lee, R. B. & DeVore, I. (Eds.), *Man the hunter.* Chicago: Aldine, 1968.

Lester, G. & Lester, D. *Suicide, the gamble with death.* Englewood Cliffs, N.J.: Prentice-Hall, 1971.

Levine, L. W. The concept of the new negro and the realities of black culture. In N. I. Huggins, M. Kilson, & D. M. Fox (Eds.), *Key issues in the Afro–American Experience.* New York: Harcourt, Brace & Jovanovich, Inc., 1971a.

Levine, L. W. Slave songs and slave consciousness: An exploration in neglected sources. In T. Hareven (Ed.), *Anonymous Americans.* New York: Academic Press, 1971b.

Levi-Strauss, C. *The elementary structures of kinship.* Boston: Beacon Press, 1969a.

Levi-Strauss, C. *The raw and the cooked.* New York: Harper & Row, 1969b.

Levi-Strauss, C. *From honey to ashes.* New York: Harper & Row, 1973.

Levitt, A. Storytelling among school children: A folkloristic interpretation. Unpublished doctoral dissertation. University of Pennsylvania, 1978.

Lewin, K. *Resolving social conflicts.* New York: Harper, 1948.

Lieberman, A. F. Preschooler's competence with a peer: Relations with attachment and peer experience. *Child Development,* 1977, *48,* 1277–1287.

Lifton, R. J. *Revolutionary immortality.* New York: Random House, 1968.

Lifton, R. *History and human survival: Essays on the young and old, survivors and the dead, peace and war and on contemporary psychohistory.* New York: Random House, 1970.

Lijphart, A. Political theories and the explanation of ethnic conflict in the Western world: Falsified predictions and plausible postdictions. In E. J. Esman (Ed.), *Ethnic conflict in the Western world.* Ithaca, N.Y.: Cornell University Press, 1977, pp. 46–64.

Linton, R. *The study of man: An introduction.* New York: Appleton-Century, 1936.

Linton, R. *The cultural background of personality.* New York: Appleton-Century Corp., 1945.

Lofland, J. *Deviance and identity.* Englewood Cliffs, N.J.: Prentice-Hall, 1969.

Luomala, K. The native dog in the Polynesian system of values. In S. Diamond (Ed.), *Culture in history: Essays in honor of P. Radin.* New York: Columbia University Press, 1960.

Macarov, D. *Work and welfare.* Beverly Hills: Sage, 1980.

MacIntyre, a. Epistemological crises, dramatic narrative, and the philosophy of science. *The Monist,* 1977, *60,* 453–472.

MacKinnon, D. W. The structure of personality. In J. McV. Hunt (Ed.), *Personality and the behavior disorders,* vol. 1. New York: The Ronald Press, 1944.

Madsen, M. Cooperative and competitive motivation of children in three Mexican sub-cultures. *Psychological Reports,* 1967, *20,* 1307–1320.

Madsen, M. & Shapira, A. Cooperative and competitive behavior of urban Afro–American, Anglo-Americans, Mexican-Americans and Mexican village children. *Developmental Psychology,* 1973, *7,* 16–20.

Maimon, S. *Autobiography of Solomon Maimon.* London: Schocken, 1954.

Malinowski, B. *Magic, science and religion.* Boston: Beacon Press, 1948.

Mancuso, J. C. Current motivational models in the elaboration of personal construct theory. In A. W. Landfield (Ed.), *Nebraska symposium on motivation: Personal construct psychology.* Lincoln, Nebraska: University of Nebraska Press, 1977, 43–97.

Mancuso, J. C. & Adams-Webber, J. R. Anticipation as a constructive process. In J. C. Mancuso & J. R. Adams-Webber (Eds.), *The construing person.* New York: Praeger, 1982.

Mancuso, J. C. & Ceely, S. G. The self as memory processing. *Cognitive Therapy and Research,* 1980, *4,* 1–25.

Mandler, J. M. & Johnson, N. S. Remembrance of things parsed: Story structure and recall. *Cognitive Psychology,* 1977, *9,* 111–151.

Mannheim, K. *Ideology and utopia.* London: Routledge & Kegan Paul Ltd., 1936.

Mannin, E. *Loneliness: A study of the human condition.* London: Hutchinson, 1966.

Mannoni, O. *Prospero and Caliban.* New York: Praeger, 1956.

Marcia, J. E. Identity six years after: A follow-up study. *Journal of Youth and Adolescence,* 1976, *5,* 145–160.

Marcus, S. *The other Victorians: A study of sexuality and pornography in mid-nineteenth century England.* New York: Basic Books, 1966.

Marcuse, H. *One dimensional man.* Boston: Beacon, 1964.

Marine, G. *The black panthers.* New York: Signet, 1969.

Martineau, H. Female industry. *Edinburgh Review,* 1859, *109,* 293–336.

Maslow, A. H. Peak-experiences as acute identity-experiences. *American Journal of Psychoanlaysis,* 1961, *21,* 254–260.

Maslow, A. H. *The farther reaches of human nature.* New York: Viking, 1971.

Masuda, M., Matsumoto, G. H. & Meredith, G. M. Ethnic identity in three generations of Japanese Americans. *Journal of Social Psychology,* 1970, *81,* 199–207.

Mates, B. On the verification of statements about ordinary language. In V. C. Chappell (Ed.), *Ordinary language*. Englewood Cliffs, N.J.: Prentice–Hall, 1964, pp. 64–74.

Mathews, F. H. The revolt against Americanism: Cultural pluralism and cultural relativism as an ideology of liberation. *Canadian Review of American Studies*, 1970, *1*, 4–31.

Matsumoto, G. H., Meredith, G. M. & Masuda, M. Ethnic identification: Honolulu and Seattle Japanese-Americans. *Journal of Cross-Cultural Psychology*, 1970, *1*, 63–76.

Maurice, F. D. & Kingsley, C. *Introductory lectures delivered at Queen's College, London*. London: Parker, 1849.

May, R. *Existential psychology*. New York: Random House, 1961.

McClelland, D. C. *Personality*. New York: n.p., 1951.

McClelland, J. L. & Rumelhart, D. E. An interactive activation model of context effects in letter perception: Part 1. An account of basic findings. *Psychological Review*, 1981, *88*, 375–407.

McCorkle, L. W. & Korn, R. Resocialization within walls. In N. Johnston (Ed.), *The sociology of punishment and correction*. New York: Wiley, 1966.

McDowell, J. The speech play and verbal art of Chicano children. Unpublished doctoral dissertation, University of Texas.

McGuire, W. J., McGuire, C. V. & Winton, W., Effects of household sex composition on the salience of one's gender in the spontaneous self-concept. *Journal of Experimental Social Psychology*, 1979, *15*, 77–90.

Mead, G. H. The genesis of self and social control. *International Journal of Ethics*, 1925, *35*, 251–273.

Mead, G. H. *Mind, self and society from the standpoint of a social behaviorist*. Chicago: University of Chicago Press, 1934.

Mead, M. *Coming of age in Samoa*. New York: W. Morrow & Co., 1928.

Meister, R. J. Introduction. In R. J. Meister (Ed.), *Race and ethnicity in modern America*. Lexington, Mass.: Heath, 1974, pp. vii–xx.

Merton, R. K. *Social theory and social structure*. Glencoe, Illinois: The Free Press, 1957.

Merton, R. K. Insiders and outsiders: A chapter in the sociology of knowledge. In T. Bottomore (Ed.), *Varieties of political expression in sociology*. Chicago: University of Chicago Press, 1972, pp. 9–47.

Metraux, A. The concept of soul in Haitian voodoo. *Southwestern Journal of Anthropology*, Spring 1946, *2*(1).

Metraux, A. *Voodoo in Haiti*. H. Charteres, trans. New York: Oxford University Press, 1959.

Metraux, A. *Haiti: Black peasants and voodoo*. P. Lengyel, trans. New York: Universe Books, 1960.

Metzger, L. P. American sociology and black assimilation: Conflicting perspectives. *American Journal of Sociology*, 1971, *76*, 627–647.

Michotte, A. E. *The perception of causality*. London: Methuen, 1963.

Middleton, J. (Ed.), *Magic, witchcraft, and curing*. New York: American Museum of Natural History, 1967.

Milgram, S. Behavioral study of obedience. *Journal of Abnormal and Social Psychology*, 1963, *67*, 371–378.

Miller, D. R. Personality and social interaction. In B. Kaplan (Ed.), *Studying personality cross-culturally*. Evanston, Ill.: Row, Peterson, 1961, pp. 271–300.

Miller, D. R. The study of social relationships: Situation, identity and social interaction. In S. Koch (Ed.), *Psychology: A study of a science*. New York: McGraw-Hill, 1963.

Miller, D. & Swanson, G. E. *The changing American parent*. New York: Wiley, 1958.

Miller, D. R. & Swanson, G. E. *Inner conflict and defense*. New York: Holt, 1960.

Minogue, K. R. *Nationalism*. New York: Basic Books, 1967.

Mischel, T. *The self*. Totawa, N.J.: Rowman and Littlefield, 1977.

Mischel, W. *Personality and assessment*. New York: Wiley, 1968.

Mischel, W. On the future of personality measurement. *American Psychologist*, 1977, *32*, 246–253.

Mischel, W. On the interface of cognition and personality: Beyond the person-situation debate. *American Psychologist*, 1979, *34*, 740–754.

Mishima, Y. *Forbidden colors*. New York: Knopf, 1968.

Mitchell, J. Cons, square-johns, and rehabilitation. In B. J. Biddle & E. J. Thomas (Eds.), *Role theory: Concepts and research*. New York: John Wiley and Sons, 1966.

Mitford, N. *The Stanleys of Alderley: Their letters between the years 1851–1865*. London: Chapman and Hall, 1939.

Morawski, J. G. History as psychology's epistemological laboratory. Paper presented at the History Faculty Seminar. Wesleyan University, Middletown, CT, April 9, 1982.

Morgan, E. *Descent of woman*. New York: Bantam Books, 1973.

Moskos, C. C., Jr. Growing up Greek American. *Society*, 1977, *15*, 64–71.

Moustakas, C. E. *The self: Explorations in personal growth*. New York: Harper & Row, 1956.

Mowrer, R. H. *The new group therapy*. New Jersey: D. Van Nostrand Co., 1964.

Mulford, H. A. & Salisbury, W. W. Self-conception in a general population. *Sociological Quarterly*, 1964, *5*, 35–46.

Murray, H. A. Preparation for the scaffold of a comprehensive system. In S. Koch (Ed.), *Psychology a study of a science*, vol. 3. New York: McGraw-Hill, 1959, pp. 7–54.

Musil, R. *The man without qualities*. London: Secker & Warburg, 1953.

Myers, I. B. *Manual for the Myers-Briggs Type Indicator*. Palo Alto, CA: Consulting Psychologists Press, 1962.

Neel, J. V. Lessons from a primitive people. *Science*, 1970, *170*, 815–822.

Neff, W. *Victorian working women: A historical and literary study of women in British industries and professions, 1832–1850*. New York: Columbia University Press, 1929.

Neisser, U. *Cognition and reality: Principles and implications of cognitive psychology*. San Francisco: Freeman, 1976.

Nelson, K. E. *Children's language*, vol. 2. New York: Wiley, 1980.

Neuringer, C. Methodological problems in suicide research. *Journal of Consulting Psychology*, 1962, *26*, 273–278.

Nie, N. H., Hull, C. H., Jenkins, J. G., Steinbrenner, K. & Bent, D. H. *Statistical package for the social sciences*. 2nd ed. New York: McGraw-Hill, 1975.

Nieburg, H. L. Theory-tales and paradigms. *Journal of Mind and Behavior*, 1981, *2*, 179–193.

Nietzsche, F. *Basic writings*. New York: Random House, 1968.

Nobles, W. W. Psychological research and the black self-concept: A critical review. *Journal of Social Issues*, 1973, *29*, 11–31.

Novak, M. *The rise of unmeltable ethics: Politics and culture in the seventies*. New York: Macmillan, 1971.

Novak, M. Cultural pluralism for individuals: A social vision. In M. M. Tumin & W. Plotch (Eds.), *Pluralism in a democratic society*. New York: Praeger, 1977, pp. 25–58.

Nowlis, V. Mood: Behaviour and experience. In M. B. Arnold (Ed.), *Feelings and emotions*. New York: Academic Press, 1970.

Nunnally, J. C. *Psychometric theory*. 2nd ed. New York: McGraw Hill, 1978.

Obidinski, E. Methodological considerations in the definition of ethnicity. *Ethnicity*, 1978, *5*, 213–228.

Ochberg, F. The victim of terrorism: Psychiatric considerations. *Terrorism: An International Journal*, 1977, *1*, 1–22.

Ogilvy, J. A. *Many dimensional man*. New York: Oxford University, 1977.

Oliphant, M. The condition of women. *Blackwood's Magazine*, 1858, *83*, 139–154.

Olson, D. R. From utterance to text: The bias of language in speech and writing. *Harvard Educational Review*, 1977, *47*, 257–281.

Open council. *The English Woman's Journal*. 1858, *1* (2), 210–211.

Ortega y Gasset, J. *History as a system*. New York: Norton, 1941.

Orwell, G. Charles Dickens (1939). In Sonia Orwell & I. Angus (Eds.), *The collected essays, journalism, and letters of George Orwell*, vol. 1. New York: Harcourt, Brace & World, 1968.

Orwell, G. Review of *Mein Kampf* (1940). In Sonia Orwell & I. Angus (Eds.), *The collected essays, journalism, and letters of George Orwell*, vol. 2. New York: Harcourt, Brace & World, 1968a.

Orwell, G. Notes on the way (1940). In Sonia Orwell & I. Angus (Eds.), *The collected essays, journalism, and letters of George Orwell*, vol. 2. New York: Harcourt, Brace & World, 1968b.

Orwell, G. The art of Donald McGill (1941). In Sonia Orwell & I. Angus (Eds.), *The collected essays, journalism, and letters of George Orwell*, vol. 2. New York: Harcourt, Brace & World, 1968c.

Orwell, G. London letter to the Partisan Review (1943). In Sonia Orwell & I. Angus (Eds.), *The collected essays, journalism, and letters of George Orwell*, vol. 2. New York: Harcourt, Brace & World, 1968d.

Osborn, H. F. *Men of old stone age*. New York, 1918.

Osgood, C. R., Suci, G. J. & Tannenbaum, P. H. *The measurement of meaning*. Urbana: University of Illinois, 1957.

Oxford English dictionary. New York: Oxford University Press, 1971.

Parming, T. The nature of ethnic identity. Unpublished doctoral dissertation, Yale University, 1976.

Partridge, E. *A dictionary of the underworld, British and American*. London: Routledge & Kegan Paul, 1950.

Patterson, O. *The sociology of slavery: An analysis of the origins, development and structure of*

Negro slave society in Jamaica. London: MacGibbon & Kee, 1967.

Pepitone, A. Attributions of causality, social attitudes, and cognitive matching processes. In R. Tagiuri & L. Petrullo (Eds.), *Person perception, and interpersonal behavior.* California: Stanford University Press, 1958, pp. 258–276.

Peplau, L. A., Russell, D. & Heim, M. The experience of loneliness. In I. H. Frieze, D. Bar-Tal, & J. S. Carroll (Eds.), *New approaches to social problems.* San Francisco: Jossey-Bass, 1979.

Pepper, S. C. *World hypotheses.* Berkeley: University California Press, 1942.

Perlmutter, P. Balkanizing America. *Commentary,* 1980, *70*(3), 64–66.

Peters, R. S. *The concept of motivation.* London: Routledge & Kegan Paul, 1958.

Pettigrew, T. F. *A profile of the Negro American.* Princeton, N.J.: Van Nostrand Reinhold Company, 1964.

Pettigrew, T. F. Social evaluation theory: Convergences and applications. In D. Levine (Ed.), *Nebraska symposium on motivation: 1967.* Lincoln: University of Nebraska Press, 1967.

Pettigrew, T. F. Three issues in ethnicity: Boundaries, deprivations, and perceptions. In J. M. Yinger & S. J. Cutler (Eds.), *Major social issues: A multidisciplinary view.* New York: Free Press, 1978.

Piaget, J. *The language and thought of the child.* New York: Harcourt Brace, 1926.

Piaget, J. *La causalite physique chez l'enfant.* Paris: Alcan, 1927.

Piaget, J. *The moral judgment of children.* London: Routledge and Kegan Paul, 1932.

Piaget, J. Necessite et signification des recherches comparative en psychologie genetique. *International Journal of Psychology,* 1966, *1*, 3–13.

Piaget, J. Le point de vue de Piaget. *International Journal of Psychology,* 1968, *3*, 281–289.

Piaget, J. *Structuralism.* London: Routledge & Kegan Paul, 1971.

Piaget, J. & Inhelder, B. *Mental imagery in the child.* New York: Basic Books, 1971.

Pitcher, E. G. & Prelinger, E. *Children tell stories: An analysis of fantasy.* New York: International Universities Press, 1963.

Platt, A. M. & Diamond, B. L. The origins and development of the "wild beast" concept of mental illness and its relation to theories of criminal responsibility. *Journal of the History of the Behavioral Sciences,* 1965, *1*, 355–367.

Pomper, Philip. Problems of a naturalistic psychohistory. *History and theory,* 1973, *12*, 367–388.

Powers, W. T. *Behavior: The control of perception.* Chicago: Aldine, 1973.

Powers, W. T. Quantitative analysis of purposive systems: Some spadework at the foundations of scientific psychology. *Psychological Review,* 1978, *85*, 417–435.

Price-Williams, D. *Explorations in cross cultural psychology.* San Francisco, Calif.: Chandler, 1975.

Priest, J. *Bible defense of slavery.* Glasgow, KY: W. S. Brown, 1852.

(The) profession of the teacher: The annual reports of the Governesses' Benevolent Institution, from 1843 to 1856. *The English Woman's Journal,* 1858, *1*(1), 1–13.

Putnam, C. *Race and reason.* Washington: Public Affairs Press, 1961.

Rabbie, J. M., Benoist, F., Oosterbaan, H. & Visser, L. Differential power and effects of competitive and cooperative intergroup interaction on intragroup and outgroup attitudes. *Journal of Personality and Social Psychology,* 1974, *30*, 46–56.

Rabbie, J. M. & Wilkins, G. Intergroup competition and its effect on intragroup and intergroup relations. *European Journal of Social Psychology*, 1971, *1*, 215–234.

Rabinowicz, H. M. *The world of Hasidism*. London: Hartmore House, 1970.

Rachlin, H. *Introduction to modern behaviorism*. San Francisco: Freeman, 1970.

Ramirez, M. & Price-Williams, D. Cognitive styles of children of three ethnic groups in the U. S. *Journal of Cross Cultural Psychology*, 1974, *5*, 212–219.

Ramsöy, O. *Social groups as system and subsystem*. Oslo: Norwegian Universities Press, 1962.

Rand, A. *The new left: The anti-industrial revolution*. New York: New American Library, 1970.

Ratcliff, R. & McKoon, G. Does activation really spread? *Psychological Review*, 1974, *81*, 454–462.

Riesman, D., Glazer, N., & Denney, R. *The lonely crowd: A study of the changing American character*. New Haven: Yale University Press, 1950.

Riordin, C. Equal-status interracial contact: A review and revision of the concept. *International Journal of International Relations*, 1978, *2*, 161–185.

Ritchie, A. I. T. *Chapters from some memoirs*. London: Macmillan, 1894.

Roberts, R. *The classic slum*. Manchester: University Press, 1971.

Rogers, C. R. *Client-centered therapy*. Boston: Houghton-Mifflin, 1951.

Rogers, C. R. *On encounter groups*. New York: Harper & Row, 1970.

Rohde, E. *Psyche*. London: Kegan Paul & Co., 1925.

Rommetveit, R. *Social norms and roles*. Minneapolis, Minn.: University of Minnesota Press, 1955.

Rose, W. L. Childhood in bondage. Unpublished manuscript, presented to Organization of American Historians, Los Angeles, April, 1970.

Rosenberg, M. A metaphor for dramatic form. *Journal of Aesthetics & Art Criticism*, 1958, *17*, 174–181.

Rosenberg, M. *The masks of Macbeth*. Berkeley: University of California Press, 1978.

Rosenberg, M. Shakespeare's tragic world of If. *Shakespeare Jahrlrich*, 1980, pp. 109–117.

Rotenberg, M. *Damnation and deviance: The Protestant ethic and the spirit of failure*. New York: The Free Press, 1978.

Rotenberg , M. *Dialogue with deviance: Hasidic ethic and the theory of social contraction*. Philadelphia: ISHI Pub., 1982.

Rotenberg, M. & Sarbin, T. R. Impact of differentially significant others on role involvement: An experiment with prison social types. *Journal of Abnormal Psychology*, 1971, *77*, 97–107.

Rubin, S. & Wolf, D. The development of maybe: The evolution of social roles into narrative roles. *New Directions for Child Development*, 1979, *6*, 15–28.

Rumelhart, D. E. Notes on a schema for stories. In D. C. Bobrow & A. Collins (Eds.), *Representation and understanding: Studies in cognitive science*. New York: Academic Press, 1975.

Rumelhart, D. E., Lindsay, P. H. & Norman, D. A. A process model for long–term memory. In E. Tulving & W. Donaldson (Eds.), *Organization of memory*. New York: Academic Press, 1972, pp. 197–246.

Rumelhart, D. E. & Ortony, A. The representation of knowledge in memory. In R.

Anderson & W. Montague (Eds.), *Schooling and the acquisition of knowledge.* Hillsdale, N.J.: Lawrence Erlbaum, 1977, pp. 99–135.

Ruskin, J. *Sesame and lilies, The two paths, and The king of the golden river.* London: J. M. Dent, 1916.

Ruskin, J. *Praeterita: Outlines of scenes and thoughts perhaps worthy of memory in my past life.* London: Rupert Hart-Davis, 1949.

Russell, B. *New hopes for a changing world.* London: G. Allen and Unwin, 1951.

Sadler, W. A., Jr. & Johnson, T. B., Jr. From loneliness to anomia. In J. Hartog, J. R. Audy, & Y. A. Cohen (Eds.), *The anatomy of loneliness.* New York: International Universities Press, 1980.

Said, A. & Simmons, L. R. (Eds.), *Ethnicity in an international context.* New Brunswick, N.J.: Transaction Books, 1976.

Sainsbury, P. The social relations of suicide: The value of a combined epidemiological and case study approach. *Social Science Medicine,* 1972, *6,* 189–198.

Sampson, E. E. Studies of status incongruence. In L. Berkowitz (Ed.), *Advances in experimental social psychology,* vol. 4. New York: Academic Press, 1969.

Sampson, E. E. Personality and the location of identity. *Journal of Personality,* 1978, *46,* 552–568.

Sampson, E. E. Cognitive psychology as ideology. *American Psychologist,* 1981, *36,* 730–743.

Sandberg, N. C. *Ethnic identity and assimilation: The Polish American community.* New York: Praeger, 1974.

Sanford, N. Surface and depth in the individual personality. *Psychological Review,* 1956, *63,* 349–359.

Sarbin, T. R. A preface to a psychological analysis of the self. *Psychological Review,* 1952, *59,* 11–22.

Sarbin, T. R. Role theory. In G. Lindzey (Ed.), *Handbook of social psychology.* Reading, MA: Addison-Wesley, 1954.

Sarbin, T. R. On the futility of the proposition that some people be labeled mentally ill. *Journal of Consulting Psychology,* 1967a, *31,* 447–453.

Sarbin, T. R. The dangerous individual: An outcome of social identity transformation. *British Journal of Criminology,* 1967b, *10,* 355–366.

Sarbin, T. R. On the distinction between social roles and social types, with special reference to the hippie. *American Journal of Psychiatry,* 1968a, *125,* 1024–1031.

Sarbin, T. R. A preface to a psychological analysis of the self. In C. Gordon & K. J. Gergen (Eds.), *The self in social interaction.* New York: Wiley, 1968b.

Sarbin, T. R. Ontology recapitulates philology: The mythic nature of anxiety. *American Psychologist,* 1968c, *23,* 411–418.

Sarbin, T. R. Notes on the transformation of social identity. In L. Roberts, N. Greenfield & M. Miller (Eds.), *Comprehensive mental health: The challenge of evaluation.* Madison, WI: University of Wisconsin Press, 1968d.

Sarbin, T. R. A role theory perspective for community psychology. In A. Adelson & B. Kalis (Eds.), *Community psychology and mental health.* San Francisco: Chandler Publishing Co., 1970a.

Sarbin, T. R. The culture of poverty, social identity and cognitive outcomes. In V. L. Allen (Ed.), *Psychological factors in poverty.* Chicago: Markham Publishing Co., 1970b.

Sarbin, T. R. Cross-age tutoring and social identity. In V. L. Allen (Ed.), *Tutoring and interage interaction.* Madison: University of Wisconsin Press, 1975.

Sarbin, T. R. Contextualism: The worldview for modern psychology. In A. W. Landfield (Ed.), *Nebraska symposium on motivation: Personal construct psychology.* Lincoln: University of Nebraska Press, 1977, pp. 1–41.

Sarbin, T. R. Hypnosis: Metaphorical encounters of the fourth kind. *Semiotica,* 1980, *37,* 1–15.

Sarbin, T. R. On self-deception. *Annals of the New York Academy of Sciences,* 1981, *364,* 220–235.

Sarbin, T. R. On the psychological analysis of deception. In D. Daniel & K. Herbig (Eds.), *Deception and counter-deception.* Elmsford, N.Y.: Pergamon, 1982 (in press).

Sarbin, T. R. & Adler, N. Self-reconstitutive processes: A preliminary report. *The Psychoanalytic Review,* 1971, *57*(1), 599–616.

Sarbin, T. R. & Allen, V. I. Role theory. In G. Lindsey & E. Aronson (Eds.), *Handbook of social psychology.* 5 vols. Reading, Mass.: Addison Wesley, 1968–1969.

Sarbin, T. R. & Bailey, D. E. The immediacy postulate in the light of modern cognitive psychology. In K. R. Hammond (Ed.), *The psychology of Egon Brunswik.* New York: Holt, Rinehart, & Winston, 1966, pp. 159–203.

Sarbin, T. R. & Juhasz, J. B. The social context of hallucinations. In R. K. Siegel & J. West (Eds.), *Hallucinations: Behavior, experience and theory.* New York: Wiley, 1975, pp. 241–256.

Sarbin, T. R. & Juhasz, J. B. The concept of mental illness. In I. Al-Issa (Ed.), *Culture and psychopathology.* Baltimore: University Park Press, 1981, in press.

Sarbin, T. R. & Mancuso, J. C. *Schizophrenia: Medical diagnosis or verdict.* Elmsford, N.Y.: Pergamon, 1980.

Sarbin, T. R. & Scheibe, K. E. The transvaluation of social identity. In C. J. Bellone (Ed.), *The normative dimension in public administration.* New York: Marcel Dekker, 1980.

Sargent, S. S. & Smith, M. W. (Eds.), *Culture and personality.* New York: The Viking Fund, 1949.

Sartre, J. P. *Existentialism and humanism.* New York: Philosophical Library, 1947.

Sartre, J. P. *Being and nothingness.* New York: Philosophical Library, 1956.

Sartre, J. P. *Sartre on Cuba.* New York: Ballantine Books, 1961.

Sartre, J. P. *Search for a method.* New York: Knopf, 1963a.

Sartre, J. P. *Psychology and imagination.* New York: Philosophical Library, 1963b.

Sasaki, Y. & Wagatsuma, H. Negative self-identity in a delinquent Korean youth. In C. Lee & G. De Vos (Eds.), *Koreans in Japan: Ethnic conflict and continuity.* Berkeley, Calif.: University of California, 1981, pp. 334–353.

Schank, R. C. *Conceptual information processing.* Amsterdam: North Holland, 1975a.

Schank, R. C. The structure of episodes in memory. In D. Bobrow & A. Collins (Eds.), *Representation and understanding: Studies in cognitive science.* New York: Academic Press, 1975b, pp. 237–272.

Schank, R. C. & Abelson, R. P. *Scripts, plans, goals and understanding.* Hillsdale, N.J.: Lawrence Erlbaum, 1977.

Schapp, W. In *Geschichten verstrickt zum Sein von Mensch and Ding.* Wiesbaden: B. Heymann, 1976.

Scheibe, K. E. Reflections on loyalty. *Trinity Alumni Magazine,* 1967, *8,* 12–15.

Scheibe, K. E. Legitimized aggression and the assignment of evil. *American Scholar*, 1974, *43*, 576–592.

Scheibe, K. E. *Mirrors, masks, lies and secrets*. New York: Praeger, 1979.

Scheier, M. F. Effects of public and private self-consciousness on the public expression of person beliefs. *Journal of Personality and Social Psychology*, 1980, *39*, 514–521.

Schermerhorn, R. Ethnicity in the perspective of the sociology of knowledge. *Ethnicity*, 1974, *1*, 1–14.

Schofield, J. W. Complementary and conflicting identities: Images and interaction in an interracial school. In S. R. Asher & J. M. Gottman (Eds.) *The development of children's friendships*. New York: Cambridge University Press, 1981, pp. 53–90.

Schwartz, T. The cargo cult: A Melanesian type response to change. In G. De Vos (Ed.), *Responses to change*. New York: Van Nostrand, 1976, pp. 147–206.

Schwarz, L. W. (Ed.), *The Menorah treasury: Harvest of half a century*. Philadelphia: Jewish Publication Society of America, 1964.

Searle, J. R. *Speech acts*. Cambridge: University Press, 1969.

Sennett, R. & Cobb, J. *The hidden injuries of class*. New York: Random House, 1972.

Sermat, V. Sources of loneliness. *Essence*, 1978, *2*, 271–276.

Sewell, E. M. *Principles of education, drawn from nature and revelation, and applied to female education in the upper classes*, vol. 2. New York: Appleton, 1870.

Shaver, P. R. & Scheibe, K. E. Transformation of social identity: A study of chronic mental patients and college volunteers in a summer camp setting. *Journal of Psychology*, 1967, *66*, 19–37.

Sherif, M. *Social interaction process and products*. Chicago: Aldine, 1967.

Sherif, M. & Hovland, C. *Social judgment*. New Haven, Conn.: Yale University Press, 1961.

Shockley, W. B. Possible transfer of metallurgical and astronomical approaches to the problem of environment versus ethnic heredity. *Science*, 1966, *154*, 428.

Shotter, J. *Images of man in psychological research*. London: Methuen, 1979.

Shrauger, J. S. Responses to evaluation as a function of initial self-perceptions. *Psychological Bulletin*, 1975, *82*, 581–596.

Shrauger, J. S. & Schoeneman, T. J. Symbolic interactionist view of self–concept: Through the looking glass darkly. *Psychological Bulletin*, 1979, *86*, 549–573.

Shütz, A. *Collected papers*. The Hague: M. Nijhoff (vol. 1, 1962; vol. 2, 1964; vol. 3, 1966).

Singer, J. *Boundaries of the soul*. New York: Doubleday, 1973.

Singer, L. Ethnogenesis and Negro Americans today. *Social Research*, 1962, *29*, 419–432.

Skinner, B. F. *Walden two*. New York: Macmillan, 1948.

Skinner, B. F. Some issues concerning the control of human behavior: A symposium. *Science*, 1956, *124*, 1057–1066.

Skinner, B. F. *Beyond freedom and dignity*. New York: Knopf, 1971.

Slater, P. E. *The pursuit of loneliness*. Boston: Beacon Press, 1970.

Slobin, D. I. *Psycholinguistics*. Glenview, IL: Scott Foresman, 1971.

Smith, G. E. *Human history*. New York: W. W. Norton, 1929.

Snyder, L. L. *The new nationalism*. Ithaca: Cornell University Press, 1968.

Snyder, M. Self-monitoring of expressive behavior. *Journal of Personality and Social Psychology*, 1974, *30*, 536–537.

Snyder, M. Self-monitoring processes. In L. Berkowitz (Ed.), *Advances in experimental social psychology*, vol. 12. New York: Academic Press, 1979.

Sofer, E. G. Inner-direction, other-direction, and autonomy: A study of college students. In S. M. Lipset & L. Lowenthal (Eds.), *Culture and social character: The work of David Riesman reviewed*. Glencoe, IL: Free Press, 1961.

Sollors, W. Literature and ethnicity. In S. Thernstron (Ed.), *Harvard encyclopedia of American ethnic groups*. Cambridge, Mass.: Belknap Press, 1980, pp. 647–665.

Soule, C. *Time for living*. New York: Viking Press, 1955.

Southern Cultivator, 1851, *9*, 85.

Spiegel, J. P. The social and psychological dynamics of militant Negro activism: A preliminary report. In J. H. Masserman, (Ed.) *The dynamics of dissent*. New York: Grune & Stratton, 1968, pp. 136–155.

Stagner, R. War and peace. In P. L. Harriman (Ed.), *Encyclopaedia of psychology*, 1946, pp. 891–897.

Stampp, K. M. *The peculiar institution: Slavery in the ante-bellum South*. New York: Alfred A. Knopf, Inc., 1956.

Stein, H. & Hill, R. F. *The ethnic imperative: Examining the new white ethnic movement*. University Park, Pa.: Pennsylvania State University Press, 1977.

Stein, N. The comprehension and appreciation of stories: A developmental analysis. In S. Madega (Ed.), *The arts, cognition and basic skills*. St. Louis: Cemrel, 1978.

Steinberg, S. *The ethnic myth: Race, ethnicity, and class in America*. New York: Atheneum, 1981.

Stengel, E. *Suicide and attempted suicide*. Baltimore: Penguin, 1964.

Stephan, W. G. & Stephan, C. Role differentiation, empathy, and neurosis in urban migrants, and lower-class residents of Santiago, Chile. *Journal of Personality and Social Psychology*, 1971, *19*, 1–6.

Stewart, S. A. Nonsense: Aspects of intertextuality in folklore and literature. Unpublished doctoral dissertation. University of Pennsylvania, 1978.

Stouffer, S. A. An analysis of conflicting social norms. *American Sociological Review*, 1949, *14*, 707–717.

Strachey, R. *The cause: A short history of the women's movement in Great Britain*. London: G. Bell and Sons, 1928.

Strickland, B. R. & Crowne, D. P. Conformity under conditions of simulated group pressure as a function of the need for social approval. *The Journal of Social Psychology*, 1962, *58*, 171–181.

Strong, S. M. Social types in a minority group: Formulation of a method. *American Journal of Sociology*, 1943, *48*, 563–573.

Stuckey, S. Through the prism of folklore: Black ethos in slavery. *Massachusetts Review*, 1968, *9*, 417–437.

Sullivan, H. S. *Conceptions of modern psychiatry*. Washington, D.C.: William Alanson White Foundation, 1947.

Sullivan, H. S. *The interpersonal theory of psychiatry*. New York: Norton, 1953.

Sumner, W. G. *Folkways*. New York: Ginn, 1906.

Sutton-Smith, B. Presentation and representation in fictional narrative. *New Directions for Child Development*, 1979, *6*, 53–66.

Sutton-Smith, B. *The folkstories of children.* Philadelphia, PA: University of Pennsylvania Press, 1980.

Suzuki, D. T. *Zen and Japanese culture.* Princeton: University Press, 1959.

Suzuki, D. T. The awakening of a new consciousness in Zen. In J. Campbell (Ed.), *Man and transformation.* New York: Pantheon Books, 1964, pp. 179–202.

Swierenga, R. Ethnicity in historical perspective. *Social Science,* 1977 (Winter), 31–44.

Symonds, P. M. *The ego and the self.* New York: Appleton-Century-Crofts, 1951.

Szasz, T. S. *The myth of mental illness.* New York: Hoeber & Hapner, 1961.

Szasz, T. S. *Schizophrenia: Sacred symbol of psychiatry.* New York: Basic Books, 1976.

Taft, R. *From stranger to citizen.* London: Tavistock Publications, 1966.

Tafuri, M. *Architecture and utopia.* Cambridge: MIT, 1976.

Tafuri, M. *Theories and history of architecture.* New York: Harper & Row, 1980.

Tajfel, H. Experiments in intergroup discrimination. *Scientific American,* 1970, *223,* 96–102.

Tajfel, H. & Billig, M. Familiarity and categorization in intergroup behavior. *Journal of Experimental Social Psychology,* 1974, *10,* 159–170.

Tajfel, H., Billig, M., Bundy, R. & Flament, C. Social categorization and intergroup behavior. *European Journal of Social Psychology,* 1971, *1,* 149–178.

Tajfel, H. & Turner, J. C. An integrative theory of intergroup conflict. In W. G. Austin & S. Worschel (Eds.), *The social psychology of intergroup relations.* Monterey, Calif.: Brooks/Cole, 1979, pp. 33–47.

Tannen, D. A comparative analysis of oral narrative strategies: Athenian Greek and American English. In W. O. Chage (Ed.), *The pear stories.* Norwood, N.J.: Ablex, 1980, pp. 51–87.

Taylor, C. What is human agency? In T. Mischel (Ed.), *The self.* Totowa, N.J.: Rowman & Littlefield, 1977.

Taylor, R. L. Black ethnicity and the persistence of ethnogenesis. *American Journal of Sociology,* 1979, *84,* 1401–1423.

Thackeray, W. M. *Vanity fair: A novel without a hero.* New York: Signet, 1962.

Thibaut, J. W. & Kelley, H. H. *The social psychology of groups.* New York: Wiley, 1959.

Thompson, P. *The Victorian heroine: A changing ideal, 1837–1873.* London: Oxford University Press, 1956.

Thomas, P. *Down these mean streets.* New York: Signet Books, 1968.

Thorndyke, P. W. Cognitive structures in comprehension and memory of narrative discourse. *Cognitive Psychology,* 1977, *9,* 97–110.

Thorpe, E. E. Chattel slavery and concentration camps. *Negro History Bulletin,* 1962, *25,* 173.

Time, 1970, *96* (August 24), 42.

Tolman, E. C. Cognitive maps in rats and men. *Psychological Review,* 1948, *55,* 189–208.

Tolstoy, L. N. *The kingdom of God is within you.* London: Heinemann, 1894.

Tolzmann, D. H. A letter to the editor of *Commentary. Commentary,* 1972, *53*(10), 22.

Toulmin, S. *Foresight and understanding.* New York: Harper, 1961.

Trilling, L. *Sincerity and authenticity.* Cambridge: Harvard University Press, 1972.

Tuan, Y. F. *Space and place.* Minneapolis: University of Minnesota, 1977.

Tulving, E. Episodic and semantic memory. In E. Tulving & W. Donaldson (Eds.), *Organization of memory.* New York: Academic Press, 1972, pp. 382–403.

Turner, J. C. Social comparison and social identity: Some prospects for group behavior. *European Journal of Social Psychology*, 1975, *5*, 5–34.

Turner, J. C., Brown, R. J. & Tajfel, H. Social comparison and group interest in ingroup favouritism. *European Journal of Social Psychology*, 1979, *9*, 187–204.

Turner, R. H. The real self: From institution to impulse. *American Journal of Sociology*, 1976, *81*, 989–1016.

Turner, R. H. The role and the person. *American Journal of Sociology*, 1978, *84*, 1–23.

Tversky, A. Features of similarity. *Psychological Review*, 1977, *84*, 327–352.

Twain, M. The mysterious stranger. In *Mark Twain's works*, vol. 22. New York: Harper & Bros., 1913.

U. S. Commission on Civil Rights. *Civil rights issues of Euro-ethnic Americans in the United States: Opportunities and challenges.* Washington, D.C.: Government Printing Office, 1980 (629–843/6080).

van Dijk, T. A. Semantic macro-structures and knowledge frames in discourse comprehension. In M. A. Just & P. A. Carpenter (Eds.), *Cognitive processes in comprehension.* Hillsdale, N.J.: Lawrence Erlbaum Associates, 1977, pp. 3–32.

Veblen, T. *The theory of the leisure class.* New York: Modern Library, 1934.

Vecoli, R. J. Ethnicity: A neglected dimension of American history. In M. Friedman (Ed.), *Overcoming middle class rage.* Philadelphia, Pa.: Westminster Press, 1971, pp. 160–180.

Vecoli, R. The Italian Americans. *The Center Magazine*, 1974, *7*(4), 31–43.

von Bertalanffy, L. *Robots, men and minds.* New York: Braziller, 1967.

Vygotsky, L. S. *Thought and language.* Cambridge, MA.: MIT Press, 1962.

Wacker, R. F. Assimilation and cultural pluralism in American social thought. *Phylon*, 1979, *40*, 325–333.

Walhke, J. H. *Loyalty in a democratic state.* Boston, D. C. Heath & Co., 1952.

Warden, C. J. The evolution of human behavior. New York: Macmillan, 1932.

Washburn, S. L. & DeVore, I. The social life of baboons. *Scientific American*, 1961, *82*, 10–19.

Watson, J. B. *The ways of behaviorism.* New York: Harper, 1928.

Watson, K. A. The rhetoric of narrative structure. Unpublished doctoral dissertation, University of Hawaii, 1972.

Weber, M. *The Protestant ethic and the spirit of capitalism.* London: Unwin, 1930.

Weber, M. *The sociology of religion.* Boston: Beacon Press, 1964.

Weber, M. *Economy and society.* New York: Bedminster Press, 1968.

Weed, P. L. *The white ethnic movement and ethnic politics.* New York: Praeger, 1973.

Weeks, D. G., Michela, J. L., Peplau, L. A. & Bragg, M. E. Relation between loneliness and depression: A structural equation analysis. *Journal of Personality and Social Psychology*, 1980, *9*, 1238–1244.

Wegner, D. M. & Wallacher, R. R. *The self in social psychology.* New York: Oxford University Press, 1980.

Weigert, E. Loneliness and trust—basic factors of human existence. *Psychiatry*, 1960, *23*, 121–131.

Weimer, W. B. A conceptual framework for cognitive psychology. In R. Shaw & J. Bransford (Eds.), *Perceiving, acting and knowing.* Hillsdale, N.J.: Erlbaum, 1977, pp. 267–311.

Weiss, R. S. (Ed.), *Loneliness: The experience of emotional and social isolation.* Cambridge, Mass.: MIT Press, 1973.

Weiss, R. S. & Riesman, D. Some issues in the future of leisure. In E. O. Smigel (Ed.), *Work and leisure.* New Haven: University Press, 1963.

Wells, L. E. & Marwell, G. *Self-esteem: Its conceptualization and measurement.* Beverly Hills: Sage Publications, 1976.

West, K. *Chapter of governesses: A study of the governess in English fiction, 1800–1949.* London: Cohen and West, 1949.

White, K. G., Juhasz, J. B. & Wilson, P. Is man no more than this?: Evaluative bias in interspecies comparison. *Journal of the History of the Behavioral Sciences,* 1973, *9,* 203–212.

White, M. *Foundations of historical knowledge.* New York: Harper, 1965.

Wilder, D. A. Reduction of intergroup discrimination through individuation of the outgroup. *Journal of Personality and Social Psychology,* 1978, *36,* 1361–1374.

Wilder, D. A. Perceiving persons as a group: Categorization and intergroup relations. In D. Hamilton (Ed.), *Social cognition, categorization, and intergroup relations.* Hillsdale, N.J.: Lawrence Erlbaum Associates, 1981.

Wilder, D. A. & Allen, V. L. Group membership and preference for information about others. *Personality and Social Psychology Bulletin,* 1978, *4,* 106–110.

Wilensky, M. *Hasidim and Mitnaqdim* (Hebrew). Jerusalem: Bialik Institute, 1970.

Williams, R. M., Jr. Race and ethnic relations. *Annual Review of Sociology,* 1975, *1,* 125–164.

Williams, R. M., Jr. Relative deprivation versus power struggle? "Tension" and "structural" explanations of collective conflict. *Cornell Journal of Social Relations,* 1976, *11,* 31–38.

Wirth, L. Urbanism as a way of life. *American Journal of Sociology,* 1938, *44,* 1–24.

Wirth, L. *Community life and social policy.* Chicago: University of Chicago, 1956.

Witkin, H. A. Cognitive styles across cultures. *International Journal of Psychology,* 1967, *2,* 233–250.

Witkin, H. A. Social influences in the development of cognitive style. In D. A. Goslin (Ed.), *Handbook of socialization theory and research.* New York: Rand McNally, 1969.

Witkin, H. A. & Berry, J. Psychological differentiation in cross-cultural perspective. *Journal of Cross Cultural Psychology,* 1975, *6,* 4–87.

Witkin, H. A., Price-Williams, D., Bertini, M., Christiansen, B., Altman, P. K., Ramirez, M. & Van Meel, J. Social conformity and psychological differentiation. *International Journal of Psychology,* 1974, *9,* 11–29.

Wollheim, R. Pictorial style: Two views. In B. Lang (Ed.), *The concept of style.* Philadelphia, Pa.: University of Pennsylvania, 1979.

Woltmann, L. *Politische Anthropologie.* Esienach & Liepzig: Thuringische Verlagsanstalt, 1903.

Wood, L. A. Loneliness and social structure. Unpublished doctoral dissertation, York University, Canada, 1976.

Wood, L. A. Perspectives on loneliness. *Essence,* 1978a, *2,* 199–201.

Wood, L. A. Loneliness, social identity and social structure. *Essence,* 1978b, *2,* 259–270.

Wood, L. A. Loneliness and life satisfaction among the rural elderly. Paper presented at the joint meeting of the Canadian Association on Gerontology and the Gerontological Society of America, Toronto, November, 1981.

Woods, F. J. *Marginality and identity: A colored Creole family through ten generations.* Baton Rouge, La.: Louisiana State University Press, 1972.

Woolf, L. *Sowing: An autobiography of the years 1880–1914.* London: Hogarth Press, 1960.

Woolf, V. *Mrs. Dalloway.* New York: Harcourt, Brace & World, 1925.

Yablonsky, L. *The tunnel back: Synanon.* New York: Macmillan Co., 1965.

Yetman, N. R. The background of the slave narrative collection. *American Quarterly,* 1967, *19,* 534–553.

Yinger, J. M. *Anti-semitism: A case study in prejudice and discrimination.* New York: Freedom Books, 1964.

Young, C. *The politics of cultural pluralism.* Madison, Wisc.: University of Wisconsin Press, 1976.

Youniss, J. The development of reciprocity and morality. Paper presented at the meeting of the AAAS, Toronto, Canada, 1981.

Zeller, A. F. An experimental analogue of repression: I. Historical summary. *Psychological Bulletin,* 1950, *47,* 39–51.

Zimmer, H. *Der Weg zum Selbst.* Zürich: Rascher Verlag, 1944.

Zimmer, H. *The king and the corpse.* Princeton: University Press, 1956.

Zimmern, A. *The renaissance of girls' education in England: A record of fifty years' progress.* London: Innes, 1898.

Zonderman, A. B. MOP: Matrix operations program. *Behavior Research Methods & Instrumentation,* 1979, *11,* 453–454.

INDEX